BRAIDED GENERATIONS

The Living, the Lost, and
the Power of Belonging

A Family Memoir
by

JEAN S. GOTTLIEB

Wingspan Press

Cover photo and rug by Kelly Wright

Published in the United States and the United Kingdom
by WingSpan Press, Livermore, CA

The WingSpan name, logo and colophon are the
trademarks of WingSpan Publishing.

Publisher's Cataloging-in-Publication data
Names: Gottlieb, Jean S., author.
Title: Braided Generations : The Living, the Lost, and
the Power of Belonging: a family memoir/ Jean S. Gottlieb.
Description: Includes bibliographical references and index. |
Livermore,CA: Wingspan Press, 2022.
Identifiers: LCCN: 2022902780 | ISBN: 978-1-63683-502-0
(hardcover) | 978-1-63683-021-6 (paperback) | 978-1-63683-981-3 (ebook)
Subjects: LCSH Gottlieb, Jean S. | Chicago (Ill.)--Biography.
| World War II--20th century--History. | Eastern Europe--Biography. |
BISAC BIOGRAPHY & AUTOBIOGRAPHY /
Personal Memoirs
Classification: LCC F869.S39 .B53 2022 | DDC 979.4/61/092--dc23

First edition 2022

Printed in the United States of America

www.wingspanpress.com

For Ezra, whose curiosity about our ancestral past unleashed this torrent. May it answer some questions and ask many more. May the life stories that have endured offer insight, solace, and laughter — and make you a respectful witness to the grief and horror our forebears endured.

PART ONE

1

My father, Oscar David Stern, was born October 13, 1888, in the *shtetl* of Novoselitz or Novoselice, near Czernowitz, a town on the Prut River that was a major center of Ashkenazi Jewish culture in Bessarabia, then part of the Austro-Hungarian Empire. (The region has been part of Romania at times, but now is in western Ukraine.) Oscar was the second child and first son of Rose (Handelman) and David Stern. His older sister, Mollie (b. Dec. 1886), and younger sisters Tillie (b. Dec. 1889?) and Rebecca (b. Dec. 1890) and his brother, Harry (b. 1893) were all born in the Old Country. Belle (b. 1899) was the only child born in America.

Rose (b. October 1867) came from a prosperous family in Bessarabia. Gently reared, she spent her time on such ladylike arts as sewing and embroidery. I don't think she learned to cook, as the family had servants. She had a personal maid who used to brush her hair. It was a luxuriant, glossy light brown, even into her late middle age. I remember that it was thick and wavy and she seemed very proud of it, although she was generally a modest, gentle, and unassuming woman.

David Stern was born December 25, 1865, in Odessa or Kiev. His father was an overseer on the estate of a wealthy Russian noble. As a youngster David helped his father look after the orchards, press olives for oil, and make wine from the cherries they cultivated. I listened avidly when he described to me his life in the Russian countryside. He enjoyed telling his grandchildren about his life in those early days. My father also had misty recollections of fragrant orchards, and all his life he retained a love of and nostalgia for groves of fruit trees. When he and Mother retired to Palm Springs, California, in the mid-1940s, my father had a small grove of orange and grapefruit trees planted on the back section of their property. He loved to escort people through his little orchard, and he delighted in picking and eating the sun-warmed fruit right from his trees.

Oscar's start in life was a precarious one. A frail little newborn, he wasn't given much of a chance to survive. In a desperate effort to save him, a cow or calf was slaughtered, its stomach slit open, and the baby was placed inside this animal's still-warm body cavity. Whether peasant superstition or the closest available approximation to an incubator, I don't know. He told me this story himself, however, and whatever the effect was meant to be, my father attributed his survival to this dramatic emergency "treatment."

As the oldest son, he was destined to become a rabbi, and by the age of five or six, he was attending *cheder* and learning Hebrew. Many decades later, when I sat beside him at the confirmation of our daughter Martha, in the 1960s, I was astonished to hear him reading the prayer-book Hebrew fluently. I asked him how he knew it so well. His response was, "It was beaten into me." He was not proud that he still remembered Hebrew; if anything, he wanted to expunge those indelible lessons. Still, I was impressed by his easy familiarity with a language that I had tried fruitlessly to learn when I was a freshman at Scripps College. It baffled me that he had never shown any interest in or reverence for at least the literary and philosophical aspects of Hebrew, which might have been meaningful to him, considering his scholarly and poetic turn of mind.

Oscar's father, my grandfather David, was a tall, imposing man with a small, childlike snub nose and hooded, almost oriental brown eyes. He had been betrothed — arranged by the matchmaker — to a woman he managed to glimpse after the negotiations had been concluded. He then did the historically essential (for his descendants) but the traditionally unthinkable: he went to his father and asked to be released from the marriage agreement. The woman, he asserted, was "too black." David's father agreed to cancel the contract, BUT, he warned his son, the next bride chosen for him would be *it* — nonnegotiable. The

4

story goes that this twenty-year-old bridegroom first saw Rose Handelman when he lifted her wedding veil at the ceremony in January 1885. There was another version, however. A friend who knew who she was arranged for David to get a glimpse of her. She was eighteen and pretty, with luxuriant wavy light brown hair. David was satisfied. Her looks indicated a gentle temperament and demure demeanor that radiated sweet serenity. And so it was: I never heard her raise her voice in anger. She and my grandfather were married for sixty-six years and the marriage appeared to be a loving partnership all their lives.

Around 1894, David, by then the father of five children, left the Old Country to escape conscription and the pogroms that brought death and chaos to whole regions. My father described a pogrom he had witnessed when he was between eight and ten years old. Terror gripped the village when, like the gust of hot wind that precedes a wildfire, the word "Cossacks" flew through every street and house. In a trice, he remembered, every lane and byway was deserted as children raced for home and adults vanished indoors as though sucked in by a vacuum. Shutters were secured, doors locked; an unnatural silence settled, along with the dust, as villagers, huddled in the back rooms of their houses, strained to hear the first dreaded drumming of the approaching Cossack horses. Oscar remembered the stifling darkness of the house; it seemed, he said, as though everyone inside had stopped breathing, in an effort to become undetectable, to disappear. They heard the Cossacks carousing through the village, breaking down the doors of houses and dragging men out into the streets where the soldiers beat them and sometimes took them away. The door of his house was smashed open with a splintering sound that my father still remembered with a shudder sixty years later. He recalled the insolence of the soldiers laughing at the frightened people from whom they demanded money or valuables in exchange for not beating or molesting them, though they often did so anyhow. In his house, though no one was killed, several of the women or girls (but not his sisters) were manhandled and raped before the eyes of the rest of the inhabitants. Oscar recalled that there was an old woman (a grandmother?), but he couldn't remember what happened to her. He said there was no screaming, but someone pleaded for mercy; for some inscrutable reason, the soldiers left my father's dwelling without killing anyone.

David, like so many others, took a desperate gamble, leaving his young wife and their five children behind under the uncertain protection of their families. He worked as a tailor's apprentice in London for about a year, saving up for his voyage to the New World. Once there, relatives or friends helped him find work so that he could start the long process of saving enough money to pay for his family's passage to America, where they would all be reunited at last.

Little is known about his arrival in New York, but apparently his first jobs were shoveling snow and then making neckties in one of the many sweatshops in the city. After he got to Chicago (where he most likely had relatives) he may have worked in a cigar factory. Then, he got into the grocery business, in what capacity I don't know. No later than 1898, he was able to pay for passage to America for Rose and their children. This included money for bribes at the various borders, food and lodging along the way, and extra funds to cover the horses and carts, boats, trains, and ships that finally delivered them (and millions like them) to the relatives awaiting them in the New World.

My father's recollections of the harrowing trip across Europe to reach Liverpool (ca. 1898) were spotty: some aspects he recalled in vivid detail; most seemed to have been lost or suppressed. Though he loved the transatlantic voyage in steerage, his most vivid memories had to do with fleeing the home of his childhood, being hurled precipitously into the hazardous, uncertain life of the refugee. The carefully planned strategy for their escape began with the bribing of the Russian sentries who patrolled the river Prut that was the border between their village and the rest of the world. Then there was the family's midnight river crossing on their uncles' broad backs.

Two uncles, brothers of Rose's, made the arrangements. They picked a moonless night. The children were awakened, bundled up, and, Oscar remembered, ordered to keep absolutely silent, barely to breathe, not to cough or sneeze. The younger children may even have been gagged. Oscar did not mention that but one of his sisters, either Mollie or Tillie, recalled it. Though the uncles had bribed the riverbank sentries, they took no chances. They waited until the soldiers were at the other end of their posted area, as far as possible from the escapees. In the pitch darkness the family was carried, one by one, across the black river, the uncles wading sometimes in almost chest-deep water, so that the children's legs and shoes got wet. My father remembered that the water was cold, and that the uncles tried to keep their splashing to a minimum as they breasted the river's current in the inky darkness. It was essential that this little band of chilled and frightened fugitives keep utterly quiet even after they reached safety on the other shore. Though the sentries had no legal right to apprehend the refugees once they had crossed the river, and though these muzhiks had been handsomely paid off, none of this deterred them, the uncles cautioned. My father was terrified; the memories of the pogrom he had experienced, which haunted him then and for the rest of his life, became part of this new, immediate fear.

A horse-drawn wagon awaited them. They were concealed beneath covers or straw. Oscar had little recollection of this part of their escape, however. The uncles had done a masterful job of planning the entire journey, and the family was handed along in clandestine stages, much as the Underground Railway had delivered Black slaves to freedom in the northern states in America, until finally they crossed the English Channel or the North Sea and reached London. There they rested and waited for passage to America. They stayed with relatives, and Oscar saw—and ate—his first banana, the most exotic food he'd ever tasted. He remembered that his mother, normally a patient, tender woman, once lost her temper and smacked one of the children with her umbrella, a sign to him of the almost insupportable stress and anxiety she was suffering. First, there had been the terrifying escape across the river late at night, now safely accomplished. Then the long trek overland across Europe. Did they have to cross the rugged Carpathian Mountains? Or had their route taken them farther north, through Poland and Germany? The record of their long trek has been lost, if one ever existed: the children were either too young or too scared to have retained those memories.

Rose and her five children still faced the ordeal of a transatlantic crossing — in steerage — to an unknown land whose language none of them either spoke or understood. After the rail journey from London to Liverpool, their port of embarkation, the trip could take up to six weeks, depending on weather and other uncertainties. For Rose, exhausted and apprehensive, it was an eternity of deathly seasickness, crowding, and inadequate food and toilet facilities. For Oscar, however, that ocean voyage was sheer delight. He shepherded his siblings around and cared for the family during the long journey. He was stimulated by the bracing sea air (he must have found a way to leave the crowded, fetid dark of steerage). The children evidently weathered the trip well, and Oscar reveled in the beauty and wonders of the great ocean and in the sense of freedom it gave him. Whatever the rigors and discomforts of that first transatlantic voyage, Oscar retained a wholehearted and lifelong love of travel.

Did a relative meet Rose and the children when they arrived in Quebec? Their father almost certainly would not have been on hand to welcome his family, since he was settled in Chicago by this time and the additional train fare would have been beyond his means. Besides, there were probably family members or friends to look after new arrivals and send them along to their destinations once they were rested.

Some Stern or Handelman relatives had settled in North Dakota and were farmers, possibly homesteaders. Rose and her brood may have gone there first, to rest up from the rigorous trip and to be reunited with David in a peaceful rural setting. Or they may have gone directly to Chicago by train. The Dakota relatives did play a part in their lives somewhat later, however. Oscar spent at least part of one summer with them when, as a college or law school student, he had a spell of frail health. He remembered driving their horse and buggy on the dusty, empty Dakota roads. There was a day of heroism and high adventure he recalled to me, when, driving the horse and buggy, he had to control the terrified animal, which had shied at a rattlesnake sunning itself in the road. His passenger, a frightened female relative, didn't know what to do. After calming the horse, Oscar climbed down from the buggy and killed the snake at a blow, probably with a shovel (a routine piece of equipment in those days when you were on the road). He proudly brought the dead snake back to the farm, where an uncle skinned it and nailed the skin to the side of the barn to dry in the sun. Oscar told me that he treasured that snakeskin relic for many years.

Once they were settled in Chicago, the parents enrolled the older children in the local public school. At that point none of the family spoke English. David may have picked up a few words during his time in London and in America, but Yiddish and Russian (and perhaps some Hebrew) would have been their only languages.

The school principal (a woman who many years later became Attorney Oscar Stern's client—they both remembered this first encounter) said to the shy, frightened yet eager ten-year-old boy, "What is your name?"

"Chaskel," he replied (pronounced "Khhoskel," with a throaty rasp at the start like clearing your throat).

"That's not an American name," she announced firmly. "You will have to change it. You may choose between two possibilities, Haskell or Oscar. Which will it be?"

"Oscar," replied my father, explaining later that he chose Oscar in honor of the king of Norway.

So he became Oscar, and somewhere between the ages of ten and eleven, he entered the first grade. He had to learn English— to speak, read, and write it—and arithmetic. I picture him being bigger than his six-year-old "classmates" even though he was small for his age (and never became a six-footer like his father).

2

The Stern family lived at 298 Center Avenue, in a house with a small yard. My father remembered it fondly; they lived there throughout his childhood and youth. Like his father, he loved cultivating the earth, and he planted castor beans along the fence that enclosed that little yard. He chose the tall plants because they were hardy and also showy. He felt that they embellished the family's yard and made an aesthetic contribution to the neighborhood.

It was a neighborhood of immigrants, other newcomers to America: Polish, Jewish, Italian, Irish, German, who settled in little enclaves, streets or whole blocks where the respective families each stuck firmly with their fellow countrymen. What all these immigrants had in common was their poverty. What made them dedicated antagonists was their innate mistrust of and hostility toward "others," the fierce rivalries and the prejudices that they brought with them from the Old Country and transplanted to America.

Oscar had to traverse a gauntlet of hostile neighborhoods to get to school. One was Italian, one Irish. Each had its own characteristic brand of bullying and extortion, and each fought the other endlessly, viciously, and single-mindedly when they weren't joining forces to attack the Jewish "Christ killers." According to Oscar, the Micks and the Dagos were all huge and muscular—they beat you up first and asked questions afterward. They would lie in wait for the newest, most terrified and ignorant children. He was small, skinny, and green, by his own account, and hated the brutish fighting that led to bloody noses and torn clothes. He was neither aggressive nor retaliatory, and he soon developed a reputation, not for cowardice, but for pacifism and honesty—he didn't lie or try to cheat these big bullies; he was quiet and studious, something of an anomaly among the neighborhood hooligans, who avoided school as much as possible. Before long, the warring factions had taken a liking to this earnest little scholar: they protected him from each other's depredations as well as from the other marauders (Polacks and Krauts) who sometimes infiltrated from other neighborhoods. He was affectionately nicknamed Sheeny Oscar, an epithet that was about on a par with Kike, Spic, Dago, or Mick. His would-be attackers became his and his family's protectors. They either walked him to school, shielding him from the gauntlet of goons that regularly prowled the route, or sometimes they got him a ride on one of their fathers' wagons.

Oscar took to school enthusiastically: this was how you became an American. Possibly it was the discipline he'd acquired in *cheder* that made him a diligent student and an eager learner. There were a few comical linguistic slipups along the way, which Oscar enjoyed recounting to us, even at his own expense. He had to learn not only to speak but also to read and write English, with its inconsistent pronunciation and Roman type. He'd practice by spelling out every word he encountered, no matter what or where. With Hebrew as his first written language, he was puzzled by word spacings. "Post no Bills" became one word, "Pawst*nah*billess," and he had no idea what it meant. He loved ice cream, which he read as "itzeh cray*ahm*." His most persistent throwback to his first spoken language, however, was his quaint use of the plural when referring to hair, as in, "I must comb my hair, they are all messed up." My sister and I teased him about this syntactical idiosyncrasy, but he was never able to shake that habit of speech.

By the age of about thirteen, three years after arriving in America and entering school in first grade, Oscar completed grammar school, then went on to attend Joseph Medill High School, which had opened its doors in 1898 and soon became one of Chicago's highly respected high schools. Located at 14th and Throop Streets (not a fashionable section of the city), it was the incubator for many dedicated and ambitious youngsters — mostly male in those days — in the fields of journalism, medicine and the sciences, law, humanities, politics and government, and all areas of intellectual exploration. Many of its graduates went on to become national figures, and the school, which closed as a high school in the 1940s, has had its name perpetuated in Northwestern University's Medill School of Journalism. (Joseph Medill, who became Mayor of Chicago in 1871 just after the Great Chicago Fire, was a champion of free public education and a driving force behind the creation of the school that bore his name. He later became owner and Editor-in-Chief of the *Chicago Tribune*.)

Oscar developed a great interest in the arts, especially classical music. He acquired recordings which he played on the family's wind-up Victrola, a tall wooden cabinet with a trumpet-shaped speaker. To play a record, you used the attached chrome handle to wind up the machine. If you cranked it as tightly as possible, you could play one record all the way through without the sound gradually slowing down and finally stopping. (It was still in his parents' apartment when I was a small child, before they moved into the cramped living space behind their Gladys Avenue grocery store. I would wind it up and play some of the recordings his family still had. My favorite was "Stop Your Ticklin', Jock," a recording of the Scottish comedian, Harry Lauder, laughing. It started sort of calmly but built to a crescendo of irresistibly contagious giggling, cackling, whooping, screeching, and gasping, and just when you thought he'd come to an exhausted end, he'd start in laughing all over again. Oscar also had recordings of Enrico Caruso that I remember listening to. They were sort of scratchy and distant-sounding, but you could still appreciate the dramatic voice.)

Oscar and his friend and neighbor, Gertrude Weinstock, shared this enthusiasm for classical music. She was a child prodigy who later took the professional name of Gitta Gradova and was a renowned concert pianist. Oscar and Gitta remained lifelong friends. A natural comic and an accomplished mimic, she presided over informal and always entertaining dinner parties. Through her we got to know some of the notable classical musicians of the twentieth century: Vladimir Horowitz, Nathan Milstein, Gregor Piatigorsky, and Mischa Mischakoff.

It was a foregone conclusion that Oscar would not only finish high school but would also go on to college. The acculturation process that had begun when he became Oscar instead of Chaskel soon led him to announce to his father that he would no longer study to become a rabbi: he would be a doctor or a lawyer instead. Rabbis belonged to the Old Country, along with the beatings and rote learning of *cheder*. In America you strove to be like the Americans: you suppressed your foreign accent and your foreign ways. The oldest son was still the Prince, however, the one for whom everyone else sacrificed so that he could go to college and become successful enough to help (and in some cases, support) the others. Hence, for three of Oscar's sisters, Mollie, Tillie, and Rhea, finishing grammar school ended their formal education. Belle, the only child born in the United States, was exempt from this requirement because she'd developed a heart murmur after contracting scarlet fever when she was very young. She was the only one of the sisters to attend high school. I was told that, during their school years, each girl had one "good" dress to wear to school. The younger girls got hand-me-downs, the outgrown dresses of their older sisters. Mollie, the oldest, got either a re-made castoff of her mother's, or, if there was money for it, a new garment was made. Rose's sewing skills enabled her to alter clothes or even to make new ones for her children. I was told that each day after school, the dresses were washed, dried, and ironed for the following day's use.

I wonder how Oscar's sisters felt about being denied the chance to go to high school because tradition dictated that boys got preferential treatment in this respect. Here they were in America, yet higher education was almost as unattainable for Mollie, Tillie, and Rhea as it would have been in Bessarabia.

David Stern ruled his family much as he would have in the Old Country. He was the Patriarch whose sons and daughters were rigidly disciplined: he did not routinely beat them, but he demanded their unquestioning obedience as long as they lived under his roof. There was a story about Mollie, who, at age seventeen or so, wanted to attend a dance. Once it had been determined that she would be properly escorted and chaperoned, she was allowed to go, but with the caveat that she was to be home no later than 9:00 p.m. — "Not One Minute After!"

Though Mollie was an obedient and conscientious daughter, she was also proud and independent. Still, I'm sure she intended to be home on time — but as luck would have it, she was late. A breathless Mollie ran up to the front stoop of their house at a minute or two past nine. The door was locked. She knocked and stood waiting with her escort. There was no response, the house was dark. She knocked again; silence. She knocked a third time and called out, "It's me, Mollie, let me in!" Still no response; she was nearly in tears. She banged on the door again — hard — and heard sounds from within. Her father's head appeared at an upstairs window. "The door is locked. It's after nine. You may not come in. Go away, worthless irresponsible creature."

Mollie, with her young escort standing terrified beside her, unwilling to desert her in this crisis, swallowed her pride and pleaded to be let in. She explained that the streetcar had been late coming and had had to make many stops. At this point, throwing dignity and independence to the winds, she burst into tears and begged cravenly to be allowed in. Where else could she go at this late hour? Rose, upstairs with David but invisible to her daughter, must have interceded, gently but persuasively (he was not a mean-hearted man), and urged him to relent. So after thundering at her and her frightened companion that if she was ever late again she would be locked out for good, he came down and let her in. Mollie apparently never missed another curfew. No one found out how David and Rose had resolved this issue. (By the time I got to know him, he had mellowed considerably; still, I could imagine him being an inflexible autocrat.)

Tall, ramrod straight, he was an imposing figure, even in old age. More scholar than seeker after the material success that so many immigrants dreamed of, he dwelt in the world of Torah and Talmud, the Holy Books in all their profound and inscrutable beauty, power, and mystery. He was in the synagogue mornings with a group of fellow seekers, reading and discussing the words, ideas, and meanings of the day's readings. His preference for that world of disciplined study led him to command his children's strict obedience with respect to school and learning, in hopes that this would bring them the worldly success that had eluded him. (He left behind a welter of failed enterprises: real estate, retail businesses, a string of failed partnerships with friends and relatives.) Still, he was scornful of his fellow immigrants, the ones who got "taken in" by American free-wheeling spontaneity, reckless adventurism, and impractical promises of riches for the taking. Those "pie-in-the-sky" dreams caused bewilderment and conflict in many immigrant households, with the children defying their parents and flouting the values they'd been raised with in order, as they saw it, to become Americans. But David Stern, surrounded by his descendants, surveyed the families of his neighbors and fellow immigrants and declared that he had the greatest wealth of all: his children, grandchildren, and great-grandchildren.

Some of the Old Country ways withstood the blandishments of the New World, however. The oldest son remained the focus of the family's ambition; no sacrifice was too great if it brought him within reach of becoming a doctor or lawyer, a rich man.

Oscar was admitted to the University of Chicago in 1905, after he graduated from Medill High School. I imagine that it was a series of long streetcar rides to the University from their home on Center Avenue. He was a student there through May 1907. He may have decided by that time to become a lawyer, and he must have applied to Northwestern University Law School. In those days, a four-year undergraduate degree was not a prerequisite for admission to law school; two years of college with excellent grades and the ability to pay the tuition was all that was required. Neither the tuition nor the distance precipitated Oscar's departure from the University of Chicago, however. He must have felt the pressure not to dally in the alluring halls of academe but to finish his education as soon as possible, become a licensed attorney, work in a reputable law firm, and provide considerable financial support to the family.

Oscar attended the University of Chicago from 1905–1907.

Presumably he entered Northwestern University Law School sometime after that. He graduated from law school in June 1910, less than two months after the life of his family was devastated by tragedy.

3

Never mentioned, the catastrophic event had been consigned to oblivion in accordance with the dictates of Jewish law. But by chance, one day, I discovered a composition book on whose title page was written "Poems – Harry Stern." I no longer recall all the details, except that I had found it slipped inconspicuously between books on a shelf in our library. It had probably been there for years, unnoticed, yet suddenly it was in my hands and I was reading the poems of this person. Why did we have this little cardboard-covered school composition book? Who was Harry Stern?

My mother told me that he was my father's younger brother, that he had died young—a suicide—and that I was never, ever to ask my father about him or to mention that I had found this book of poems. Of course, I was mystified, curious, but also frightened. I knew I had stepped into forbidden territory, a dark, horrific place. She explained that no one ever mentioned his name, and that I must honor this silence no matter what. There was something about the way she spoke that both aroused my curiosity and prevented me from pursuing this dark mystery any further. Sometime after my discovery, the notebook disappeared, I don't know when or how; perhaps in the course of one of our several moves it got thrown out or lost. But Harry Stern stayed with me: Was he the reason my middle name is Harriet? That I have a cousin also named Harriet?

Finally, many years later, when my father was in his late sixties and signs of oncoming Parkinsonian dementia were seeping into his personality, a sense of urgency overtook me. I needed to know about his brother Harry before it was too late. Harry Stern, whatever his story, mustn't vanish without a trace or a recollection. On one of my parents' visits to our house, I led my father into our library, shut the door, and said, "Daddy, I want to ask you something about your family in the past. Will you tell me anything I want to know, answer anything I ask you?"

And even though he might have sensed what was coming, he replied, "Yes."

"Will you tell me about your brother Harry and what happened to him?"

My father was an emotional and expressive man, one who pinched cheeks (and behinds and Mother's breasts, much to her [feigned] annoyance). He talked baby talk to us, gave us pet names, and was unabashedly sentimental. It must have taken courage and strength to allow those memories to return in their full, appalling detail, but he was a man of his word, and we loved each other, and he knew I was asking him for the important reason that even the bad, hard parts of family history must not be lost; the memories of even the greatest sorrows and the unhappiest people must be cherished.

There was silence between us as he gathered himself to speak of the unspeakable.

Harry was (approximately) five years younger than Oscar. The two brothers were close. They shared a room, of course, possibly even a bed, given the living conditions in immigrant households. (Oscar's four sisters all slept in one room—did they have two beds to share?)

Unlike his brother, Harry was not a studious type. As far as I know, only two photos of him survive, and I saw them some years later, after my father's death. One was the requisite posed portrait, with everyone dressed in their best clothes (evidence of their prosperity and security in America). It was taken in about 1901 or '02: Belle, the baby, appears to be about two years old. The other, which I saw only once, shows Harry in his early teens. Both reveal a serious demeanor, but it's hard to extrapolate a personality from either of these pictures: consider that studio photos required the subject to hold still for a minute or two while the flash powder was ignited, exploded with a sudden huge

BANG, and the film in the big camera on a tripod received its image. Everyone looked solemn in those pictures. A round-faced boy, with his hair slicked down, wearing a stiff-looking wool suit, Harry gazes expressionlessly ahead. In the later picture, a snapshot taken outdoors on the front steps of a building, Harry's head is down; he is avoiding eye contact with the viewer.

He may not have been a scholar, but Harry was a poet. Was he a dreamer? Did he rebel against the strait-laced Old Country lifestyle at home, where girls were lucky to get an elementary school education and it was taken for granted that they would defer to their father, their mother, and their brothers (in that order)? Oscar was the exemplary son; Harry, in contrast, may have felt like the black sheep for his lack of interest in school, his withdrawal from the family in favor of his friends, a group of carefree boys and girls who liked to dance, romp around, have a good time. Was he scorned by his strict patriarch father as a layabout and good-for-nothing? Was there a showdown between Harry and his father? Or was there just an increasingly chilling atmosphere of criticism, disparagement, censure of the boy's attitude, behavior, and choice of friends?

Oscar and Harry were a study in contrasts. Oscar was quiet and studious, and Harry, a surly adolescent around his parents, was close to his brother, and evidently gregarious among his peers. He was probably no older than sixteen when the real trouble started. He had lost interest in school, a bitter disappointment to his father and a source of mounting tension between them. Oscar may have tried to intercede by urging tolerance on his father's part and some academic effort on Harry's. But the alienation ran deeper: Harry was keeping company with a Gentile girl, a *shiksa*.

David Stern was a dedicated student of the Holy Books, though he cared little for the ceremonial part of Jewish life that demanded faithful attendance at services in the synagogue. (He would escort his dear Rose to shul on holidays or on the Sabbath, and while she was inside making her devotions, he would stalk up and down outside like a picketer, muttering imprecations and berating rabbis as a bunch of parasites and hangers-on who never did an honest day's work but lived off the guilt-ridden contributions of their impoverished but faithful flock.) Still, that his son should even be *acquainted* with a non-Jewish girl was intolerable and unforgivable. Given Harry's age and his temperament, such sternness and rigidity simply made him more defiant. What might have been a casual flirtation took on the character of a serious romance. We don't know her name or anything about her, though Harry probably confided in Oscar and may have described her (I seem to remember my father telling me she was blonde). I don't know whether Oscar or any of his sisters ever saw or met her. I wonder whether some of the poems in that lost composition book were written to or about her.

A showdown was building between father and son. Finally, David handed Harry an ultimatum: quit school if you won't pursue your studies, get a job and help support the family, or leave home and find yourself another place to live. As for the *shiksa*, you must give her up absolutely, completely, and immediately or be irretrievably cast out of this family.

Harry left school and got work as a clerk in a shoe store. His father accepted this but was not happy with his son's career choice. Still, he'd set forth the options and Harry was complying with the terms of their agreement—except with respect to the *shiksa*. He was still seeing her, defying his father and the ultimatum. The unacknowledged stress and tension in the household was exacerbated by David's tormented efforts to maintain his authority as patriarch whose command was being eroded by the incomprehensible behavior of this boy. Had he been corrupted by American freedom?

Rose, the loving soother of ruffled feelings, mediator, fashioner of compromise, tried to intercede. She was always such a gentle soul, sensitive to the emotions of both her children and her husband. I am sure she felt the danger that loomed over Harry and the family, and her most intense efforts focused on a way to avoid the impending showdown. Harry, the moody, conflicted boy, was aware that Oscar was the "good" boy; but this did not affect the closeness of these two deeply attached brothers, whose emotional profiles, though sharply contrasting, were complementary. Oscar understood the defiance in Harry, and Harry understood the compliance in Oscar. Their father David lived a life of discipline and probity. How did this happen to him, that his son should provoke a climate of conflict and bitterness that set the whole family on edge? He believed that a father's obligation was to rule his children — wisely but uncompromisingly, for their own good. How had that basic tenet gotten so deformed that it was fomenting rebellion in this lad?

And then, one fateful day, Oscar returned home from University and found Harry in their room, writhing in agony on the bed. "Help me! Help me!" he begged his brother. Panicked and terrified, Oscar ran to the nearest source of medical knowledge, the pharmacy, and begged the druggist to advise him what to do: Harry was in terrible pain — what could be the cause? What could he do to help his brother? "Oh my God, he came in this morning and bought some cyanide — to kill rats in the house, he told me." For a frozen moment Oscar and the druggist stared at each other in silence. Then, galvanized, Oscar ran out of the shop. By the time he got home, all he could do was hold his brother in his arms as excruciating death overtook Harry. My father never mentioned whether anyone else was in the house. Neither time nor place existed for him then, only the fading moans of his dying brother penetrated his awareness.

Harry died on April 30, 1910, as recorded on his death certificate. (I found it, by searching public records, more than 100 years later.) His tragic death shattered the very foundations of family life, as each member wrestled with the meaning of that death, that pointless, unnecessary, premature end. A suicide in an observant Jewish household erases the individual as though he or she had never existed. All evidence of the person and his or her life in the family and in the world is expunged. So Harry's name was never spoken again. I shudder at the thought of those sisters, the surviving brother, the parents, all emotionally cut off from one another, forbidden from sharing their bereavement, though that might have been a small but real comfort. No one ever mentioned Harry's name, not the sisters to one another in secret, not the parents, no one. I don't know whether Mollie, Tillie, Rhea, and Belle ever mentioned Harry to their children. There was no grave to visit, no stone beside which to grieve and lay flowers, no memories to be called back in tears or laughter or wistfulness.

When my father described that day to me, his voice became unsteady and he wept as the memories engulfed him; the pain and horror of that afternoon remained a livid wound even though he had tried to consign it long ago to deepest oblivion. His grief became my grief, but mine was suffused with guilt for having made him bring back this nightmare. After my father told me that tragic story, we never again mentioned Harry's name. Yet the person I never knew, that phantom poet-uncle wasn't eradicated, as he'd been in Oscar's family. He has remained a presence. I hope that at some level my father derived comfort from sharing that terrible story with me, knowing that I would tell my children, and that we of the later generations would always honor his memory and his brief, troubled life. It is said that there is a grave in Forest Park Cemetery. If there is, what I find will be added to this memorial honoring him.

Telling that story to me had been so full of anguish for my father that I couldn't bring myself to ask him for details about his brother—what kind of person he was. I got the sense that he could be charming and lighthearted, that he was gregarious and that he was little given to despondency—until the conflict with his father swamped the entire family. Perhaps part of my father's attraction to my mother was that both the sparkling and the dark side of her temperament reminded him of Harry.

The little composition book of Harry's poems became especially poignant in my mind. Oscar must have hidden that last remnant of his brother and kept it near him in secret for all those years. And then it disappeared after we left the Belden Hotel to move to 70 E. Cedar Street when I was about fourteen. I never saw it again.

I wonder—and marvel—at my grandmother's stoical acceptance of the cruel and total banishment of her son Harry from everywhere and forever. But Grandma Stern was a quietly resourceful woman who may have devised ways to maintain secret and silent communion with her dead son. She loved to go to "lunchings," a rare opportunity to dress up and be with her friends. It was a chance to breathe air that wasn't drenched in sorrow. She was a faithful member of Hadassah and seemed to know that companionship and the community of other women would nourish her and be a comfort even if her mourning remained locked away. She was also a faithful attendee at funerals. "I'm going to *na* funeral," she'd say, and off she'd go, with my grandfather's tender blessing, all dressed up in her hat and gloves. Was it a chance to put herself nearer to Harry?

Once I knew about that tragic episode, I reexamined the Friday nights I remembered, where she'd have prepared what I now realize was Shabbat dinner with all my dad's favorite dishes, and Grandpa would bring out his potent cherry *vishnik* that he brewed himself. Grandpa David Stern was a scholar of sorts. He spoke with stentorian authority, and he knew his scripture (sort of — I'm no judge), whereas Grandma Rose Stern understood the emotional meaning of every aspect. Not a scholar but a servant. Her benign and sweet stewardship of the household, observance of all holidays, and unobtrusive but consistent obedience to Jewish life came effortlessly from love and comfort in the gifts that seemed to accompany observing it. (Completely different from my mother's mother, Grandma Rose Preaskil, who was secular as hell, shrewd about how to get by, jolly, and pretty much without scruples.)

I would watch Grandma Stern with curiosity and considerable awe when she went into the tiny triangular bedroom, just big enough for their double bed and a chest of drawers. There was a mirror over the dresser and an immaculate white dresser scarf that she must have embroidered herself. Two brass candlesticks flanked her comb and brush on the dresser. She would cover her hair with a veil or scarf, and facing the mirror, she'd light the candles in the two brass candlesticks. She would murmur something that I couldn't hear. I never asked her what she was saying. It felt like a very private moment, reverent but also somber. Was Harry in her heart then? He was probably always in her inner being. How can you deny a life lived — especially one so cruelly brief and self-destroyed? Standing and watching her made me feel a stirring, some strand of affinity with my grandmother and possibly many others I'd never known. Even though ours was a totally secular, resolutely American life, this little Friday night ceremony resonated in me.

4

The shocking death of Harry Stern, with its grief and shame, upended the apparent order and serenity of the Stern household. It bore witness to the harshness of the immigrants' complex challenges, fears, and desires: the frequently raw conflict between children and their parents over the pursuit of life, American style, that was so alluring to the ambitious, naïve young immigrants.

In June, only weeks after his brother's tragic death, Oscar graduated from Northwestern University Law School. He was twenty-two years old. In twelve years he'd learned English, completed elementary school, high school, college, and law school. He was awarded the Order of the Coif, a legal honor society comparable to Phi Beta Kappa. (He always wore his Coif key on his watch chain, which was attached to a gold pocket watch tucked into the pocket of the vest that was a part of every suit he owned.) He was also awarded a collection of books, a prize from a legal publishing company in recognition of outstanding scholarship. That prize was abruptly revoked, on the flimsiest of pretexts: Mr. Stern had already been the recipient of the academic honor of the Order of the Coif, and the company (lamely) decided to bestow the book prize elsewhere. The unspoken reason, delicately hinted at by the Law School's Dean Wigmore, was that the company preferred not to present the award to a Jew, but this was never verified. John H. Wigmore, an eminent legal scholar and dean of Northwestern Law School from 1901 to 1929, was very fond of my father, this ambitious immigrant lad who was a first-rate scholar and student. He was quite exercised at the behavior of the publishing company that took back its prize, and he wrote a dignified and sympathetic

25

letter to my father in which he subtly questioned the propriety
of the company's action.

My father saved both Dean Wigmore's letter and the
awkward one from the donor, asserting that since Oscar had
already had the Order of the Coif bestowed on him, the book
prize should be given to someone else. Why did he preserve
this specimen of covert anti-Semitism? Perhaps it served
both as a reminder of one of life's realities and as a spur to
his ambition to become a successful attorney. He understood
that the best revenge on the anti-Semites was success: to
become a distinguished — and affluent — professional. Maybe
his experience as Sheeny Oscar, mascot of those Irish and
Italian ghetto toughs, gave him security and self-assurance
that armed him against Jew-haters. Or perhaps it was the iron
determination instilled in many refugee immigrants: get out,
work hard, look ahead, not back.

Instead of a public denunciation of that publisher, Dean
Wigmore took a positive action: he recommended his new
graduate to the law firm of Judah, Willard, Wolf and Reichmann.
Wigmore extolled Oscar's academic and personal qualities,
characterizing him as just the kind of young lawyer who would
be a credit to the firm. Interviewed by Alexander Reichmann,
the formidable senior partner, Oscar was hired and spent his
entire professional life with that firm. He practiced law for over
fifty years and became a partner; he saw his name become part
of the firm name, Judah, Reichmann, Trumbull, Cox, and Stern.
(I remember meeting Alexander Reichmann when I was quite
young: he was a monument of a man, seated behind an equally
imposing heavily carved desk that seemed to me to be as big as
a freight car. He had a large gray moustache, and he wore a suit
with a vest, a style my father adopted from then on.)

The problems of older immigrants were at least as formidable as
those of the young. Many of them had families to support and
were desperate to find work. They had little, if any, command of
English and few marketable skills, but they were — had to be —
ingenious and resourceful: friends, family, and neighbors helped

one another out. Yet despair often hounded older workers who could not find — or keep — a steady job.

The grandfather of Anna Preaskil (Oscar's future wife) was one such unfortunate. His name was Harry (short for Harris, born Hyman) Silverman. He was a *shochet*, a kosher butcher, and steady employment was evidently a challenge, judging from records that show him working first in one place, then another, or sometimes not working at all. The Silvermans lived near their daughter Rose and her husband Louis Preaskil, and my mother, a small child at that time, remembered her grandfather vividly. He was warm, animated, and easygoing, and he'd come to their house after work so that he could see his granddaughter. He'd sit her on his lap and let her help him make his cigarettes with the cigarette-rolling machine that he used. But his life, like that of so many of his fellow immigrants, began to unravel as he grew older and therefore less employable. He was probably drinking as well. Silverman's life of poverty and despair ended with his suicide in 1903. He was fifty-seven years old.

Both Oscar Stern and Anna Preaskil had endured tragic suicides in their families. Never mentioned, the grieving festered, a corrosive in the hidden family memory. It has been my mission — an imperative — to restore those two poor souls to their respective families, to acknowledge their lives, offering them, belatedly, the sympathy and affection that family members should have for one another.

Anna Florence Preaskil, the first child of Rose (Silverman) Preaskil and Louis George Preaskil, was born in Chicago on June 17, 1894. Louis (born 1867), the oldest child in his family, had been the first of the three Preaskil brothers to escape Lithuania and impending conscription — he was eighteen — as well as anti-Semitism and poverty. His father was a woodcutter who had lived on a farm in a "mixed" (presumably not all-Jewish) rural area where Dave, Louis's youngest brother, remembered having to watch out for wolves as he walked to school. When their parents became too old to stay on the farm, they moved to either Vilnius, the capital, or Vilkomir, a *shtetl* about forty-five miles to its north.

Louis sailed from Liverpool on a ship called the *Spain* and landed in New York in September 1885. He found some sort of work that enabled him to share a "warm bed" room with another immigrant. One "tenant" had a day job and slept in the room at night; the other had a night job and occupied the bed during the day. It was rare for the two occupants to meet, or even to know who the other one was. Though it may be apocryphal, a story has come down through the family that once Louis, who had the night job, was too ill to work, but since he had noplace to go, he had not yet left the room when the day-job worker, a young woman, arrived. There are no further details.

Louis was in New York for a relatively short time, just long enough to make the fare to Chicago. Why he picked Chicago I have no idea: Did he have relatives here? There is no record of that, or of how he got into the grocery business. He may have started out as a peddler selling produce door-to-door, with a pushcart and then a horse and wagon, but soon he opened a grocery store, generally a good option for an impoverished immigrant, who would at least have his stock to help provide food for his family. Louis's siblings, Julius, Ida, and Dave, followed him to America and to Chicago later, when the boys approached conscription age. Dave, the last to make the trip, came with an aunt when he was fifteen, in 1891, the same year Louis married one Jennie Gros (whose name is all I know of her) and became the father of a son, Fred.

Louis, Julius, Ida, and Dave started out living near each other in Chicago's Jewish ghetto around 14th and Jefferson Streets. Julius started out as a housepainter, and when he was able to afford it, he opened a paint store. Dave at first continued his Old Country craft of harness making in Chicago. Like his oldest brother Louie, he was a dedicated tinkerer who was good at fixing things and making trinkets; his descendants still comb antique shops and house auctions for his trademark, a little brass fitting, either an oak leaf or a Star of David with the initials "D. P." that he affixed to his harnesses. As horse-drawn conveyances began to be replaced by gasoline-powered "horseless carriages," however — only a trickle in the 1890s, but soon to be a flood — Dave saw the handwriting on the wall, and got out of harness-making and into hardware. He opened a store at 14th and South Halsted near a burgeoning development of light industry and soon became a prosperous merchant, his success reflected in the substantial brick building he bought — the only one in the neighborhood — which had his store on the ground floor and the family's dwelling upstairs. Both he and Julius seemed better than their oldest brother at anticipating economic trends. Both moved their families and businesses out of the ghetto before Louis did.

It was cheap and handy to occupy the second floor of the structure that housed your business downstairs. Julius and his wife Rose lived above their paint store in a wooden building. Louie may have lived above his little grocery store, which backed up to a stable, with Jennie and their son, Fred. Jennie was pregnant again. In December 1892, their second child, Samuel, was born — but Jennie died giving birth to him, or shortly after, leaving Louis a widower at twenty-four with a frail infant, a toddler, and a business to run. With no mother for his boys, helpmate for his store, or wife for himself (he was known for his vigorous sexual appetites), Louis faced a crisis. He desperately needed a woman.

Rose Silverman, my mother's mother, arrived in America from either Ukraine or Poland sometime between 1889 and 1892. Her father, Harris (born Hyman) Silverman, had immigrated in 1891; did his wife Anna accompany him? Harry had married Anna Newman in the Old Country in 1866. At least two of their children were born there: Rose (my future grandmother) in 1871, and Louis in 1875. (One recorded arrival of a "Rosa" Silverman in 1893 might be my grandmother.)

In Chicago, Rose Silverman lived in the ghetto around 14th and Jefferson. This is my mother's account of how Rose and Louis Preaskil met: one day Rose walked into Louis's grocery store, and there behind the counter was this tall, good-looking young man. It was obvious why he was known as "Handsome Louie." Rose was smitten, and Louis was in dire straits. It isn't

clear exactly how soon after they met the marriage took place —
there is no record of the date — but it was probably early in 1893.
So young Rose Silverman married the handsome widower and
presumably assumed the care of Fred and the ailing Samuel, if
the infant was still alive. The newborn survived his mother by
only a few months, dying in April 1893. His death certificate
lists the cause of death as "gastro-enteritis, duration of disease
10 days." (Commonly called "summer complaint," it was a
notorious killer of infants and young children in those days of
unpasteurized milk, no refrigeration, and only sketchy ideas
about basic sanitation. Bottle feeding, if there even was such a
thing, was fraught with health hazards, and what poor ghetto
family could afford — or find — a clean and healthy wet nurse?)

How much did this independent twenty-two-year-old know
about the care and feeding of infants? Did she ask neighbors or
family for help or advice? I picture the young, newly arrived
Rose, who spoke no English, who may have come to America
alone, suddenly the stepmother of one or two small children,
having to look after the babies, mind the grocery store, keep
house, and sleep with her sexually insistent husband. She
became pregnant almost immediately, and gave birth to Anna —
my mother, their first child — on June 17, 1894, little more than a
year after baby Samuel's death.

5

By the time she was two and a half Anna had a little brother, Samuel Ira (born December 1896). In their tiny, cramped living space above the Preaskils' store there was no such thing as privacy, and Anna heard not only the horses downstairs, stamping, snorting and farting all night, but she could also hear baby Sammy, who slept in a cradle at the foot of his parents' bed, cry and whimper in the night. His exhausted mother attached a string to the cradle and tied the other end around her toe so she could rock the cradle and soothe him by moving her foot back and forth without having to get up. What else did Anna hear?

In later years, when my mother was an adult, Rose told her that my grandfather's insatiable sexuality resulted in numerous pregnancies. He was always after her, she said with a certain pride—suggesting that she was neither timid nor a prude. She certainly found her handsome husband irresistible. The only problem was that she had no idea how to avoid getting pregnant. She was skeptical and mistrustful of what little information might have been available. This was before the day of the crusading Margaret Sanger and her clinics offering sex education and contraception advice to all comers. If there were helpful nurses or midwives or philanthropic society ladies who counseled women, Grandma Rose would have had nothing to do with them. Buttinskis, she called them derisively. Or Bolsheviks, decadent purveyors of Free Love. Her prejudice against "free advice" from some wild-eyed radical or meddling blueblood doomed Rose to a life that included numerous abortions, after Sammy and perhaps even before. Abortion was dangerous, illegal, and hideously unpleasant, but it was better than being constantly pregnant and having a houseful of children.

My mother told me that her heart used to ache as she watched her mother, clutching a thin sweater (AND the cash box), scurry downstairs to the store before daybreak to prepare for the day's trade. It grieved her that Rose worked such long hours, on her feet all day. Nonetheless, Rose showed herself to be an energetic businessperson, who preferred the store to the housewife's lot. She was never much interested in homemaking and domestic matters (in contrast to Rose Stern, Oscar's mother, the angelic homebody and fabled cook). Louis was getting into the wholesale grocery business, at least part-time, and Rose had to tend the store while he took the horse and wagon to the market on West Randolph Street to buy produce for the store and for the door-to-door trade in his neighborhood. Freddy was not required to help, and Sammy grew into a dedicated mischief maker and devil-may-care type who knew how to avoid anything smacking of responsibility. When Sammy was old enough for school, Anna had to help him get dressed and then get ready for school herself. Did she prepare breakfast for her father and her brother Fred, or was hers one of those chaotic households in which there were no set mealtimes and family members foraged for themselves?

When Anna was eight or nine, she would come straight home after school so that she could help out in the grocery store by doing her mother's bidding. "Making *fagelach*" was one of her principal tasks. "*Fagelach*" is the Yiddish word for "little birds," and Rose taught her daughter this technique, of which she was probably not the originator, but at which Anna became singularly adept. First, I provide some background about the family, and then an explanation of "*fagelach*" and what it was all about.

It was not until Anna herself was about to be married that her mother told her that Freddie was her half-brother, that he was born of a different mother. Did Anna ever learn about the baby Samuel who had died? Or was she told only about Louis's previous marriage and half-brother Fred? Why were these parts of family history so assiduously concealed? In my mother's family, deception, superstitious anxiety about the Evil Eye— and outright lying—were commonplace. They were survival mechanisms that did away with those long, embarrassing, compromising explanations of things that weren't anybody's business. A little obfuscation to modulate a hard truth prevented unpleasant confrontations that wouldn't solve anything anyhow. This seemed to be Rose's pragmatic philosophy, part of her character. It was not uncommon among the immigrants for whom just "getting by" was challenge enough.

Still, neither Dave nor Julius nor Ida and their spouses felt the need to deceive, connive, conceal in the way that Rose did. But then, they were close to one another, while Rose, always assertive and independent, apparently didn't foster closeness with her in-laws. Her behavior shaped her family and its values. Life, according to her, ran most smoothly when any problems or misfortunes or failures were papered over with whatever sort of lie seemed to serve. That climate of moral opportunism perpetuated itself beyond Rose, beyond Anna, and like a birthmark, put its imprint on me and even, perhaps, on my children. It was an alluring way to get what you wanted, to make life over to match your wishes and illusions. If you could get away with something, it was imperative that you not let the opportunity slip away. A little undetected cheating wasn't really cheating, it was like reaching for the brass ring on the merry-go-round, it was taking advantage of any opening, any opportunity that came your way.

Now, my mother's family (like my father's) lived in the multi-ethnic ghetto. The working poor, mostly Polish, Russian, Irish, and Italian immigrants, patronized the Preaskil grocery store because it was in the neighborhood and, more important, because my canny grandmother extended credit to her regular customers when they were short of cash between paydays. My mother, who had learned a few words of Russian, Polish, and Italian, could make a shy immigrant woman feel quite at home by spinning out some simple platitudes in the customer's native tongue. The grocer's pretty little daughter soon became a local favorite and something of a public relations phenomenon.

This is how one "made *fagelach*": Each customer had a little charge account book that he kept. The store had a duplicate book with the customer's name on it, kept by my grandmother. The customer, the poor, ignorant (and maybe illiterate) Wop or Polack, not too good with numbers, would come in with his little account book and make his purchases: two cents' butter, five cents' sugar, four cents' flour, and so on. My grandma would enter the item and its amount in each book. She would compare the two books to be sure they were the same. Every week or two, perhaps on payday when at least part of the tab would get settled, my grandmother would total up the accrued outstanding charges. She would go through the columns of previous charges in each book to make sure both books had identical numbers — the customer wasn't likely to remember the exact amount (if he or she could read — or add — at all), and then she would deftly change a few of the numerals in each book: sometimes a 1 became 11; a 6 was transformed into an 8 — just a few cents here, a few cents there could increase the total and improve the store's cash position in a modest way. Do this "creative reconciling" with every poor *schlemiel* who bought on credit, and you not only made a little "free" profit, you also had the satisfaction of knowing how much smarter you were than those poor suckers: "A few cents here, a few cents there, they'll never know."

My mother was taught by her mother to be careful not to make too many changes, to be sure that both the customer's and the store's totals tallied. Though Anna became adept at this swindle, she was uncomfortable about deceiving the store's impoverished customers. She knew them, and she enjoyed talking to them in their own languages. They admired this conscientious schoolgirl who faithfully helped her mother every day. But her sympathy for overworked Rose stifled her ethical concerns and convinced her that the few little pennies didn't matter, and that if the customer *could* be fooled, he *should* be fooled. Did my grandfather know about this practice? Did he condone it, or did he leave the running of the store to his wife, who had such a good head for business? The 1900 census shows Louis Newman, possibly Rose's younger brother (using their mother's maiden name), also working as a clerk in the Preaskils' grocery store. In the records I have, he appears only this once.

Sammy, Anna's younger brother, grew into the feckless and delightful apple of his mother's eye. Fun-loving, carefree, mischievous, an accomplished and pragmatic liar, he brought warmth, brightness and laughter with him. He had a limitless supply of jokes of all kinds, including many (not for my child's ears) that were truly vile. One of his favorites, told with his special leering twinkle, was when his ma said to him, "Sammele, eat up your dinner," and he replied with his roguish innuendo, "I'm gonna eat every potato and pea on my plate."

He teased Anna mercilessly. He'd snatch a treasure from her—among his other talents was a light-fingeredness that would have made him a fine pickpocket—and holding it behind him or just out of her reach, he'd dance around her, intoning, "Want it back? Sayyyy—ubble ubble bubble." She'd repeat the formula and he'd command, "Sayy—eena neena nyahh nyahh." So she'd repeat the words and still he'd tantalize her, staying just out of reach. "Sayyy—Polamasky," he'd finally announce, and that was the truly magic word.

"Polamasky!" she'd shout, laughing, knowing what was coming. Whatever he'd snatched would then be handed (or hurled) back with impish grin, courtly bow, and a couple of little soft-shoe dance steps.

Sammy was an artful dodger from his earliest childhood: he and his pal Benchky Fine—what a pair! These two loved to play in the local coal yard, probably pegging chunks of coal at passing horses to see if they could make them shy or bolt; or at passing pedestrians in an attempt to dislodge a hat or give a lady a *cknock* in the bustle. It was like being a sniper: you hid behind a pile of anthracite, sticking your head out just long enough to take aim, and then you ducked back behind your barricade. An alternative activity, when there weren't many passersby, was to pocket a small piece of coal and write dirty words on walls and other conspicuous places. Sammy would come home from these forays with Benchky full of a sense of accomplishment, and as grimy as a coal miner. Exasperated, always tired (often pregnant or recovering from the most recent abortion), Rose would yell at him, "Sammy, didn't I tell you don't play in the coal yard, don't get yourself so filthy dirty, I can't get your clothes clean? Look at you! What's the matter with you? You didn't hear me what I told you? How do you get so dirty so quick?"

"It ain't my fault, Ma," he'd say. "Benchky Fine put coal in my hands." That became a signature pass-the-buck mantra in our family. Any time you wanted a fireproof, foolproof rationalization you just trotted out Uncle Sammy's creative riposte, "Benchky Fine put coal in my hands."

Though endowed with charm, a nimble wit, and high sociability, Sammy lacked the ambition to "better himself" — and his family — that his business-loving mother had hoped for. Maybe he took after his father, Handsome Louie, in that respect. Energetic, ambitious, and a quick study though scantily educated, Rose wanted a successful man, a go-getter. She had married a dreamer. While his grocery store provided a secure, if modest, living for the family, with both his younger brothers so successful and his sister Ida married to a well-to-do businessman, Louis was the family loser. If not her husband, well then, a son would do. (In reality Rose probably would have steamrollered any assertive male go-getter who developed in that household. It was Anna who would turn out to be the closest approximation to a go-getter, concentrating her ambitions on becoming a lady — speech, manners, dress — and landing the sort of reputable good provider her mother could be proud of.) Rose kept nagging Sammy that he should be helping out the family by getting a good-paying job and getting rich. But Sammele loved a good time, and a good time wasn't to go every day to the same place, same job: work! Sammy didn't see "better" as "richer." He saw it as going dancing, walking around looking at the girls, having a good laugh. Laughter was success to him.

But his ma was relentless. And one by one, his pals drifted — or resolutely marched — into the workaday world. So, probably around 1916, when he was nineteen or twenty, Sammy enlisted in the U.S. Navy. "A sweetheart in every port" must have been an alluring prospect, both geographically and romantically. There's no record of the duration of his service or where he served, and I don't recall any seafaring adventure stories from him (unusual for him not to have tales to tell!). But there is a photo of him, white sailor's cap at a jaunty angle: he was obviously proud to wear that sparkling white uniform with its bell-bottom trousers. Sammy had entered the Navy already a very good ballroom dancer; he emerged a polished and stunningly graceful one. All the girls loved to dance with him—his rhythm and grace carried his partners along and made them feel light as butterflies. Soon after he returned to civilian life and got a job as a salesman in a shoe store, he found the PERFECT dance partner, who also became his life partner (though I have no date for their marriage). Her name was Esther Stone.

Esther was a Chicago girl—born and raised on the South Side. I don't know whether she went to college, but she was smart and well-spoken, a stylish, slender blonde. She and Sammy had no children, but theirs was a sturdy, smooth-running relationship. And they made a dazzling couple on the dance floor. When those two went to a ballroom or a nightclub and got moving to the sound of a good little jazz combo, other couples would move aside to watch as they glided, twirled, and improvised. The jazz band would give them an assortment of rhythms—rhumba, blues, waltz, jazz, tango—that showcased their versatility, the band and the two dancers improvising together as the onlookers swayed to their rhythms. Their dance floor grace and delight won them wide admiration even beyond their own community: they were referred to as "the Jewish Veloz and Yolanda"—an internationally famous ballroom duo in the 1930s and '40s.

Predictably, my mother was jealous of Sammy's devil-may-care attitude and the seemingly serene way he and Esther just "got along." She had only withering contempt for Esther, whom she described as a hatchet face (there was some truth to that, but her dance floor grace made you forget the face and admire the feet) and a snob who lorded it over Sammy, ordering him around as though he were a servant—HER servant. Anna was ambivalent about her brother, too: disparaging his irresponsibility, relishing his naughtiness, envying his happy-go-lucky joy in the here

37

and now: no yearning for a better life — or even a bigger, fancier car! When she was smoldering with fury at his dirty tricks, he'd mutter some vile *double entendre* under his breath and she'd laugh in spite of herself. It was a classic example of sibling rivalry. Fred never figured in this family equation, somehow. He married Mignon, a ferret-faced dyed redhead — another sister-in-law for my mother to disparage — and the blueberry business that he owned supported him and Uncle Bush adequately, if not lavishly.

I adored my Uncle Bush. Sammy got that nickname from my father (who gave nicknames to people he loved) because he went quite bald at an early age. He was a merry, quick-witted purveyor of jokes ranging from dirty to *very* dirty. He loved the easy way out in everything and anything, including his relationship with Aunt Esther. Visits with him were merry, which discouraged squabbling or mean-spiritedness, and his tendency to be a gentle crook added both spice and laughter to the aura that surrounded him. He should have been a song-and-dance man, not a toiler in his half-brother's blueberry business. A quick wit, a way with words: I cherish little snippets of wordplay, like "Jet propulsky!," that he showered on us.

In 1977, when Bush was dying, I urged my mother to come to the hospital with me to say goodbye. "Sammy? Why??" she asked. She always had a hard time with "elemental" emotions: *turn away, don't look.* But she came with me, and I got the sense — afterward — that she was glad she'd gone: Hail and farewell, Sammele Preaskil!

6

Louis's two brothers, Julius and Dave, and their families maintained close ties. They lived and had their businesses on the Northwest Side; Julius eventually sold his paint store and established a lumberyard that became another successful "Preskill" enterprise (there are many variant spellings of the surname). They visited and spent time together; their wives probably swapped gossip and recipes, and their children may have attended the same schools. But Louis was "out of the loop," physically—and perhaps emotionally—removed from his brothers and their world. His family lived south of Randolph Street, where he had his store and had established a delivery clientele. That physical distance might have influenced the relationship, or it may have been Rosie, his energetic young wife, who was a businesswoman, not a domesticated stay-at-home mom proud to be married to a "good provider." The wives may have done charity work, but as far as I know, they were in the classic pattern of homemaker: always there with fragrant, freshly baked cookies when the kids came home from school, the house always redolent with the pungent odors of a substantial dinner in process. Rose Preaskil liked the store—that's where she ran the show—and she loved making money.

Dave was married to Ida, who was my mother's favorite relative. Ida's last name was Glickson, but the name Rosenzweig also surfaced now and then. Only during this writing did I find out why: a Dr. Rosenzweig, her mother's first husband in Lithuania, was Ida's biological father. But Rosenzweig had proven "insufficiently pious," in Ida's mother's view (was that code for playing around?), and she had divorced him and taken Ida, a small child, to *her* mother's house in Poland. There she met and married Glickson, and the new family emigrated to Chicago. Ida took Glickson's last name — he was the father who raised her — but Rosenzweig was never completely out of the picture. Dave and Ida had four children: Roland, known as Rollie (b. 1903), Esther (b. 1907), Alfred (b. 1911), and Leonard (b. 1918).

Julius, the second of the three Preaskil brothers, was also married to a Rose. Imagine what confusion might have reigned in this extended family, with its multiple Idas and Roses, save for an ingenious identification system that kept each one firmly attached to the right spouse: my grandmother Rose (Silverman), wife of oldest brother Louis, was referred to as "Rosie Louie's"; the Rose (Lipmann) married to Julius was called "Rosie Julius's"; the Preaskil men's sister, another Ida, was married to Louis Lasar, so she was "Ida Louie's"; while my mother's beloved Aunt Ida (Glickson), married to youngest brother Dave Preaskil, was called "Ida Dave's."

It was Dave and Ida's third child, Alfred, who, in just a few words, explained the workings of this simple but foolproof system to me when I interviewed him shortly before his death in 2002. He and his wife Frances were living in an Evanston retirement facility. At ninety-one, Alfred was courtly, articulate, informative, and utterly charming. He recalled his aunt, my grandmother Rosie Preaskil, as "lively, full of fun, the one who loved to give presents," and he remembered his cousin Anna (my mother) as "fascinating." My mother maintained a certain distance from all of these cousins, however. Years later, the one member of the Julius Preskill family she singled out for mention was daughter Minnie, who was two years younger than her (born, like Sammy, in 1896). Minnie didn't marry until she was thirty-two! How Anna would have relished an additional decade of carefree flirtatious freedom instead of the drab, isolated life of motherhood and housewifery. Otherwise, I scarcely knew the names of these relatives: I remember the names of Hy (b. 1898) and Matt (b. 1906), Minnie's brothers, but knew little about them and nothing of their sister Ruth (b. 1905).

Louis, ever the dreamer, aspired to become a man of commerce, a successful businessman, more like his brothers. To that end, he entered the wholesale grocery business. To finance this venture he went into partnership with a man named Glass, evidently a prosperous entrepreneur (he lived in one half of a double house in the more upscale part of the Near West Side, on Douglas Boulevard). With the partnership's name, "Glass & Preaskil," emblazoned on the side of his wagon, Louis drove to Chicago's wholesale produce market, on West Randolph Street, where he bought his inventory of comestibles. He must have gradually built up a substantial clientele, possibly one that included restaurants

With Rose Preaskil—pregnant again—running the grocery store and Louis delivering his stock with the horse and wagon, Grandma Anna Silverman became the de facto housekeeper for her daughter. Grandfather Harry, the *shochet*, was chief kosher butcher in the Stockyards and also a "freelancer" in neighborhood shops, slaughtering and dressing meat and poultry according to kosher law. The little that can be gleaned from census records suggests that in his later years he may not have had steady work, perhaps because of his poor health (and heavy drinking). His granddaughter Anna adored him, remembered him lovingly: kind, gentle, and funny. He had a little hand-operated cigarette-rolling machine, and he used to hold her on his lap as he sat in the family kitchen and let her make cigarettes for him while he told her stories and jokes. His wife, temperamentally his opposite—an outspoken, dominating woman, sharp-tongued, tiny but dynamic—was critical of her husband's gentle temperament and his line of work, dismissing slaughter as a "low-life" occupation. It was not—a *shochet* was a respected religious officiant, and Harry was well-known and admired throughout the ghetto.

In 1903, Harry Silverman was out of work once again. The *Chicago Tribune* reported that after "nearly thirty years" overseeing kosher slaughtering in the Stockyards, he had lost his job due to "a factional fight . . . between two elements in the Orthodox Jewish church [*sic*]." Harry's patron, Rabbi Hirsh Album, for many years the Orthodox Chief Rabbi in Chicago, had been deposed, replaced by a Rabbi Jacob David Ridbos (or

Ridbaz). The *Tribune* reported, "[M]any Jews . . . still maintain that Rabbi Album is the only accredited chief," and the ensuing bitterness spawned hand-to-hand combat in the ghetto streets, the factions wielding boards, sticks, and tree branches as weapons to dislodge or defend the "interloper." With backing from big shots in New York and Pittsburgh, Album's "usurper" held firm — and circulated a letter warning that meat killed by Album-sanctioned *shochets* was *trayf* (not kosher). "Silverman was one of these." In the insular world of the ghetto, that was tantamount to being told, "You'll never work in this town again."

By then Harry was a sick man, plagued by "asthma," a hard, habitual drinker in the best of times, and, at fifty-seven, too old for the strenuous work of butchering livestock. His wife's criticism may have contributed to his descent into depression and heavier drinking. And then he took a last, terrible drink: in the early morning hours of September 29, 1903, Harry Silverman "stumbled into the front room of his home, 200 West Fourteenth Street," the *Tribune* reported the next day, "and fell unconscious on the floor," gasping and choking. Doctors summoned to the home were unable to save him, and "he died two hours later," in agony. He had swallowed carbolic acid, a horrific suicide. "It was said that he had left a letter saying that without the position of kosher rabbi *[sic]* there was nothing left to live for." It was a shocking blow to the community and to the precarious stability of his family.

Harry's widow, destitute, illiterate, spoke only Yiddish. She would have to be taken in by Rose and Louie, though he and his mother-in-law were implacable enemies: they NEVER spoke a word to one another, though they lived under the same roof for over twenty-five years! But sheltering his mother-in-law burnished Louie's reputation as a generous and dutiful son-in-law. Anna moved into the Preaskil household and became resident housekeeper while Rose ran the grocery store. Louis plied the wholesale grocery business.

To vulnerable nine-year-old Anna Preaskil, her grandfather's suicide was devastating and incomprehensible. In keeping with Jewish law, *Shochet* Silverman was erased: his name and person gone forever. My mother memorialized him in her secret self by remembering the benign man who made her laugh, and let her help him make his cigarettes. Religious "Law" eradicated the man, but for Anna he was an immortal presence, and she passed him along to me.

Anna Preaskil was growing up in a crowded household. Barely two months after Harry Silverman's suicide, on December 6, 1903, Rose gave birth to a baby girl, Evelyn. Since Rose had to get back to the store as soon as possible, the baby became her big sister's responsibility, added to school and helping her mother in the store.

Within a year or two of her grandfather's death, however, Anna's life was suddenly changed. She was introduced to Hull House, the settlement house founded and run by the redoubtable Jane Addams. I don't know how my mother discovered Hull House: Did some schoolmate tell her about it or take her there? Mama Rose, ever skeptical and suspicious about whatever was outside her own world and experience, had no use for the place — oh, sure, she knew all about it, run by a bunch of society women or Bolshevik freethinkers with weird sexual proclivities. But Anna discovered a whole new world there: drama, the arts, gracious living, courtesy, respect, the excitement of beauty and beautiful things, the possibility of her own perfectibility. And personal hygiene.

The first time she went to Hull House, a shy, skinny ten- or eleven-year-old standing at the back of the room avidly watching a bunch of youngsters like her rehearse a play, she was completely mesmerized, she told me, lost in the fascination of the play, rapt as she watched people her own age performing on a stage, and wearing *costumes!* Her father had taken her to concerts occasionally, and sometimes to the theater, both of them all dolled up. Anna was always thrilled and a little scared at leaving her familiar neighborhood. But she cherished those memories of streetcar rides to downtown Chicago (which was as foreign to her as Rome or Paris), mingling with the crowds of elegant-looking people, and being with her handsome father.

Still, as she watched that rehearsal at Hull House on a winter afternoon, she was so transfixed that she never noticed the woman who came up beside her. "Are you enjoying the rehearsal?" the stranger asked. "Would you like to try out for one of our performances?" Anna was speechless. The woman continued, "My, but you have such lovely hair." In fact it was an unruly mess, long, quite curly, and in need of care. It was immediately evident that it was so tangled no brush could penetrate it. The lady then observed gently, "Perhaps if you'd let me wet it, we could brush it out and I could show you a couple of hair styles." Anna was both shy and dazzled: she had never had anyone make such an offer to her. Vanity triumphed and she acquiesced.

Of course it turned out that just wetting this matted mop wasn't enough. So my mother got her hair washed and brushed by this lady until it shone. The lady was charmed by the pretty girl with all this gorgeous black curly hair. "Let's see how you'd look in the queen's costume for one of the plays we're going to do," she said. By now Anna trusted her and was also thoroughly captivated by the thought of being in a play and being the *Queen*. The next step, once Anna had disrobed to try on the costume, was to get her bathed and to wash her clothes, so that she and her clothes would be as fresh and clean as her hair.

It was winter, my mother recalled, and in *her* family you didn't change your clothes very often, and your underwear hardly ever, sleeping in it and not removing it (which meant you didn't bathe) until the first thaw, for fear of getting a chill and catching who knows what. Their "apartment" was poorly heated, with no more than a single wood stove in the living area. They relied on warmth from each other, and perhaps the horses stabled below contributed some body heat. How this woman, whoever she was, overcame Anna's reluctance and her strongly ingrained traditions and superstitions, which included wearing a small bundle of garlic or herbs around her neck to ward off unspecified disease, is a mystery. But my mother told me she'd always had this feeling that there was something better in life.

Her Aunt Ida's house, a frequent stop on her way home to

help her beleaguered mother, was tranquil and orderly and fragrant with the aroma of freshly baked cookies, a glimpse into a world beyond her own raucous, crowded warren. Not all households were like hers: you didn't have to eat your meals at a kitchen table covered with greasy newspaper. Not all families were cowed by fear of the "evil eye;" nor did they live with the guilty shame (yet exultant curiosity) she felt, that nameless yearning to find out about things like sex and sexuality that you weren't supposed to know. Making *fagelach* and being ruled by superstitions, evasions, and lies didn't make her life or her family's life easier, happier, more gratifying or successful. But until she found Hull House, she said, she had no idea that another kind of life might exist for her. The trips downtown with her father were forays into someone else's world; now, she realized, she could learn ways to enter that world, guided by the people and the activities at Hull House.

Predictably, her mother was horrified and furious when Anna came home, freshly bathed, shampooed, and coiffed, clothes washed and ironed, eyes sparkling with the excitement of it all. Rose hollered imprecations that having allowed these Anarchists to undress her, exposing her to who knows what cold drafts and diseases, the next thing, and it had already started, these free-love aficionados would corrupt her, this rehearsal business was only a devious first step. But Anna knew that she had to find a way to return to Hull House without further antagonizing her mother. As long as she still helped in the store and continued faithfully making *fagelach*, perhaps she could avoid suspicion by lying only when necessary and simply sneaking a little extra time for her new discovery, claiming she had after-school work she was doing for her teacher. Rose had no time for the school or her daughter's teacher; in fact, she was skeptical of these educated women, all radicals who promoted free love and all manner of depravity. She preferred to leave them to their radical goings-on. As long as her daughter was obedient, conscientious, and helpful, Rose preferred to avoid contact with those corrupt females. Anna, meanwhile, had discovered enchantment: her heart and imagination turned toward the wonder world of Hull House as a flower turns toward the sun.

Hull House radically and permanently altered both my mother's outlook on life and her self-esteem. There was beauty in the world and she now knew that she could experience it. She and her father continued to cross the invisible boundary between the ghetto of 14th and Jefferson Streets and Chicago's bustling Loop to visit the Art Institute, attend concerts, and go to their odds-on favorite, the theater, where Anna's newfound affinity for the stage blossomed into a deliriously happy (if only temporary) escape from the sordid world of *fagelach* and all that stood for. I don't know for how long Anna was able to continue sneaking off to Hull House or whether she participated in many of its activities or programs. It had worked its magic on her, however, and her downtown excursions with her father offered a further opportunity to study the glamour, urbanity, and elegance of Chicago's high society.

7

Anna was surrogate mother to Evelyn: her little sister, her darling, her beloved albatross. If ever there was an ambivalent relationship, this was it. Trying to keep track of Evelyn as a two- or three-year-old was a challenge. This kid sister was inquisitive, independent, mischievous, and generously endowed with the family trait of devious opportunism. Dangers lurked everywhere in their neighborhood of muddy (or dusty, depending on the season) streets, choked with horse-drawn wagons that yawed wildly as panicked horses plunged, terrified, in an effort to avoid one of the frequent and spontaneous collisions. The day the family got dressed up to be photographed turned into one of those unanticipated calamities.

The photographs were taken in a studio in front of a backdrop of some sort: draperies, Oriental rugs, a misty street scene of some generic foreign country. The photographer put his head under a black cloth that covered the light-sensitive film at the back of the large wooden box camera. He had flat tins of flash powder that he ignited at the moment he opened the camera's shutter. Fancy photographers had assistants who touched off the powder on signal, but this guy was evidently a one-man operation. While everyone was preoccupied with the goings-on, Evelyn wandered over to the workbench and found a glass jar filled with colored water from the paintbrushes the photographer used to tint his portraits. Evelyn promptly drank this beverage. Pandemonium ensued. It was Anna's fault, Evelyn was her responsibility, why wasn't she watching the baby instead of primping and fussing with her hair? The photographer was excoriated for carelessly leaving dangerous—even poisonous—chemicals in reach of Rose's baby. Amid the hysteria and shrieking, Evelyn stood calmly, showing no ill effects, but that didn't prevent Anna from getting smacked a couple by her mother, or Louis getting yelled at on general principles. They all dashed out of the studio, unphotographed.

On another occasion, Evelyn climbed up the front of a tall cabinet filled with glassware and dishes as though it was the North Face of Everest. I don't know whether this calamity occurred at the same unhappy photographer's shop or somewhere else, but once again the family was engrossed in some transaction, giving Evelyn enough time to dart over to this cabinet and start climbing it. In a commotion of splintering glass and crockery the cabinet toppled over on her. Luckily, its doors and drawers flew open as it fell, so Evelyn avoided being crushed by this huge, heavy piece of furniture or even cut by shards of glass. But once again, Anna was screamed at. It was her fault that Evelyn had had a few unsupervised moments.

There were also the many times that Anna and Evelyn would be walking on the streets, Anna taking Evelyn somewhere (to Hull House for an interval of stolen rapture?). People couldn't help but notice the pretty young twelve- or thirteen-year-old with the little toddler in tow. And then, in a moment of unpremeditated mischief, Evelyn would lie down on the dirty wooden sidewalk proclaiming that she was tired and wanted Anna to carry her. No coaxing, begging, or bribing could prevail upon Evelyn, who was too big and heavy for her sister to lift, let alone carry. In desperation, Anna would finally have to drag Evelyn to her feet, only to be excoriated by passersby for bullying such a sweet little tyke. It was apparently one of Evelyn's favorite ploys, always good for sympathy from strangers and a good scolding for Anna, maybe even seasoned with a couple of hard smacks. Such sweet revenge!

Lest it appear that, except for Hull House, Anna's life was one of dismal drudgery, there were times when she, like her brother Sammy, enjoyed rollicking good fun. She was something of a tomboy and had a reputation as a daredevil show-off when the occasion arose. She loved to roller-skate, and became an accomplished hitcher of rides, hanging onto the backs of wagons, careening along on her wooden-wheeled skates and being shouted at by alarmed pedestrians. On the rutted streets of her neighborhood this was a dangerous pastime, frowned on by the police and discouraged by everyone, but Anna managed to keep her mother in the dark about such a forbidden adventure, and this and similar stunts earned her the admiration of some of the more influential boys in her school.

Then, about the time that Anna completed grade school (there is a photo of her in an elaborate white graduation dress sewn by her mother), another calamitous, life-altering event shook the family. Rose had become pregnant again. Maybe she was afraid to tempt fate by having another abortion; maybe she wearily decided to have this baby; maybe the pregnancy sneaked up on her (she might have entered menopause by this time—but such matters were not spoken about).

In the ghetto most babies were delivered at home, just like in the Old Country, and the lying-in usually required nothing more than the services of the neighborhood midwife. This time, however, the midwife could tell that something was seriously wrong. As her labor progressed, Rose began to hemorrhage. Fortunately, when the midwife sent for a physician for this emergency, Chicago's most eminent obstetrician, Dr. Joseph DeLee, who donated services to poor women in need of specialized care, dispatched a well-trained young doctor to take the call for help. The doctor arrived at the house in time to take over the case. My mother must have witnessed much of the horrific scene, since she and the midwife were both pressed into service.

They laid Rose on the kitchen table on newspapers (the closest thing to a sterile disposable surface handy to hot water). By the time the doctor arrived she was well along in labor and bleeding heavily. The kitchen was awash in blood, "like a slaughterhouse," my mother told me. The doctor knew immediately what the problem was: a *placenta praevia* birth, an abnormal situation in which the placenta is expelled before the baby. The hemorrhaging is generally fatal to the infant and often to the mother as well, unless prompt and appropriate measures are taken. Rose's baby, a boy, was born dead. The young doctor fought to save the mother's life at a time (around 1906 or '07) when blood transfusions were scarce and would have had to be administered in a hospital, not in a ghetto kitchen — to a charity patient at that. How he managed to stanch the terrible bleeding my mother was not able to describe. The whole desperate picture, though it left an indelible mark on her, was wrapped in a fog of terrorized forgetting of details.

Rose, ever the unsinkable optimist and scrapper, survived but was uncharacteristically weak for many months after this ordeal. Without the blood transfusions that are now so commonplace, her recovery was very slow. (As far as I know, after that catastrophic delivery she never became pregnant again, whether because of age, damage to her organs, or even the charity physician's intervention.) My traumatized mother, due to enter high school, found herself thrust into the role of manager of the household and the family until Rose regained her strength. (I can only speculate that beloved Aunt Ida and other relatives offered what help they could to the beleaguered teenager during this crisis.) Anna's entrance into high school was postponed for a year. There is no mention of Grandma Anna Silverman in all this: Where was *she?*

Now, there are several stories about why Anna stayed out of school for the entire academic year. At the onset of puberty Anna was apparently completely ignorant about her approaching menarche. (She did not get informed about birth control, reproduction, menstruation, or any biological function related to sex, either at puberty or when she was about to marry my father.) Maybe Anna was witness to enough in that crowded house to have some rudimentary impressions about sexual intercourse, but such observations wouldn't have given her a clue about the menstrual cycle. She told me that her first menstrual period terrified her. Had she "done something to herself"? What? How? Why was there blood "down there"? Was she one of those poor ignoramuses who tried sitting on a hunk of ice to stop the bleeding (especially after what she had witnessed with her mother's delivery of the dead baby in the blood-soaked kitchen)? I guess she finally told her mother about this mysterious bleeding, though she never told me how she finally learned how a girl handled the phenomenon of menstruation and what it was. Did Hull House come to the rescue? I find it hard to imagine that a shy girl from the ghetto would have had the equanimity to ask one of the Hull House ladies about such an intimate matter. It's possible that her beloved Aunt Ida was her informant.

In any event, I became the beneficiary of her poor preparation. At age twelve or so, I was told — more or less — what happens (you bleed a little), though she didn't, or couldn't, explain the physiological whys and whats. I was informed about the "sanitary napkin" and the rudiments of personal hygiene during menstruation. What got the greatest emphasis was the fact that once you began having periods (my mother always referred to her periods as "being unwell") it meant that you could get pregnant, so watch out for boys, all of whom are predatory and have only one thing in mind. Don't let them fool around with you and don't you fool around with them, either. "Fool around" meant any activity having anything to do with "down there."

Another possible explanation for Anna's delayed entrance into high school is that the onset of her puberty coincided with her mother's final labor and delivery: the death of the infant and Rose's precarious and slow recovery. That lethal coincidence may have triggered Anna's first bout with the depression that dogged her all her life. Growing up with the model of Rose's hard lot: the unwanted pregnancies, the poverty, the grueling, endless work, the handsome but unassertive husband, the failures, superstitions, nameless anxieties, all of these could have contributed to her fear of becoming an adult, her conviction that she could not confront and surmount the challenges she would face. One would hope that Aunt Ida might have stepped into the breach to help, but her own family's needs would, of necessity, have taken priority.

During her year of absence from school, Anna had to help manage the household and look after her siblings. Did her maternal grandmother Anna Silverman (who was still living with them) shoulder some of these burdens: deal with Dour Fred, Feckless Sammele, and Evelyn the Irrepressible, as well as with Handsome Louie, the wall of stony silence between them still unbreached? The family all had to be looked after, and there was also the grocery store, in which Louis probably worked (half-heartedly) only when his daughter Anna was at school. Did this mean that she, like her mother, was tiptoeing downstairs on those dark winter mornings, cash box in hand and thin sweater around her bony shoulders, to open up the store, greet the customers, and make a little discreet *fagelach* to honor the commercial tradition Rose had inaugurated and passed on to her?

My mother also told me of another disturbing experience that she would only hint at. It apparently took place just as she was finishing grade school, and it might have contributed to her need to "hide out" for a year. She would never describe it to me, wouldn't divulge detail. This was unusual in a woman who was outspoken with me about the abortions she'd had after my sister's birth, and about her triumphs flirting with guys and getting them sexually aroused. She would dance suggestively with them and note with satisfaction that "it felt as though they had a bunch of keys in their pocket." Or she would say they got "hot under the collar." She mingled naïveté with a kind of animal knowledge, a combination that probably bewildered her even as she enjoyed the power to arouse young men that her attractiveness and sexual flirtatiousness gave her.

There was a male teacher, she recalled, who told her what a pretty little thing she was. She mentioned that he often made flattering remarks to her, but she was very close-mouthed about him. I got the feeling that he might have made some explicit (and probably unwelcome) advances to her, in response, at least in part, to her behavior. She did tend to act seductively (was this "flirting"?) and then be surprised or perhaps somewhat uneasily triumphant when her behavior elicited strong sexual responses from the men she "playfully" tempted.

During this difficult time in Anna's life, her beloved Aunt Ida and Uncle Dave's warm, stable home was a much-needed refuge. It may have been kindly, sensible Aunt Ida who helped her niece Anna through the terrible year after her mother's *placenta praevia* delivery. Ida may have been the person to whom Anna turned when her own body, with its mysteries and developing sexuality, bewildered her. Anna went to Aunt Ida's whenever she had the chance because Ida, always welcoming, always good-natured, would have freshly baked cookies for her and always had time to sit and talk to her. Ida encouraged her to pursue the dreams and values that Hull House had instilled in her, to return to school, to get a life, to aim higher.

8

Around 1909, when she was about fifteen, Anna felt ready to enter high school. Her mother had recovered her health and buoyant spirits. Anna had apparently overcome the frailty and anxiety that may have been related not only to her own budding sexuality but also to the lingering trauma of having to assist at the bloody, frightening birth that had almost cost her mother Rose her life. But much as she wanted to rejoin the world of her contemporaries, Anna still felt inadequate, a condition she blamed on the cramped horse-smelling flat they still occupied. She couldn't possibly make new friends at Medill High School, noted for its high academic standing and accomplished graduates, and bring them home to such malodorous squalor. She wanted her family to leave the ghetto and move into "decent surroundings," where, as a high school girl, she could confidently entertain her friends.

Her mother may have cared little about where they lived — the store was what she concentrated on, making enough to support the family while her husband Louis tried to make (and later lost) a fortune. No one else, with the possible exception of Anna's father, seemed to be sensitive to the environment in which the family subsisted. Her association with Hull House had opened her eyes to the world beyond the ghetto she lived in (and that had formed her mindset). It fired her ambition to become the person who could — and would — inhabit the world of graciousness, comfort, refinement, and importance that she wanted for herself. A better place to live was the prime requisite of that new person. Appearances were everything, that's how others judged you, and the first impression had to be a high-octane knockout or you would be consigned to the drab shadows of eternal wallflowerhood. (Her conviction, which began early and stayed with her all her life, that appearances were of the highest importance was passed on in no uncertain terms to Darlene and me.)

Her mother realized shrewdly that when the time came to attract a decent husband, maybe when she was seventeen or eighteen, her daughter would suffer a competitive disadvantage in the race to grab off a good provider if they were still living piled on top of one another in that dark, evil-smelling flat. It was a financial gamble—no one could be sure that their prosperity would continue—but at that time Glass & Preaskil was riding high. Maybe she'd have to be a little more energetic with the *fagelach*, although the immigrants weren't so scared and ignorant any more. Louis couldn't deny his Anna this fondest wish of hers, and besides, he, too, liked nice things: cars, clothes, substantial carved furniture, accoutrements like the ones his successful brothers were accumulating. (In 1915, with the wholesale grocery business of Glass & Preaskil prospering, he bought a fancy touring car, a Hudson Super 6, the first one in the neighborhood. Learning to operate it must have been an adventure in trial and error. He told his brother Dave how he managed: "See, Dave, I hold her steady at fifteen miles per hour.") He also enjoyed gourmet food and exotic dishes. He and Rose had already abandoned the religiously observant life that his brothers continued to adhere to. My mother's cousin Alfred Preaskil remembered that his uncle Louis once invited Dave and Ida, Alfred's parents, and the four children over to partake of a wonderful special grocery item, a new delicacy he'd come upon while studying the inventories of his competitors. It sounded both exotic and interesting, he told them. What was it? Canned lobster! *Trayf*!! This was all the more scandalous given that Anna's maternal grandfather, Harry Silverman, had been a *shochet*, a kosher butcher.

Louis's partner Glass lived in a two-flat building on Douglas Boulevard, the upscale neighborhood to which my mother aspired. She coaxed and begged her parents to leave the muddy, crowded, unsanitary ghetto of 14th and Jefferson. In this period of prosperity, miracle of miracles, the Preaskil family moved into 3511 Douglas Boulevard, the companion flat in Glass's building, probably around 1911.

It was the realization of Anna's fondest dream. Douglas Boulevard was the Gold Coast of her world. With its broad, manicured parkway and gracious buildings, it was a prestigious address. For Anna, thanks to this move, high school began on an auspicious note. The year out of school had restored her. I don't know whether she had a whole new group of friends as a consequence of the move to a new neighborhood, which would have allowed her to re-create herself, or whether, having lost a year by staying out of school, she was with different but not totally unfamiliar people. In any event, she blossomed in this new milieu.

A pretty girl, noted for her liquid and expressive "bedroom eyes," she sparkled with animation and flirtatiousness. She was an accomplished dancer, a collector of boyfriends, but still a hoydenish tomboy who thrilled at the chance to strap on her wooden-wheeled roller skates and hitch a ride on the back of a horse-drawn wagon. Though she was an inveterate tree- and fence-climber, she also reveled in the chatter and gossip of her legions of girlfriends. Her mother despaired. Would this wild one ever settle down and become a demure lady? There was more to life than being popular, Rose cautioned. But Anna's life was a whirl of good times, and settling down was not in her lexicon. Those years, she told me, were the happiest of her life.

It must have been some household the year that Anna entered Medill High School. Did widowed Grandma Anna take over as cook, housekeeper, and housemother/disciplinarian so that daughter Rose could run the store? After all, there were the two boys, Fred and Sammele, who went their own carousing ways but had to be fed and supervised; there was Evelyn, who required considerable surveillance; and there was Anna, a hoydenish, impulsive young adolescent, just emerging from a dark interval in her life. The family was embarking on a new life in a new neighborhood. Grandma Anna must have been ideally suited to step in and run things: she'd have been on everyone's case. She would probably have appropriated space for herself in deference to her age and her position of authority. Louis's and Grandma Anna's mutual antagonism remained undiminished, however, and the atmosphere of despair, poverty, and depression was slow to dissipate.

When she applied herself, Anna was an able and ambitious student. Her circle of friends included both "sports" and go-getters who were planning to attend college — the University of Illinois in Champaign was the academic Mecca for these first-generation cultural "pioneers." As the dynamic center of her circle of friends, Anna wanted to join them at Illinois, to become a coed, with all the liveliness and fun that implied. She BEGGED her mother to let her go. Neither of her brothers showed the remotest interest in academics; their preference was for the University of the Wide World and the City Streets. Anna would probably have been a top-notch student. But their mother Rose, who, though nobody's fool, was herself only marginally literate, said a categorical "No!" to college for her daughter. She was suspicious of book-learning carried to such extremes; Anna couldn't convince her that any good would come of all that education. College was for Bolsheviks, anarchists, do-nothings, free-love seducers with only one thing in mind — despoiling young girls foolish enough to fall for such educated degenerates and debauchers. Better to position yourself to find a good provider for a husband instead of bumming around with that bunch of college smart-alecks. Anna should volunteer at a reputable place like the Marks Nathan Orphanage, learn to be a gentle and demure young lady, and meet a young man with a good reputation and good prospects, not one of those longhairs or fast college sports she'd been hanging around with. When she found the right man, one approved by her mother, she should get him to propose. Then her virginity would be safe and her future secure.

Well, that was still far off; she was just beginning those "best years of her life" — high school and the year or two after, before she got married and had to "settle down." High school was heaven.

She was the magnetic, lively energizer of her group, the movers and shakers at Medill High School. The boys lined up for the chance to walk her home from school, and she and her circle of good-looking, fashionable girlfriends schemed and plotted their strategies in the flirtation game at frequent "hen parties." Anna became editor of the school yearbook, involved herself in many school activities, including the drama group, and was definitely the social Queen Bee. She was chosen for the role of Portia in Medill High School's production of *The Merchant of Venice*. She still could—and did, with only token encouragement—deliver Portia's famous speech, "The quality of mercy is not strained," in its entirety when she was well into her eighties.

One of her admirers was a boy from her neighborhood who wanted to be a writer. Anna's mother shook her head in disgust. She proclaimed that he'd never amount to anything. That was the verdict of Rose Preaskil (whose own two sons were hardly exemplars of studiousness or good citizenship). She felt sorry for his mother to have such a do-nothing dreamer for a son. The boy and my mother were very fond of each other—he was a sweet kid, had a way with words, was most likely good-looking and sexy. There was more than a hint of a romance between them. Once, this impoverished young man managed to accumulate enough money for a pair of tickets for a play. He invited Anna to go with him. He'd budgeted his money so that he'd have enough for the tickets, the streetcar to the theater, and a couple of seltzers after. He'd have to walk the mile or so from his house to hers to pick her up, but he'd be able to take the streetcar back to his place after he'd brought her home at the end of the evening. (Please note that, unlike the strictly regulated Stern household, the Preaskils apparently had no curfew, at least none that anyone ever mentioned.)

Anna unwittingly upset all his delicate calculations by exclaiming, as they entered the theater and were being shown to their seats, "Oooh, I'd love one of those tiny boxes of chocolates the ushers are selling." The young man gulped (reconfiguring his money to ditch the two seltzers and the streetcar ride back to his house from hers) and bought her the candy. I don't remember whether she told me what performance they saw, but they both enjoyed it, munching happily on the chocolates as, spellbound, they watched the actors. Did they hold hands? I never asked, my mother never said.

To prolong the magic evening, after the show they bought one small ice cream at the nearby soda fountain. That still left two nickels for the streetcar fare back to Anna's house for the two of them. They didn't share the ice cream; he said he didn't care much for ice cream. Anna, oblivious to the perilous state of his finances – and maybe caught up in the wonder world of an evening at theater – was still in a daze on the streetcar ride to her house (unknowingly leaving him penniless). As they walked to her doorstep (Did they hold hands or kiss? Whoever knows is now long gone) and said goodnight, she remembered long after how dazzled they both were. The young man, trudging off into the darkness and still spellbound by the evening at theater with Anna, walked the mile back to his house. He didn't tell her of his financial straits on that magical night until many years later.

His name was Samson Raphaelson, and he did, in fact become a successful screenwriter and playwright: *The Jazz Singer*, a Broadway show patterned on the life of Al Jolson, was his first big hit. He and his wife Dorshka spent their winters in Palm Springs, California, in their later years, as did my parents. Rafe and my mother used to reminisce mistily about their shy yet ardent high school romance. Anna remembered that later on in high school, when Rafe was still too poor to buy her a birthday present, he wrote a poem for her, "Nineteen Tonight." She treasured that memento, would speak with tenderness about him and that charmed period. They must have been pretty sweet on each other through much of high school, Anna and Rafe. In his later years, he became blind, but no adversity dimmed his and her recollections of what Anna called the best year of her life – age nineteen. If that's really true – and she said so to me more than once – it's sad to think that everything in her life from 1913 on was anticlimactic.

The Block brothers (there were at least three of them and they may originally have been her brother Sam's pals) were among her racier boyfriends. They spent much of their time joyriding around in a snappy sports touring car (top down, of course). When Anna volunteered at the Marks Nathan Orphanage, they'd stop in to see her, and once they mentioned that they had a friend, a newly minted lawyer named Oscar Stern, who wanted to meet her. She didn't say no, but neither did she express great interest. In any case, young Stern managed to cook up some legal business at the orphanage as a way to meet the vivacious raven-haired Anna Preaskil. Since he had the OK of the Block boys, she turned her full, 1,000-watt charm on the hapless fellow. She apparently knew that he'd done brilliantly at Northwestern University Law School and had been hired right out of school into a prestigious Gentile law firm. Though he was favorably impressed (maybe even dazzled) by her, he was far too shy to ask her out. There is no record of her reaction to this serious, scholarly young attorney.

In her flighty way and busy life, she soon forgot about quiet, unassuming Oscar Stern. At nineteen or twenty her world consisted of a whirl of dates, dances, and drives with the Block boys and their fast-track ilk. She told me that on weekend nights she'd have two or three consecutive dates, at one- or two-hour intervals depending on the attractiveness of the petitioner. A lucky fellow got the 10:00-to-midnight slot; others, in descending order of favor, got the 8:00–10:00 p.m. period, with the 7:00–8:00 p.m. time, only an hour, an entry-level interval reserved for the untried or those whom she couldn't stand for more than a short time.

It was all fun, maybe more fun than college would have been. Still, she never got over the feeling of inadequacy that she attributed to being deprived of the College Experience. She never felt at ease with college-educated people and believed that higher education mysteriously endowed them with intellectual brilliance that was beyond her reach. All her life she compensated for her perceived lack of "intelligence" by attracting as friends those who were more like the flashy and superficial good-time Charleys of her late adolescence. Still, she yearned to become a refined yet self-assured young lady, poised and elegant, an eye-to-eye, mind-to-mind equal of the aristocratic Goyim who had revealed that other world to her at Hull House. Though she felt contempt for her "home world," which made her restless and unhappy, she was still most comfortable there, surrounded by her self-assertive ghetto gang, a lively combination of the Douglas Boulevard swells (some of whom, like her family, were recent transplants from 14th and Jefferson) and their city-wise Yid cohorts, with their coarse jokes and innuendos, raucous laughter, and spontaneous vulgarity.

In an effort to master this conflict, Anna threw her formidable energies into a life of trivial social intrigue even as she was ineluctably drawn toward the world of luxury and elegance. She observed the exquisite clothes and the refined surroundings of the patricians whose activities filled the society pages of the newspapers (some of whom she may have recognized as volunteers at Hull House, where she'd shyly watched them from a distance). She yearned for that elevated way of life, which seemed unattainable without the education her mother was denying her. If she couldn't become a businesswoman, a scholar, or a teacher, she would have to MARRY success: find and appropriate a man adept at getting ahead in the cultured and "civilized" world to which she aspired, a man whose reputation she could embellish with her good looks, magnetic charm, personality, and intelligence.

9

While her mother didn't object to her having a good time and a busy social life—after all, how else would she get to look over the field of eligible males and pick a winner?—Rose warned Anna, "You're going to end up an old maid. Other girls are getting the boys with good futures while you're just playing around. You'd better think about settling down and finding a good provider."

Enter a besotted young dentist named Kahn. I know very little about him, where Anna met him, or even what his first name was. There's no record of how long they had known each other or what sort of person he was. He was Anna's future, according to her mother, though Anna seemed to have little, if any, feeling for him. He evidently proposed and was accepted. He was suitably dull but obviously would be a good, steady, dependable breadwinner. Her mother was satisfied. "After all," said mother Rose, "a girl like you with a reputation as a hoyden should take what she can get. Now a really promising fellow like that Oscar Stern you once met, he wouldn't come near you. You're much too wild for such a dignified lawyer. You could never get HIM to propose to you."

The challenge rankled. "I'll bet I can get him to propose—if I ever get to see him again."

"Go on," said Rose, "You're not even his type."

"Oh yeah? Wanna bet?"

"You don't bet on things like that," answered her mother, who might have had a gambling nature but preferred cheating to losing.

Engaged or not, Anna curtailed neither her dating patterns nor her social life. She claimed that the Blocks and the others were pals, not suitors, so Dr. Kahn evidently didn't interfere with her last chance to have a little fun before she settled down into what she must have pictured as the end of the spontaneous joy of youth and the unwilling assumption of the drab mantle of a settled married woman — a dentist's wife.

Then, seemingly out of the blue, Oscar Stern telephoned her. Did she by any chance remember him? Yes, she said, she remembered him; after all, he had an impressive reputation — how could she forget him?

It had been a couple of years since they'd met. He had been taken with her, hadn't forgotten her — and in his methodical way, felt that he was now, at the age of twenty-seven or twenty-eight, well-enough established professionally in the Chicago law firm of Judah, Willard, Wolf, and Reichmann to contemplate marriage. He may have been earning as much as $25 per week by this time, and he had a promising and secure future at the firm. Still, he may have needed a little prodding from the likes of the Block brothers, who evidently knew of both his interest in her and also his shy hesitancy.

So Oscar reentered her life, and, as they say, the rest is history.

Oscar asked Anna to go out with him on Saturday night. I'm so sorry, I can't, she said, I am all booked up (another of those three-tier evenings), and she simply couldn't work him in. He persisted, however, overcoming his natural urge to give up — something about her made him even more eager to take her out because she was so busy. Well, what about Sunday? he asked. Could we go for a walk on Sunday morning?

Now, after dancing until at least Saturday midnight with the liveliest of the weekend's dates, Sunday mornings were generally reserved for rest and recovery, but there was her mother's challenge and she didn't want to discourage Oscar entirely — just entice him a little. Sunday morning would be fine, she said, but there was something else at noon. "That's fine," said Oscar, "I'll call for you at nine o'clock, and we'll have time for a nice walk in Garfield Park."

NINE O'CLOCK?? WALK?? GARFIELD PARK?? What kind

of man IS this? Maybe a short stroll to the drugstore for an ice cream soda, or maybe they could stop at a nearby bakery for a roll and some coffee, but after the previous night's exertions a walk wouldn't be high on her list of preferences. Still, she could hardly wait to brag to her mother that Oscar Stern, the Unattainable One, had actually called her and made a date. So she said, "Fine. I'll see you at nine on Sunday." Of course, mother Rose couldn't understand why Anna wouldn't break one of her prime-time dates for Oscar, but Anna, in a moment of high ethical propriety, said she wouldn't go back on a commitment. No one mentioned Dentist Kahn.

Sunday morning at 9:00 a.m., Oscar and a bleary-eyed Anna set out for Garfield Park. It was probably early spring, maybe a mild April Sunday in 1916, with a pale sun and trees just budding out. She remembered that Oscar strode along inhaling the sweet air while she lagged along somewhat wearily. As they approached a bench, she suggested that they sit down for a spell. Oscar, taken aback, said, "Why, we've only walked a little way." Was this the athletic girl he'd heard about from the Block boys? But sit down they did, possibly a foreshadowing of who called the shots, even though he had had the last word about the time and place of their date. They evidently found enough to talk about, though what they discussed was not reported to me by my mother, who remembered the scene clearly. Oscar put his arm along the back of the park bench, an uncharacteristically impulsive move on his part, even though he didn't actually make contact with her. This hoyden, this three-date-a-night wild one, turned to him and, feigning maidenly surprise, exclaimed, "Oscar! You have no right to put your arm around me!"

"I will have if you give me the right," he blurted out.

"Are you proposing to me?" she asked before the poor guy — this careful, methodical lawyer — could catch his breath. "I accept," she announced, and snuggled up a bit to prove it.

"Now, Anna, let's not be impulsive, you may want to think this over, I don't want to rush you into anything."

"You're not rushing me, Oscar, I have always admired you."

And so it came to pass. This is the story my mother told me, and my father never disputed it. There is no report on Oscar's state of mind. He tended to be a deliberate sort of person, so she must have quite overwhelmed him. Anna remembered being elated, skipping along as they started back to her house. In the entrance hall they stood before the pier glass (a full-length mirror that commonly hung in the foyer, where you could make a final check of your appearance before you left home). Standing side by side, studying their reflection, Anna was nearly as tall as Oscar. Ever the impulsive one, she put her arm around his waist and lifted him a couple of inches off the floor. "Oh, I wish you were just that much taller," she said.

Flustered, probably feeling trapped, blindsided by this powerful Katinka in stylish clothing, Oscar said, "Well, maybe you'd just as soon call it off."

"Oh, no, please, Oscar, I was only kidding around," she replied hastily. Mollified at last (was there a warm kiss? No report on this), Oscar left, promising to return the following day—perhaps to go through the formality of asking her father for her hand, though there was no mention of that.

As soon as Oscar left, Anna hollered, "Ma! Ma! Where are you? Ma! I'm engaged to Oscar Stern!"

Mother Rose chided, "How could you be engaged to Oscar Stern, you just went out the door with him a few minutes ago. You don't joke around about something like that. Besides, you're already engaged to Dr. Kahn. You should be more serious."

"No, really, we are engaged. He's coming back tomorrow, you'll see. What did I tell you? I win the bet, you didn't think he'd ask me, did you? Well, he did. I had to help him along a little, but we are engaged!"

And what of Dentist Kahn? He was blown off in some unspecified and cavalier fashion. Anna barely remembered him, what he looked like, what kind of a person he was. But among the memorabilia she kept over her long life, there was one postcard that I saw from Dr. Kahn. Just a few curt words, yet she kept it, and it is there, in an album. She once told me that he never married and that he died fairly young.

There's no report on Oscar's state of mind. How did he feel

about this precipitous "engagement"? How did his parents and sisters react? Well, this was America, where the young were allowed to arrange their own marriages. And Oscar was twenty-eight years old, a settled, practicing attorney in a respected firm, with offices at 134 S. La Salle Street.

The engagement period was brief but eventful—one might characterize it as tempestuous, to say the least. Anna's conduct as an engaged young woman was not a model of subdued decorum. At twenty-two, she was queen of a lively social whirl, with the added attraction of her impressive catch of this respected professional. In deference to her new status, she claimed that she had given up her practice of several successive engagements on a single night (the first might have been a shy newcomer, the second an attractive, excellent dancer, and the third, someone who'd drive her around in his sporty roadster). Instead, her social life became a succession of rollicking good times with her large, exuberant gang of young men and women. She asserted that moving in this crowd protected her from any opprobrium that might still attach to her former one at-a-time dating practice.

Oscar, who took a strictly conventional view of the conduct of engaged couples, was critical of Anna's happy-go-lucky behavior. He may also have had some second thoughts about marrying this impulsive live wire, much as he was attracted to her. He hesitated to confront her with any implied accusation of "entrapment" that might have been associated with their precipitous engagement—unless her undisciplined behavior provided him with an opportunity to postpone or cancel it. Her indiscriminately flirtatious conduct tested his patience and tolerance and he (infrequently) surprised her by getting angry, showing a flash of spirit that both frightened and impressed her. But he was not the type to face her down and announce authoritatively, "Now see here, Woman!" He must have realized early (and often) that he had a tiger by the tail.

There were at least two occasions during their engagement when it looked as though they'd never make it to the altar. The first time was when Oscar discovered a little pot of rouge in the pocket of Anna's coat. He objected to "painted women," who were just one step away from streetwalkers and other females of dubious respectability. After all, none of his sisters, models of modesty, used cosmetics. They were the women she should strive to emulate, not the painted and powdered floozies who had no sense of decency and propriety. (When Darlene and I were in high school and used lipstick, he still expressed a sort of defeated disapprobation.) Anna recalled that he told her he was horrified that she put that "dirt" on her lovely face. If she was one of those loose painted women, the engagement was off (was he trying to extricate himself?). He didn't wish to associate with a common harlot, he announced, and he walked out of her house. Anna, knowing danger when she saw it, ran after him, out into the street, shamelessly begging him for one more chance — she'd never, ever use paint on her face again! He cared about her, didn't he? He wouldn't want to disgrace her, would he, by calling off the engagement? (Note that she didn't say, "break my heart": there may have been a bit of ambivalence on both their parts.) He informed her that this was her last chance to live a seemly and dignified life as a woman engaged to a distinguished member of the bar, and paint had no part in such a life. After some tearful (and seductive?) coaxing, Oscar relented — a lifelong pattern in their marriage — and said, "Well, I'll give you one more chance."

Anna met Oscar's parents and his sisters shortly after the engagement. Oscar's patriarchal father David (who never lost his interest in pretty girls) took an immediate liking to this stylish, animated young woman, who definitely had a way with men. The four sisters, Mollie, Tillie, Rhea, and Belle, were cool to this vamp. They had their own ideas about what sort of person would be good for their brother (poor innocent!) and make him happy; this one was definitely not it. They'd chosen one of their informed and socially responsible friends who, they felt, would be worthy of Oscar, but he had not cared for their choice. (There was a young woman he'd met on a trip to Colorado Springs, however — several photographs of her appear in an album. Her name was Mary C. Raff. The photos show a shy, demure — and very pretty — young girl; a cloud of dark hair frames her face, very like Anna Preaskil, except that Mary's face expresses shy serenity, whereas Anna's has a spark of fire in eyes that seem to smolder with challenge.)

So what does he do? Oscar brings home this flashy, flighty thing—probably just a gold-digger. Mutual reserve, bordering on antipathy, established itself right from that first encounter with Oscar's sisters. Anna sensed their disapproval, and she thought they were stuffy and definitely frumpy. They weren't interested in dancing or flirting; they were serious and studious (dull, she thought). Of course, they had had to go to work as soon as they finished grammar school so that Oscar could attend college and law school. The American promise of higher education for all wasn't available to the daughters of impoverished immigrants, whose hope for the future lay in their educated (hence employable) brothers (or sons), whose income would be sufficient to support the whole family. I marvel that the sisters never expressed resentment or disappointment at this state of affairs. Oscar felt warmly toward them and maintained as much of a relationship with his sisters as he could, given Anna's disdainful lack of interest in his family.

Apparently "one more chance" didn't mean the same thing to Anna as it did to Oscar. She took it as a challenge: not to see if she could tread the straight and narrow path of righteousness for an engaged female, but to devise a way to go on doing pretty much as she pleased without getting into hot water with her fiancé. Thus another pattern that carried through the often turbulent years of their marriage was put in place.

Her girlfriends got together and arranged an engagement luncheon for her at the LaSalle Hotel, the location of one of Chicago's most prestigious downtown restaurants. There were six or eight lively, excited young women in the group, all in their late teens or early twenties, all stylishly dressed for this special occasion, with the bride-to-be wearing a corsage the girls had given her. They must have been quite a dazzling contrast to the many Chicago businessmen who were the majority of diners there at lunchtime.

There they are, in the elegant, pinkly lighted dining room,

laughing and chattering, a vivacious contrast to the men in somber business garb and the sprinkling of older ladies in their hats and gloves. I picture them seated in the center of the room, their youthful exuberance and brightness a halo surrounding them with radiance. An orchestra is softly playing demure dance music in the background.

One of the men from an adjacent table comes over, smiling. "What kind of a celebration is this?" he asks.

"It's an engagement party," they tell him, "and she's the honoree," pointing to Anna and her corsage.

The gentleman steps over to her and says, "Congratulations."

"Thank you," she replies, sizing him up.

"Such a festive occasion," he remarks. "Would you care to dance?"

"Ooh, I'd love to," she responds, jumping up. He was a marvelous dancer, she recalled, smooth, firm, with a terrific sense of rhythm. She'd already discovered that Oscar was not a dancer. He just didn't have that spontaneous responsiveness to the beat of the music that her brother Sammy had been born with, and that this stranger in whose arms she was enjoying an ecstatic whirl around the dance floor also had. They exchange names and he asks her how old she is. "Twenty-one, almost twenty-two," she replies.

He looks down at her—he's pleasantly tall—holds her a little closer and murmurs into her ear, "What a pity that a lovely young thing like you should get married and spend the rest of her life in the kitchen or cleaning house. I could take you on a little trip, show you some wonderful times. You'd see and do things you never even dreamed of. How about it? You're too young to throw your life away on household drudgery."

"Well, gee, thanks," she says, "but the wedding date is already set, so I can't do that. But thanks for the dance." And she goes tripping back to the table and her awestruck girlfriends.

Was she aware that she might have behaved indiscreetly? She just loved the power she had to attract and arouse men. She wasn't exactly naïve, but what knowledge she had seemed to have been the result of experimentation rather than information.

The stranger had evidently touched a responsive chord in her: she didn't look forward to becoming domesticated, to having the centerpiece of her day be serving her husband a nourishing, tasty dinner in a spotless house. "Between the dishes and the douches you're always in hot water," was the way she described domestic bliss to me.

That evening when she and Oscar were sitting contentedly — and demurely — in her family's parlor in the gracious apartment on Douglas Boulevard, he asked her how the engagement party had been. "Oh," she bubbled, "it was wonderful." She described the elegant dining room, the lighting, the food, the dance orchestra, the clientele; and then out of innocence (or devilment), she told Oscar about the nice man who invited her to dance, what a good dancer he was, how he flattered her by telling her how pretty she was and that she was much too young and pretty to settle down and get married. She skipped the part about his offering to take her on a trip to some unspecified (but glamorous) location. Now, my mother told me, all those years later, that she thought Oscar would be pleased that she'd had such a good time, that he'd be proud that his fiancée was such a charmer that even total strangers took note of her, that his luck and good judgment in picking her for his own was corroborated by an unbiased stranger.

Instead, Oscar, who had a fierce and unforgiving temper (which he could usually control), shot to his feet, outraged. "How could you? That's IT! Acting like a common streetwalker, consorting with a total stranger, *dancing* with him in a public place for all to see! You, an engaged woman, behaving shamelessly before your girlfriends and in public! It's over! I'm through with you! The engagement is off, over, canceled, finished!" And he stormed out of the house.

10

Anna saw immediately that her world was in dire jeopardy. Not one to hesitate in a crisis, she dashed out of the house, calling after him, "Oscar! Oscar! Come back! I'm sorry. I'll never do it again! NEVER! Please, please come back!"

She said she never gave a thought to how this must have looked in that dignified, upscale neighborhood where people didn't go running and yelling down the street. For someone who was always painfully conscious of how she appeared to others, this was one time when she threw caution to the winds. Getting Oscar to relent was all that mattered to her. Fortunately, she was both longer-legged than he and athletic enough to be able to overtake him as he strode furiously down Douglas Boulevard.

She tugged on his coat sleeve, pleaded, may even have sobbed and wept, hurried along beside him, begging him, words of contrition tumbling over one another breathlessly. He didn't give in readily, probably had no intention of taking her back, but her powers of persuasion (and the implied promise of submissiveness to his every desire) were irresistible.

This may not have been the first episode in which she won him over, but it wasn't the last. He was adamant, however, announcing severely to her that one more misstep would be the end, the absolute end. He made his point; she realized that this was serious. She'd finally been shocked into the reality of being engaged, of intending to marry, and what it all meant. There were no more lapses of taste and judgment. Their wedding was only a few weeks away.

Then there was the whole business with the engagement ring.

Oscar picked out a nice if modest diamond solitaire, something in keeping with his position as a very junior lawyer — tasteful but not showy. He may have had advice from his sisters and their friends, or from someone whose sense of style was equally clueless. He presented it to Anna, who was not inclined to suppress her opinions. She took one look at this little ring in its box and her face fell. She had something different in mind, she announced, something a little more "high style" (and bigger). Why didn't they return this one and consult the Block brothers, whose high-stepping lifestyle would surely include knowing a jeweler who could provide something a little showier, let's say, but still tasteful. Crestfallen but game, Oscar acceded to her wishes. "After all," she reminded him, "I'll be wearing it for the rest of my life." He wanted her to be happy, didn't he?

Did they patronize Moony Weinstein's father? It was someone the Block boys knew, and of course she saw a diamond solitaire that would compare favorably with — if not outshine — the engagement rings her girlfriends had gotten. It would be respectable if not spectacular. Though she did wear it always (until it was stolen when, late in her life, she was in the hospital), she always referred to it disparagingly as "the chip." It was a nice, pretty good-sized round diamond, but she instilled in Darlene and me the firm conviction that a big diamond meant big love, there were no two ways about it. The only diamond worthy of being a girl's best friend was one you didn't need a magnifying glass to see, one that gave you a signal from across the room

As the time for the marriage approached, Oscar's eagerness was almost exactly counterbalanced by Anna's dread and apprehension. Her wedding picture portrays a solemn young woman. They were married on June 29, 1916. Details about the wedding were never imparted to me, but the wedding announcement is in *The Sentinel*, the premier Jewish weekly of Chicago, June 30, 1916:

Mr. and Mrs. L. G. Preaskil, 3511 Douglas boulevard, announce the marriage of their daughter, Anna Florence Preaskil to Oscar D. Stern, which was celebrated Thursday, June 29, at the B'nai Abraham Temple. Rabbi M. Ungerleider officiated.

There were portrait-head photographs of bride and groom: Anna in a simple square-necked gown, Oscar in suit coat and stiff high celluloid collar. Oscar was twenty-eight, Anna twenty-two. They honeymooned at Starved Rock, a resort in downstate Illinois, about ninety miles southwest of Chicago—for a week? Ten days? It was a voyage of discovery: both were virgins.

At twenty-eight, Oscar was ready for marriage, and long past ready for sexual intercourse. He had had some undisclosed physical problem, acute enough for him to consult a doctor (was it Dr. Louis Handelman, his relation who later delivered Darlene?). The doctor advised him to get some sexual experience, preferably with a professional, stating that celibacy was not a "natural" or healthful way of life. He diagnosed Oscar's ailment as sexual deprivation, counseling him that sexual intercourse was the treatment of choice for his "indisposition."

If a picture is worth a thousand words, the photos from Anna and Oscar's honeymoon are a veritable encyclopedia of combined bewilderment on her part, and a jaunty—if a trifle anxious—obliviousness on Oscar's. My mother remembered it as a time of endless copulation for which she was both emotionally and physically unprepared. Fifty years later she would reminisce to her granddaughter Annie, "Ock and I had kissed and necked, we touched, breasts, I touched him all over, but we had agreed – we drew the line. Then on our honeymoon – in Starved Rock – we were both green." Neither of them had had premarital instruction; no one revealed to either Anna or Oscar the mechanics and mysteries of sexual intercourse. How to give and receive this primal pleasure appeared to have been unmentionable in both their households. What little they knew they must have learned from street-corner conversations or, in Anna's case, from overhearing her brothers' lurid and lascivious descriptions of their sexual exploits. For her, it was in keeping with the lack of instruction and information she'd suffered from at the onset of her menstrual periods. Her mother Rose apparently believed that all the previous generations of women had learned what they needed to know by getting married, and there was no reason why her daughters shouldn't continue that tradition.

Some discussion among peers might have supplied fragmentary information to Oscar, but he was intensely focused on his career as a lawyer—and too shy, proud, and repressed to admit his ignorance. (No wonder my father later became the owner of Havelock Ellis's multi-volume classic, *The Psychology of Sex*. A fascinating set, it was kept on a high shelf in our bookcase, supposedly out of the reach of the inquisitive young; I eyed it with considerable curiosity and did succeed in looking through it, but I couldn't really make much sense of it. By the time I was old enough to appreciate it, it had disappeared, along with most of my dad's painstakingly accumulated and wide-ranging library.) "You'll find out" was what each of them was told: that was how it had always been. Their complete lack of knowledge was a challenge that imposed a steep learning curve on the couple.

Anna was jolted by the discovery that flirting was one thing, teasing and arousing men, inspiring that predatory glitter in their eyes, was one thing—but the "payoff" was something else, something entirely different, fascinating yet revolting. She recalled being "so sore I could hardly walk for the first couple of days." And yet, many years later, they both recalled that honeymoon interlude with misty smiles and lascivious nostalgia. "We just stayed in our room," my mother told Annie. "There we were – two starved people in Starved Rock. And I couldn't walk. It was wonderful. We'd go to the dining room and the waiter would say, 'Mr. and Mrs. Stern, come right this way,' and I was so proud to be *Mrs. Stern*, and he liked it too, having a little missus."

Her lack of preparation, needless to say, extended to pregnancy and how to prevent it. "My mother had told me women had to douche, and she gave me a douchebag, and

I thought the long nozzle was just to make it handy, so I just sprayed myself with it – in that area – I didn't know you had to put it way in.

"So of course I got pregnant right away."

Oscar's first day back at Judah, Willard, Wolf, & Reichmann as a married man was a grim one. It began with a stern lecture from Mr. Alexander Reichmann on the subject of appropriate attire for a Member of the Bar in one of Chicago's most respected and prestigious firms. In an attempt to snazz up her unassuming new husband, Anna had exerted an unfortunate influence on Oscar's wardrobe. Guided by the Block boys in matters of all the latest styles, she realized too late that an attorney and a racetrack tout inhabited totally separate worlds. Oscar had been too innocent to object.

"Go home and change into a dark suit, with a dignified cravat, a vest, and dark shoes, well-polished," Reichmann, the firm's elder partner, and a German, admonished. Henceforth Oscar's suits were made to order by one of the City's most austere and conservative tailors: his suits were of the recommended conservative cut, the fabrics elegant but understated. Only a connoisseur would recognize the pedigree of his wardrobe, and that was as it should be. Mr. Reichmann, mollified, saw that this young man was a quick study, modest (as became a Jew in this rarefied atmosphere), a fine legal mind, loyal and even-tempered. Oscar spent his entire professional life with that firm: in practice fifty years, and he became a partner of the firm.

One's name was also an important part of the impression one made: Oscar's bride decided that from now on she would be called Anne, no more foreign-sounding Anna. Henceforth, and for the rest of her life, she was Anne Preaskil Stern.

The David Stern family: Left to right: Oscar, Mollie, mother Rose, Tillie (back), Belle (front), father David, Harry, Rhea

A pensive Oscar Stern as a college or law student

A rare glimpse of young "Handsome" Louis and Rose Preaskil

Bun & Sam (Bush)   July 27-18.

Polamasky! Anna and brother Sammy Preaskil, 1918

The Julius Preskill clan, Julius and "Rose Julius's" front and center

Anna Preaskil, 20, volunteers at Marks Nathan Orphanage, 1914

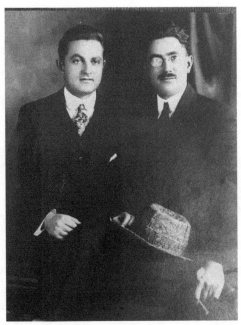

Oscar Stern, young attorney, with an unnamed friend

Oscar and Anna's wedding photos, 1916

ave — Deer Park — July 1916

Two starved people at Starved Rock

Deer Park — July 1916

Round two!!

And how!

Just one more. Daddy

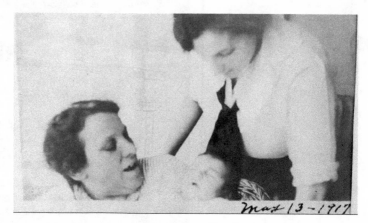

Rose–Anne–Darl

The fashionable young mother: Anne with Darlene

Aug. 26, 1917

Daddy and his Dolly Grapes

Darlene, apple of Grandma Rose's eye

Jean: Mother's little baby

Darlene, soon after we moved to the Belden

Mother dressed me like a life-size doll

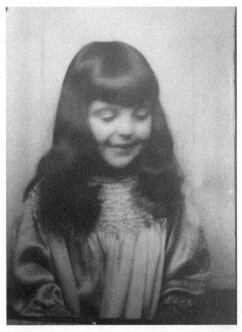

Thick black wavy hair that fell to my waist
(dress from Mayme Abbott)

Darl was a reassuring presence

Union Pier   Aug 1920

7/23/29   Atlantic City

Archie Paley

Uncle Archie Paley was tall and handsome

Among Park's Easter Flowers

Jean Stern, daughter of Oscar D. Stern of the Belden hotel, in a garden of Easter flowers at the Lincoln park conservatory. Easter is March 31.

Lincoln Park was MY park

Her hair, dyed an unforgiving black, made her look even harsher

Mother, our anti-Pygmalion, kept Darl a shy,
undeveloped girl and me an eternal toddler

Tapped by a magic wand
Before and after

Dress-up for my camera in room 1102

Mother's and Daddy's was not a tranquil marriage

July 1935 - Beverly Hills

The notorious Jackie Paley

1-18-50

Wed by 'Contract,' Couple Marks Jubilee

A Chicago husband and wife whose marriage was arranged by their parents two years before they ever got a glimpse of one another, celebrated their 65th wedding anniversary Wednesday.

They are Mr. and Mrs. David Stern, of 126 S. Central av. He is 84; she, 82.

"We grew up in Bessarabia, then a part of Russia, and our parents contracted our engagement through a marriage broker," Stern related.

"We were children when we married, 19 and 17, but we had been engaged four and a half years."

* * *

THE ARRANGEMENT wasn't as heartless as it may seem to moderns. Stern's parents had earlier selected another girl, the daughter of a wealthy man, as their son's fiancee.

But, when they quietly pointed out his prospective bride to young David one day, he said a little sadly, "It wouldn't hurt if she were better looking."

His parents thought over his lack of enthusiasm and notified the marriage broker they had changed their minds. And one day they found for him a country beauty who became his wife in 1885.

* * *

SITTING side by side in their tiny kitchenette apartment, the Sterns agreed that they have had a very happy marriage.

"You may not believe this, but I love my wife more now than when we were newly married," the grey-haired husband said.

"If he had not taken such good care of me last year when I was sick, I would not be here today," confirmed the wife.

* * *

STERN came to Chicago from Europe in 1898, and was followed a year later by his wife and five small children. He worked diligently as a carpenter and contractor and at other occupations.

"The first requirement for a husband is that he be a respectable, hard-working man, not a drinker and gambler," he says today.

"And for a wife—she should meet her husband at night with a smile."

No bitter quarrels marked this marriage, but Mrs. Stern recalls some disagreements occurred when she thought her husband was overly strict with the children.

"No one is perfect," concedes the bride of 65 years ago. "But when my grandchildren and great-grandchildren marry, the most important thing is that they have a real love for their partners."

There are 10 grandchildren and 10 great-grandchildren.

Grandma and Grandpa Stern's 50th anniversary

The Stern clan
Back row, L–R: Buds Handelman [Becker]; Dave Greenberg; Arline Dreebin
[Nudelman]; Oscar Stern; Anne Stern; Conrad Jacobson; Bert Dreebin
Middle row: Tillie [Stern] Greenberg; Mollie [Stern] Handelman; David
Stern; Rose Stern; Rhea [Stern] Dreebin; Belle [Stern] Jacobson
Front row: Harriet Handelman [Rubenstein]; Dick Jacobson; Jean Stern
[Gottlieb]; in my lap, Marilyn Jacobson [Nasatir]; Paul Greenberg; Bob
Greenberg [the two cousins I got drunk that day on Daddy's *vishnik*]

Eighth grade was a watershed year:
Sarah Greenebaum, teacher extraordinaire

Peter Kuh

Betsy Kuh

A radical and a model

PART TWO

11

A nne and Oscar began married life in a sunny third-floor apartment on Magnolia Avenue. She soon realized that she knew next to nothing about how to be a housewife worthy of her attorney-husband; she needed help transitioning from social butterfly to efficient housekeeper. So she called on her mother-in-law, Rose Stern, to teach her the art of making simple but delicious meals, and her grandmother Anna Silverman to show her how to clean house and do laundry efficiently.

Newly pregnant Anne had terrible bouts of morning sickness. Cooking was an effort of will to overcome nausea, and the accompanying fatigue made the calisthenics of laundry (up and downstairs from third floor to basement and back) almost beyond her willpower to manage. She had none of the anticipatory joy of even the most ambivalent mother-to-be; she just kept throwing up and being tired. Having an apartment to clean and a husband who expected a tasty, hearty dinner after his day at the office, some enjoyable lovemaking, and clean, crisply ironed shirts to wear to work were all things to which she was a complete stranger. Except for infrequent meetings with her girlfriends when she was feeling up to it, she felt isolated in their tiny walk-up apartment. She couldn't imagine how she'd get through the lonely, nauseous days, she was so frightened and depressed.

Oscar, in contrast, blossomed under the releasing delights of regular sex. For all his prim exterior, he was an expressive, demonstrative man, a lover of physical contact, which now repelled Anne, in her morning-sick state. Her mother reassured her that it would get better when she felt better. She'd get used to the sexual demands of her husband — all women adjust to it one way or another. Would Anne ever get used to ever-present sex, let alone learn to relish it? The answer is a resounding AND HOW!

I have always wondered whether there were other men in her life, or whether my dad turned out to be a pretty good lover. He was certainly not physically repressed: a great pincher, squeezer, kisser, he was tender and expressive. I think probably he loved happiness and laughter especially intensely because he could not expunge the terror of that childhood escape, the river crossing in the dark night, and he, the oldest boy, caring for his seasick family on the long ocean trip; and then the hideous death of the brother whose sins were that he wrote poetry, loved a good time, and had a Gentile girlfriend.

Oscar, child of an orderly, serene household, wasn't prepared for Anne's lack of housewifely skills and her general personal sloppiness. He was shocked to discover that she simply stepped out of her clothes when she undressed and left them in a heap on the floor. At first he picked up after her, neatness being second nature to him. He tried reminding her to put her things away in orderly fashion so that they'd be presentable for a second day's wearing, but to no avail. Finally, he simply let the mess accumulate, which was a worse trial for him than for her. She told me that the moment of truth came when she wanted to go out somewhere and had no clothes in wearable condition. Who, Oscar wanted to know, had picked up after her in her parents' house? He finally instilled in her a minimal tidiness, but it was never second nature to her. What little acquired orderliness she developed she credited to her husband's firmness and persistence. (She really should have had a lady's maid!)

In an attempt to instruct her in housekeeping and general household management (a futile effort to transform her into a paragon of serene housewifely orderliness), Oscar gave Anne a weekly "allowance." She was to run the apartment, her little fiefdom, with this money and to acquire the frugality practiced by his mother and sisters. She was uninterested, not a good student of domestic arts and home economics. Her days of dealing with money and accounts and making *fagelach* were behind her, and that experience may have killed whatever appetite she might have had for scrimping and saving. After all, she'd married a "good provider" just so she wouldn't have to be pinching pennies all the time.

Improvident, impulsive, she immediately began skimming this allowance so that she could purchase an inordinately beautiful hand-embroidered banquet-size tablecloth. An itinerant peddler had played to her greatest vulnerability: the need for the outstanding, the one-of-a-kind, the gorgeous, the luxurious. After bargaining down the substantial initial payment on this white elephant, she gave her peddler installments of 25 cents per week, sneaked out of her household allowance. Oscar had not asked for an accounting of her disbursements, so she was able to conceal the transaction. She knew he would be horrified by the out-and-out extravagance — and uselessness — of this item. But she HAD to have it. Thus was initiated another marital convention: when she had to have something she usually got it, by hook or crook. The moment of disclosure tended to lose its scandalized aura when she deployed her array of seductions on Oscar, who seldom if ever won these jousts. The tablecloth cost $300 — in 1916! She never told me how she paid off that enormous sum. It was trotted out and used only once that I know of: at Darlene's wedding in 1940! Just to launder it, let alone iron it, required specialized equipment, and its delicacy demanded that it have only the most meticulous handling. Yet she never regretted that purchase, but spoke of it with pride: she had shown how self-disciplined she could be when the stakes meant something to her.

With the happy news of a blessed event had come the Stern family's dictum of the doctor who would deliver their grandchild: Dr. Louis Handelman, Rose Stern's cousin. He was a fine physician, they promised her, a professional (no old-country midwife), just as competent as those fancy specialists and a lot less expensive: he would give them the family discount for his services. Still a neophyte when it came to family politics, Anne had accepted this recommendation, though she'd had her own dreams of an aristocrat's cossetted lying-in. She had little, if any, prenatal care; everyone assured her that having babies was what women were meant for.

After a hard and protracted labor, Darlene Grace Stern was born on Easter Sunday, April 8, 1917. I believe it was a hospital delivery. Anne told me that she was terrified, didn't like this doctor—he had dirty fingernails, she said—and was not at all comforted by the testimonials of Oscar's family. The horror of her mother's terrible childbirth experience ten years earlier was still vivid in her mind, and in her terror and isolation the miracle of childbirth, which she only poorly understood, seemed instead shameful, dirty, and pain-filled, the culmination of nine months of discomfort and grotesque distortion of her once-lovely body.

The arrival of Darlene catapulted Anne and Oscar into full-fledged adult family life, for which neither of them was prepared, especially Anne. Nevertheless, Darlene was a healthy baby, Anne had no trouble nursing her, and everything seemed to go well at first. But some time after Darlene's birth, Anne was found to have a large "staghorn" kidney stone in her left kidney that required surgical removal of the entire organ. I have no information on how this came about; perhaps it was related to her lack of prenatal care. Though she never spoke of it, I remember seeing the large neat (but ugly) scar, like a ladder, along her left side, from under the rib cage almost to her backbone; it both repelled and fascinated me. I'd ask her: What was it? What happened? But though she didn't conceal the scar from me, she wouldn't tell me anything about it.

Possibly staying with Rose and Louis for help with Darlene while she convalesced (or Rose may have moved into their small quarters on Magnolia Avenue), Anne recovered from her surgery, but it probably contributed to the depression that then engulfed her. Alone in the little apartment all day, having to drag the baby up and downstairs if she wanted to get out, cooking, washing, at the beck and call of this tiny wailing tyrant of an infant, she sank lower and lower. Oscar was powerless: nothing he did could dislodge the depression that gripped her.

So they gave up the apartment on Magnolia and moved in with Rose and Louis. The new grandparents were thrilled to relieve Anne of her responsibilities, and they adored the wide-eyed, sweet-tempered baby, growing into a shy little girl. Rose swung into action and assumed the care of her first grandchild, and Darlene basked in the unconditional love that is a grandparental specialty. The bond forged between Rose and Darlene was full-hearted, adoring, unequivocal, and permanent.

Rose encouraged Anne to enjoy herself and go out with her girlfriends: no household chores. That way grandmother and granddaughter could enjoy the spontaneous delight of being together by themselves. Apparently Rose took on the housewifely role that she'd disdained when her own children were young, cooking and doing laundry as well as caring for Darlene. Anne took full advantage of being back "home" and having the luxury of her mother's help. For her it meant a return to the world of the living and a faint echo of the carefree times before her marriage. Some of Anne's pals who were married were also new mothers, some had nursemaids for their babies, but none had Anne's easy life: she was free as a bird. Sometimes she and her girlfriends would meet in Garfield Park with their babies to gossip and giggle and compare husbands. Sometimes they could still arrange a luncheon, but nothing like the infamous party at the LaSalle Hotel, which they all recalled with mischievous relish.

Anne blossomed. She loved the life back home with Mom and Dad. Oscar was less enchanted. Whereas Anne seemed to have settled back in with an air of complacent permanence, he saw this return home as a temporary expedient. He felt that they were a family now, and should have their own domicile.

I don't know for how long they stayed on, living with the Preaskils. When they moved in, the family was riding high. The partnership of Glass & Preaskil had flourished, and during the early years of World War I, when the opportunity presented itself to trade in commodities, they ventured beyond the bounds of the wholesale grocery business to become a player in the high-stakes speculation in commodity futures — in this case, sugar. Louis had at last become a go-getter. Glass & Preaskil is mentioned in the financial pages of the *Chicago Tribune*. As wartime shortages of sugar increased and prices escalated, the wholesale grocery firm held a large sugar inventory, and the partners hatched a daring scheme to corner the market. For a time, they appeared close to succeeding. Louis boasted to his brother Dave, "I've taken care of my children and grandchildren." They would be financially secure for life, thanks to the proceeds from this business triumph.

But then, in 1918, as World War I drew to its bloody close, anticipation of the Armistice opened the floodgates of foreign sugar that had been unavailable. The speculative bubble burst, sugar prices collapsed, and Glass & Preaskil went bankrupt.

Louis's dream of an economic coup was ended. The business was all but wiped out. Louis was crushed by the personal economic calamity and by the disgrace. He seemed to lose interest in the struggle to recover: he let Rose run the grocery store, and presumably went back disconsolately to the door-to-door horse and wagon business. He never regained the motivation to return to the hurly-burly business world. Rose continued to run whatever small economic enterprise they had; when Darlene was still very young, they gave up the grocery store and opened a small hardware store on Clark Street and Wrightwood.

I don't know what happened to Glass, Louis's partner in bankruptcy, but Louis and Rose moved out of the Douglas Boulevard duplex and into a modest apartment just a few blocks from the hardware store. Perhaps that was when Oscar finally (and uncharacteristically) put his foot down, and the little family of Oscar, Anne, and Darlene went off on its own. It was probably before Darlene had started school (she went first to the Swift School, then to the Lincoln School, both public schools). Their new apartment was a third-floor walk-up on Kenmore Avenue. By then Anne had gotten the hang of motherhood, and she had a little more sense of freedom now that Darlene had matured from the unpredictable and incomprehensible shrieking and wailing of infancy to the companionable chatter of childhood.

Anne continued to take Darlene to visit Louis and Rose often, giving all of them precious time to do what they loved: Darlene and her grandparents to delight in being together, and Anne to get a much-needed break from the daily routine she was learning to tolerate. Darlene remembered spending lots of happy hours in the hardware store with Grandma and Grandpa. She reminisced about those times. She was allowed to ride the little kids' tricycles that were part of the inventory, and she was given the run of the store, playing with whatever hardware items could be converted into toys.

12

Darlene, a gentle, sweet-tempered child, something of a poet and a dreamer, had become a companion to her mother, so their lives went along tranquilly. After the traumatic childbirth experience with Darlene, Anne was adamant: No more children!

Why did she not consult the enlightened women at Hull House, who are celebrated as pioneers in spreading the word of safe, clean contraception? Margaret Sanger had opened the first (illegal) birth control clinic in the United States the year before Darlene's birth, promoting the diaphragm, which she had learned about in Europe. Hull House opened the second such clinic in the nation—but not until 1923, the year of my birth. During World War I the Navy, desperate to control an epidemic of venereal disease sidelining sailors who'd visited prostitutes, had started issuing condoms to its troops, and after the war they were sold in drugstores, purportedly for disease prevention only. I do not know whether Anne and Oscar ever discussed sex and children candidly, or whether they ever talked about sex at all, except in lascivious banter. Female contraception, in those first years after the war, was still illegal and all but unavailable. Perhaps Anne continued to rely on the douche, which she might have learned to use correctly by then. Still, she soon found herself pregnant again. She turned to her mother for help.

Rose's solution for unwanted pregnancies was abortion. She had had many—married to an insatiable man who couldn't keep his hands off her, whom she couldn't or didn't want to turn down, she had fought off the notion of being "domesticated" (like Oscar's mother), a homemaker with babies. As a regular customer, Rose knew all the abortionists. So (my mother shocked me with this confidence late in her life—it evidently haunted her), Anne obediently followed her mother into that dark and unsavory world: down a dark, muddy alley, furtive, posted with "lookouts" watching out for cops who might be patrolling these notorious little warrens, a peephole where you had to identify yourself. It was an ordeal: Mother was petrified and repulsed, it was dirty, the abortionist did his terrible business deftly but hurriedly; gave Anne some pads to blot up the bleeding; were there pills for the pain? She never said. Clinging to each other, Anne moaning softly, she and Rose would slowly make their way back home.

She said she only did this twice. After she had me, she finally went to a proper OB-GYN and got fitted for a diaphragm. Contraception was still technically illegal, but court cases in Illinois the year I was born opened a loophole for private practices and their married patients; Margaret Sanger was (illegally) importing diaphragms from Europe and Japan, and in 1925 she helped open the first U.S. factory to manufacture them. I remember at age twelve or thirteen helping Mother hunt for her diaphragm, which she had trouble inserting. It would bounce under the radiator, and we'd have to hunt in all the carpet fuzz that the hotel maids at the Belden Stratford didn't vacuum out from under there.

Abortion, of course, remained a crime on the law books but a fact of life. In the thirties and forties, Anne and Oscar were friends with a Dr. Hugo Foster; I remember meeting him and his wife, Helen, more than once when I was about eleven. It was some time after that that Mother told me—salaciously—what he did for a living: he worked for the Syndicate—exclusively— as their "in-house" abortionist and OB-GYN specialist. How that came about I don't know; he was evidently a really fine M.D., and that's how he got the offer, but it was the end of a real professional career for him. He and his wife lived on the Gold Coast, possibly at 20 East Cedar Street, which must have been something of a gilded cage: he "belonged" to the Syndicate and was probably monitored constantly, but he and his wife were allowed to socialize with some of his friends. Daddy was never really comfortable socializing with them, or with Arthur Greene, a shady big-money financial manipulator; Mother may have been titillated by the whiff of "off the straight-and-narrow" that they represented. But nobody had to worry about getting nabbed by the cops: these men never got even a speeding ticket! Nor did their names EVER get in the newspapers, which is why I was unable to find any mention "on the record" of Hugo Foster.

Anne finally decided she wanted to have a son—for Ockie, to console him for the loss of his brother. But she was also one of those women who begin to yearn for another baby when the older child goes off to school and the house suddenly seems very still and empty. Her girlfriends had become absorbed in the routines of marriage and motherhood; inevitably, they saw less of each other as their lives diverged. Now that Darlene was in school, Anne discovered that having and being with her child was a delight like no other. This time they'd have a boy, and Darlene would have the fun of helping her mother with the new baby, which would be better than the dolls she loved to play with.

By the time Anne decided she wanted a second child, she had also firmly fixed in her mind just *how* she was going to have it: an eminent specialist would be her doctor from the beginning of the pregnancy through the delivery, which would take place in one of the city's premier hospitals. I must have been conceived a couple of months before Darlene's sixth birthday; I was born at 5:00 a.m. on November 17, 1923, at Presbyterian Hospital. I was a breech presentation (rump first), delivered by Dr. Edward Allen, an attending physician in the practice of the city's eminent, high society obstetrician, Dr. N. Sproat Heaney. Dr. Heaney was chairman of the Department of Gynecology and Obstetrics at Rush Medical College and Chief Gynecologist and Obstetrician of the Presbyterian Hospital. (Though Mother told me that he had delivered me, the birth certificate is signed by Dr. Allen.)

Everything about this pregnancy was in marked contrast to the first one: there was hardly any morning sickness; she'd wanted and planned for the baby and looked forward to presenting Oscar with a son. She was so confident and relaxed that when she felt the beginnings of labor, she and her twenty-year-old sister Evelyn took the streetcar from Kenmore Avenue, in Rogers Park on Chicago's North Side, all the way to Presbyterian Hospital, south of the Loop. Anne and Evelyn giggled and joked as they made the long trip from one end of the city to the other, the vivacious, raven-haired, very pregnant young woman and her lanky attractive kid sister, who was carrying the little overnight case.

The labor was quick and painless, the delivery easy despite my rump-first position. Needless to say, I was not a boy. But Anne said she heard the doctor say, "This is the most beautiful baby I have ever seen!"

One is justified in thinking that this is what doctors say and feel about all babies; otherwise they'd go into a different line of work.

Anne felt exhilarated, marvelous, after I was born. The easy delivery, the high-class ambience of Presbyterian Hospital, all contributed to putting her — temporarily — "on top of the world." If she or Oscar were disappointed that they had had another girl, they evidently got over it.

In December, just a month after I was born, Evelyn, Anne's beloved sister, married Archie Paley. He had been in the Navy at some point (there was a photograph of this good-looking young man in a sailor's uniform). Archie had grown up in a large, rollicking ghetto family, big on practical jokes, noisy and extroverted, the bunch of them, led by mother Fannie, a zesty, earthy, outspoken matriarch. This was a family of hustlers and entrepreneurs; they became successful Chicago cigar makers. (The Paley extended family included the elegant William Paley, later head of CBS, and Jay Paley, who became a Hollywood movie mogul.)

Anne's elation was only temporary, alas. She developed a breast abscess, which she claimed was caused by scooping ice cream out of big containers for the guests at Evelyn's wedding.

As a result of the abscess she stopped nursing me, an activity about which she may have been ambivalent anyhow. The post-partum depression that then engulfed her was so severe that she was sent (by whom I don't know) to the euphemistically named North Shore Health Resort, a sanitarium in the Evanston area. This was her first stay in the place, but not her last.

Possibly the depression that incapacitated her and left Oscar to deal with a young infant and a seven-year-old school child inspired the move to the Belden Hotel. Her depression eventually dissipated, giving the family a brief, blissful interval of domestic tranquility; still, Anne needed the comfort and elegance of being waited on; she wanted a prestigious address; Lincoln Park, not Rogers Park, was what she strove for. As far as she was concerned, Rogers Park, a Jewish enclave, was only a short step above the ghetto of her childhood. If the cost of an apartment at the Belden seemed unreasonably high to Oscar, raised in the prudent sanctuary of an orderly household, he realized nonetheless that he had to have a functioning wife to care for him and his two girls. And clearly Anne couldn't (or wouldn't) function in the workaday environment of a walk-up on Kenmore Avenue. She wanted beauty and elegance and class and *service* — and when the Belden Hotel was finally ready to be occupied, she got it. I was about eighteen months old when we moved in.

13

For Darlene, at age eight, the experience of moving was difficult. Both her school and friends from her old neighborhood were left behind. The break with whatever social life she had had in Rogers Park was pretty complete: parents in those days did not ferry their young to friends' houses for "play dates" with any regularity — at least, our mother didn't. I don't know whether we had left a neighborhood teeming with children, but Darlene, a shy, introverted dreamer of a girl, couldn't bring herself to intrude into the self-contained world of the Belden, even though there were quite a few families with children. There were the Philipsons, the Eisenschimls, the Lustgartens, each with children Darl's age. But she was too painfully shy to go downstairs and make friends with this gang that played catch, jumped rope, or roller skated around the Belden Avenue side of the building, where the doorman and lots of action could be found.

It was not your uppity hotel, despite the liveried help and polished brass doors: no one objected to the swarm of boys and girls who played hopscotch on the sidewalk near the entrance to the building or made exuberant drawings with colored chalk. The wall of the hotel had a series of decorative curves and channels, and a favorite game of "baseball" or catch for anywhere from a solitary player to five or six (the sidewalk was a generous double or triple width at the hotel entrance) involved throwing the rubber ball so it hit these curves a certain way. Then it would fly back at you in an unpredictable trajectory: sometimes a fly ball, sometimes a grounder, sometimes a line drive. An intricate system of scoring was devised, and this baseball game was a favorite with both girls and boys.

After two or three weeks of clinging to her mama and staying indoors and being too shy to initiate any move toward this bunch of youngsters, my sister clearly needed a boost of some sort. So according to Darl, who both laughed and cringed at the memory, Mother took her by the hand, marched her down the corridor and into the elevator, down the lobby stairs and over to where the gang was playing. Cutting the most sympathetic and friendly-looking girl (Ruth Philipson) out of the herd by walking up to her authoritatively, Mother announced, "This is my daughter Darlene Grace Stern. We just moved in a couple of weeks ago and she doesn't know anyone yet. She'd like to play with you but she's too bashful to ask." She then said goodbye to Darl, who was in an anguish of embarrassment, rooted to the spot, and marched back upstairs, leaving the poor kid to face this group of five or six kids all alone. (Anne would never have found herself in this sort of predicament: she was spontaneous, outgoing, and at least on the surface or with people she felt were her peers, she was an exuberant initiator.)

The gang apparently stood around assessing this newcomer, a couple of them whispering and sniggering. Was it the chorus-girl first name of Darlene that got them? Or was it her inappropriate middle name, Grace? She was gangly, leggy, anything but graceful, which became apparent almost instantaneously. (She became an accomplished ballroom dancer as an adult, but in her childhood and early adolescence she suffered all the torment of the lifelong wallflower.) She told me later that if she hadn't been so completely demoralized, she'd have bolted and run back upstairs, away from this clique that was waiting for a signal from somewhere about whether she was to be "in" or "out." Ruth Philipson, who'd already felt the power of Mother's basilisk eye and who was a naturally compassionate person, walked up to poor Darl and said something cautiously friendly: "Wanna play hopscotch?" or whatever the game of the moment happened to be. Darl was still mute with terror and embarrassment, but, she recalled, Ruth took her hand and said, "C'mon, we could use another player." And so the ice was broken. Darlene became close friends with Ruth and with the two older Eisenschiml kids,

Jerry and Rosalie. Ralphie was younger, only a year or so older than me, and he and I became pals later, but he was too young for Darl's "gang."

Once Darlene had pioneered entry into hotel social life by getting to know the children, Mother and Daddy became acquainted with the parents. The Eisenschimls were an interesting family. Otto, the father, was a chemist whose hobby was the study of Abraham Lincoln's assassination. He wrote a book, *Why Was Lincoln Murdered?*, with which my father was very impressed. The family was its own musical ensemble. Mrs. E. sang, I think; Rosalie played violin, and Jerry, viola or cello. Papa may have been the pianist. When he was old enough, Ralphie joined the family chamber group. Ralphie taught me a lot about music, trying to teach me to read the notes by following the conductor's score while he played a classical recording on their Victrola. The Lustgartens were another family chamber music ensemble. Alfred, the oldest, played violin; Ruth, the middle child—who was Darl's age—played piano; and the youngest, Edgar, played cello. Mama and Papa, who'd emigrated from Germany or Austria years earlier, also took part in the musical ensemble. I was very impressed with the kind of family life in which people made wonderful music together. They enjoyed playing and I loved listening. What a civilized family activity, I thought later on.

With the move to the newest and most attractive hotel in the city, the Belden Stratford, Oscar Stern and his family entered a different world. Even its pretentious name conjured up elegance. In my baby talk years (which lasted much longer than they should have) I called it the Beddy Tefford. It was an imposing thirteen-story structure with a gray glazed terra cotta exterior, and it boasted distinctive arched windows on the top floor. A courtyard separated its two wings. Darl later told me that that courtyard, which was just outside the windows of our apartment, had been intended to become a tea garden, but the Depression put an end to that plan and the courtyard was just a sooty windswept space paved in reddish brick.

At the time, a number of similar apartment hotels were being built around the city. The Belden, the Parkway, and the Webster were within a few blocks of each other, on Lincoln Park West, facing Lincoln Park. The Park Lane, where my Paley cousins, David and Elaine Lowenberg, lived, was at Surf Street and Sheridan Road, less than a mile away. Their mother, Miriam, Archie Paley's sister, was married to Iz, an architect, who designed and built functional (but unimaginative) buildings.

An innovative type of living arrangement, the apartment hotel was a mix of transients and families whose year-to-year leases gave them the status of permanent residents. There were also a few elderly single ladies who, like Harry Gottlieb's great-aunt Susie Cahn, lived independently but with the support of housekeeping and dining facilities on the premises, perhaps the ancestor of "independent living" housing currently in vogue, except that there was no umbrella institution hovering over them to scoop them into the safety and regimentation of today's nursing home when they became mentally or physically incapacitated.

I was too young when we moved into the Belden to have any memory of our first apartment, 515, which was on the fifth floor, at the back end of the courtyard that separated the two wings of the hotel. Anne put up with its perpetual sooty gloom for as short a time as possible after our momentous move. Did she implicitly threaten a recurrence of her depression, or were they on a waiting list for a better (and more expensive) apartment? By the time I was two or so, she got the place she wanted.

Apartment 122, on the first floor, had generous casement windows with curved tops that repeated the architectural motif at the top of the hotel. The living room and my parents' bedroom, which faced Lincoln Park, had a gracious treetop view of the much-loved (and climbed-on) statue of Shakespeare, with the park's exquisitely tended gardens visible through the lush foliage. Although the apartments were furnished, Anne had no use for that "hotel stuff," and she set about acquiring an array of interesting—and pricey—antiques.

The child of ghetto poverty, and indifferent to the

virtues of neatness and domestic order, Anne was an ardent and determined seeker after the fairy-tale existence of the Aristocracy. Her dream was to live in an elegant apartment, with domestic chores performed by a superbly trained corps of invisible lackeys. They would attend to all tiresome domestic details as though they were clairvoyant. For her the Belden was the perfect answer. The hotel supplied all linens and towels, and two maids came every day.

To Oscar, the Belden was finally a home to which they could invite his friends and colleagues, the people he associated with: college-educated, mostly German Jews from the North Shore, people he met through the firm and at the Standard Club. He'd applied—and was accepted for membership—as soon as he was able to afford the initiation fee, using the credentials of his prestigious law firm to pass muster despite his Russian Jewish immigrant origins.

I remember some of his friends. There was Oscar Blumenthal, a brilliant mind, fated to become a casualty of the Great Depression. Sigmund David was a suave, sandy-haired man (possibly a lawyer) whose lovely dark-haired wife Louise died young of cancer, leaving him with four small children: three girls and a boy named Alan. (It turned out that the Davids were acquaintances of the Gottliebs, and Harry Jr. was a contemporary and possibly a schoolmate of Alan David.) I remember Louise—pale with a cloud of dark hair, ethereally beautiful. She spent the final months of her short life smocking and embroidering a whole series of dresses for her daughters in an array of sizes so that they'd continue to have lovely wardrobes—clothes that could be passed along from the older to the younger girls—after Louise was gone. I remember visiting their sumptuous house in Winnetka. Louise made a profound impression on me—her dignity, her graciousness, her suffering, the air of sorrow that hung over them all, the beauty of the place, its tranquility and order in the face of this oncoming death which would disorder everything. They had an automatic record player, a Capehart, the first of its kind I'd ever seen. You could put on several records, a whole opera or symphony, and it would automatically turn each record over so that you could play an entire piece without having to jump up and change the records.

Then there was Walter Bachrach and his twinkly wife Alice, known as Allie. They were warm and spontaneous and unpretentious, maybe less formidable in Anne's view. Walter was his own person — some might say eccentric: he would excuse himself from his guests and leave his own dinner table after the main course had been served, and go to bed, leaving Allie to carry on for him for the rest of the evening. She didn't seem in the least perturbed by this, but I was quite surprised at such conduct, even though I was probably no more than four or five.

14

There were two stages in my early childhood life before I entered first grade, while Darlene was in school. The first was when I was Mother's little baby, prior to and early in our move to the Belden, but after her depression had lifted, when she began to enjoy "playing house," and I was small and tractable enough to be a prop in that fantasy. She'd doll me up, put me in my fancy "English cab" buggy (an elegant baby carriage, similar to those used by royalty), and we'd amble around the neighborhood. The Anne who loved the high-stepping life hadn't been expunged by motherhood; that aspect had merely entered a dormant phase.

I was probably not quite two when she embarked on a misbegotten adventure. Dreams of culinary glory may have clouded her judgment: Mother enrolled in the School of Domestic Arts and Sciences, a castle-like building that must once have been a residential estate. With its imposing exterior of rough-hewn limestone blocks, trimmed with darker stone around the windows, it sat on a huge lot at the corner of Commonwealth and Belden Avenues. Its imposing entrance opened onto a large foyer beyond which were huge, sunlit rooms bustling with people in cook's whites. The school was an institution for aspiring culinary professionals and a few "high society" matrons (doyennes of establishments requiring regimental-size staffs). Its students learned everything from how to set an elegant formal table to the creation of elaborately decorated cakes and pastries.

I have memories of that experience: the walk from the Belden to the school, always with a sense of keen anticipation—I thrilled to the bustling activity and the sensory excitement of all those aromas: baking bread, roasting meat, the heavenly sweet bouquet of chocolate and cakes and cookies. But Mother "resigned" after just a few sessions, much to both the school's relief and her own: her presence there was unsuitable for her, and disruptive to the professionals-in-training.

I've been told that I was a stunningly beautiful child. I can't really tell, because I live on the other side of my face, hence what I go by is what is mirrored in the words and expressions of others more than by what looks out at me from the looking glass. Mother dressed me like a life-size doll, in fabulous starched dresses and white Mary Janes. I had long black sausage curls, bangs (which were invariably crooked), and large hazel eyes fringed with heavy black lashes. Passersby would stop us on the street and exclaim over this exquisite little girl. They'd bend down and ask, "What's your name, dear?"

I'd reply in the baby talk I'd carefully cultivated long after I could speak English, "Din Dun," my infant pidgin version of Jean Stern. Then they'd gush about me to Mother. I learned to flirt, learned the power of being beautiful; it gives you a head start on others who lack this gift of nature, poor things. I also learned to be a conniver, a manipulator, a liar when it suited me. People believed me because I was so pretty.

I had thick black wavy hair that fell to my waist, and Mother fussed over it as though it were hers. She'd brush it into long gleaming sausage curls that she shaped around her finger and then secured with a bobby pin. All this took much too long, and the end result fed Mother's vanity more than mine. Mother and I had quite a few battles over my hair. Once a week we had this battle royal when it was shampoo time. It was a very vocal war we fought, me howling, Mother yelling, and lots of soapy water flying. I had to kneel on a chair or bench and lean over into the washbasin. My neck got tired, my arms, back, and knees got tired. Rinsing all that hair was horrible but the washing part was the worst: I almost always got soap in my eyes, which brought on thrashing and screaming. She'd kind of drown me in rinse water, then throw a towel over my head to muzzle me. By that time I'd had enough, but we still had to do this sausage curl thing. I tended to be very squirmy by then, and Mother was pretty exasperated, too, so there was some hair yanking and other rough stuff. It was weekly warfare. The bathroom looked like the aftermath of a major naval battle: trails of wet soapsuds running down the walls, the floor awash in scummy water. As captain of my ship, I would not surrender.

The only other battle that compared to it for ferocity and hysterics—and it was an even higher order of combat—was the one that accompanied the frequent (or so it seemed to me) administration of enemas. I don't know how Mother determined that I needed to be "cleaned out." If I'd had a cold, might be catching a cold, or if she suspected that I might be constipated (a condition I went to great lengths to conceal from her for obvious reasons), there she'd come with the dreaded enema bag and this determined look on her face. The enemas were always wrestling matches: I fought with everything I had, fought like a cornered beast. It was a day of liberation for me when I finally got too big and too strong for Mother to be able to hold me face down across her lap while she inserted the hated enema tube, but those experiences left a permanent psychic scar. Doctors who assumed that I'd accept the enema as a routine part of pre-surgical or pre-childbirth preparation found themselves confronted with glaring ferocity and categorical refusal of any such procedure. Most of them gave in.

By now I was no longer Mother's passive and compliant infant, but had become a vociferous and demanding runabout. Anne's parents, who had delighted in looking after Darl when she was little, had since lost interest in grandparenthood as a vocation, and were busy running the hardware store, which my father partially bankrolled. The solution, my mother concluded, was to free herself from the monotony of child care by hiring a surrogate. So, the second stage of my early childhood began with a "nursemaid."

I remember the first one only because of the terror she inspired in me. This was her very first day on the job. I was put into my crib for a nap—how old would I have been?

Perhaps I was two, or three. I was a dedicated thumb-sucker, which Mother seemed mostly to ignore. Periodically she'd put evil-tasting stuff on my thumb or cover my hands with sort of mitten things, but if I cried, she'd desist and lose interest in the whole effort. This nursemaid, however, put me to bed and threatened to cut off my thumb if I persisted in sucking it. So I ducked under the covers to suck away in peace. But that nurse-witch tiptoed in on me, the sneak, flung back the covers and caught me in the *flagrante delicto* of thumb-sucking. Off to the kitchen she went and came back with a long butcher knife.

I became hysterical, screaming and screaming until my throat was raw. Darlene protected me from this sadist who said she was just trying to put a little scare into me. I cowered in my crib, afraid to leave its relative safety, and wouldn't let that fiend near me. Darlene reported the story to Mother when she came home from whatever frivolous interlude she'd been enjoying — a luncheon? mah jongg? shopping? — and the offender was summarily dismissed. I still remember the waves of icy, then flaming terror that washed over me, and how I clung to Darl, who sheltered me psychically and physically, comforting and defending her little sister.

Darl was a reassuring presence. My earliest recollections of her are of great tenderness toward me. She was protective, amused by me, marveled as I developed. We had this deep affection for one another — from her heart to my heart — something that our mother, ambivalent, untamed, not reliably available emotionally, was unable to provide in a sustained way. For all that I was a conniving nuisance, the one who had permanently encroached on her only-child ascendancy, Darl loved me unconditionally, and she elicited from me worshipful, overwhelming love.

And envy and jealousy, which I tried to suppress.

My admiration of Darlene was more than tinged with jealousy, it was marinated in it. It was wrong to hate her — but she was so accomplished, so smart, so admired by our parents, while I was dismissively referred to as "Little Jean." I envied her those almost seven blissful years she'd enjoyed before I came along, when she'd been the cosseted darling of parents and grandparents alike. Daddy had a real soft spot for his little poetess — in his wallet he had little smudged, folded slips of paper on which she'd carefully copied out her poems for him. With her six-and-a half-year head start on me, I felt I had to play catch-up, to try to be as smart and accomplished as my beloved big sister. But I wasn't a high-principled poet/idealist like she was. I felt I had to resort to shortcuts to get ahead of her somehow.

What was her reaction to having a little sister, after being her Daddy's beloved "Dolly Grapes" and Mother's boon companion for almost seven years? Did she ever envy me, the little attention grabber? I was unaware if she did. Too bad, I'd have loved having the power to make her even just a teensy bit jealous, but I never had that satisfaction. It wasn't part of her temperament, though it was part of mine.

She was gawky, skinny, shy, with string-straight hair that she wore in the flapper-style bob of the day. Always gentle, she was somewhat shy and reserved with others, which made her appear tentative and unsure of herself. But she was without malice. To me she seemed a model of honesty and integrity: she couldn't be sneaky or self-serving — but she had a hot, quick temper that hit like a lightning strike. She also had a strong sense of the ridiculous and the playful: any time I could get her to laugh — even when I had pestered her until she finally lost that famous temper — her anger would blow away in gales of laughter. Mostly, times with Darl were magically delightful. Her gentleness far outweighed her infrequent explosions.

Darl's and my best times as roommates happened when she would read to me at night. She'd be in her bed and I, enraptured, in mine. I must have been between four and six by then, and she'd read me *Winnie the Pooh*, much to our mutual delight. We'd be helpless with laughter over Piglet and the Horrible Heffalump, and we loved dear tiresome Owl. Our Aunt (Rhea) reminded us of Eeyore — we called her "Reeyore" (but not to her face, of course).

Darl also read lots of poetry to me, and I was a rapt audience. That she was a poet herself I never appreciated when I was little.

But she was my first and most tender teacher, and she instilled in me an abiding love of poetry, which I strongly associate with those lovely nighttime interludes when we were both in our beds, giggling over Winnie or making mind pictures as she read Coleridge's word magic: "In Xanadu did Kublai Khan/ A stately pleasure dome decree . . ." (Poetry and *Winnie the Pooh* side by side weren't the least bit incongruous.) She had several anthologies that we must have gone through from cover to cover more than once, and we got to know many of the poems by heart: Blake, Kipling, Tennyson, Shakespeare, Vachel Lindsay, Eugene Field, Yeats, Teasdale, Edna St. Vincent Millay, and many others. Darl put beautiful language and the wonderful density of poetic thought into our lives. It was as natural as breathing to say those words and think those thoughts. At a time in her life when she felt inadequate and unsure of herself, being my mentor and being so terribly important to me gave her value that she must desperately have needed. It didn't seem to matter that I was so much younger. Our minds and spirits met and coalesced through poetry and stories.

That was the upside of room sharing. But much of the fun and many of the wonderful times we shared were at *her* pleasure. Sometimes when I wanted her to read to me, she'd be annoyed and say "no" and I had to put up with that. She established turf boundaries in no uncertain terms: I was not to TOUCH anything belonging to her without her express permission—while she always assumed, as *droit du seigneur*, full access to *my* possessions (which got difficult later on, when we were close enough in size for her to wear my underwear). So I learned early that *her* dresser drawers were emphatically off limits, on pain of something even worse than death—rejection, total freeze-out rejection of me by her.

I could inventory my parents' dressers (Daddy's top drawer was the most interesting, full of souvenirs and little treasures)—and did—mulling over some of the mysterious things I found, like the little hinged celluloid cutout of two people, face to face, who did some sort of dance when you jiggled this device. One of them had a sort of stick down by its lower abdomen and it jabbed it toward or into the other one, which seemed to have a pair of bumps on its chest. I never told anyone I'd found that little device, but after a lot of speculating and thinking about it, and looking at it and jiggling it, I realized that one of the two, the one with the stick thing, was supposed to be a man and the other a woman, though I wasn't sure about what sort of dance they were doing.

My father also had an ivory elephant, yellowed and very old-looking, that I loved to hold in my hand and study. It was both warm and cool and its tiny sorrowful eye gazed at me with hypnotic intensity. There were also keys and exotic coins, everything kept in meticulous order, so I had to be careful to put things back just so. I don't think Daddy ever knew that I did these regular inspections of the top drawer in what he called his chifforobe. (That's one old-fashioned word I remember; another was "duofold," a name for a sofabed, I think.)

Darl put up with lots of snooping, lying, and duplicity from me — but more of that later. How must it have been for *her*, sharing a smallish room with a demanding, cloyingly affectionate, nosy sister who was so much younger? What a trial it must have been for her: such a lack of privacy, such close quarters, especially living with me, a spoiled, demanding, cheating, lying little opportunist. Darl's forbearance was truly remarkable. And it remained steadfastly so almost always, in spite of the tests to which I subjected her. Nothing could erase the pleasure of being together, sharing confidences, laughter, and worries.

15

After the thumb-sucking episode, Mother gave up on nursemaids for a while, until I got over the immediate terror and the nightmares subsided. Though I had always been outgoing (read "showoff"), sure that everyone loved and doted on me, I became shy and suspicious of strangers, especially if I thought they might be coming to take care of me. For a while Mother was patient and sympathetic — perhaps she felt guilty because she had been in such a rush to pursue her own pleasures that she hadn't taken proper care in choosing someone to look after her precious Jeanie. Now she and I were going to be pals, it seemed. She may have imagined a reprise of her happy interlude with Darlene. But Mother was older, and I was younger and less compliant than my big sister. I had to go with her wherever *she* chose to go. It quickly became clear that we wouldn't be spending a lot of time looking at the animals in the zoo or going to the playground. We would be going downtown so that Mother could resume the life of a lady of leisure, shopping and strolling on Michigan Avenue, whether I liked it or not.

Sometimes we went to Marshall Field's. One of Mother's bewildering routines was the tissue-paper-wrapped package caper. One day she would buy some item or other. When we got home she'd decide she didn't want it and would wrap it in tissue paper and return it to the store on our next trip downtown. Maybe Daddy tried to rein in her extravagance by making her take things back. You had to go to the returns booth and explain why you were returning the item, a humiliating experience for an elegant lady like my mother.

Sometimes she bought things that mystified me. Having

inventoried her dresser drawers—as I had Daddy's (his were neater and more interesting, but Mother's, which were quite tumbled around, had her distinctive sweet/salty odor which I liked)—I recognized one item she bought quite often, a "sanitary apron." This garment mystified me. It was pink and sort of rubberized. She wore it backwards, an apron behind her, not in front. I remember glimpsing the dense black triangle of her pubic hair as she hauled on her girdle. It awed and sort of frightened me, it was such a strong contrast to her pale flesh. I looked, then looked away in confusion and embarrassment and tried to act like I hadn't seen it, because she was not casual about nudity or exposure of her body. (My father, in contrast, was more in the Greek tradition with respect to nudity. He never objected if I came into the bathroom when he was lying, relaxed, in the tub. I was mesmerized by the sight of his genitals floating and swaying in the water, like sea plants.) While Mother was buying these sanitary aprons in Marshall Field's Notions Department, I'd stand there fidgeting and puzzled, trying to understand her underwear. What were those aprons for? She wore different underwear than I did: there was that girdle with garters attached to hold up her stockings, then the sanitary apron, then a slip—but she didn't wear panties, just all this other equipment. I wanted to ask her why she didn't wear panties and what the sanitary apron was for, but I felt inhibited about asking—or maybe I did ask but got fobbed off.

Marshall Field's elevators were operated by men in livery who wore white cotton gloves, like the elevator boys at the Belden Hotel. They announced the number of the approaching floor and droned out a rapid catalogue of the items for sale there, just before the elevator came to its bouncing stop. The elevator was an ornate iron cage, rather like a birdcage for people, and it was a great temptation to stick your hand out and try to touch the walls of the elevator shaft as they slid by. There were all sorts of yankings away from the dangerous fascination of those walls, plenty of "Jeanie! NO!" as I was hauled firmly into the center of the car. There, you could look up at the mosque-like glass dome of the elevator's ceiling and watch the play of light as the elevator glided from the brightness of the sales rooms to the darkness of the thick concrete floors that held the whole building up. Toys were on the fourth floor, and if I behaved reasonably well, we'd spend some time there, gazing raptly at the gorgeous dolls fit for royalty only, the palatial doll houses, the delectable stuffed animals in all sizes, extravagances beyond my wildest dreams. You could get in and pedal the fire engines, finger the elegant *trousseaux* that accompanied some of the dolls, and — my runaway favorite — you could fondle the little yellow ducklings that were real products of the taxidermist's art and were available only around Easter. Mother would buy me one every year. I loved those fuzzy little creatures with their bright black glass eyes, their wrinkly desiccated feet, and their baby downy fluff that smelled like butter. (I never mourned their short lives, sacrificed just to become Easter souvenirs.) The best thing about these ducklings was that Darlene was mortally afraid of them. They were my weapon of choice for overcoming her in those brief, heady moments when I could get the upper hand in a dispute by threatening to throw my duckling at her. She may have had superior strength and brains, but with my duckling missile I could triumph, if only briefly.

It seemed to me that we went downtown every day. It was like a very boring job. First, we had to be all dressed up: Mother wore a hat and gloves; I wore one of my many beautiful little dresses, either starched cotton with lace and appliqués or the heavy satin ones that Aunt Mayme Abbott got for Darlene and me. They were hand smocked by nuns in some convent somewhere, and always inspired admiring comments from passersby. Although Mother was an inveterate taker of taxis, in some misguided spirit of frugality (so the money could be spent on worthier things like clothes?) we would walk over to Stockton Drive, a block or so from the Belden, and catch the bus downtown. Thus began my ordeal. I would get nauseous almost the moment we boarded the bus. Mother would try to distract me, but it was hopeless. Many times we had to disembark right after she had given our fare to the conductor. In those days there was a driver, who did nothing but operate the bus, and a conductor who wore a little silver change maker strapped around his middle and who gave us our tickets and made change. If I was showing signs of imminent sickness, the conductor would usually refund the fare or hand us transfers as we dashed for the exit. We'd sit on a park bench for a while, with me gasping like a fish out of water, swallowing convulsively, trying to control my urge to vomit. The smell of gasoline has always had bad associations for me, and as a child I hated car trips and invariably got carsick. So the trip downtown on the bus was sort of a gamble: how close to our destination would we get? I felt Mother's exasperation, which only made matters worse, so there were many days when the trip downtown was just endless misery. We never aborted the trip and returned home, however.

Sometimes we went to one of the ladies' dress shops on Michigan Avenue, where the window-store mannequins gazed out at us loftily from behind the plate glass. One in which I spent a good deal of time was a store called Rikka Kaplan. It was at the corner of Michigan Avenue and Randolph Street and was later replaced by the Crerar Library (now also just a memory). This was a very exclusive location, and you could tell how elegant the shop was by the clothing displayed in the windows. Mother must have been one of their best customers, and she had a favorite saleslady who would lug out armloads of coats, gowns, or suits to show her as she sat on a chair in the spacious salon. If she expressed interest in an item, the saleslady would hang it on a nearby rack and return the rejected items to the stockroom in the back. Then she'd reappear with more clothes and the entire performance would be repeated. It was pretty boring to me, as Mother and the saleslady would analyze the garments in great detail: "It can be shortened; the color is so flattering; try it on, Mrs. Stern, I'll call the fitter." And Mother would be undecided — should she try on whatever it was? Were there other things she should look at first? What else did they have? All of this took hours, it seemed to me, and I'd get restless and was probably a terrible nuisance.

I seem to remember once when no one was shadowing me, I figured out how to get into the big plate glass show window that faced Michigan Avenue. I recall looking up at the mannequins, fondling the luscious silks of their gowns. They wobbled dangerously on their frail metal stands, as I tried not to bump them while, ever the showoff, I pranced and waved and simpered at the growing crowd of pedestrians, gawking, open-mouthed, at this unscripted spectacle in the shop window. I was soon nabbed by a saleslady and taken firmly in hand by my disgraced mother. I think that shopping trip may have been aborted.

But there were others, and after that experience, I was both better-behaved and more zealously monitored. The poor saleslady assigned to manage me had to forgo her chance to wait on the next customer (and maybe make a sale and land a prized commission, which was how it was done in those days — I learned a lot during my forced attendance in upscale dress shops). She'd try to distract me, either by walking me around the store and pointing out objects of interest (not a successful ploy) or by taking me upstairs — the most entrancing part of the shop — where the workrooms were: hat-making and button-anchoring were done there, as well as the intricate alterations on garments pinned up by the fitters and then expertly sewn for the purchaser.

To me, the hat-making area was the most enthralling. Long tables were covered with little boxes of neatly sorted buttons, flowers, feathers, trinkets of all kinds that could be sewn onto a hat. There were wooden hat blocks, adjustable to whatever hat size was called for. There were hat "blanks," some felt, some straw, that were ready to receive the embellishments that transformed them into elegant *chapeaux*. I especially loved playing with the feathers and buttons and other tiny ornaments, taking them out of their boxes and creating my own arrangements, otherwise known as making a mess. But Mother was a good customer, so they had to put up with me.

Her natural tendency to be an impulse buyer had to be balanced against Daddy's inevitable disapproval of her profligacy. She always had to wheedle and bargain to wean him away from his innate frugality, so she tried to be cautious about having the fitter pin up a garment that she wasn't sure she was going to buy. She'd devise a strategy for presenting bills to Daddy that would downplay her naturally extravagant tastes. This strategy never included much self-denial, however. She identified with the lavish-spender *grande dame* image, and fiscal self-restraint was not part of that picture.

Aunt Rhea, Daddy's favorite sister, was the bookkeeper at Rikka Kaplan, although Mother and I never saw her there; I didn't even know she worked there until later on. She was the prettiest — and unhappiest — of my father's four sisters. She had married good-looking Harry Dreebin, and they had two children: Bert, who grew up to be as handsome as his father, and Arlene, who inherited our grandmother Rose Stern's serene and loving disposition. When the children were little, Aunt Rhea took them to Union Pier for the summer, where the family congregated for a few weeks of simple outdoor life in a modest little "resort." One of the early summers there, which I don't remember but heard about long after, had a scandalous conclusion. When Aunt Rhea returned to Chicago and her husband Harry, who hadn't been able to join his little family on their holiday, she found a bottle of medicine used for treating syphilis in the medicine chest. Horrified by what had obviously been his adulterous behavior while she was gone, and convinced that above all she had to protect her children from disease and degeneracy, she ordered Harry to leave immediately — and permanently. He had probably picked up this syphilis from one or more summer visits to a brothel, and my father, an implacable enemy of marital infidelity (who more than once intervened in the affairs of various relatives to impose his unrelenting morals on them), demanded that his wronged sister and her vulnerable little ones be assured a safer, purer life. So Aunt Rhea divorced Harry. She became the sole support of her children — which she never let you forget. When men asked her out (and they did because she was so pretty, intelligent, and modest), she'd remind them bitterly that they'd have to entertain her children also, which invariably scared them off.

I don't know how Rhea felt about her rich sister-in-law

and bratty niece sashaying into the store and laying waste the workrooms and stockrooms while she toiled for a barely living wage, among the invoices and accounts, in a dark, isolated back room, hidden from the bustle and glamour of the shop. Of course, if she kept the books she must have known how much money Mother actually spent for all those endless hours of looking and trying on (and being flattered). Since a garment that had been altered couldn't be returned, there were no tissue-paper-wrapped packages going back to Rikka Kaplan's.

Even as a three- or four-year-old, I was astonished — and impressed — by my mother's insouciant extravagance, truly something to behold. It would continue unabated even into the Depression. There was the $600 hand-woven jacket and skirt, the fur-lined cape, the silver fox jacket, which Daddy was told about after the fact and to which he responded much too mildly, to MY way of thinking. He had to supply financial help to his relatives: Aunt Rhea was a struggling single parent, and I'm sure he contributed to her support. In that era of no Social Security, when both sets of grandparents had little if any savings, Daddy paid their rent and gave them a stipend to which those of his brothers-in-law who were able contributed. After all, Oscar was the rich one — look at how his wife dressed and where they lived, in that fancy hotel. Darlene was by now enrolled in a private school, Francis Parker, which meant there was a pretty high tuition to pay. And Mother was getting ready to employ another nursemaid to look after me. She seemed oblivious to Daddy's warnings of imminent fiscal peril. Sometimes Darl and I overheard strident arguments that seemed to be about money, but Mother always managed to wheedle what she wanted out of Daddy. I felt that she took advantage of him; she was a slick arguer, and she'd brag to us that *she* should have been the lawyer. If mastery of verbal thrust and parry weren't enough, well, she had other ways of prevailing, which involved a certain amount of suggestive posturing that he could never resist.

Aunt Rhea was always embittered and unhappy. Arlene told me that her mother never, ever spoke words of endearment or gratitude to her, and that Bert, a sweet but feckless fellow who was the favorite, fared little better. Rhea was not given to demonstrations — or words — of appreciation or affection. Arlene did much of the housekeeping and cooking by the time she was in her early teens. She felt sorry for her hard-working mother and tried to help the unhappy woman. But Aunt Rhea was a fault-finder: Arlene, sweet and gentle — and very efficient — was inevitably criticized for minor omissions and trivial details: the stew wasn't salty enough, the soup was cold, the dinner could have been more appetizing, the tablecloth was crooked. I didn't know about any of this until much later when Arlene and I reminisced.

16

However long it was that Mother and I were "shopping pals" was too long for me. I was even ready to try another nursemaid.

The next was the one I loved the best, Anna Bracher. She was calm and serene, a young Czech or Slovak immigrant who had a golden heart that matched her golden curls. I don't know how long she stayed with us, but she was fun and sweet yet still expected—and taught me—a standard of conduct and three- or four-year-old decorum (whatever THAT would be) that made me adore and respect her. She was immune to my blandishments, tantrums, and conniving. I was devastated when she left us. I never knew why. She was young and blonde and pretty and vivacious: could Mother have been jealous of my attachment to her? Or concerned that Daddy might find her temptingly attractive? Mother was noted for her possessiveness and jealousy. Few could ignore the sweeping searchlight of her suspicious glare, deployed at potential rivals.

After Anna was gone there was a succession of nameless, faceless ones. I became a veteran of the revolving door nursemaid wars. I'd lost the desire or ability to make an attachment: why go to that trouble if they were just going to leave me?

Once—I was probably around five—I was left in the muddled and not very competent care of a new "nurse." I don't remember her name or what she looked like. I think she was Scandinavian. She'd cause great giggling from Darl and me because of her accent: "Yean, puut on your pee-yamas," she'd say. I'd say, "What?" just to get her to repeat it, and Darl and I would try not to laugh out loud because we didn't want to hurt the feelings of this pathetically gullible woman.

So, I am home alone with this new nurse. Darl and Mother were both out. Sly little devil that I am, I say to her imperiously, "Please get my two Bye-lo dolls down from the top shelf of the closet."

"Vy they up there?" she asks, a little suspicious.

"Oh," I reply airily, "To keep them away from my sister." Pretty clever on such short notice, I think, to come up with that answer.

Whatever-her-name-was (Ingrid? Astrid?) dutifully retrieves Joan and Peter, my sister's precious and gorgeous prize dolls. I coveted them, had yearned to fondle them, with their smooth porcelain baby faces, for ages, but Darl, possessive, selfish girl, wouldn't even let me touch them: "Keep your grubby hands off my dolls, you'll get them all dirty and sticky," she'd say, whisking them out of my reach. I'd often watch enviously from a distance when she and her friends played with them. These dolls had lifelike bisque china heads, with blue eyes that opened when you sat them up and shut when you laid them down. Their cloth bodies, covered in utilitarian muslin and stuffed with cotton, were soft and tender to the touch (ah yes, I'd sneaked an occasional furtive feel), and they had composition hands and feet attached to their little stuffed cloth limbs which were sewn onto their bodies so that the arms and legs flopped in a lifelike way. In addition to a gorgeous doll buggy to wheel them around in, each one had a miniature steamer trunk just like our big one, with drawers for their dainty booties and bonnets and nighties and hanging space for their dresses, coats, and jackets. Joan had a pink Chinese silk embroidered jacket; Peter had a blue one. Joan's christening dress and bonnet were trimmed in pink ribbon, Peter's in blue.

Many of their beautiful outfits were gifts from Mother and Daddy's friend (and soon our dance teacher), Merriel "Mayme" Abbott. "Aunt" Mayme was a veritable fairy godmother. She loved to shower us with lavish gifts, always in "good taste": she gave me a gold charm bracelet, and then regularly gave me charms for it; she gave us look-alike dresses she had made in some convent in France (she took the dance troupe she had trained to Europe every summer). I remember the dresses so clearly I could draw you a sketch of them: a heavy silk satin, one peach color, the other lavender, all smocked around the neck and the cuffs. I think it was for my Sunday school confirmation that she gave me a beautiful Black Sun Press edition of *Alice in Wonderland*, with lithographs by Marie Laurencin, a treasure I still have.

The dolls' wardrobes bore the inimitable stamp of Aunt Mayme's taste. She must have had some of those clothes made especially for Joan and Peter. They had knit rompers, play clothes, little fur-trimmed coats, buntings and mittens for cold days—wardrobes fit for the twin prince and princess that I pretended they were. Oh, what joy to have those two dolls all to myself! I was delirious with the greedy pleasure of handling all the forbidden treasures, many of which I'd never even been allowed to look at. Though the trunks of doll clothes weren't kept out of my reach, they were meaningless to me without the dolls to dress them in, so I'd never bothered much with the clothes. Because the dolls themselves, with their beautifully modeled fragile china heads, were kept out of my lustful reach, they were my obsession; they cast a spell over me, and now, having them in my possession, even temporarily, made me feverish with excitement. I laid the two beauties on my bed and proceeded to unpack their trunks of neatly laid-away clothes. I dressed each of them in a succession of exquisite matching outfits, throwing each ensemble into a disordered heap after they'd modeled it for me. The lovely doll clothes were strewn over both Darl's and my beds, as I flung myself into the magic world of dolldom.

Then I pretended that one of the twin babies had misbehaved. I picked it up, scolded it, and rapped its head on my knee to punish it. Horror of horrors! Its blue eyes fell back inside the china head, leaving two blank black holes. I had jarred loose the mechanism that held the eyes in place. And just at that moment, I heard the front door open and then close. It was probably Darl returning. In a panic, I flung doll clothes under the bed, behind the pillows, any place I could find to cram the evidence of my guilty transgressions out of sight. The two poor dolls, both stripped of their fine clothing and one of them now eyeless, I stuffed behind the pillows on my bed. Darl's suspicion of my wickedness preceded her into our room—I think the place must have positively reeked of my guilt. She took one look at our rumpled room, pillows disarranged, doll trunks gaping open with doll clothes hanging out of the drawers like tongues, and at me with GUILT, TERROR, and SHAME written all over me, and said, "Jeanie. What have you been doing?"

"Oh, nothing," I replied tremulously, a guilty flush like a red flag suffusing my fat sweaty face. (I was never a good liar. Even though I practiced a lot, I could never manage the cool poker face of the accomplished prevaricator.)

"What have you been doing?" she repeated as her eyes swept the room like searchlights, noting the bits of clothing peeping out from under the bed and from behind the pillows. "You've been playing with my *dolls!*" she exclaimed. Enter Astrid or Ingrid or whatever her name was. "Did you give her my dolls?"

"See told me dey vas hers," she says.

The jig was up. What a nightmare! From the Heaven of being busy, loving manager of Joan and Peter, I fell through icy space into the searing, utter Hell of Darlene's righteous fury and the nursemaid's outrage at having been duped by a lying spoiled-brat little sister. And to cap the trauma, when Darl took up her darling dollies and saw that one of them was now eyeless, *blind*, the curtain dropped on my life of guileless innocence forever. I was morally damaged goods, maybe even a criminal marked for life—and wait! Just at this moment Mother returned home.

She strode into our room and took in the scene of the crime. I was so frightened and appalled at my own evil that I was beyond tears. My happy life with my sister was over! Mother descended on me mercilessly, shaming me, expressing horror that I played the nursemaid for a fool and got possession of my sister's dolls by *lying*, the most heinous part of the whole criminal performance (this from the disciple of *fagelach*, the one who complained loudly when she was short-changed but who remained mute when a monetary error was in her favor). And what's worse, I had broken the doll. Luckily, its eyes could be replaced at Marshall Field's doll hospital. But the lying was another matter. My reputation was irremediably sullied, and a suitable punishment had to be meted out. I was to have my lying tongue cleansed by a good washing with soap. That's how you removed the dirty evil.

It was Palmolive soap (which I've avoided using ever since). Mother thoroughly lathered up a washrag and in spite of much yelling and gagging, she gave my poor tongue a good scrubbing. . . . Darlene's righteous indignation dissipated, the doll's sightless eyes were replaced, but that whole scene, its pinnacle of delight plunged into clammy Palmolive-flavored shame, remains indelible in my catalogue of disgrace.

There's a postscript to the doll episode, a bittersweet one, kind of anticlimactic. By the time Darl turned fifteen, she'd really outgrown Joan and Peter, the Bye-lo dolls, their trunks full of lovely clothes, and the beautiful gray English cab doll buggy. She gave the entire treasure to me: dolls, clothes, little bassinettes, high chairs, and all. In the perverse way such contests often conclude, once Joan and Peter became truly mine, their allure diminished. I played with them lackadaisically now and then, but mostly they were consigned to dusty neglect and finally to oblivion. I wish I had them now; they were really works of art, and so were their clothes.

The only other nursemaid I remember was Brigitta Skarbina, another immigrant, this time German, this time slightly older. Brigitta came into my life somewhat later, I think, perhaps when I was five or six. She was around for a couple of years and may have been the last of the nursemaids, which is why I remember her. She was OK, but no one ever filled my heart the way Anna had.

Brigitta may have been with us on the chilly late autumn day when Darlene and I were returning to the hotel from a walk in Lincoln Park. We had sister krimmer coats. Krimmer was a soft curly gray lamb's fur—named, I now know, from the German for the Crimea, where the lambs' pelts came from. We gave no thought to animal rights in those days—who did?

Animals were grown to be meat or fur or to be looked at in the zoo—that's how it was.

William Shakespeare lounged in his bronze chair at one of the walkways that led into the park. You'd think it would have been a statue of Lincoln rather than Shakespeare, but the Bard seemed to set the right tone: a magic and contemplative air that made you feel the presence of *A Midsummer Night's Dream*. He was seated in a relaxed and easy posture, his finger between the pages of a small book. Darl had climbed into his chilly bronze lap (a favorite exploit) and then been cajoled down again while I, chubby, too small for this climb, envious, frustrated, and impatient, fidgeted around the granite base of the statue, many of whose surfaces were worn to a deep golden luster by the hands and behinds of all the girls and boys who regularly swarmed over his lap, his arms, and even onto his bald pate (those were the daredevil show-off boys).

Well, that was the story of my short life: everything I wanted was beyond my reach or my ability. And as Darl glided gracefully down from Shakespeare's welcoming lap, perhaps a little smugly, I felt the fire of impotent jealousy rising within me. I can't remember whether she tweaked me a little about my chubbiness and other shortcomings, but I got into the towering, helpless fury of the little sister who's outmatched. On blind impulse, I grabbed her arm and bit as hard, as hard as ever I could, the power of all my anger and self-pity focused in my jaws. Our nursemaid companion, whoever she was, gasped as Darl shrieked in pain at her fat little sister, who was clamped onto her arm like a bulldog. She shook me loose, leaving me with a mouthful of faintly mothball-flavored fur, and flung off her coat so she could study her injured arm. "Ooh, Jeanie, look what you've done! You've bitten clear down to the white meat!"

All that rage drained out of me as though someone had pulled the plug. Terrified and contrite, I burst into hysterical wails and tears and pleaded with her to forgive me. "I'm sorry, I'm sorry, I'm sorry," I blubbered. But then she began laughing and I realized that I'd only nicked the surface of her skin, that my little milk teeth had barely made it through the fur and the sweater and the shirt underneath her coat. Duped again! Gullible little dummy! But I was so relieved that I hadn't given her a mortal wound that though my tattered self-esteem prevented me from joining in the laughter, at least I stopped crying.

On Sunday mornings, we almost always went to the park with Daddy. He was up early. On Sundays, when he didn't have to go to the office, he would be cheery and eager to help us get dressed up in our dresses and Mary Janes (patent leather "party shoes"). He'd wear his gray Homburg hat with black headband and discreetly turned-up brim edged in gray grosgrain ribbon, his gray pin-stripe suit, and in the vest pocket, his gold watch and chain (with the Coif key, of course), and this dapper outfit would be topped off with gray spats and his ivory-tipped Malacca walking stick. The wood had an exquisite pattern and was light as a feather.

The three of us would head over to the zoo to see the foxes and bears and visit the lion house, but most important, we'd stop at the octagonal kiosk to buy candy: Malteezers were a favorite (chocolate-coated malted milk balls), but I often made the tough decision in favor of Cracker Jack, not that I liked it as well as the Malteezers, but you got a prize in the Cracker Jack box. Darl more often went for the Malteezers, disdaining those cheap trinkets that were almost always a disappointment. Those were exuberant mornings. Daddy loved to extol the Marvels of Nature—in this manicured park!—and he seemed happy and carefree and quite enchanted with our company. I don't remember any fights with Darl on those Sunday outings. Daddy's relaxed pleasure set the tone.

I remember rare occasions when Mother came to the zoo. The only part of the place that interested her was the monkey house, and she managed to make watching the monkeys an embarrassingly pornographic experience: she always hoped that the monkeys would masturbate or engage in some sort of sexually explicit behavior, and then she'd snigger like a teenager and make unflattering comparisons to us human cousins of the chimps, gorillas, baboons, and others. She always had some coarse remark to make about the baboons, who cheerfully displayed their rainbow rumps, as if especially for her.

17

Every summer we would drive to Union Pier, Michigan, for the Stern family gathering. From Chicago to Union Pier is less than seventy-five miles, but in those days nobody but race car drivers drove much more than 30 miles an hour. Our big green Cadillac had little vases for flowers clipped beside the big square windows (that you could open by turning a crank), itchy plush upholstery, and silk window shades with braided pulls that had little tassels on the ends.

I dreaded those interminable two-hour drives to Union Pier. They were trips heavily punctuated by my serial throwing up. Despite the bath towels we traveled with (which were unfurled to protect the upholstery, not me), that car seemed always to be wreathed in the sour aroma of my puke. It was—excuse the expression—a tossup whether *being* in Union Pier with my cousins made the nauseous anguish of *getting* there worthwhile. We usually made one stop to refuel about halfway there, but that was almost worse than the endless jolting ride on rutted sand roads which, it seemed to me, consumed the major portion of the trip. The "gas station" was this dark converted barn that reeked of gasoline with a faint under-perfume of livestock. To this day the smell of gasoline still inspires in me a distant but persistent clutch of nausea. The gas pump was a cylinder the top half of which was glass that had a spiral thing inside. When you cranked a crank, the spiral twirled and this reddish fluid moved up in the glass section and you could see the fuel moving, sort of like blood. I could either get out of the car and try to find a place that didn't reek of gasoline, where I could gulp sweet uncontaminated fresh air convulsively and try to beat down the nausea, or I could stay in the back seat of the car, overwhelmed by the pervasive odor of my disgrace, but at least the gasoline smell was weaker.

In Union Pier we'd join Daddy's sisters and Grandma and Grandpa Stern and stay in this little circle of teeny cottages called "Peep o' Day." Each of my aunts had one for her family: Aunt Mollie, Aunt Tillie, Aunt Rhea, Aunt Belle, and their children, my cousins whom I seldom saw: Aunt Tillie's two boys, Bob and Paul; Aunt Mollie's daughters, Buds and Harriet. The cabins were not much bigger than doll houses, each with its tiny kitchen corner, and bedrooms smaller than our closets at the Belden Hotel; their damp lumpy mattresses on the spavined cots smelled of mildew. There may even have been an outhouse instead of proper plumbing, and I faintly recall that we pumped water from a well. You had to cook on grease-coated gas burners in the room that was kitchen, dining room, and living room all rolled into one stuffy little space; the cooking pots were dented and stained. Because the cabins were so small, I think each family made a dish and then we all ate together outdoors, picnic style. Grandma Stern, still the premier cook, always made superb things: succulent chicken, strudel, and other specialties of hers whose names I remember, but I don't know what they were: knadlach, knishes, special kinds of meat that the daddies liked.

We would visit for an uncomfortable week or so, which Mother hated: the cramped, primitive cabins, the hot, dusty air vibrating with the drone of hostile insects like bees and mosquitoes. A few years later, Mollie bought an old building nearby and turned it into a successful and profitable resort hotel, the Lake Manor Hotel, where, at the end of the summer when the paying guests had left, the extended family would gather for our holiday together. Mother still didn't care for the whole scene. She didn't enjoy vacationing with her in-laws, and between us she nicknamed Mollie's establishment the "Lek Manure Hotel," "lek" being Yiddish for "lick."

Mother and Daddy made brief excursions with friends to a popular spa at French Lick, Indiana, mini-getaways without Darl and me. But there were several magical summers when Mother and I went to New York City to stay with Aunt Evelyn and Uncle

Archie. I must have been between three and five. Most of those years Darl went to summer camp, a place called Pinemere, in Wisconsin. Even though I had bouts of feeling queasy during the overnight train ride, those trips are indelibly fixed in my memory as times of adventure and delight.

The club car had a little outdoor observation platform at the very back end of the train, and I loved sitting on the folding plush chairs, breathing in the pungent smell of hot-metal-tinged fresh air and being mesmerized by the castanet sound of the wheels on tracks that seemed to spool off into a vanishing point we were streaming away from. Those rides tended to be pretty sooty, because at least the first year or so that we went to New York, trains had no air conditioning, so you had to open the heavy, stubborn windows to keep from suffocating, in exchange for which you got delicately coated with a fine grit of black coal dust from the steam locomotive. Then there was at least one summer when some sort of super-refrigerated air was pumped into the entire train and you were not allowed to open the windows at all. That was when the refuge of the little outdoor observation platform was especially precious to me, because the air in the train got sort of used up by the time we went to bed; it was dank, clammy, and very stale. I got to sit out on that platform both before and after dinner in the diner, alone, as I remember it, but that can't be right. I could have climbed over the waist-high railing of this balcony-like platform and been dashed to pieces on the disappearing train tracks while Mother disported herself in the club car. Either I have edited her out of my remembrance of that welcome release from stale air, or one of the kindly dining car waiters would have gotten a break from work to be out there and watch with me as the trees flew by and the tracks sang their syncopated song. Locomotive smoke seemed as fragrant as spring flowers compared to the fetid air inside the train.

Even so, I loved the mystery of sleeping in the lower berth with Mother. I liked the porter's economy of motion when he made up the berth, snapping the sheets to make them obey him and lie smoothly on the unfolded seat that was transformed into a cozy den for the night. I liked peeking out the window at the night villages we hurtled through, train whistle mournfully tooting, and the crescendo-decrescendo sound of the bells at the crossing gates as we flew past. On some trips I got to have my own space in the upper berth, and I especially liked the cave-like sensation of being up there in its disorienting total darkness that fell on you as soon as the porter snapped heavy green curtains shut after you climbed the little ladder and settled in for the night. You had your own swaying hideaway with its little mesh hammock for your shoes and undies. But in the lower berth, the muffled clackety of the wheels and the huge spans of empty black night were a kind of lullaby, punctuated by sudden clusters of brilliant lights at stations whose names I will never know and towns and isolated farmhouses whose denizens had lives that would never intersect with mine. And then suddenly it was morning and light seeped in around the heavy shades that covered the train windows (that I had peeked around during the night).

I would feel a keen excitement as we approached New York: first there were the little towns or suburbs; then this incredible confluence of intricately intertwined railroad tracks. And as we sat in the bright dining car, suddenly the windows became opaque black and we were plunged into the great tunnel that dived under Manhattan. What a dramatic way to enter New York! Much more exciting, I think, than floating in over the smoggy jumble of snaggle-toothed skyscrapers, for the train emerged from the black tunnel into the gloom of huge, bustling Grand Central Station. That's how it seemed to me: Grand and Central.

I must have been three when I made my first trip to New York. On that occasion, I was Mother's cute little albatross. She might have loved dressing me up and showing me off, but most of the bumming around that she and Evelyn loved to do was not feasible with me along: my shopping threshold was low, and I was not compliant when it came to situations I didn't enjoy. I don't know whether she was ever able to find someone else to mind me, so I remember that she was often annoyed and impatient. Though in subsequent summers we stayed with Aunt

Evelyn and Uncle Archie in their grand apartment at 44 West 77th Street, that first trip Mother and I stayed by ourselves in a tiny apartment. That was the occasion of the Pea Soup Episode.

One day we went to the fruit and vegetable store and she announced, "I'm going to make you some delicious pea soup for your lunch." We also bought some luscious peaches, as peaches and cream was one of my favorite desserts. So we get back to our little apartment and first she shells the peas, then she washes the peas, then she cooks the peas, then she strains the peas, then somehow she turns them into soup. Then she puts the bowl of soup in front of me. I look at it suspiciously. Do I want to eat something called "pea," even if I have watched the entire process of creation from pod to plate? Furthermore, it is thick; it is also green. Do I want to eat something kind of mealy and green? My gorge rises at the prospect and tells me I definitely do not want to eat it. I don't even want to taste it — not even a single spoonful.

First Mother coaxes — "Just a teensy taste, you'll see how delicious it is" — then she cajoles, then she gets a bit short-tempered and orders me to taste it. I refuse. She tries to lever the spoonful into my mouth. I clamp my lips shut. I positively lock them against this thick green stuff. Then she threatens: "This is your lunch. If you won't taste the soup, I'll toss it down the sink and there will be no peaches and cream for dessert and you will go to nap with no lunch because I am NOT fixing anything else. I spent all morning shopping, shelling, cleaning, and cooking the peas and making the soup, so you eat it — or else!" I simply could not make myself swallow even a tiny taste of that stuff, which seemed to become less and less appetizing the more I was being forced to put it in my mouth. So, true to her word, she picks up the bowl of soup and pours it down the sink drain.

Suddenly, I was ravenous — and scared. Would I starve, fat little me, without a morsel of lunch? I was sure something terrible would happen to me if I had no food. "Oh, Mommy, I'll eat it, I'll eat anything you fix me, even more soup!" I am weeping inconsolably, hysterically, and I am making plenty of noise. Even if she'd had the ingredients, there was absolutely no chance that Mother would do a reprise on the pea soup, and I think I must have sensed that, but I really did think at that point that I would eat anything she set before me — even boiled turnips! The screaming, screeching, and yowling developed its own momentum and I was pretty sure that I had more screaming to express before reaching the crescendo of my hysterics. The only way to shut me up was to feed me, so Mother rummaged in our little icebox and found some hamburger, and I had hamburger AND peaches and cream for lunch, and tranquility was restored. Still, if that episode, which we both remembered wryly, taught me anything, it was that getting hamburger instead of pea soup didn't make me smug, triumphant, or self-satisfied; I'd gotten lesson Number 1 in psychology: there is a disturbing cost to pushing limits, even if you "prevail."

18

Uncle Archie was tall and handsome — even though he had *three* front teeth (one of his nicknames was Middletooth Archie). His and Aunt Ev's apartment was a splendid, high-ceilinged affair with a large living room that looked out on West 77th Street. The formal dining room was all dark wood paneling, and most of the floors were covered with Oriental rugs. Bedrooms — I don't remember how many — opened off a long hall that extended back from the dining room, with the master bedroom at the far end of the hall. I remember that on one visit that included Darl, I slept on two chairs pushed together facing each other; on another occasion Darl and I shared a single bed. I preferred the two-chair arrangement.

The apartment was just a couple of blocks from New York's marvelous Museum of Natural History, which, like Chicago's Field Museum, was a totally fascinating place to browse in. I spent hours in each of these museums; there were so many different kinds of exhibits, from the hundreds of slightly dusty-looking stuffed animals to the dioramas of cavemen to the meticulously arranged cases of butterflies. I was dazzled by the variety, color, and size of the creatures in the collections in both museums, and I wasn't in the least bothered by the pins through their abdomens that affixed them to the display boards. As a butterfly hunter and collector myself when I was older, maybe seven or eight, I would spend many hours capturing these beauties in Lincoln Park, transferring them from my butterfly net to the little jar which contained a cake of poison whose fumes killed the poor things rather quickly, then taking my trophies home, dipping them in alcohol to fix the colored powder on their wings, and finally laying them on cotton in a glass-fronted frame. None of this struck me then as wanton cruelty—in fact it still doesn't.

When our daughter Annie was four or five, I introduced her to butterfly collecting. But her heart was never in the collecting, killing, and mounting part of this hobby. Once in a while we'd capture a caterpillar, put it in a jar with cheesecloth over the mouth of the jar, so that the creature could breathe, and then wait and watch—for days, or weeks, it seemed—to see if it would make a cocoon. Our efforts were successful once or twice: the cocoon was duly spun; we again waited many more weeks, it seems to me, until, finally, the butterfly, its wings pleated shut, would painstakingly drag itself out of its confinement, exhausted, and as we watched, the wings would slowly come to life, open out, tremble a little at first, as the life-fluid filled the wings' black veins. And then there was the thrill when we removed the cheesecloth cover from the jar's mouth and the newly minted butterfly climbed onto the edge of the jar, seemed to hesitate for a moment of orientation, and then was effortlessly airborne. Mostly, though, we were satisfied with observing the wonders of the insect and bird world that we found in the heart of Chicago, in Lincoln Park.

Aunt Evelyn and Mother were a hilarious duo: lots of giggling and comparing bust sizes, and other stuff of which I faintly disapproved. They were a striking-looking pair—sharp dressers—and I'm sure they did their share of flirting, probably egging each other on in the kind of sibling competition that added spice to whatever devilment they were up to. Aunt Ev, who was a discriminating (and affluent) collector of antique furnishings, had an admirer, a dealer in antiques named Arnold Prelucker. I don't know whether he was more than an admirer or whether theirs was just a business relationship, but he must have filled the artistic, culture-hungry void in Evelyn's life that Uncle Archie, the stockbroker, a golfing, cigar-smoking extrovert, wasn't even aware of. My father, by contrast, offered Mother a richer diet of culture and intellect than she was comfortable with. She developed exquisite taste in clothes and home décor, but never extended it to art, literature, drama, fine music, even jazz, any one of which would have suited my father, who yearned for immersion in aesthetic pursuits. Though they attended concerts and later on the Ballets Russes, she clung to her supposed intellectual inadequacies, which became the justification for expressing her artistic talents principally through self-adornment, which included a suitable backdrop; hence, whatever apartment we lived in was invariably tastefully furnished and decorated.

She had an eye for design, and in later years she sewed needlepoint canvases that became coverings for bricks which we used as bookends or doorstops. The patterns were her own unscripted creations, traditional needlepoint in vivid color combinations and imaginative patterns. She made many of these, and they are now keepsakes treasured by her grandchildren as an expression of her artistry and originality.

One of the best things about those sticky, steamy summers in New York was my Sundays with Uncle Archie. If I'd been a good girl all week—and he made a point of interrogating Mother and Aunt Ev (and sometimes even me!)—I'd get to go out with him on Sunday morning. We'd go to Broadway. There was a guy who sold newspapers in one of those little kiosks with a chest-high counter. They'd stand me up on a high stool and I would "sell" the newspapers to passersby. It invariably drew a crowd, this gorgeous little girl selling papers—so pretty, and all dressed up (Mother saw to that). Looking back on those wonderful Sundays (my first experience in Retail?), I now suspect that the newspaper guy was Archie's bookie and that they were transacting "business" while I distracted the non-horseplaying clientele. After all, Uncle Archie had a seat on the New York Stock Exchange, and they were rich, and he must have liked gambling and risk—he seemed like the type.

After we sold papers for a while, we'd go to Kediff's cigar store, which was on the way back to their apartment. Uncle Archie was one of the Paley clan of Chicago, which consisted of six or seven grown kids. There was Ben, a violinist who had had a terrible auto accident, and no one was sure whether he'd ever be able to play the violin again. He, like the rest of the family, was an accomplished prankster. You could see where he got his madcap ways: from Mama Fannie! She was a magnificent specimen of the Jewish matriarch, big and bosomy, loquacious, uninhibited, spontaneous, and dominant. She adored babies, and her rapacious ways with them appalled prudish me. When Archie and his wife and their toddler came to visit her and her rowdy clan in Chicago, nothing could stop Fannie. She scooped my little cousin Arlyn (an introverted only child) up into her big, fleshy arms, pressed the wide-eyed child against her bosom, pulled down the little panties and squeezed the baby buttocks, planting kisses on them, caressing them with her big false horse teeth, laughing Yiddish endearments all the while. The Paleys all hooted and laughed: that's our Ma! Once the baby got over her initial shock, she howled a quavering soprano shriek and tried to squirm away from that mountain of soft flesh. Bubbe Fannie was laughing and shouting who knows what as she rocked and pawed the little tyke. No one except Aunt Evelyn, Arlyn's mother, seemed shocked or disapproving. "That's Fannie for ya, ha, ha, ha." Evelyn snatched her child away, spat a few Yiddish insults at her mother-in-law, and stalked off. Horrified, I was grateful that Fannie wasn't MY grandma!

It was a family of extroverts, and no one was safe from their mischief. One of their favorite stories, recounted with relish, was about the time they were driving to Union Pier, all of them, including Fannie, crammed into the family touring car. On their way, Fannie announced that she had to pee. So the driver said, "OK, Ma, I'll pull over and you go to the side of the car away from the road, just at the edge there, and go ahead." So Mama disembarked, hoisted up the voluminous skirts, hauled down the bloomers, squatted, and was just feeling the blessed relief of peeing—when the car, wheels spitting dust, sped just far enough down the road to leave her there, bare-bottomed, with the shouts of laughter from her faithless children floating back to her. Of such naughty practical joking did their family amusement consist. But they had also turned their energy to finding a business that would make money for them. I don't know how they got into the cigar-making line of work, but they were successful enough to have their own brand of cigar, which they named La Paulina, after Paulina Street, where their original factory was located, on Chicago's Near West Side.

My memories of Kediff's are mostly visual and olfactory. The place was a dark warren, long and narrow with little on-street frontage, like a deep cave. The place stayed cool even on a hot day, and it always had a dank smell of dust and cigars. From my close-to-the-ground perspective, I could see into the showcases, which were just about at my eye level. I recall a jumble of razors, matches, small cheap tin toys, not too different from the Cracker Jack prizes, pocketknives, knickknacks, marbles, and souvenirs. Behind the counter, the wall consisted of ranks of shelves with neatly stacked cigar boxes, a veritable library of cigar boxes. A few aristocratic cigars may have been displayed in the glass cases to tempt customers, but most of his more expensive stock was safely behind Mr. Kediff. The countertops were littered with book matches, a few small stuffed animals, cigarettes, and those little punch-out rolled-up paper "chances": you punched a key into a little hole in a board and you got this rolled-up paper. Sometimes it awarded you a prize, but most times you just got a bright saying. There were glassed-in shelves above the cigar box "library" that had somewhat larger stuffed animals, a mongrel assortment of undistinguished-looking dolls, and a few games and puzzles, but way up at the top, out of reach even of Mr. Kediff or Uncle Archie, practically in Heaven and sheathed in dusty cellophane, were the big, beautiful, enviable, and unattainable dolls. I had plenty of time to sneak furtive, yearning glances at those large, gorgeous treasures while I stood waiting for Uncle Archie and Mr. Kediff to stop chatting about the stock market or politics or neighborhood gossip, whatever the endlessly boring topics were that seemed to interest them.

If I'd been especially good all week—which meant that in the evening after supper, when Uncle Archie jerked his thumb back toward the bedroom, I'd get up right away and head back to bed, no fussing or stalling—I could get a present at Kediff's. I always eyed those big beauties in their dusty cellophane shrouds up there in doll heaven, but I felt it would've been greedy and indecent to signal that I wanted one. So I generally settled for a modest trinket. Except once, there was a handsome yellow teddy bear sitting right on the counter. He was medium size; he had a collar or a ribbon, I don't remember which, and he looked just exactly like Winnie-the-Pooh. Shyly, I indicated that that's what I wanted. Uncle Archie pretended to reflect—had I really been THAT good all week? After all, this was somewhat bigger than the usual present. Finally he said, "Okay." How I treasured that gentleman teddy bear! He suffered through baths, haircuts, all manner of mauling all the years of my childhood. I think I still had him, a battered, straw-filled critter, when Harry and I got married.

19

Aunt Evelyn and Uncle Archie lived only a short walk from Central Park, in those days a safe, verdant fairyland of trees and little hillocks and strange outcroppings of ancient rock, all of this right in the middle of bustling New York. When you got deep into the park the city sounds were muffled by all those leafy trees. Perhaps it really happened—as I seem to remember it—that I was allowed to go to the park unaccompanied by an adult. I did that in Chicago's Lincoln Park when I was eight or nine, but I was a good deal younger during those New York summers, I'm guessing five. I don't remember anyone watching out for me, though someone must have helped me across Central Park West to get into the park on that hot summer afternoon when I went fishing in one of the Central Park lagoons.

I must have planned for this adventure, because I had some string, some sort of homemade fishhook or a bent pin, some dough balls carefully crafted out of my uneaten bread pieces and cemented with spit, and a little bucket. I found a stick in the park, and tied my string with the baited hook to it. As luck would have it, I actually caught a couple of lethargic and not-too-smart carp! I dipped some water out of the pond into my bucket, getting my shoes muddy in the process, and managed to slide the fish into it.

As I was admiring my catch and imagining how I'd tell the story of my exploit to Aunt Ev and Uncle Archie, who'd applaud both the fisherman and her prey, a policeman suddenly appeared. "Little girl," he announced, "you can't keep those fish. They are Park property, you know. It's against the law for you to take Park property. You'll have to put them back in the lagoon."

They were *mine*, I protested. I'd caught them and I wanted to take them home to show my family. My lower lip trembled with the gathering emotion of self-pity and longing, followed by pathetic tears (a generally successful ploy with my parents when I wanted something they said I couldn't have). "Can't I keep them, just this once? I didn't know they belonged to the Park. I'll take good care of them, really I will."

"Well," he said after thinking it over, "just this once, but don't let me catch you keeping any more of them fish — ever. Just these two is all, and don't you forget."

So I hot-footed it back to 44 West 77th St. flushed with triumph, strutting past the impassive liveried doorman (who, I imagined, was secretly impressed only he didn't dare show it), into the cool wood-paneled lobby with its marble floors and Oriental rugs, into the elevator, excitedly slopping dollops of water out of the bucket. I was sure the elevator man was impressed and I was bursting with pride in my accomplishment, never anticipating the domestic crisis I unleashed with that bucketful of two small carp.

Aunt Evelyn took one look and announced, "Jeanie, you can't keep those fish here. They won't survive all crowded in that little bucket and we have no place else to keep them."

"Yes we do," I countered. "We can keep them in the bathtub until we get a fishbowl."

So Aunt Evelyn, who usually had a great sense of humor — and of the absurd — and who was always much more indulgent and devil-may-care than her older sister, but who was inexplicably touchy about her apartment, went off to consult Mother. Though Evelyn was a softy, my mother was both more outspoken and less easily suckered by me, having become inured to my manipulations. But I must have done the trembling lower lip thing, eyes brimming with bright tears, with the two little carp making very tight turns in their cramped bucket. There was more than one bathroom in that glamorous apartment, I seem to remember, but it must have adjoined Evelyn and Archie's bedroom, and if we did put the fish in our bathtub, then all of us would have to troop through their bedroom whenever we wanted to take a bath.

I switched my facial expression from pathetically pleading to angrily resolute: after all the policeman said that even though they were Park property, I could keep them, just this one time. That was the Law speaking, and I owed those fish a good clean life in our bathtub where I would feed them dough balls and make sure they had fresh water to swim in, not the murky, weed-choked stuff in those lagoons.

There must have been a good deal of controversy among Mother and Ev and Archie over those fish, but it was out of my earshot. The power of my desire to keep them allowed me to be oblivious to the dispute which smoldered around the little creatures and me and made the very air in the apartment tremble. So the pair of carp came to live in the bathtub, where they seemed quite happy with this large white expanse to swim in. But contentment for me and my new pets was short-lived.

First, there was my sister Darlene (this must have been one of the summers when she'd come with us), who both feared and hated all animals. She balked noisily at sharing the bathroom with two wild, dirty fish (how could they be dirty? They lived in WATER!). Then there was the maid who refused to enter that bathroom to clean it as long as those smelly things were in there (they didn't really smell—they were just sort of fishy). And finally there was Uncle Archie: sure, he'd been in the Navy and was less offended than the others by creatures of the water, but he objected to having the sanctity of *his* bathroom violated by his in-laws traipsing in and out to take baths.

All my family seemed to have it in for those fish, thought they were disgusting, inappropriate, out of place, and they felt that giving up our bathtub for them was going too far, I shouldn't be indulged any longer. If my father the nature lover had been in New York, I might have had a potent champion on my side, I thought, but he was in Chicago working and I was alone, with no one to stand up for me. My recollection is that the fish got to spend a pretty tense night or two with us, but then the boom got lowered on me: What was I going to feed my little charges? Surely, they couldn't survive on a nutrient-deprived diet of dough balls. Did I really think that they could live for any length of time in the sterile, weed-free environment of a *bathtub*? Besides, we humans needed that tub more and more urgently as time went on.

I got an ultimatum from the person I revered. Uncle Archie informed me gently but firmly, "Either you put your fish back in the bucket and return them to their pond in the park or they get flushed down the toilet" (that would certainly have created a major plumbing crisis as the fish were probably four or five inches long). So I think I must have returned them to the park. There had been, I realized later after they were gone, a kind of smoldering tension in the household while those fish were in residence. But I think the domestic crisis they exposed may have revealed some of the unraveling of what had formerly seemed to me to be a satin-smooth family fabric: there was tension between my mother and her sister and between Evelyn and Archie—but more of that later.

I think that was the last summer we stayed with them in that apartment. There was no more Kediff's, no more hawking newspapers on Broadway and 42nd. There were long stretches of summer in Chicago when Darl went to Camp Pinemere, which she loved, and I wallowed in boredom and self-pity. My friends were all away, my sister loved camp, and I aimlessly wandered through Lincoln Park and the zoo and the conservatory. Or I made doll clothes for my Raggedy Ann doll, or I read. My memory is one of loneliness and solitude. Where was my mother? I've no idea. I was growing, and the world was changing. October 1929 would soon bring down the stock market in the great crash.

But there was one more trip, 1928 or '29, before the Crash, when Daddy joined us for at least part of the summer, and we took the train from New York to Atlantic City. We stayed in a fancy hotel on the Boardwalk, the Ambassador. That was the summer Daddy taught me to swim and not to be afraid of the water. He communicated a calm assurance and confidence as my "swimming coach," in contrast to Mother, who, though she was a "natural" athlete (taking into account her enthusiasm for dancing, which Daddy did not share), was pathologically terrified of the water and never learned to swim. Unimpressed by Daddy's faithful adherence to his athletic "program"— he went regularly to the gym at the Standard Club, where he played squash (the lawyers' game of choice), swam, and did calisthenics—she criticized him as an indecisive Milquetoast. His (ineffectual) defense was that it was the nature of the judicial temperament to look at things "on the one hand . . . but then again on the other . . ." She dismissed that, contending that without her advice he couldn't manage his life.

But he taught me to swim there in Atlantic City—I was five or six—by leading me gently into the water, and when the shallows became the first wrinkly beginnings of surf, he'd lift me up and carry me out beyond the breakers, where the water was about up to his chest, but calmer. He'd lower me slowly into the water until I was almost up to my armpits but not touching bottom. He'd hold me firmly so that I wasn't afraid. "See how light you feel," he'd say, moving me up and down in the water so I could feel its buoyancy. "The water holds you up. It won't let you sink if you relax. Here, I'll show you. Just lie back on my arms," and I would lie supine in the gently heaving water. I could feel his arms supporting me. "Just pretend you're lying on your bed." After a few nervous failures when he told me he was going to take his arms away, I found myself floating effortlessly—just as he said I would. How astonishing! What a thrill! Then he taught me the crawl, which I wasn't very good at.

I loved the beach even though it was crowded. I remember sunburn and that coarse, hot Atlantic Ocean sand and the water with those big combers. I had the beginner's mistaken confidence that I'd overpowered the ocean, so I had a knockabout near miss on a day of booming Atlantic surf. I plunged confidently into the water—between combers as Daddy had taught me— so that I could do some body surfing, riding just behind the curl of those big breakers. I managed a couple of exhilarating rides, finishing up with a nice glide into the shallows. Then on the next try my timing went awry and I found myself being tumbled in a misty underwater gloom filled with sand and pebbles. It was like being in a giant washing machine, tossed end over end, helpless to find which way was up to the surface, as in wide-eyed terror I was turned every which way in the sandy whitish mist. I did what Daddy had taught me to do: I relaxed my body and let this maelstrom take me on its roaring foaming ride to shore—for as long as I could hold my breath. Luckily I got spat out on the gravelly strand, chin scraping the pebbles, flung out like a useless rag just before my lungs had reached their limit.

Although there were lifeguards stationed at regular intervals, I wasn't sure that anyone was aware of my frightening experience. Maybe almost being eaten by a wave is a common and not very dangerous adventure, but it felt terrifying to me. If my parents had been aware of my plight they probably would have forbidden me ever to go into the water again any deeper than to my ankles, so I never mentioned it to them, but it was a lesson to me; it made me cautious, if not actually timid, and it gave me lifelong awe of and respect for the power and mystery of the ocean. Mostly I was happy there in Atlantic City, playing by myself, pleasantly anonymous in the crowds of beachgoers.

The Ambassador Hotel was like the Belden: white-gloved "elevator boys," as we called them, deep carpets in the ornate lobby, rooms that looked out onto the beach and the endless ocean. That wonderful ocean smell and sound which filled our apartment when the windows were open (which they often were, as this was before air conditioning) brought with it a mysterious and exhilarating sense of the sea's vast expanse, on the other side of which was Europe, separated from us by half a world of water.

The preparations for summer vacation in Atlantic City were formidable: we brought enough luggage for a six-month stay. I don't know how long we planned to be there, but Mother was never one to travel light. She operated on the "what if" principle: What if the laundry didn't get returned? What if one trunk or suitcase got lost? What if we were invited to some Special Event and didn't have a suitable outfit because we'd left it at home? So we had a huge steamer trunk, rather like a portable closet. It was at least four feet tall, opened like a book, and had hanging space on one side and drawers on the other. The hanging space was crammed with my starched and ironed dresses — as many as fifty of them — brought along for a summer on the beach!!

It seemed to me that I spent nearly all day every day in my bathing suit, but I guess we must have gotten dressed up in the late afternoons and gone for walks on the fabled Boardwalk, browsing among salt water taffy emporiums, souvenir shops, and ring-toss games, and taking in such curiosities as the side show on the Boardwalk. The barker stood out in front, proclaiming the wonders and mysteries within his little fiefdom: wild animals, Siamese twins, a strong man who could bend an iron bar as though it were rubber. The most entrancing "exhibit" was Gertie, the ferocious African cannibal. She prowled up and back in her "cage" wearing a leopard-skin toga of sorts. Her kinky hair was pulled up into a sort of knob on top of her head, and the knob was decorated with beads, bones, and other appropriately savage-looking jewelry. I don't remember ever going inside to see the entire show; my parents weren't interested, and neither was I. Gertie was the principal attraction for me. I'd hang around there for hours, watching her pace up and down and mumble unintelligible sounds mixed with occasional shrieks and whistles. She fascinated me.

After several visits, she seemed to recognize me, and we got to know each other. Even though she was billed as a savage who ate people and could only make animal-like noises, it turned out that, in fact, she was a local girl from somewhere in New Jersey. We had several brief but pleasant conversations when there weren't any other customers and the boss wasn't there. I can't remember what she told me about herself, but when she wasn't being an African savage, she seemed to live an ordinary, rather unremarkable life.

20

I must have started first grade at the Francis Parker School (it did not then have kindergarten) in September of 1929. Darlene had already begun high school there after skipping a year at the Swift School, a North Side public grammar school. As the stock market tottered at its perilous peak, Daddy was now sending two children to one of the most expensive schools in Chicago.

What possessed Mother (agreed to by Daddy) to send us to the Francis Parker School, that bastion of enlightenment, which had a 10 percent Jewish "quota"? It was one of a very few prestigious private schools in the city, it was exclusive, it was expensive. These were the all-important characteristics that distinguished the aspiring dreamer Jew from the one who'd settled for a lesser level of social and economic status—the neighborhood dentist, the small-time merchant entrepreneur, those who were satisfied simply to live worlds away from the terrors of *shtetl* life that had driven their parents to America. Oscar Stern belonged to the dreamer group; Anne Preaskil did too, but she felt much less comfortable in the lofty precincts she aspired to, and had a morbid fixation on the lurking anti-Semitism that she knew lay in wait to keep us out. Still, she and Daddy persevered in their determination to send us to Parker. In spite of the underground river of prejudice whose existence she didn't doubt for a moment, it was the best education to be had.

Even though it was just a short block through the alley from the Belden Hotel to Francis Parker, Mother made Darlene walk me to school when I was in first and second grade. She'd drag me along at a panting jog trot so we'd make it before the bell. Darl especially hated walking me to school in the winter, when

I was so bundled up (bulky coat, stiff, itchy woolen leggings, mittens, and galoshes) that I could barely get one leg in front of the other. Our milkman still drove a horse-drawn wagon which he parked in the alley, and I always wanted to stop and pat Babe, his big patient horse. I'd have a couple of lumps of sugar clutched stickily inside my mitten for him. Darlene, never an animal lover, despised Babe—his smell, the dopey, lovelorn expression in his big brown eyes; she wouldn't even touch his velvety, taupe-colored muzzle. She was actually afraid of him. Darl would give my hand a good yank, and in retaliation I'd let my grasp go all limp and boneless so that my mitten, soggy with horse snot, would slip off into her hand. She'd drop the mitten, fling my hand away, and stalk off, leaving me to flounder after her. (Years later, I was repaid for my sins when I had to get our six kids into their winter outfits and they'd let their knees go limp as noodles when I tried to shove their feet into their always-too-tight overshoes; we referred to that limp-fish syndrome as Spaghetti Legs.)

First grade at Francis Parker was intriguing but scary. I wanted to feel comfortable but didn't, really. Miss Hattie A. Walker, a diminutive and very old lady with white hair piled up on top of her head, was firm and businesslike, not tender or loving or even very friendly. But after all, this was school, the beginning of a sort of impersonal "work life."

Learning to read, discovering quite suddenly that I was *reading*, was like a sunrise: awe, surprise, delight. When those inscrutable symbols on the page suddenly became words that spoke to me, it was an epiphany: my life was forever changed. "The Little Red Hen" was the first story I actually read, my eyes grasping meaning and the story speaking to me through my eyes, telling itself to me. That hen's self-importance as she strutted around the barnyard in her apron seemed almost lovable—and kin to me because I, now a reader, felt self-important, too. Then I had to write about what I had read, and that didn't give me quite the same rush as reading. I misspelled the word "farm," writing "fram," and Miss Walker reproached me sharply. I was stung. I don't recall being praised for mastering the mystery of reading, which seemed to me much more important than the triviality of a carelessly misspelled word. I didn't like being corrected then— and I still don't much care for it.

I thrilled to words, any words: labels on medicine bottles, street signs, newspapers, all of them decoded themselves before my eyes. Furthermore, wonder of wonders, Darl and I could now take turns reading to *each other*.

Though I was not quite six years old, the stock market crash of 1929 crashed into my life. Terrifying! Friends and associates of my father's were completely crushed, reduced before our eyes to pale, shrunken shadows. Many of these were men I had seen at lunch with Daddy and Mother at the Standard Club, where they'd been jaunty, smartly dressed businessmen and professionals. A couple of Daddy's friends jumped out windows, preferring death and the legacy of debt they burdened their families with to trying to make their way back to the respect that accompanied economic solvency. I don't think survivors could even collect the life insurance of a suicide, so some of the formerly affluent found themselves both disgraced and destitute.

Daddy was deeply shaken by the suicide of one of his closest friends: Oscar Blumenthal, a jolly man who used to awe and entertain me at lunch by making all manner of objects out of folded paper. I was especially impressed with a little paper washing machine he made; it stood on four legs, a little square tub, and it delighted me—watching him make it and then hand it to me with a ceremonious nod of his head and a twinkle in his eye. He jumped to his death from his office window in the Loop— 134 South LaSalle Street, headquarters of many of the city's prestigious law firms. How did I find that out? Did I overhear a conversation? It haunted me: Oscar Blumenthal was a short, plump man, always wore a vest like Daddy did. I pictured him, in my mind's eye, hurtling through the downtown air outside his office building, which faced on LaSalle.

My dad had speculated in the stock market, doing what many others had done: he'd bought stock on margin, a hazardous activity unless you were a stockbroker. So when the Crash came and the money owed for all such shaky investments was called in by the creditors, he couldn't pay up. My poor naïve father evidently thought it was "Pay up or go to jail!" He was pale and anxious: what was he to do? Mother was angry: she hadn't known about this poor judgment. They were both seriously frightened. Fortunately, the senior partner of Daddy's firm, Noble Brandon Judah, generously offered to lend my father the money to satisfy the creditors, and let him repay the debt in installments, as he was able. I remember Colonel Judah: an aristocrat of the old school. His father may have founded the firm. But he was friendly — even to a little girl like me: courtly but good-natured. He made an indelible impression on me.

Paying off the accumulation of his misplaced confidence in his fiscal acumen was long and arduous for Daddy. He wanted to keep us at Francis Parker School; he wanted to stay at the Belden; to keep the Standard Club membership, and so on. It was Mother who clung to the lifestyle; Daddy understood that about her. I remember once, while everything still seemed to be crumbling around us, Daddy came home one night all excited, and announced to us that he'd bought a stock, United Founders, which was absolutely guaranteed not to go down. (How could he have believed that?) Of course, it immediately got swallowed up in the general financial collapse, sank into oblivion, and added to Daddy's alarming indebtedness.

Just when the tension had begun to ease, in 1938 Noble Judah died, at the age of fifty-three, while my father was still paying off that debt. Noble's widow Dorothy, heiress to the National Cash Register fortune, did not have his open-hearted generosity. She was small, ferret-faced, with very black hair — dyed, no doubt. Why do I remember such details? She is not remembered fondly by me. She demanded that the debt be paid off immediately and in full, as she was a vulnerable widow who couldn't afford to carry this burden. Ha! I remember their estate in Lake Forest, which we visited at least once when I was quite little — four, perhaps. You drove a half mile at least along a glorious drive flanked with cypress trees. Athwart the end stood this chateau. That's where they lived, and they also had a stable with horses housed in a matching though smaller building.

I don't know how all of that was resolved; possibly one of the other partners stepped in to say that the original agreement couldn't be broken. After all, they were a bunch of lawyers, familiar with litigation. Or perhaps the firm took over the debt. In any case, Dorothy Judah was out of the picture.

Though Darlene and I suffered no changes in *our* lives, the Great Depression was a time when business failures left their mark even on someone as young as I was. We couldn't avoid seeing what was happening all around us. Even though I was only six, I remember the numbers of men, often in well-made overcoats and shoes, lined up in front of the places where there were jobs on offer; I remember well-dressed men in fedoras and Harris tweeds selling apples on downtown street corners and around Lincoln Park. I was frightened—of something nameless that just seemed to be in the air.

Meanwhile, first grade at Francis Parker was a year of extremes: exhilaration and shame. I was trying to get the hang of the school rules, and to understand the difference between a tolerable lapse, a misdemeanor, and a serious breach of propriety, safety, honesty, or socially appropriate conduct. I knew the school motto: "Everything to help and nothing to hinder," and the school word, "Responsibility," which tolled like a bell in my mind.

The worst failure was the time I wet my pants—publicly, avoidably—in music class.

21

Miss Luella Cornish, our music teacher, was as kind and smiley as Miss Hattie Walker was tart. There were about twelve of us in that music class. As we entered the music room, which was right next to the girls' bathroom, I knew that I needed to go to the toilet, but I was afraid that a pit stop would make me late and that would draw unwanted attention. The thought of asking to be excused in the middle of class was out of the question: everyone would know where *I* had to go, and there would be a lot of whispering and sniggering. So instead—what was I *thinking*?—I figured I could hold on and brazen it out until class was over.

Actually, music was one of the most enjoyable classes (unless your bladder was about to let go), and singing with my classmates gave me the illusion that our shared experience transformed these relative (and moderately hostile) strangers into friends. I wanted to blend in and be easy and casual and have the kind of pals my classmates seemed effortlessly to have. But at the same time, I wanted to stand out, to be special. Well, I got my wish in that music class.

It got really hard to focus on anything but the need to relieve myself. I sat in the back row, which was on a raised platform, and things were at the stage where I was furiously swinging my legs, which made the whole platform squeak enough so that people were looking at me quizzically. When we stood up to sing, I hopped and shifted from one foot to the other, but that didn't help either. Miss Cornish finally noticed my distress and asked, "Jean, do you need to be excused?"

"No," I replied, desperately dancing up and down.

Then, when we sat down again, it happened. I felt that terrible warm relief and horrified shame as my distended bladder let go. It sounded like Niagara Falls or drumbeats in the jungle as the stream poured onto the platform and then to the floor beneath. All those surprised faces turned toward me like little moons, and I heard someone make the dread announcement: "Jean wet her pants!"

Murmurs and giggles surrounded me, and through my nightmare I heard Miss Cornish, "Jean, have you had an accident?"

"No," I replied stoutly, denying reality.

Whoever was sitting next to me said "Yes you have. You've wet your *pants!*" Miss Cornish gave me a look and asked me to see her after class.

I was totally destroyed. No worse disgrace than what I had already suffered could possibly overtake me. So I endured the interminable rest of music class, standing soggily, then sitting back down in my little puddle in the chair, with the small lake on the floor beneath the platform, and the pervasive effluvium of urine in a cloud around me. My classmates weren't staring at me anymore; worse, they were looking away in disgust. I still had to get through the interview with Miss Cornish when the class ended. Why couldn't I just run out of the room and never, ever come back?

I stood there, sopping and smelly, as she asked me the superfluous question: "Jean, did you have an accident?"

Crazy me, I replied, "No, I sat down in a wet chair. It was already wet."

She sat at her piano looking at me reproachfully. "Jean, that chair was *not* wet when you came in here. Now, having an accident is one thing; it can happen to anyone, but lying, well, you think it over. Lying is not an accident, and we don't tell lies, that is a bad thing. Now, did you have an accident?"

"*No,* Miss Cornish," I repeated, on the verge of desperate tears, "I sat down in a wet chair." How had I gotten into this nightmare? Why couldn't I just have wet my bed in the comfort and privacy of my own home, instead of out in the world where I was now doomed forever to the contempt and disgust of my peers—a liar, a failed bluffer, a baby who couldn't even control her bladder?

Miss Cornish shook her head, more in sorrow than in anger, as they say, and I scuttled, dripping, from the music room, telltale drops of pee leaving a trail behind me. I headed for the comforting dark of our little first-grade cloakroom, with its cubbies, like small upended coffins, that held each child's outer garments. I quickly climbed into my woolen leggings, grateful for their concealment, itchiness or no itchiness, and tucked my sopping, stinking dress inside. It wasn't a comfortable solution to my shame; instead, it felt rather like how I imagine a hair shirt might feel, and it was much too warm to wear indoors, but it hid the most glaring aspects of my disgrace, and except for the occasional sly, knowing glance from one of my music class colleagues, I was left blessedly alone. When that interminable school day finally ended and I escaped the knowing sniggers of my classmates, I made my moist way home, vowing never to return to that school that had been such a wonderland of new learning for me but which now seemed to be totally ruined. I had no future.

Dealing with my *wisenheimer* sister was yet another nightmare hurdle in this day of scalding shame. When Darl got home from school it was almost dark, and I was still in my leggings. Brigitta had tried in vain to get me to take them off. Darl took one look at me, flushed, sweaty, and faintly malodorous, and asked, "Jeanie, why are you still in your leggings? It's much too hot to be wearing them in here."

"I'm fine," I replied. "Leave me alone."

Darlene, like Mother, had that instantaneous clairvoyance that made it impossible for me to lie successfully to either of them. I was probably a pretty clumsy dissembler, but even so, it seemed to me that they both had this sixth sense and would immediately see through any little lie I tried to sneak past them. "Why won't you take them off? What's *wrong* with you? *I* know, I'll bet you wet your pants at school! *Did* you? Is that what happened? I'll bet it is. Come on, let's get you out of all the icky wet clothes and into the bathtub. You'll feel so much better. Tell me—what happened?" Still stubbornly refusing to admit my shame, though I yearned for the fragrance of a cleansing bath, I maintained my uncharacteristically stony silence. How long could I keep up this lying and denying and being in pee-soaked garments?

Then Mother came home and the whole charade ended; the jig was immediately up. "Jeanie, you've wet your pants," she observed, "and you can't go around in those damp clothes, you'll get a rash." Turning to Darl and Brigitta, who were watching to see how this would play out, Mother said to them, "Why didn't you get her out of these smelly leggings? How could you let her go around like this all afternoon?" While she was reproaching them, she was peeling the damp garments off me, leading me into the bathroom, and running warm water into the tub, even as I continued a token resistance. Darl and Brigitta looked at each other, shrugged, and didn't even try to explain.

Somehow I would have to deal with this shame I'd brought on myself, which I was sure would dog my entire school career forever. I would have to admit that there's no denying Nature's bodily imperatives. And I'd have to confront the fact that I'd compounded the shame by lying. It was the lying, I realized, that was the worst of all, the indelible stain, even if I never lied again, which I knew was impossible. Though I'd always been too transparent a liar to depend on it as a means of avoiding ridicule, unpleasant confrontations, or harsh reality, I thought there was no other resource to call on when I needed self-protection. But now, in this school where the Protestant Ethic loomed over us all the time, I knew I'd doomed myself to perpetual disapproval from my teachers. My only hope was to tell myself that if *I* "forgot" my shame, everyone else would, too. I'd furtively study my friends to see whether there was any trace of that awful time lurking in their expression or in some chance remark. No matter, *I'm* doomed to remember it.

This brings me to another public embarrassment which, though it was less raw, has left its own psychic scar.

Every Morning Ex, which was our all-school assembly, much anticipated by everyone, began with Miss Cooke, our teeny, twinkly but firm gray-haired principal, ringing her metal triangle to bring us all to silent attention. We had all sorts of programs for Morning Ex (short for exercise, though these assemblies exercised the mind, not the limbs): plays, speeches, performances by various classes or outside speakers. Two I remember vividly: Vachel Lindsay reciting his poem "Boomalay-Boomalay-Boomalay-BOOM," all of us delightedly shouting that chorus after he recited each verse. The other was *Nanook of the North,* an early documentary movie filmed by Robert Flaherty (in remote northern Canada in 1922). We were captivated by its depiction of an Eskimo family's day-to-day life in the Arctic wilderness.

This occasion of my public embarrassment came at the close of a Morning Ex organized by the senior class. They read or recited some of their favorite poems. Sensitized to poetry by Darl's and my nighttime reading sessions, I listened avidly, hoping that they might pick one that I knew and liked. Ours was a school where poetry was brought to life not only by speakers like Vachel Lindsay but also by teachers like Mr. Merrill, who loved and were familiar with the language of poetry (and the poetry of language).

Miss Cooke concluded by asking, "Is there anyone who would like to share a poem with us?" My first-grade class sat on small wooden chairs in the front row of the auditorium, and it may have been the physical proximity to our principal, this petite but cosmic ball of energy, that inspired me. My hand shot up. "Jean," she announced.

I rose. "My poem is 'Little Lamb, Who Made Thee,' by William Blake." I breezed through the first stanza, but then I suddenly realized that that was all I knew. The expectant silence of the audience terrified me. I was sure they all heard my pounding heart. I rummaged desperately through my disordered memory—no more verses of 'Little Lamb' arrayed themselves before my mind's eye. After what seemed an interminable pause, Miss Cooke spoke, with disapproval, it seemed to me. "Is that all of the poem you can share with us?" I stood, mute and disgraced before all 300 students of our school. Miss Cooke looked down at me with a severe expression on her face, "Next time we have a poetry Morning Ex, Jean, I will call on you and expect that by then you will have learned the rest of 'Little Lamb' and will recite it for us so that we can all enjoy the whole lovely poem with you."

For months after that public disgrace I assiduously dodged Miss Cooke. When I saw her little gray head bobbing down a corridor I'd duck into a doorway, dodge down a hallway, melt into the center of a group of students—any trick to make me invisible to her. I lived in dread that one day she'd beckon me into her office or call on me in Morning Ex—"Jean, you've had time to learn all of 'Little Lamb, Who Made Thee.' Please recite it now, will you?" It never occurred to me that she had completely forgotten that episode that was the stuff of nightmares for me. I was both disappointed and relieved when I realized that she had. I could easily have memorized the remaining verses and my anxiety would have vanished. I never did. I never have. Once in a while I reread that poem—I still love it—but I will not memorize it, out of some perverse "in memoriam" to Miss Cooke.

In second grade I added extortion to my library of shameful behaviors. I had a would-be admirer, Malcolm Greenebaum, a fat boy with pale blue eyes and crinkly blond hair that lay on his head like rows of little waves on the beach. He said he liked me. He followed me around. He was not particularly interesting or glamorous, but I sensed opportunity. "If you want me to love you, bring me a present."

He brought me a little box. It had a diamond ring inside. I liked it a lot more than I did Malcolm, but a deal's a deal, so I told him yes, OK, I loved him—wondering what obligations loving him would entail.

I showed the ring to Mother when I got home. Her eyes widened and a look of amazement crossed her face when she opened that little box. "Where'd you get this?" She seemed quite alarmed.

"From Malcolm," I replied.

She phoned Malcolm's mother. "Have you lost a diamond ring?" she asked. Then she turned to me. "You shouldn't have let Malcolm give you this ring."

"Why not? I told him I'd love him if he brought me a present, so he did."

"But," Mother remonstrated, "not a diamond ring!" On the other end of the line Mrs. Greenebaum evidently said yes, her diamond engagement ring was missing. And Mother said that we had it and she would see that it was returned to Mrs. Greenebaum. I was disappointed to lose my present, but I hadn't wanted anything that "important." I'd imagined something like a Cracker Jack prize, and besides, the ring was too big for me. I never thought there was anything the matter with exchanging "love" for a present, especially if you didn't love the person; putting it on a transaction basis seemed more honest than pretending to love him when you didn't.

The extortion episode caused something of a commotion. Our second-grade teachers, a pair of tall, "American Gothic"-looking sisters called the Misses Enoch, were evidently drawn into this; they probably became custodians of the ring until Malcolm's mother could come to school to reclaim it. They were kind of stern and disapproving that such goings-on were happening under their noses. But to me it seemed like a tempest in a teapot. Why was everyone so disagreeable about this? Malcolm was sympathized with as more a victim than a thief, but *I* wasn't the one who took the ring. The only good that emerged from this episode was that I didn't have to love Malcolm.

22

My cousin Arlyn, the daughter of Archie and Evelyn, had been born on August 19, 1929; her middle name was said to be "Bear Market" (I've never found out whether it appeared on her birth certificate). The next time we visited the Paleys for a summer interval, in 1930, they'd rented a house in Pelham, a suburb of New York. That time both Mother and Daddy came, and though (it's clear now) incipient tensions already were simmering between Mother and Evelyn and between Evelyn and Archie, Daddy was a distinctly soothing influence on family relations. Unfortunately, he tore a ligament in his leg playing tennis and had to lie around keeping his foot elevated, which further disrupted an already ragged household.

I remember reading aloud to him. The book he chose was *The Epic of America*, by James Truslow Adams. I didn't understand much, if any, of what I read, but he seemed to enjoy it and I was proud that I could entertain him. Arlyn had a German governess named Hannah, and as she was just beginning to talk, her first language became German. I must have stayed on with them after my parents left; I am not sure of that, but I was there long enough to learn some infant German. Arlyn and I communicated easily, as little children can, but I got proficient enough to speak German with Hannah, too.

It must have been the following summer, 1931, when we went to Atlantic City: Evelyn, not-quite-two-year-old Arlyn, her nursemaid Hannah, and Brigitta, who came along to keep an eye on me (and Darl, to some extent) so that Mother and Aunt Evelyn were able to live like flappers. I have a dim memory of Hannah and Brigitta prattling in German.

This time, Mother and Aunt Evelyn and the whole entourage

stayed in a modest, cramped apartment in a building called the Biarritz, which we disdainfully pronounced ByRitz, and which Mother referred to as "Rapuchik's Hotel." It was a dump, a comedown after the Ambassador, but this was the Depression. It had a little Pullman kitchen, an array of rollaway cots and Murphy beds to accommodate all of us, and a cramped, stale griminess that was utterly lacking in elegance, tranquility, or privacy. If ghetto-sensitive Mother hadn't had Aunt Ev to prowl with and Brigitta to give her freedom, I think it might have been a terrible summer. But because it was a summer spent mostly on the beach, it was a blissful time for all of us.

It seemed to me, however, as self-appointed watchdog over Mother, that she was much too flirty with every passing Romeo. She and Aunt Ev spent their time with a pretty unsavory crowd of beach bums, most of whom appeared to be guys for hire, or on the lookout for good times and some free eats and drinks in exchange for escort service for a rich dame. They buzzed around these two good-looking broads like bees around daisies, and my heart burned with righteous indignation and disapproval. I was Mother's Virtue Nazi, guardian of my poor, hard-working father's interests, trying to keep his flighty, improvident wife on the straight and narrow. I might as well have been trying to empty the Atlantic Ocean with a sieve. I was a persistent Puritan, however, and simply transferred the snooping, nosy behavior I usually reserved for Darlene to Mother, whom I felt it was my duty to spy on as self-designated protector of Daddy. My method was not subtle, and Mother was especially unappreciative of my efforts to cut her out of this herd of good-time Charlies and joy-boy idlers when, on the day of her birthday, I skipped up and down the beach, proclaiming in a loud sing-song, "Mother's thirty-sev-en, Mother's thirty-seven!"

She and Evelyn would go out at night, and at the time I had no idea what they did—I just instinctively felt that they were up to no good. Once, however, they woke me up when they came home in the middle of the night. They had two big beautiful dolls, like the ones in Kediff's up on the doll-heaven shelf. One was dressed in pink, the other all in blue. "We won these in a game," they announced happily. "You can have first pick because you are the oldest, and Arlyn will get the other one. Which one do you want?"

It was the first time in my life as the kid sister that I got first dibs on anything—even those times when I'd created a row, my parents gave Darl first pick. Being confronted with the heady and unaccustomed role of having first choice, I couldn't make up my mind! On the one hand the doll in pink looked so dainty and charming; but on the other hand the blue was such a lovely cool color and it matched her eyes. So first I'd decide on one, then in a moment or two I'd change and go for the other. Aunt Ev and Mother got sort of impatient with me, so I settled on one of them—let's say it was the one in blue (I can't remember any longer)—and still stunned by this dream-come-true good fortune, I trotted back to bed, happily clutching my doll.

These dolls were even bigger than the dusty creatures on the top shelf at Kediff's. Arlyn, being littler, wasn't awakened in the middle of the night like I was; anyway, she was getting my reject. I felt pretty smug about that. But then the next morning Darlene weighed in with *her* choice, and of course she preferred the one in pink—and gave me all sorts of irrefutable reasons why it was the superior choice: pink is a girl color and this was obviously a girl doll. She had other pro-pink arguments, and my confidence in the rightness of my choice of the one in blue was demolished. By this time Arlyn was fastened onto the pink-clad doll. All my pride and pleasure in having had first choice evaporated; the blue doll looked positively homely to me.

Then Darlene, that slick rhetorician, having demonstrated the power of her persuasiveness, took pity on me and went to work on gullible Arlyn on my behalf, saying that the pink doll would get dirty faster, its hair wasn't as nice as the blue doll's, it had some imaginary blemish—and Arlyn gave up the pink doll without a murmur, especially after Darl told her that I really didn't *like* the pink doll and had been thrilled that I'd gotten first choice and didn't have to be stuck with that awful pink one, such an ugly shade of pink, and so on. So after I crowed, "Nyah, nyah, I wanted the pink one all the time and now I've got it and no trade-backs," Arlyn burst into frustrated tears—she'd been had—but Evelyn and Mother soothed her by promising that next time they went to the Steel Pier and played those games where you throw something and if you hit the target you get a prize, NEXT time Arlyn would get first choice.

I marveled that Mother and Evelyn could throw well enough to win not only once but twice; I didn't think they had such remarkable throwing arms either for strength or accuracy. But of course Darlene, the sophisticate and authority in all such matters, explained that the two of them had gone on a date with two of the beach bum gigolos that I so despised, and the guys did the throwing and the winning (and Mother and Ev did the paying). There was a whole exuberant bunch that all went out together. A couple of the other women looked like chorus girls and probably were. There was a lot of inside joking and laughing among this crowd—maybe it took Mother back to her high school days. Darl's knowledge wasn't extensive enough for her to speculate on what other activities they might have engaged in besides drinking, fooling around with the games on the Steel Pier, and going dancing, or if she had any ideas, she wasn't telling.

In spite of the crowded living, we had a happy summer. It had gotten off to an inauspicious start, however, as these voyages always did, because packing was such a production. Mother was an anxious traveler; she liked *being* in places like New York and Atlantic City, she just didn't like *getting* there. She protected herself from the waves of anxiety by insulating herself with enough luggage for a small army. In fact, we were akin to a small army. Even when we were living in the shabby little Biarritz, we wallowed in lavish wardrobe luxe. There's a photo of me on the Boardwalk, simpering for the camera, all duked up in a dress I remember: a lovely little white linen shift with large orange circles appliquéd around the hem. I wore a wide-brimmed white hat, my white Mary Janes and socks, and I definitely was a show-stopper. And knew it. And expected it. Sometimes we took a ride in one of the wicker rolling chairs that were trundled up and down the Boardwalk by men (usually Black) who reminded me of both the caricature Black comic Stepin Fetchit and the weary men in broken shoes who led sleek little ponies, with us in the saddle, around a small ring at the Lincoln Park Zoo. Those chairs were like giant baby strollers, with room for three, or possibly four, passengers. The men who piloted them wore starched white jackets, reminiscent of colonial servitude, over their frayed clothes, but that touch of sartorial hypocrisy, designed to suppress any individuality that might assert itself, couldn't cover up their knobby, work-hardened hands, or their dull-eyed resignation, as they shuffled and plodded among the sightseers idling along. I was both embarrassed and delighted to be pushed by these poor old men, the justification being that they were making "an honest living" and may have been rescued from the dismal hobo jungles that the Depression spawned. Was it worse than being "Gertie"? Hers seemed to me a sort of celebrity life, boring but with a touch of glamour. I turned aside such thoughts and simply enjoyed the sea smell, the perpetual sound of surf as an accompaniment to life near that big ocean, the feel of being at the edge of America, all of it filling the eyes and the lungs and the spirit with the signature of big sky and big water. Gulls wheeling around and calling was part of the special windblown ocean atmosphere.

Mother loved to get both of us all dressed up and then stroll along the Boardwalk attracting admiring stares from the "tourists." Once, as a special treat, she took me to lunch at the Canary Tea Room, a perfect little restaurant on the Boardwalk. You could watch the endless procession of walkers and gawkers through its sparkling plate glass windows and see the water beyond in the brilliant ocean light. It was a place to which you wore a hat and gloves — a haven of old-school propriety. Hat and gloves at midday in this beach paradise? Well, that's the way it was at the Canary Tea Room. The floor was black and white squares of spotless, gleaming linoleum, and all the décor was canary yellow: the tables, the dishes, the linens, the upholstery on the chairs, even the sheer organdy curtains at the windows. The waitresses wore prim, immaculate yellow uniforms, the walls were yellow, the place practically screamed "gentility," except that it would have been very un-genteel to scream. One had to behave with appropriately perfect and immaculate manners in the Canary Tea Room, the home of unremitting decorum. Why did Mother take me there? Was I in training to become a Princess?

After studying the menu she ordered weakfish (that's sea trout), and I recall that it arrived on its oval (yellow) platter whole, with its wide-open eye staring at us reproachfully, it seemed to me. That may have unnerved Mother, who was never much of a carver. She really didn't know how to handle this pretty little fish that gazed up at her from its bed of parsley with lemon garnish. At her first effort to slice into the fish, it slipped out from under the knife and fork, leapt from the plate, flew off the table and skidded across the checkerboard squares of the floor. It seemed as though all the diners' well-hatted heads swiveled around in unison to gaze at us disapprovingly. So much for propriety!

Although she tried to make light of it, I could tell that Mother was flustered, as though she'd been caught impersonating a Lady, and now we were both exposed as the imposters we were. Her ghetto ignorance and lack of refinement were fated to betray her and reveal the coarse sloven from 14th and Jefferson who didn't even know how to handle a knife and fork well enough to slip the tender flesh of that delicate fish from its dainty bones. And so it fled from us and announced to all the world that we were really two filthy ragged immigrants with dirty fingernails and smelly hair who'd thought they could disguise themselves as English ladies. Her discomfiture went beyond the sort of jokey, casual self-deprecating laughter that a really confident person would have displayed. I was infected by her sudden hot flush of shame and felt as though *I* was the one who had revealed our ghetto origins to a scandalized public in the tea room — I, the pampered child, gently reared in the luxury and elegance of the Belden Hotel! Well, at least I didn't have to eat that weakfish, whose huge hypnotic eye stared me down. I don't remember what we ate; the whole experience reeked of disgrace, and we never returned to the Canary Tea Room.

23

Perhaps it was that first summer when Mother, Darl, Brigitta, and I made the trek to Atlantic City directly from Chicago—well, more or less directly (we had to change trains in New York, of course)—that I Got Lost.

We had the usual mountain of luggage, including at least one steamer trunk, enough to take us on a globe-girdling safari. (What on earth did we do with all those clothes?) The logistics of changing trains in Grand Central Station with all that baggage was a formidable challenge, but this was the Depression, and there were a lot of Red Caps, porters (generally Black) who'd hustle your luggage with their hand trucks or dollies, manhandling the trunks and big suitcases into the baggage car at the front of the train to Atlantic City and the rest into the luggage racks or the storage space of our coach. Then, at your destination, your very own baggage, all of it, would be mysteriously assembled on the station platform waiting for another Red Cap to haul it to a taxi or a wagon, depending on how much stuff you had to transport to wherever you were staying. Grand Central was so huge and so bewilderingly chaotic, with people rushing in all directions and the arrivals and departures of trains being announced from so many different tracks all at once, that I was terrified I'd get lost, so I clung like a limpet to Mother, who was trying not to lose any of our extensive collection of freight.

The train to Atlantic City was a sharp contrast to the stylish carpeted elegance of the 20th Century Limited, THE New York-to-Chicago train for the rich and famous. First of all, this train didn't even have a name, that's how proletarian it was, with its woven straw seats whose backs could be moved to allow you to face either forward or backward, more like a streetcar than a proper train. I'm not even sure we had reserved seats; it may have been catch-as-catch-can, first come, first served. It was noisy, boisterous, crowded with vacationers, with their boxes and bundles, cardboard valises, baby carriages, and baskets of food to eat on the way, all of which lent the trip a frenzied, carnival atmosphere totally unlike the well-bred tranquility of the 20th Century.

As the train started up, with a lot of metallic clanging and jerking (not smoothly and silently like the 20th Century), I noticed a woman with an enormous green parrot in a cage not far from our seats. "May I go see the lady and the parrot?" I begged. Glad to be on the last leg of this trying journey and knowing that she and Evelyn would be reunited at our destination so there'd be help with all the baggage, Mother seemed more relaxed. "Sure, go ahead," she said, "Just don't wander off anywhere, and be sure to come back here before we get to Atlantic City so we can all get off together." I don't remember whether Evelyn's modest travel entourage — she, Arlyn, and nursemaid — were on the same train from New York or whether they had arrived earlier, to get settled into our apartment (and nab the choicest locations for themselves), but in any case we were all to meet in the Atlantic City railroad station.

The lady and her raucous pet with its scimitar beak were given a wide berth by the other passengers, so there was plenty of seating space beside her. Ever the animal fancier and deprived of those delights by Darl's unreasoning terror of all furred or feathered creatures, I asked the lady whether I might sit with her and her bird, and she seemed genuinely pleased by my obvious admiration for her companion. I probably asked the usual questions: How old is it, what's its name, is it a girl or a boy, what does it eat, how long have you had it? — but I don't remember the answers. Certainly, riding with her and hearing about her bird transformed what might have been a tedious trip through the less picturesque parts of New Jersey into a fascinating adventure in ornithology.

As the conductor announced our approach to Atlantic City, I returned to my seat beside Mother and tried to tell her about this marvelous bird, who actually had talked to me! She wasn't in the least interested, of course, and besides, she was gathering herself for the descent onto the train platform, the task of rounding up all the luggage, and the search for Evelyn, her presumptive deliverer—what if she wasn't there to meet the train?? Preoccupied, she cautioned me to stay near her while she focused on these other matters. And so we descended onto the platform at Atlantic City.

Since this was just an intermediate stop, there was a good deal of bustle and chaos as the disembarking passengers scrambled to collect all their bundles and not leave anything behind. What with all the people pouring onto the platform with their parcels and children and suitcases, the shouting of cab drivers and Red Caps offering their services, the train exhaling loud screeches and whooshes of steam from its air brakes (a sound that terrified me), and Mother preoccupied with rounding up all our extensive luggage collection from both the baggage car and the luggage racks, a performance that was of no interest to me, I decided to wait for my new friend and her bird to descend from our coach. I wanted to say goodbye to her and to the parrot. She was among the last of the passengers to disembark, and we embraced and said our goodbyes and I peeked beneath the cover of the parrot's cage to say farewell to him, too. The cover prevented him getting too agitated by all the noise and the crowds, she explained.

At that moment the conductor shouted, "Boooard," swung onto the steps of the rail car, and with shrieking and clanking of metal, the train began its gradually accelerating departure from the Atlantic City station.

The crush of people—scissor-like legs rushing past me, piles of baggage—blocked my view. I wormed my way among all these big people in search of Mother, who, with our mountains of luggage, ought to be as easy to spot as Mount Everest. But there were so many people rushing in all directions, calling and searching for porters or buses or family members, that I couldn't see more than a few feet in any direction. I wove in and out among the crowds the length of the platform in one direction but didn't see her, so I retraced my steps and went all the way to the other end—still no sighting of her or Darl or Brigitta. By this time the crowds were thinning out, so I had a longer vista, but I was also beginning to feel scared—had I been left behind? Forgotten??

Pretty soon I was one of just a scattering of people on the platform, and I could see all the way to the end in both directions. There was absolutely no trace of my family or of our enormous pile of luggage and steamer trunks. There were a few cab drivers standing aimlessly beside their vehicles hoping to pick up a straggler. I started walking toward one end of the platform again, gulping air convulsively, heart pounding, trying not to cry. I approached one of the cab drivers, "Have you seen my mother? She's a lady with black hair." He just kind of sniggered and shrugged. I was not only scared, I was also insulted: he seemed to be laughing at me, not being sympathetic at all, thought I was funny, this chubby little kid huffing and puffing up and down the platform. By this time I wasn't walking, I was dog-trotting, as though I'd find her if I got to the end of the now-deserted and silent platform sooner. My dignity and reserve, such as it was, had blown away in my gasps as I tried not to wail, "Mommy!" All pride vanished and I was asking every stranger if they'd seen my mother. No one had.

Not knowing what else to do, now in a genuine panic—I was deserted!—I ran toward the opposite end of the platform, past the blur of the few cabbies and bus drivers still lounging about, all of whom seemed to be laughing at me and my plight, but I no longer cared. The station seemed to close in on itself and go to sleep, waiting until the next train with all its attendant bustle pulled in, whenever that might be. Porters dissolved back inside the little station building, cabbies climbed back into their cars to rest or to drive to some other promising location. It was the end of the world, and I was all alone. I turned and, hiccupping little sobs, headed disconsolately back toward the other end of the platform, now so miserably familiar to me, too frightened to stand still. Walking at least made me feel as though I was trying to do *something*, even if it was something pointless. Where was

I to go? I had no idea where we were staying and there was no one to help me. I was alone in an uncaring world.

And then, at the far end of the platform, way ahead of me, I saw her—Mother—running toward me. Any tattered remnants of concern about dignity flew to the four winds and I flung myself into her arms. "Jeanie! Where have you been? Where did you go? Where were you?" she asked as she hugged me tightly.

Where did *I* go? Where did *she* go? I was there all the time, sobbing and gasping, heart pounding. "I was looking for you," I answered between teary sobs, "And I was so scared my breath was whistling!"

It turned out to have been one of those classic comedy scenes: Aunt Evelyn, with Arlyn, was at the station waiting for us in her snazzy convertible, and some of the baggage was loaded into its trunk, while a few more pieces got put in the trunk of a cab in which Darlene and Brigitta waited. An extra truck took the remaining trunks and bags, and once that was attended to, Mother got into the cab with Darl and Brigitta, assuming that I was in the convertible with Evelyn and Arlyn. Just as the caravan was about to pull away, Mother decided she wanted a cigarette, but she didn't have a match. Ordering her cabbie to wait a moment, she went over to Evelyn's car to borrow a light. When she looked in and didn't see me, she asked, "Ev, where's Jeanie?"

"Isn't she with you in the cab?" said Evelyn.

"No," replied Mother, "I thought she was with you."

"And I thought she was with you," said Ev.

Their eyes locked in alarm, and they both dashed off to search for me. Kidnapping was one horror that crossed their minds, they told me later. How could this have happened? Why wasn't Brigitta keeping an eye on me? Because she'd been put on baggage detail along with everyone else.

The uncertainty of Mother giving me over to a succession of women who seemed like strangers, who WERE strangers, reinforced my fear of abandonment, of being lost, of which perhaps my mother's disappearance into the sanitarium when I was an infant, too young to remember, was the inception, and this memorable episode of "losing" my whole family in the Atlantic City railroad station was the vivid, unforgettably terrifying climax. That episode left me with a lifelong separation anxiety. It's probably why I don't like meeting people at airports or railroad stations or even for a simple, innocuous lunch date. I tend to be anxious that I will be stood up, that they'll never show up and I'll be abandoned. For many years I was chronically late for appointments, and I suspect it was to give the other person time to be there first so that I could avoid that feeling that I might be deserted — again.

It was that summer that Darlene, who was about fourteen, had what was probably her first boyfriend. If Mother could flirt around and get a boyfriend or two or six, why not Darl? I was still safe in the peace of prepubescence (though there was a boy, Buddy Deutsch, who became a pal; we made sand castles and played in the water and had sandy-tasting lunches in the damp shade under the Boardwalk, where you could escape the sun). No one in that Rapuchik's Hotel had much privacy, but Darl had found someone who lived in the adjoining warren of an apartment, and she and he would send signals to each other by tapping on their common wall. How much they actually got to see each other, I don't know. Somehow my surveillance of Darl was less thorough that summer — I was distracted by Gertie, the beach and its many enchantments, and keeping a watchful eye on Mother, to whom I gave espionage precedence over my sister. Toward the end of our vacation the signaling became more fevered; there was some furious rap-tapping for the final couple of days. When the day of departure came at last, Darl was not only uncharacteristically weepy, she also threw up, a most extraordinary action for her. I was both pleased and alarmed to see her so miserable and upset, my big sister, always the soul of self-possession.

24

Once I started school at Parker and the nursemaids became obsolete, Mother, ever ingenious at avoiding household activities, hired a cook, Olga Fruland, a tiny, birdlike, red-headed Norwegian from Stavanger. Olga arrived from faraway Humboldt Park by bus (*two* buses, actually) every morning at 7:00 a.m., fixed breakfast for Daddy and us, and got Darlene and me off to school. (Mother loved to sleep late. I don't remember her ever being up to see us off to school.) Olga not only shopped and cooked but also stayed and washed up after dinner, leaving the kitchen spotless and ready for breakfast, which she returned to fix for us by 7:00 the next morning.

Olga was reserved, as Norwegians can be, but she was lively, quick, bright, and not reserved with me. I loved her. I hung around the kitchen whenever I could, and she taught me by letting me watch her make schnecken and cookies and marvel at her skill rolling butterballs between two wooden paddles. (After persistent pleading, she let me try to make them: they demanded a dexterity and confidence that I never acquired.) Once she took me on the long bus ride to her house in Humboldt Park. That was my first inkling of how vast Chicago was: Humboldt Park seemed as far away as California!

I met Olga's husband, Eli, who was a tailor, a tall, dour Scandinavian. I didn't like him, and I learned later that he was a drunk and may even have abused Olga. She had an affair with our Bowman Dairy milkman (who must've delivered more than milk to our apartment). Eventually she divorced Fruland and married her milkman, and theirs was a happy union. I am glad she got away from Mr. Fruland. Olga was a marvelous cook, the envy of all Mother's friends, some of whom tried to entice her away from us, but she was with us for ten years or more. She worked for us until 1940, after we had moved out of the Belden Hotel.

As far as I was concerned, my whole life had been lived in the Belden. I had been eighteen months old when we moved in, so I had no memory of any other home. The hotel seemed to me like a self-contained city. It had an elegant dining room, complete with a string ensemble that played banal semi-classical music at dinner. Among its other amenities was a drugstore with a soda fountain where I spent many absorbed hours crushing the paper jackets of drinking straws, then putting a drop of water on the accordion-pleated paper and watching it writhe and curl like a worm. In the time-honored tradition, my chums and I often blew these jackets at each other when the proprietor wasn't looking. Near the front entrance of the hotel was a barbershop; the beauty shop was off the South Parlor, a ground-floor party room. The newsstand, a sort of counter that opened off the drugstore, sold candy bars and odds and ends that the drugstore didn't stock, though both of those operations were under the same person's harassed management. Adjacent to the lavish marble-clad lobby was a well-stocked commissary. If you got marooned in that hotel, you'd survive quite handily and find almost limitless ways to amuse yourself, too.

Life at the Belden was always interesting. In spring, summer, and autumn we played hopscotch and roller skated on the wide sidewalks in front of the hotel entrance; we kept track of all comings and goings—the interesting commercial vehicles as well as the inhabitants of the hotel. In bad weather the Belden became our indoor playground. We mostly ran around and played games, passing through the marble lobby with its gold leaf and vaulted ceiling without really being aware of its majesty, or its pomposity. Our roving gang ran up and down the broad carpeted corridors, probably a great nuisance to our fellow residents; we cruised the red-carpeted stairways to the mezzanine, a maze of game rooms and splendid banquet rooms and ballrooms, each with its own French doors, where weddings and private parties were held, and we little resident urchins could gawk at the elegant women in their fairy-tale frocks.

The hotel's most interesting working innards were behind big double doors off the lobby: the package receiving room, where the doormen and others congregated for their breaks and you could pick up gossip; the kitchen, which prepared meals for the dining room and also catered private parties; the housekeeping department, which laundered all the hotel linens in huge steamy cauldrons (in the basement, which was dark and wet and which I seldom visited) and ironed the sheets on industrial-size mangles back in the maze that was the underside of elegant hotel life.

We even explored the thirteenth floor, the very top of the building, supposedly off limits but accessible to those in the know. Besides the handyman's room where the electrician and the troubleshooters worked, there was an upholsterer's workroom and a carpenter's shop, where daylight streamed through huge arched windows into the loft-like space that smelled of newly sawn wood. The thirteenth floor also housed the elevator machinery whose braided metal cables wound and unwound majestically on their huge metal spools. (It later became the title and the setting for Darl's Young Adult mystery novel, *The Mystery of the Thirteenth Floor*.) Along with other alcoves and byways, it presented spectacular opportunities for hide-and-seek.

So the day I decided to run away from home, I didn't have to run far.

I must've been seven, perhaps a little younger. Darlene, at the moodily magic age of fourteen, seemed to command all my parents' concern and attention. She was skinny, had totally straight hair, didn't stand up nice and straight (like I did), was awkward, had become withdrawn—not from me or from her gang of lively friends, but from Mother and Daddy, with all their anxious prying. But it was *her* they focused on, not me. I felt as if no one cared about me, no one noticed whether I was there or not. It was like being not only invisible but also—and worse—unloved, ignored, passed over, a cipher. Well, if nobody cared whether I was there or not, if, therefore, nobody cared whether I lived or died, I'd show 'em. I'd vanish, and they'd look all over and wouldn't find me. They'd be all worried and upset and they might even call the police to help search for me.

I did hardly any advance planning for my "disappearance." I might have grabbed a candy bar or a small bottle of milk, but that was all. It was autumn; the days were becoming shorter, and it got dark before six. There may still have been a few leaves on the trees in Lincoln Park. I had no intention of wandering darkening city streets. I didn't really want to venture into the World Outside, to be a runaway and forge my own life on the run, in hobo camps or abandoned buildings. I just wanted to put a scare into them. I figured out a perfect hiding place right in the hotel.

There was a little cubbyhole concealed by brass grillwork just inside the entrance to the hotel on the Lincoln Park side of the building, where there was no doorman. Part of this ornamental grillwork concealed the radiator that warmed the area between the outer and inner doors, our refuge on cold winter days when we'd run into that entryway to warm fingers that ached from the cold after an interlude of snowball throwing or mittenless tag on the sidewalk. But you couldn't see into the space behind the brass grille, which ran the entire height and length of the wall between the inner and outer doors to this entry. It hid both the blessed radiator and the empty space beyond it. It was one of the numerous little mystery places we knew about in the hotel. So around four o'clock I crept out of our apartment, not even taking my coat—a dead giveaway that I was somewhere on the premises. But that didn't matter to me. I just wanted them to miss me and want me back and to greet me with tender and joyous relief.

I rode down in the elevator, strolled casually out of the lobby, and, making sure no one saw me, opened the door in the grille and slid into this somewhat cramped and quite grimy unused space. I was feeling pretty satisfied with myself. No one had seen me leave our apartment, and the elevator boys wouldn't have taken notice of me going downstairs at four—we kids were always going up and down on our mysterious errands of mischief or sociability. We must've been a great trial to those elevator boys, going up and down, down and up, all afternoon after school, collecting each other, going back for some forgotten item, changing our mercurial minds about whose apartment we were playing in that day. At least it kept the elevator operators from falling asleep on the job.

There wasn't a stool or a seat in this little space, so when I got tired of standing I sat on the sooty floor. It was one of those hidden, neglected places that would've scandalized Mrs. Cash, the hotel's chief housekeeper and our chief Tyrant. I could peek out through the grillwork, but this little dungeon was so dark that no one could see me unless they came up close and peered in. I could watch the dusk – and then the darkness – settle over the park and its trees. Pretty soon the green of all that vegetation dissolved into the night and everything seemed quite black out there, except for the streetlights and car headlights. I was wondering whether they'd noticed I was missing. Were they getting ready to sit down to dinner? What would they think? Would they get alarmed that I'd been kidnapped? I hoped they were crazy enough with worry and anxiety to compensate me for the discomfort of the hard, dark, dirty floor and cramped space. I wondered how long I'd been there. Why were there no police stamping around and searching for me? Why weren't my friends out there trying to hunt me down? Where were my distraught parents and worried sister?

I felt as though I'd spent many hours in there – too many – and I was beginning to realize that I couldn't wait much longer to be found, as I had to go to the toilet. Whenever one of the big brass outer doors opened, my heart leapt and I imagined the joyous reunion with my loved ones, those careless, unfeeling Philistines! But it was just some hurried businessman rushing in out of the dark to join his eagerly waiting family, someone whose arrival would be greeted with shouts of joy and open arms, while I, poor neglected waif, languished in the sooty dark, unmissed, uncared for. I was tired, had to go to the toilet, I was hungry: what time was it anyhow? It felt like ten o'clock.

I slunk out of my hiding place and made my way upstairs as

inconspicuously as possible. I was perversely glad not to run into any nosy acquaintances, because I wasn't prepared to explain my smudged and disheveled appearance. When I opened the door to our apartment, I half expected it to be deserted, with Mother, Daddy, and Darlene having fanned out in search of their darling Jeanie. As the door shut behind me, Mother called out, "Is that you, Jeanie? We wondered where you were." Oh, *did* they? Not enough to come looking for me, not enough to be all tear-stained and worried. They were just sitting around in the living room, Daddy reading the stock market page of the *Chicago Daily News*, Mother reading some novel or other and smoking, Darl curled up in a chair with a book. They all looked quite unperturbed, looked up at me kind of absently. "Wash your hands," Mother instructed, "dinner will be ready in just a few minutes."

So what time *was* it? How long had I been gone? It wasn't even six o'clock yet! Why had I thought I'd been in hiding for three or four hours when it had been less than two? Hadn't anyone worried that it was dark and I wasn't home yet? Why hadn't one of my friends phoned looking for me and maybe given Mother a little prick of alarm? But no, they scarcely looked at me, they didn't even notice how grimy and sooty I was from my little secret cubbyhole. No one cared about me—not my friends, not my family. I was an outcast, a failure. I couldn't even run away from home properly.

I was too ashamed of my incompetence to tell my family what I'd been up to. I'd muffed the whole runaway effort so badly that they'd probably never even realize that they had almost lost me forever. The worst would be if I told them that and they laughed at me. So I slunk to the dinner table and never said anything to any of them about my disgracefully failed enterprise, not even to Darl whom I trusted above all others. If she had even just smiled, I couldn't have stood it. It was just one of my compost heap of embarrassments, failures, and shames that I seemed to have more of than anyone else I knew.

But if the capacious Belden offered refuge to the morose, it was also a veritable Mecca for mischief, an ideal school for hoodlums in training. There was lots of trouble after Pauline Marks and Dorie Pearlman and Carol and Billy Kobin and I were caught skipping down our corridor with pencils in hand, making a long wavery line on the wall that recorded our skipping. We were spied on by a neighbor, Dorothy Horwich, who lived across the hall from my family on the first floor with her henpecked husband, Morrie. Dorothy had fierce black patent-leather hair and dark eyes that darted like adders and never missed a single detail. She reported us to Mrs. Cash, the chief housekeeper, and our parents all got a stern warning.

We were not deterred for long.

Pauline Marks, a few months younger than me, but taller, was my dear friend and most enthusiastic accomplice in rascality. There was one Halloween when we scrawled soap graffiti all over the ground-floor windows of a neighboring apartment building. Our most audacious prank, however, was perpetrated during one of the ladies' luncheon and card party events often held in the hotel's South Parlor, just off the lobby. A lovely, airy room, it boasted the hotel's signature tall windows and French doors, and was often occupied by dressed-up ladies who gathered in this popular destination for a tasteful luncheon served by the white-gloved dining room staff, followed by a genteel and sociable afternoon of cards.

On this sunny winter afternoon, we peeked into the South Parlor, sizing up the ladies in their frilly dresses, all of them twittering to each other like the birds in the zoo's Birdhouse. Since you had to enter the South Parlor if you were going either to the ladies' room or the beauty shop, the room remained more or less accessible to the public, which we knew, of course. So we sauntered in, eyeing the crowd of ladies and evaluating their tailleur — we were very interested in clothes and how stylish they were. (We made lots of gaudy dresses for our paper dolls.) With elaborate casualness, we strolled toward the ladies' room. There was a cloakroom adjacent to the ladies' room. There was also a water fountain and paper drinking cups. Pauline and I entered the cloakroom, meandering along the ranks of neatly hung coats, stroking the fur ones, fingering the collars on the fur-trimmed ones. The ladies' hats were ranged on a shelf above the coats—all ladies wore hats in those days—sort of bowl-shaped, with floral or feather trimming.

What got into Pauline and me? Whose fiendish idea was it? Mine, I confess. I fancied myself the brains of the partnership: I was a better student—but not a shrewder analyst of acts and their consequences. "Paul" was a terrific sidekick: cheerily compliant. First we got the idea of turning these bowl-shaped hats upside down. Surveying our arrangement, it seem clear that each of those hats cried for a cup with a little water in it to be carefully placed inside their upturned hollows where the cup would be invisible to the ladies. As each reached up to put her hat on when the party ended, she'd get a bit of a drenching. It seemed like a great idea, though as we placed our little water cups in each hat, we realized that we couldn't have the pleasure of witnessing the reaction of our victims or the havoc that would ensue. We'd just have to complete our work and take it on the lam.

Once we'd done all the hats we could reach—I must have handed some of the cups to Pauline because I couldn't reach the shelf—it struck us quite spontaneously that something needed to be done with—or to—the ranks of coats. One of the more elaborate fur coats was some sort of smooth black fur, seal perhaps, and it sported a snow-white ermine cape, fringed with finger-slim white ermine tails, each one delicately tipped with black. We ceremoniously dipped every single ermine tail—and it seemed as though there were a lot of them and we were beginning to get a bit nervous—we dunked each one in water, and then, in a final flourish, dashed the remaining cups of water, plus a few more, against the linings of the coats where the damage wouldn't be immediately visible but would become apparent only when the ladies removed their coats from the hangers and started to put them on.

Once our job was completed, we realized, with a sudden rush of horror, that this was a big, bad mistake. Panicked, we left the scene of the crime as unobtrusively as possible, then darted up one of our "secret" sets of stairs, up several flights, where we hid for a while, alternately giggling and feeling heart-poundingly scared. Pauline was one of those people whose bladder reacted convulsively to fear or anxiety, so we had to rush to her apartment on 7 so she could go to the toilet.

The redoubtable Mrs. Cash, bewigged gargoyle of the Linen Room, wasn't long in tracking us down, naming us the culprits, and giving our parents a threatening lecture, this time a REAL ultimatum: one more such prank and we'd be evicted. Further, our parents were liable for sizable bills for cleaning and fur-restoring. There was talk of not letting Paul and me play together anymore, but she and I managed to talk our way out of such a draconian punishment.

I often stayed overnight at her apartment, because she had her own big bedroom, while I shared with Darlene. The Markses made me feel comfortable and at home, and I always loved being there. Paul's mother, Gertie, was the most glamorous "older woman" (maybe forty) I'd ever seen. She was an exquisitely coiffed platinum blonde, like the movie star Jean Harlow, and she had a perfectly gorgeous figure which she pampered and dressed in the height of fashion. She and Meyer, her darkly handsome (but so dumb even an eight-year-old could tell) husband, loved to dress up and go out to speakeasies, dance halls, secret gin mills, gambling joints and roadhouses, all the night clubs around town. They were a dashing couple, she so fair and slender, delicate perhaps, and he so dark and big and strong-looking. I remember them going out one night when I was staying at Pauline's, and the two of us just staring, completely gaga, as Gertie swirled into their living room in a form-fitting long black velvet number whose entire bell-shaped hem was edged in luxuriant silver fox. Meyer was no slouch, either, resplendent in a perfectly tailored tuxedo. Every winter they took Paul out of school and they all went to Palm Beach, Florida for at least three weeks, maybe longer (could that cavalier attitude toward her education have contributed to Pauline's mediocre school record?).

I was wistful and envious of a family that seemed to think it wasn't a vacation unless you were all together. (My parents never took me with them on their winter vacations to Palm Springs, California.) Pauline's older brother, Julian, was dark and handsome like his father. He wasn't around much; he had a roadster and may have been in college. When her folks went out of an evening or maybe to French Lick, Indiana for a weekend, a wonderful young woman of about seventeen came and stayed in their apartment. She and Paul and I would make paper dolls and impossibly gorgeous extravagant clothes for them by the hour. I remember a silver dress she made for one of the dolls, and some futuristic-looking outfits that we both vied for. There was a lot of swapping, but Paul and I didn't fight — she was easy to be with and a good friend, one I trusted, as she had no malice.

But tragedy stalked her family. Gertie got breast cancer and was dead a year later. Meyer lingered on for a few years, a lost soul without his Gertie. He lost all his money during the Depression, and had to move out of the Belden. He may have committed suicide. After Gertie's death, he had turned Pauline over to Gertie's sister and brother-in-law, asking them to raise her. The brother-in-law had a band at the Embassy Hotel on Diversey, and he didn't make much of a living at that time. Then he and his wife and Pauline moved to California. Pauline became a sort of indentured servant, and later she told me that life with them was hard and unhappy, even after her uncle became a very successful musician. His name was Jule Styne, and he became composer and conductor for many Hollywood films. Pauline's brother Julian was a flier in World War II and was shot down and imprisoned in Germany for at least a year and a half, a perilous existence for a Jewish soldier. Later, Pauline's young daughter was killed in a boating accident in Lake Tahoe, run over by a speedboat. Pauline's marriage failed, and there were at least two more marriages. In later years she lived in a mobile home with her dogs, but was finally hospitalized with a fatal kidney ailment. Though she lived in modest poverty in her last years, she was unfailingly cheerful, still exuberant and full of laughter, the way she had been as a kid. I really loved her.

25

ecause Darlene was mortally afraid of animals, we had never had a pet, despite my pleading. In second grade we read stories about farm animals, and as a progressive school, Parker believed city kids should experience the real thing. In a little shed and fenced-in yard behind the school building, we had three hens plus the inevitable rooster, of three breeds: White Leghorn, Rhode Island Red, and Plymouth Rock, a handsome black-and-white tweed-feathered bird. Our teachers that year, the Misses Enoch, who were sisters (one's name was Ora, I've forgotten the other's), must have had a farm background, because they taught us how to care for the chickens and harvest their eggs. Every day we'd collect the warm eggs from under the hens, not my favorite job. I was a little leery that a hen might peck me with that sharp beak (though they never did—maybe they were too dumb?), and I didn't care for the chicken smell of musty feathers and excrement. We also had a goat, whose pale eyes with their strange vertical pupils gave him a shifty, unpredictable look. He seemed emotionally unreliable, impulsive, as though he could be standing there placidly one moment, and then the next, with no warning, he might haul off and butt you or kick you.

It was a dog I longed for. Even though Darlene was especially afraid of dogs, I begged and begged to have one. I promised to take care of it, it wasn't fair for me to be deprived just because of her irrational fear. I was seven or eight at the time. After lots of thinking and study of various breeds, I said I'd love to have a Scottie puppy. Now, that's a nice small, sociable dog, suitable for a hotel apartment; it's a non-shedding dog, easy to care for—I had all the "pro" arguments lined up. It seemed as though my pleas and my watertight case in favor of a dog had finally gotten through to Mother and Daddy. They located a kennel out in the country and we went out there on a Sunday to pick out a puppy. In my keen anticipation, I'd gone to the pet store and gotten a collar and leash and a food bowl and a water bowl. I could hardly contain my excitement.

We got to the kennel and saw the litter of irresistible puppies: they were about eight to ten weeks old, weaned and ready to be adopted. After careful study of the little squirmers, I picked one out. I was delirious with delight, ready to cuddle the little darling in my arms on the way home. But then there was this conference between Mother, Daddy, and the breeder. I don't remember where Darl was. I was totally focused on my pet-to-be, and Darl had just dropped out of my mental picture frame. Next thing I know, Mother is explaining to me that we simply cannot do this. Care for the animal will surely fall to her or Darlene (unthinkable!) or whatever maid happened to be the current hire. I'd be in school all day, I'd want to play with my friends after school so I wouldn't be home to walk and care for the dog, I'd get tired of the puppy (preposterous! Get "tired" of a living creature? I didn't get tired of my sister or my friends, did I? And the puppy would be my friend), so we cannot do it, we cannot take the puppy home after all.

"But you *promised* me," I trembled.

"I know, but that was a mistake. I shouldn't have let you talk me into it, and you know, we have to consider Darl, too, since you share a room—and where would the puppy sleep?"

"But you *promised* me, you told me, look, I even have the leash and collar because you *promised* me. Maybe Darl would get used to the dog, get over being afraid of dogs. This one's so little and cute, how could she help but love it? Please! You *promised!*" I felt the helpless tears of betrayal welling up. And I was whisked into the car and we left, puppyless.

Having that promise broken—even if it had been made in a moment of weakness, even if the arguments against having a dog really outweighed the ones in favor—was a crushing, disastrous disappointment from which I felt I'd never recover.

How could I trust a woman—my mother—who was so duplicitous, who would go back on her sacred word like that? Daddy would've liked a dog, I knew he would, but he'd never cross Mother—there'd have been Hell to pay—and he seemed helpless to defend me and the promise she made to me in the face of her absolutely unshakable decision that there should be no dog. Smoldering anger, resentment, self-pity flamed through me. I knew that the puppy would have been a nuisance to *her*, that was the real reason we didn't get a dog. No one was asking *her* to walk it or feed it (Heaven forfend!) but even so, "no" was her final, implacable word.

A gulf opened between Mother and me, and she knew it. She may have misjudged how much that almost-my-puppy had meant to me. I now realized that in her list of priorities, she and her pursuits were paramount, unless my needs or wishes meshed with hers. I didn't want to have any more to do with her than I absolutely had to. She tried a few third-rate blandishments, but I was unmoved. Did she ever say she was truly sorry? I don't remember, but I was utterly disdainful of her efforts to "buy me off." No bribe would have restored my disillusioned soul, and part of the injury done to me was the realization that at the center of her caring for me was empty space, not warmth. Warmth and unconditional love came effortlessly and consistently from Daddy—Mother was a harder case, and I understood that now as I hadn't before.

And then, in early spring (the puppy debacle had occurred in the fall, I think), she comes home one day with a big box. "Jeanie, I have a surprise for you! Open the box." My heart was dead to joy or anticipation; I knew it wasn't a puppy, whatever it was, and nothing else would have stirred my dormant spirits. I knew a cat was also out of the question: *no* one would have liked a cat, except me, and I knew that Darl would have been even more hysterical about a sneaky cat than a dog.

So I opened the box, and there, gazing expectantly up at me, was—a rabbit! An Easter Bunny! White, with an albino's pink eyes. I couldn't resist the cute furry thing, who sat up on his hind haunches and looked at me and squeaked and wiggled his little pink nose (actually, I've no idea what its gender was). He was certainly the least practical animal of any Mother might have selected. It was almost surely an impulse buy, fueled by guilt.

Where could we *keep* him? What did he eat? We seemed to be a family that regarded the bathtub as the animal shelter of choice, whether for Central Park carp or Clark Street pet shop bunnies, so into the bathtub he went. It seemed to me the height of cruelty: he needed to hop around and have exercise, and the poor thing couldn't even get any traction on the slippery porcelain surface of the tub. He kept sitting up on his haunches, little pink paws crossed over his chest like a supplicant, squeaking, looking pathetic, obviously yearning to get out and be free. Not able to stand his pleadings, I lifted him tenderly out of his cold white prison.

Big mistake. Liberating that poor nameless creature was a *big* mistake. He took off like greased lightning as soon as his haunches hit the carpet, hippity hopping into some of the most damnably ingenious and inaccessible recesses you can imagine, spaces that were too small for you to get your little finger in: between the radiator and the wall; under the refrigerator or icebox or whatever it was; underneath our living room couch, which HAD no underneath, or so we thought until the bunny revealed it to us. What I learned in a hurry is that rabbits have this genius for hiding—after all, they are pretty defenseless little morsels, so their protection is this ability to flatten out, squeeze down, become one step away from invisible—unreachable. Therefore, as soon as we let him out of the bathtub, the entire family had to begin trying to recapture him. Even Darl was pressed into the hunt, in her own best interest, since the alternative would have meant having this furry thing loose in the apartment all night, maybe waiting to attack her or, worse, to be stepped on.

It took us a couple of hours to tire him out enough for him to make a tactical mistake and let his guard down so that we could sort of corral him, and I could lay hold of him. This adventure taught all of us a lesson or two, and we acquired (the hard way) new respect for the native elusiveness of this little fluff ball whose brain probably wasn't as large as a radish. We realized he'd have to live in the bathtub almost all the time; further, during his brief and infrequent periods of freedom, he'd have to be confined to Darl's and my room so that recapturing him didn't become an all-day exercise in frustration.

After a couple of days of all of us having to bathe in Mother and Daddy's tub, of Darl getting quite whiny about having the rabbit's pink attentive gaze on her while she performed her private and personal activities in our bathroom, of the hotel maids getting pretty surly about having to clean up copious (and ubiquitous) rabbit droppings from accessible and inaccessible places around the apartment, tempers were fraying dangerously. Then, one night, as this hapless creature was lolloping around in our room, I noticed, during an intermission in the recapture effort, that his little pointy chest and his chin had lost most of their fur. Horrors! You could see his naked pink skin there — the fur seemed to be falling off almost as I watched, aghast. He seemed perfectly lively, his usual evasive self, but as we stood, transfixed, watching this nightmare, his fur fairly dissolved from his chest and shoulders. It looked like some sort of galloping mange.

I became really frightened: what if he died right there and then in front of me? What if he had some terrible — and contagious — rabbity disease that I or my family might catch and from which we might all die an agonizing death? In a panic — it was dark night, after dinner — we did the only thing you know to do when you live in a hotel: we sent for a bellboy. The bellboy, with great savoir-faire, pulled on his immaculate white cotton gloves, plucked up the hapless bunny (who might have been slowed down a little by this unnamed ailment), gently popped him into a pillowcase, and headed toward our front door. I ran after him, asking him what he was going to do with the bunny.

Tomorrow, he said, he would see that the bunny went to Bunny City at the zoo — a fanciful rabbit "village," consisting of miniature pastel houses embellished with a variety of architectural flourishes. Bunnies were always hippity-hopping in and out of the doorways of their little houses; there must've been hundreds of rabbits there. He'd consult with the keeper and make sure that my bunny got medicine for whatever his ailment was. I tried to believe that it was our rough wool carpet that had worn his soft bunny fur off his chin, but secretly I knew better. He was a sick rabbit, and the zoo would either isolate him and try to diagnose his problem or, as euphemistically spoken, "put him to sleep."

Did the bellboy actually take the bunny to the zoo? How could I ever know? I'd had one betrayal and there was no reason to believe that the bellboy would honor his word. Maybe if Mother or Daddy had tipped him he'd do what he said. I didn't want to ask and find out they hadn't. I used to go to the zoo and look for my poor little bunny in Bunny City, but I never saw him there, though how, among the hundreds of bunnies bounding and scurrying everywhere, I'd ever have singled out mine, I can't imagine.

That was my first — and last — warm-blooded live pet. It may help explain why, when I became a mother and boss of my own establishment, we had cats, dogs, birds, lizards; once, briefly, a "rescue squirrel," our failed effort to raise a newborn who'd evidently fallen or been pushed from the nest . . . and a fox cub, who transported me across time.

26

At least I felt that the Lincoln Park Zoo was *my* zoo, which meant that I had thousands of pets. It was one of the incongruities about living at the Belden, with Lincoln Park spread before our door, just across the street: that the sounds of wilderness and jungle from the zoo wafted into our apartment in this elegant state-of-the-art building just about every night. Lying in my bed and waiting for sleep to settle over me, I'd hear the coyotes baying and yipping, answered, it seemed, by the deeper, throatier howl of the wolves. We often heard the lions roaring from the lion house. It was farther away, but that building had acoustics (thanks to interior walls of iridescent tile and brick) that magnified and transmitted the lion crescendos perfectly.

Those wilderness night sounds in the middle of the city were among the marvels of Lincoln Park. They sent a little *frisson* down the spine; the scalp tingled as one's hair obeyed the ancient reflex to stand on end. Another marvel was the Edenic character of the park in those days. The trees were so much more lush and robust than the spindly, struggling trees in the poor neighborhoods west of us. I wandered the whole place by myself: I could walk through the conservatory, first into the moist green gloom of the tropics; then into the fragrant airiness of rooms filled with blooming flowers, especially refreshing when you came in out of the slushy chill of a gray winter's day; and for another contrast to alert the senses, into the room of steamy sinuous paths that wound between mossy waterfalls where immense vines dangled from palms whose fronds almost touched the glass conservatory ceiling that was nearly hidden by the tangle of greenery reaching toward the light.

For me, however, the animals in all their immense variety — a veritable Noah's Ark — were the most captivating. I had a proprietary feeling about those animals — they were *my* animals; I knew them. We saw each other almost every day.

The lion house had a lingering cat kind of smell. The lion concert built to near hysteria when one of the lions began roaring, for then the others would take up the chorus one by one until, if you were in the lion house at feeding time (which I often was), the very walls would tremble and the faint of heart would head for the exits with their hands clapped over their ears. I rather liked that buildup of roaring; it was like a church organ at full volume. These big, supple, menacing-looking creatures would be pacing excitedly up and back, up and back, roaring louder and louder as the keeper approached each cage with the occupant's servings of huge bloody-looking chunks of meat. He'd poke these gory gobbets in under the bars with a long stick that had pincers he could release in a hurry. Once all the lions and leopards were served, it became very quiet as they focused intense and undivided attention on their meal.

Though I was awed by the lions, the most menacing creatures were the black leopards; there was a pair of them. They were slender, sinewy, and moved like well-oiled machines. Their pale-yellow eyes were both calculating and expressionless. They seemed like dedicated killers.

The red foxes — a prolific lot — were caged right next door to the wolves and coyotes. The foxes are like fashionable models, their brilliant reddish coats, slender legs, masked faces, brushy tails all very elegant, and they are high-strung creatures, much more restless and tetchy than the wolves. Foxes have a distinctive rank odor. The timeless power of olfactory memory smote me forty-some years later when our daughter Martha brought a fox cub home from college. Stepping into our basement, where he lived briefly, I got time-warped back to the zoo and that cage of restless, dainty-looking, strong-smelling creatures, and I was a little girl again, with mittens on strings, and chapped wrists.

The bears, which captivated most visitors to the zoo, struck me as lumbering, emotionally undependable creatures. Their apparent clumsiness, I thought, could've turned in an instant into slavering savagery. All you had to do was to look at their equipment: claws like obsidian scimitars, and when they yawned and you looked into that huge pink cavern of a mouth, ringed with square powerful teeth and incisors like daggers, you knew they weren't all roly-poly sloth.

The guanacos, llama-like creatures, had their own house and outdoor space, and a good thing, too, as they were virtuoso reproducers. Every spring there'd be a clutch of wobbly-legged little ones, nuzzling each other sociably, and dancing nimbly among their numerous relatives.

But my favorite of all the creatures was the yak. Under a heavy curtain of wavy silky brown hair, little feet peeked out, ridiculously little feet, with dainty ankles and delicate hooves. The yak looked like a giant walking permanent wave. It was his face that struck my heart with tenderness, though. He had a benign pug-nosed gentle expression; his soft, compassionate brown eyes gazed at you with liquid sympathy. He never seemed to be cross or in a hurry.

Now, the camels were another story entirely. They were on my list of detestable creatures, even if they had remarkable stamina as desert pack animals. They were mean and sneaky. They'd wait until the keeper was behind them, then they'd shoot out a knobby, powerful leg with its large round foot and try to give him a good kick. They had haughty, supercilious faces and could deliver a nasty bite with their grinder-type teeth, perfect for masticating the harsh vegetation of the desert. The cleft upper lip also enabled them to spit prodigiously; they had many ways of being mean.

Some children go through a phase when they are afraid that there are monsters under their bed. For me it was camels— horribly lifelike camels, because I had seen the real thing. I was afraid to put my feet down on the floor: I could see those ratty, motheaten-looking, molting camels under there, way back against the wall, their knobby legs folded up under them, their malevolent amber eyes glowing in the dark, waiting for my little foot to appear in their line of sight, then uncoiling the long, muscular neck, and with their cleft front lip and mean yellow teeth, taking a good chunk out of my little foot. It made me shudder. Darlene was the only one who could — and did — comfort and reassure me that there weren't any camels under my bed. She never laughed at me or ridiculed me; she honored my fear and didn't demean it or me. Maybe she needed someone to do the same for her. Scared as she was of real animals, Darl was fearless in the face of phantoms and ghosts.

Of the more pet-size animals, I'd watch the raccoons in their oval outdoor cage as they busily moved things around, a sort of commune in which everyone had to be gainfully occupied: gnawing sticks, eating carrots, pushing bunches of twigs from one place to another. Only the occasional big fat old one would be sprawled asleep on a branch of the large dead tree in the center of their cage.

Thanks to a little, wizened man I saw feeding the squirrels one day when I was roaming my park, my "pets" came to include these semi-wild fellow city dwellers. Though I'd seen lots of people feeding squirrels, this man caught my attention. He was sitting on one of the green wooden benches, surrounded by squirrels and birds; the squirrels were climbing all over him and poking into his pockets, the birds were hovering around his hands. He radiated the kind of magnetism that seemed to draw animals to him. I thought of Saint Francis.

Intrigued, I approached hesitantly, watching him with interest. "Would you like to feed the squirrels?" he asked me. He had a soft German accent. "I'll show you how to make them feel safe enough to sit on your arm or in your lap."

Thus began a remarkable friendship. It lasted for at least a couple of years. It eventually reached out to embrace my parents, though not my sister. Her life had moved into a different milieu, of which the park and its many marvels were no longer a part.

The man's name was Anton J. Steiner. He was German, and he worked in a bakery not far from the Belden Hotel. His job was to apply lettering and decorations in colored icing on cakes and pastries. He had very distinctive writing that was a mixture of classic German black-letter script and some sort of calligraphy: spidery yet sturdy and precise. I know because he made an incredible treasure for me: an herbarium. He spent much of his spare time, when he wasn't in the park communing with the little free-roaming animals, in the forest preserves collecting plants and wildflowers. He pressed his specimens and when they were suitably prepared, he fastened them onto the pages of a big loose-leaf album. Then he labeled them, in his wonderful cake-decorator's script, with both their common names and their Latin ones. Each page was then covered neatly with cellophane.

How I wish I still had that meticulously assembled volume, which he inscribed to me. Many of those little plants and flowers may have disappeared from the forest preserves by now, victims of the depredations of civilization and urban sprawl. It was even more of a treasure than the Bye-lo dolls. I loved leafing through it and studying the names. One of my favorites was a delicate lavender flower, "hepatica trillium." Though we didn't move often, there was always book attrition, and so that monumental work of patience and scholarship disappeared along with the little notebook of Harry Stern's poetry and that complete set of Havelock Ellis's *The Psychology of Sex* that Daddy tried to shelve out of reach but I secretly examined.

Tony taught me to sit very still, to move slowly so as not to startle the animals, and to be patient. "Then they will come to you and trust you," he said. And it was true, they did! It took me a few days to acquire this skill, but Tony saw that I was an eager pupil. Then one day as we were sitting there among the birds and squirrels, he said, "Would you like to learn how to pick up a snake?" I was enthralled. He'd seen a little garter snake in a nearby flower bed, and somehow he got close enough to pick it up gently and slide it from one hand to the other as though it were dough or taffy. I learned how to do that, too, and I liked the cool, dry feeling of the muscle that was the snake as it let me pass it back and forth between my hands.

Tony got to know some of my playmates who lived at the Belden, at any rate those who shared our affinity for animals. The twins Carol and Billy Kobin, relatively recent arrivals in the hotel community, took an immediate — and reciprocated — liking to Tony. So did their big, brusque German governess. She cut quite a figure beside this little elf of a man because she looked like a tank wearing shoes. Tony taught us lots of interesting facts about animals and plants. He never talked about where he came from in Germany or why he came to America. He just never talked about himself.

I asked Mother and Daddy if I could invite him to our house for dinner, and much to my surprise (and their credit), they said yes. They knew about my friend and may have wanted to get a look at him. Possibly Daddy had met him once when we were in the park, I can't remember, but Tony had said he had some sort of legal problem, and I knew Daddy would be glad to try to help him. All this seems so impossibly remote from today's world. I can't imagine how I was allowed to roam all over Lincoln Park all by myself, or how my parents tolerated my making friends with a strange man who played with animals, but that friendship influenced my interest in and attentiveness to nature, even though I viewed and experienced it in Lincoln Park, so manicured and artfully tended. It was also my earliest exposure to the art of calligraphy, though it wasn't the literary, but the bakery type.

I don't remember anything about the night he dined with us, though I know Daddy did help him with whatever legal problem he had — an immigration issue? It couldn't have been a debt difficulty, for Tony was frugal and methodical — I knew that about him. Perhaps he had some dispute with his employer. It seems that Daddy and I both felt admiration and sympathy for this mouse of a man.

27

Because it was the home I'd always known, and also because many other families with children lived there, living in the Belden didn't seem extraordinary to me. We kids were so accustomed to playing in the pretentious lobby, we didn't even notice its faux eighteenth-century vaulted ceiling, painted à la Fragonard, with plump cherubs floating among pink whipped-cream clouds; its crystal chandeliers and gilt torchères; the lavish Oriental rugs that lay on marble floors.

When the Stern clan came to the Belden, which was not very often, they tried to act matter-of-fact about its opulence. They were so Old Country: my aunts dressed in frumpily shapeless garments (no sense of style whatsoever!). They looked out of place at the fashionable Belden. On the one hand, Mother and Daddy delighted in impressing our relatives with these emblems of social and economic status, noting with a certain smugness how they gawked at the marble-clad lobby and all the liveried help scurrying about. On the other hand, my parents were still conscious of their own humble beginnings, only partly concealed by the adoption of an attitude of airy nonchalance amid all this splendor. It was, however, an adoption, not a birthright, and once the relatives swarmed over our preserve, the pretense of being "to the manor born" was rattled, if not dispelled.

In fact, I think my aunts and uncles were much more urbane than my parents gave them credit for. They probably took the Belden's faux eighteenth-century gilt and marble and all the fairy-tale pretension that went with it pretty much in stride; they were more indulgent than envious about Mother's need to be rich, upper class, glamorous. Aunt Tillie and Aunt Belle were secure in their lives of more than merely modest comfort and success, satisfied with the gratifications of family life and with participating in community affairs. The other two aunts, interestingly enough, were divorcées: Mollie, the eldest, an independent go-getter, gave her feckless husband Handelman, a longtime minor Chicago political functionary, the heave-ho. Somewhat later, she moved to Arizona, opened a dude ranch, of all improbable ventures, and made quite a success of it. She died in Tucson in 1968. Rhea (Dreebin), the "wronged" wife of the one-time philanderer (who contracted a venereal disease for his trouble), felt impelled on moral and contagion grounds to force him out of her life. These two women sought independence or righteousness rather than connubial comfort or conspicuous wealth.

Not Mother: she thrived on luxury: mink coats, high-end automobiles (we had a spinach-green Cadillac first, and then later a two-tone grey Packard, both with silver "ODS" monogram medallions on the doors); sterling silver tableware *and* butter plates (the regular, nightly setting for dinner), with fragrant home-baked tiny rolls and the little fluted butterballs that Olga rolled so deftly between the wooden paddles and then embellished with a jaunty sprig of parsley. In the spirit of our dining ritual — and because he seemed to like it — Daddy always came to the dinner table in coat and tie. This stilted elegance was seen by Mother as the mark of success in America. Much of the impetus for our near-ritual dinner service may have been inspired by Olga, in her immaculate uniform with starched organdy apron, who served (from the left) the elegant dinners she prepared and then deftly cleared the table (from the right).

Two maids came to our apartment daily: a (white) room cleaner, or "chambermaid," who dusted and used a carpet sweeper (I don't remember vacuum cleaners, except for the loud pneumatic hoses the tall Black "vacuum man" wielded in the carpeted corridors) and changed the towels and bed linens; and her Black second, the "bath maid," who scrubbed the tile floors in the bathrooms and the kitchen, cleaned the bathtubs and toilets, and emptied the drip pan under the icebox (refrigerators came later). The bath maids fascinated me. The only other dark-skinned person I'd ever seen was Al Jolson, and I knew that he painted himself black. So I asked the bath maid if she'd let me look up the sleeve of her uniform to see how far up her arm the dark color went. I got my first lesson in comparative ethnography from her as she explained to me that her skin was dark all over: up her sleeves, on her tummy, on her back, everywhere except for the soles of her feet, the palms of her hands, inside her mouth—and the rest she didn't mention. She was very matter-of-fact, telling me about her dark skin. She didn't laugh at me or get embarrassed. Instead, she said that the color didn't come off when she dried her face with a towel; it didn't come off on her collars and cuffs; she was born with dark-colored skin.

The bath maids wore starched caps that covered all their hair; the white chambermaids wore little starched tiara-like things. Mae Hogan was our chambermaid during the bleak years of the Depression. I knew that she had a lot of children and that she lived across Clark Street, walking distance from the hotel, in a modest neighborhood of rooming houses and workingmen's apartments. I used to follow Mae around the apartment, chattering at her while she worked, and we made friends. I didn't get to know any of the bath maids as intimately. There seemed to be more turnover among them, or perhaps I was discouraged from making friends with them. Most of them were polite—speaking when spoken to—but sort of remote.

When we went to the "normal" houses and apartments of our friends, we took them as they were; we didn't think about how big and pretentious—and different—our home was by comparison. We took it for granted that their houses didn't have a front desk with ranks of little mail cubicles, nor were there switchboards with operators, or doormen, nor did most of them live in houses with elevators and certainly not with white-gloved "elevator boys." Everyone's house had beds, bathrooms, kitchens, as ours did, but I never thought about how differently we lived, with the maids who came and swept and scrubbed every day, the fresh sheets on our beds and fresh towels in our bathroom every day. It seemed normal to us, and the contrast between the luxury of my childhood lifestyle, with all that hotel staff just to look after us, and the modest apartment of, say, Mary Ann Burgoon, my close friend for many of our school years, just didn't register with me on an economic scale.

Olive O'Neil, Mary Ann's mother, sang professionally and accompanied herself on the harp. I never went to any of her performances, but she, *her* mother (Mary Ann's grandmother), and Mary Ann lived in a modest third-floor walkup apartment on Lakeview Avenue. Mary Ann's grandmother looked after Mary Ann and kept the house. When I'd go there after school, Grandmother (if I ever knew her name, I don't remember it) always had freshly baked cookies and cool, sweet milk waiting for us. I really admired the life Mary Ann led in that apartment, and I wished I had a grandmother like hers—always cheery and soft-spoken, with her immaculate apron and her 100 percent American looks and voice—instead of those Yiddish-talking women I was stuck with.

"Take a *hawnyon*," Grandma Stern would start out, almost without fail, whenever you asked her for a recipe. Even for apple strudel, an onion? we'd kid her. Bubbe and Zhazh, as all their other grandchildren called my Stern grandparents, never lost their Yiddish accents. I avoided calling them by their Yiddish nicknames. Grandma was a superb cook. I think she must have learned by doing, because she'd come from a household in which there were servants. But she made knishes, a flaky strudel dough filled with potato or onion or cheese, and apple or cherry strudel for dessert. They were heavenly. Grandma also made her own gefilte fish: going to the fish market and selecting carp and whitefish and I don't know what other unlovable sea creatures, bringing them all home, simmering them with onion, garlic, carrots, and spices, and grinding the lot so that it was very fine. I wouldn't even look at her gefilte fish as a kid; I only came to appreciate it later, when the handmade stuff was rarer than a natural pearl.

I remember some big celebrations, probably Passover Seders, when everyone was there and the bustle of preparations was formidable. I remember climbing the steep carpeted stairs to Grandma and Grandpa Stern's second-floor apartment and entering a whirlwind of activity: Grandma and Aunt Mollie, her eldest and also a virtuoso cook, carefully stretching strudel dough over a floured tablecloth, the dough pale gold and almost translucent as they worked it thinner and thinner. It smelled deliciously of butter, a fragrance that melded with various delicacies—cheese and raisin, apricot, apple, even potato—that were being prepared by my other aunts as fillings for the strudel. Those feasts, with everyone pitching in and knowing what they were supposed to do and how to do it, were choreographed by Grandma, who never appeared to be the one in charge, but whose quiet, gentle purposefulness had instructed each of her daughters so well in the sacred art and work of cooking that she and the four of them functioned as one in the kitchen. With zest and competence, they created festive, delicious repasts. My cousin Arline, who lived with the grandparents when she was a child, was the heir not only to Grandma's recipes but also to her methodology and, best of all, to her remarkable disposition, which I am sure contributed to the heavenly quality of her cooking.

Grandpa was a demonstrative type—he loved to pinch our cheeks and give us sloppy kisses. Grandma, however, was less openly expressive. Radiantly placid, soft-spoken, tender and self-effacing, she looked like an angel all her life. Her disposition was taken by Mother as a personal reproach. No one could really be as saintly as Grandma appeared to be. It had to be an act. In fact, all evidence from family members confirms that she was without guile: patient, gentle, protective of her children and grandchildren, utterly devoid of malice or the desire to dominate.

My other grandma was another story. Full of life and pepper, she was assertive, even pushy, self-confident, good-humored, full of fun, bossy and outspoken. She overflowed with vitality, life, and merriment. Grandma Rose Preaskil dismissed Grandma Rose Stern as a mousy homebody. What *she* loved most of all was making money in America, being a businesswoman. Between her and Grandpa Preaskil, Grandma was indisputably the boss, the One in Charge. She "wrote" the signs that went in the shop window of their small hardware store with the jaunty self-assurance of the born entrepreneur. People would gather in front of the window puzzling over the items on display, with their crookedy hand-lettered signs: "LEKTRIK RION" is one I recall, placed in front of the electric iron on offer.

Grandma Preaskil tried going to night school to learn English reading and writing as well as speaking, but she quickly lost patience with the instructor, because he kept correcting her when *she* knew that her English was perfectly intelligible to anyone who made a little effort. Mother got exasperated with her for being so bullheaded. It all came to a head the one time Grandma took the train alone to New York to visit Evelyn. Mother could see the handwriting on the wall, as it were, when Grandma would have to order her breakfast in the dining car. In those days waiters did not take verbal orders; you wrote your choice directly onto what would become your bill. So Mother advises Grandma, "Listen, Ma, you let the waiter write out your breakfast order for you. Otherwise he won't be able to read what it is you want."

"Vot you min?" says Grandma, affronted. "I write just fine."

"No you don't, Ma, you don't spell right or anything."

"So," says Grandma, "Vot I'm gonn hev fa brekfuss—a piss tohst, a cop cawfee."

"Okay," says Mother, "I'll pick the easy word. How do you spell 'toast'?"

Grandma thinks a minute and then says, very deliberately, "Tee Ho Hess Tee."

"No, Ma, that's wrong!"

Grandma replies insouciantly, "So? I forgot de vye" [the Y].

I probably have a skewed view of Grandma Preaskil because she was so wholeheartedly crazy about Darl, and couldn't have cared less about this pampered little fatty that was me. My affinity was for Grandpa Louis, the wood carver, tinkerer, maker of things. He was more of a dreamer than an entrepreneur, and kind of a depressed guy in later years. He didn't seem very interested in the "hodverry" store and its small-time commerce. He'd go in the back of the store and take a nap.

During the Depression my Preaskil grandparents lived in a modest apartment only a few blocks from the hardware store. The store — probably rent free — occupied the ground floor of a yellow brick building at the corner of Clark and Wrightwood that Oscar had bought before the Depression, when he'd dabbled in occasional little deals. (That building is still there!) Rose's mother, Anna Silverman, had commandeered the only bedroom in their flat, right off the kitchen — probably once a maid's sleeping quarters. I remember that room: it was tiny, with just enough space for a bed, a chest of drawers, and a rocking chair. Rose and Louis slept on a sofa in the living room that opened out into a double bed — not much privacy. Anna was still housekeeper for her daughter and son-in-law, the role she had assumed when they took her into their lives after Harry Silverman's suicide in 1903. Louis and his mother-in-law were still not speaking to one another.

Great-grandmother Anna wore several unclean, malodorous old-country woolen petticoats under a greasy skirt or dress. Over these she tied an equally soiled apron. This was her garb, winter and summer. She had very few teeth, spoke Yiddish but no English, and spent her days, when she wasn't cooking or cleaning, sitting in the rocking chair in her bedroom, crooning to herself. But she'd brighten up when Darl visited her after school. Anna would get up, reach for Darl's hands, and they'd dance — hop and stamp and twirl around, Anna cackling and singing Yiddish songs. It didn't matter that they couldn't talk to each other; they'd just dance and laugh. Darl loved her, and remembered her as animated and fun-loving, lively and full of laughter — a side of the old lady I never experienced. She disgusted me. I was probably jealous because they had such good times together.

One day Great-grandma Anna, in her late eighties, decided to wash the kitchen floor. She was alone in the apartment, and for some reason she put on Handsome Louie's size 13 rubber overshoes. (He was a tall man with big feet and she was tiny and frail, under five feet.) So she slopped the water on the floor, started swinging the mop around — I imagine her crooning to herself — and she slipped on the wet floor. Down she went, and she couldn't get up: she had broken her hip!

This was evidently around noon, and Rose and Louis wouldn't get home from the hardware store until after 5:00 p.m. Even if Anna could have gotten to the phone, she couldn't have made herself understood to the operator. She lay on the floor, helpless, for several hours. When they came home and found her, she wasn't in good shape — in shock, most likely. They called Anne and Oscar at the Belden, not far away, who in turn called Dr. Phil Lewin, their friend who was an orthopedic surgeon; he ordered an ambulance to come get her, and she was rushed to Michael Reese Hospital. Phil operated on her, set the hip, and put her in a cast. Unable to tolerate the cast, she went into shock again, and they had to hurriedly cut it off. The dancing days with Darl were over; she would never be able to walk again. Anna would spend her last years bedridden.

Since she needed full-time care, Anne and Oscar rented a small, sunny apartment somewhere on the West Side — far from my grandparents and us — and moved her in with the first of a succession of good-natured but browbeaten Eastern European immigrant women, who lived with her for as long as they could put up with her shrieked vituperations. She was always sure they were robbing her, stealing her money from its hiding place under her mattress while she slept.

We were forced to visit her, which was, for me at least, a frightening ordeal. I had never seen anyone with such a wrinkled hide — her face was seamed and cratered with wrinkles; she had no teeth, so her mouth and chin were totally shriveled. She had a voice like a crow, all cracked and harsh, and because she was probably sort of deaf, she *yelled* all the time — hollered an appalling string of Yiddish curses at whatever cheerful Polish or Bohemian girl was looking after her. It was possibly for our benefit, because then my mother, more out of guilt than benevolence, would take out an extra $5 bill. Once, when I was still quite small, Mother made *me* come close and hand the money to her. It was a punishing experience for me. Great-grandma Anna lay in a bed with sliding sides, a kind of crib for grownups;

I approached and tentatively reached the money through the bars the way you'd feed a wild animal at the zoo. She scared me! She snatched the bill in her dried claw, like a monkey's paw, gave me a beady-eyed look, and, when she thought no one was looking, slipped it under the mattress.

She seemed frighteningly sharp and alert—more scary than if she'd been comatose. She always knew my name and my age, and would recite this to me in Yiddish, almost in an accusing way— *I know how old you are!*—to prove that we couldn't put anything over on her. She may have lived four or five more years; the little apartment, to my relief, was not near enough for us to go see her very often. When Anna Newman Silverman died, in 1935, her age was estimated to be ninety-three.

I wanted a granny who looked like Mary Ann Burgoon's. She was the picture-perfect American grandmother: snow-white hair with rows of gentle little waves in it, drawn back in a neat bun. She had a friendly round face, pug nose, round pink cheeks, twinkly bright blue eyes, and she wore silver-rimmed glasses. Round as a pumpkin and pillow-soft, she looked most of all like Mrs. Santa Claus. She was always cheery and soft-spoken, a welcome change from my mercurial household.

28

I loved playing at Mary Ann's after school not only because of Grandmother and her cookies, but also because of Mary Ann's mother's harp. It was a full-blown concert harp with a gorgeous classical gold column at the front and a smooth, tiger-striped glossy wood sounding board. One time – and one time only – when Mary Ann's mother was at home, she let me play her harp. I was enthralled. The vibrations from the strings and the rolling sounds you could draw out of the instrument ran through me like an electric current. I could make delicate little silvery sounds on the tiny short harp strings at one end and all sorts of glorious orchestral-sounding chord colors and trills by running my fingers along the full range of strings, until my thumbs fairly got blisters. No wonder the harp is the instrument you see in illustrations of Heaven. Mrs. O'Neil had to pry me loose from the captivation of the instrument; I couldn't tear myself away.

I don't remember what kinds of games Mary Ann and I played at her house – dolls, probably – or what we played when she came to my house after school. Her granny preferred to have her come home, so it's likely that I was there more often than she came to visit me. We lived about four blocks apart and were really close chums from about the third grade well on into high school.

Mary Ann's mother was slender and dark-haired, not gorgeous or flamboyant but attractive, though she always looked sort of careworn. How, I think to myself now, could she possibly have supported the three of them by singing and playing the *harp*? Not your standard vaudeville act or night club performance. Did she give concerts? Did she provide genteel accompaniment to diners in upscale restaurants? I saw Mary Ann's father only once, and the memory is hazy. Mary Ann looked more like him than like her mother; he had a broad open face and so did Mary Ann, and they both had ginger-colored curly hair; Mary Ann's was a mop like Little Orphan Annie's, and freckles marched across her pug nose, which was more like her father's. Her mother's face was a long, pale and delicate oval, a Modigliani kind of face. Mary Ann had greenish eyes and a sweet disposition like her granny's. She never got upset or angry, never yelled and stamped her foot the way I did. One thing I was often aware of when I was with her was how spoiled and headstrong I was compared to her; she was so gentle, soft-spoken, tractable.

She and I went all the way through the Francis Parker School, from kindergarten through twelfth grade, and we graduated from high school together in 1941. I saw her only once after that, probably ten years later. Harry and I were living at 1353 E. 50th Street. I remember that I was nursing a baby—probably Martha—when Mary Ann visited me. She'd moved to New York, had been married and divorced, and did some sort of theatrical work (following in her mother's footsteps?). She still had the red hair and the freckles. We'd been such close friends in our school years, but on that visit we were sort of at a loss for words: our lives were so totally different. Here was I, the militantly domestic stay-at-home mother of three, and Mary Ann was the single career woman. Still, it was important to both of us to see one another again, not to recapture what was past but to discover that time and distance, though they made us a little awkward with each other, had left our affection untouched and in place. Then, a few years later, I heard that she had died.

My mother was naturally musical, and, not to be outdone by the cultured, German Jewish Eisenschimls and Lustgartens, she HAD to have a piano. Fortunately, the living room of our apartment was large enough to accommodate a baby grand. It was a Kimball, I think—Mother always bad-mouthed it because it wasn't a Steinway! All the white keys were chipped. Had I taken a hammer to them when I was little? Or was the instrument damaged goods bought cheap because Daddy said we couldn't afford such an extravagance? Both Darl and I had to take lessons to justify this piano, but Mother was the one who got the greatest benefit out of the instrument. She could read music and also play by ear, with fluidity and a certain expressiveness. Two pieces in her repertoire, which she sang while accompanying herself on the piano, were "Please" ("lend your little ears to my pleas") and "Pale Hands I Love" ("Beside the Shalimar, where are you now, who lies beneath your spell?"). We suffered through frequent renditions of both of these numbers.

Though Darl was conscientious about practicing (she was such a *good* girl!), it never took. I don't remember playing the piano at all, though for a short time when I was four or five, Mother took me downtown to some sort of class with kids much more musically proficient than I was. The teacher, a lady named Rose Dumoulin, tried to encourage Mother to keep me at it, saying I was "musical," but that's what they all say. Rose may have been a friend of Mother's, and though she was eager for students, I didn't like the class or my classmates, and I probably refused to go after just a few lessons.

In contrast, I loved dance. Both of us took lessons, Darl for a shorter time than I did. Our dance teacher was Mother and Daddy's close friend Mayme Abbott, whom we called Aunt Mayme, married to "Uncle" Phil Lewin, the orthopedist who treated Great-grandma Anna's broken hip (and, twenty years later, my polio). Besides teaching dance, Mayme was in show biz of the pop type — "Entertainment," it was called: stage shows and vaudeville. She managed floor shows for the Empire Room at the Palmer House. The Merriel Abbott Dancers, who were more like chorus girls than ballerinas, toured Europe for a number of summers, performing in Paris and other entertainment capitals. All those nubile female dancers — Mayme's lesbianism, or at least bisexuality, was not self-admitted but obvious. When I was old enough to be aware of such things, I suspected that she and Mother had some sort of a relationship, but it may have been just a flirtation.

Mayme radiated the authority of a drill sergeant. She taught with a cane in hand, and it would be a slight tap or a sharp rap against the metal radiator or a chair depending on how clumsy (or lazy) the student was. She wasn't into yelling, but she could speak sharply: "Get your leg UP, lummox!" The little girls, three or four years old, were plainly terrified of her—and awed. I never felt that way about her. I was NOT scared of her; I sort of liked her—she got those snotty young girls to behave. And she could be funny and good-natured. But I adored Uncle Phil, a wonderful doctor, who loved his profession and was kind to his patients (including, eventually, me).

Mayme adored Darlene, even though Darl was a "lummox," awkward and stiff, not a natural like me. I had limberness and grace, and, though I hated the drudgery of practice, I really loved dance—especially classical ballet. It inspired both a profound respect for ballerinas and a critical eye for the proper toe stand and the performance of the five positions and the classical steps (the plié, the entrechat, and the rest). My hunch is that Mayme herself had very little formal ballet training; the class was a mishmash of tap, toe, and the whole gymnastic-dance repertory: cartwheels, handsprings, backbends, frontovers, backovers, the splits, headstands . . . and the traditional ballet positions. I studied this demanding mongrel dance with her from the age of five until I was fifteen.

Mother, meanwhile, had begun taking voice and piano lessons from a formidable Italian baritone, Concialdi (who had no first name that I can recall). He was giving Mother lessons in exchange for my father's legal services negotiating the seemingly endless stream of contract disputes he was embroiled in. A tall, imposing, handsome Italian, his longish dark wavy hair streaked with silver, he cut a distinguished figure in his gray Homburg hat, black overcoat with a broad beaver collar, and long white silk scarf. With the silk handkerchief in his breast pocket and the fine-looking walking stick he affected, "Conchy," as we fondly called him, really looked like a prosperous impresario—until you got up close and saw that his big, doe-eyed Italian face was a trifle pinched and sallow, and his shirt collar and trouser cuffs were thrift-shop threadbare. This was in the depths of the Depression, there were no jobs, and it was clear that Conchy was desperately poor — and *hungry*.

Fortunately for both us and Conchy, he combined the infinite patience required to be Mother's music teacher with flamboyant culinary skill. He began coming on Thursdays not only to give Mother her lesson, but also to create fabulous spaghetti dinners for us. Thursday was cook's night off — a much-needed break for wonderful Norwegian Olga, who on all other days of the week arrived in time to fix Daddy's breakfast and stayed through our dinner to do the cleanup — and before Conchy, Mother would have to prepare dinner on Thursday nights. Her menu alternated dismally between salami omelettes (the memory of which makes me gag even now) and (canned) salmon patties, which were almost as bad. That's where Conchy came in.

Mother paid for the groceries and Conchy bought them in the Italian section of the city. It meant a good nourishing meal for him and all of us, but, even more wonderful, it filled our apartment with exquisite aromas of tomato and garlic as he joyfully pursued his first love, cooking, all the while accompanying the clatter of pots and pans with his fine, rich baritone voice. As I walked down the long corridor to our apartment after school, my senses would be assailed simultaneously by the tantalizing fragrance of a fine garlic-laced Italian sauce in progress and by a full-throated baritone solo. Opening our front door, I'd be enveloped in the rich aroma, as though those tomatoes had just dropped from the vine, and I'd be transported by Conchy's passionate rendition of *Pagliacci*. It was like walking into Naples — our dark first-floor apartment was suddenly filled with brilliant Italian sunlight.

Mother loved not having to cook, and Conchy was a whirlwind in our little kitchen. Expansive and happy, he'd get a nice pink glow from the cooking and the anticipation of a good meal. I was always a great hanger-around in the kitchen with Olga, but Conchy was an especially exotic treat. He was the kind of person who did everything with a flourish. I'd watch him assemble his sauce, spoon waving through the air like a conductor's baton, ingredients never measured (the way of the timid, he said) but flung pell-mell into the pot, stirred energetically as the big baritone voice filled the whole apartment with arias by Verdi, Puccini, Mozart—an exposure to the magnificence of classic opera immeasurably more thrillingly alive, immediate, than Daddy's scratchy old Caruso recordings

Besides being happy to have a good meal, Conchy was a lively dinner companion. He taught us how to twirl spaghetti onto the fork by holding the tines against a spoon. He regaled us with interesting tidbits about the Italian language, about the ways of the brilliant, wonderful Italians—descendants of the noble Romans and brilliantly gifted Neapolitans—and about personal style, which, undimmed by poverty, was as natural to him as feathers on a bird. And he was full of stories—about his childhood, about his years as a performer in opera and as a vocal and acting coach, about movie stars. One of his students was Walter Pidgeon, a handsome actor who had an unfortunate stutter and a reedy, nasal speaking voice that wasn't acceptable on movie soundtracks. Conchy ironed out the stutter and transformed Pidgeon's speaking voice into a mellifluous low tenor/upper baritone, he told us. I saw Walter Pidgeon in the movies, and it was true, he had a crooner's voice and clear, crisp, stutter-free diction. I felt a proprietary sense of pride in that makeover, since I knew the Pygmalion to Pidgeon's Galatea.

It cheered us all to have Conchy around; we basked in his extroverted and expressive Italian ways. The house definitely seemed brighter with him in it.

29

Mother may have wanted Darl and me to go to the Francis Parker School mainly for reasons of status, but, incidentally or not, she and Daddy gave us the gift of an unforgettable education. Francis Parker and John Dewey were the founders of the progressive education movement that waxed and waned with progressive politics for much of the twentieth century; in fact, Dewey, who founded the University of Chicago Laboratory School, considered Parker the "father of progressive education." Both gravitated to Chicago (Parker in 1883, Dewey in 1894, the year of my mother's birth) and made it the seedbed of the progressive movement. Dewey was deeply influenced by Hull House (as was my mother, in her own way), and when he settled in Chicago he enrolled his children in Parker's school, then called the "Practice School." As is evident from their schools' names, both intended them as laboratories for working out new, nonauthoritarian ideas that "rejected rote learning and enlisted the natural curiosity of children in the schooling process."

Our second-grade teachers, the Misses Enoch who introduced us to chickens, were very pleasant and businesslike, but they also showed a streak of childlike imagination. They had a large sand table in our classroom which they populated with biblical characters, desert scenes of kings and nomads, palm trees, camels, and at the appropriate season, the Holy Family. There were little mirrors to signify oases, there were shepherds and their flocks, there were Arabs in flowing robes; the whole scene was a mishmash of sacred and secular, ancient and contemporary, and we told stories as we moved these figures around. It was a vivid way to bring to life an exotic place and time, and it helped me overcome a terrifying movie experience I had suffered.

My parents often took me along to the movies, because they wanted to go and had no one to leave me with. I didn't like movies, or at any rate the cinematic preferences of Mother and Daddy. I had — and still have — a pathological fear of loud, sudden noises: bursting balloons, gunshots, even thunder, and the movies of those days seemed to specialize in very noisy soundtracks, as this was in the early days of talkies and the novelty of sound was still being explored and exploited. I was hustled out of some of Chicago's most elegant movie palaces, screaming hysterically at the commotion of cannons, explosions and other overwrought booming. I would always ask, "Will there be shooting?" when we headed off to the movies, and I was always soothingly assured that there wouldn't be, and there always was — a lot. Talk about betrayal!

One particularly terrible film starred Janet Gaynor and Charles Farrell, the smoochy love duo of that particular season. The movie featured these two in some sort of Arab encampment. It reminded me of my fascination with a wrought iron "lamp" in the form of an Arab tent (one of Mother's antique finds) that stood on the commode at our front door. An odalisque clad in semi-transparent veils reclined on striped cushions inside its shadowy interior, and a lascivious-looking sheik stalked toward her with a knife gleaming in his upraised hand. (What a welcome to those who entered the portal of *our* tent, I think now!) A tiny bulb that hung from the ceiling of the fringe-trimmed tent gave this dramatic setting in painted iron a mysterious smoky look when it was lit. I used to stand and study the suspenseful scene and touch the wicked point of the knife and try to imagine what came next.

In the movie, the lovers in the desert sat on a log, and the poisonous snake that lived in the log came out and bit Janet Gaynor, who had to be rushed back to civilization to save her life. Charlie Farrell carried her to their tent to get the car keys or something, and they started off across the trackless sand dunes. Of course they were promptly attacked by shrieking

Bedouins, guns blazing and scimitars flashing. Then everyone was engulfed in a howling sandstorm, but through the raging wind I could still hear the guns, louder than ever. I don't know whether Janet Gaynor survived or not, as the gun battle was the signal for us to leave.

At least my familiarity with the miniature desert in our second-grade classroom made a more benign aspect of desert life available to my imagination. On our sand table, just like those rolling dunes but much smaller, I furtively made a small happy ending to the movie whose conclusion I never saw: Janet and Charlie were back in their desert paradise, sitting on the log (the snake had been dispatched), holding hands and looking into the sunset. All the Arabs were now peace-loving.

French lessons at Parker began in second or third grade with Miss Barnes. She taught us folk songs and we played Lotto in French, a foundation for the serious study of the language and culture that would come later. In third grade we studied Old Chicago with Mrs. Carley, and Fort Dearborn and the Chicago Fire of 1871 both came alive for us. The high point for us third graders was May Day, when a high school senior was elected May Queen by vote of the whole school. We were the class that performed the Maypole Dance in her honor. As a group of eight-year-olds we were well-coordinated enough to master the dance that braided lovely multi-colored ribbons around the Maypole.

Miss Davis became a legend in her own time, revered by generations of fourth graders whom she immersed in the study of everything about ancient Greece short of learning the language, or so it seemed. We were on a first-name basis with a large swath of the Greek Pantheon, familiar with the Roman as well as the Greek names of the gods and goddesses; we made— and wore—the short garment of the common people, the chiton; we made flutes and played "Greek" music; we created dramatizations of many of the Greek myths; we studied the Trojan War, read Greek poetry, learned about the great Greek dramatists and philosophers and scientists.

Any day when I came home from school, walking down the hall to our apartment I might hear a lovely sweet cascade of music. Conchy's Thursdays were only a small part of it. My father did legal work (I suspect at modest fees) for several internationally known musicians, work he loved because it put him in closer touch with the world of artists and the arts — and because he had a lasting and innate sympathy for immigrants, famous or not. He was the Chicago legal counsel for such luminaries as Nathan Milstein, Vladimir Horowitz, and Mischa Mischakoff, who would go on to become concertmaster of the NBC Symphony under the baton of Arturo Toscanini, but who at that time was a timid young immigrant violinist in his early twenties, newly employed by the Chicago Symphony. Mischa sometimes had dinner at our house, which was a treat, because he always came early, around four, and would stand at our living room window, gazing out at Lincoln Park and playing his violin as though he were serenading the view.

These musicians came to Daddy through the recommendation of his childhood friend Gitta Cottle (neé Gertrude Weinstock), known professionally as Gitta Gradova. (At her impish invitation we called her Gittel Cottle, and even Gadiddle Gadoddle.) She herself was a brilliant concert pianist who retired at the height of a stunning career, ostensibly to give full attention to her two children, though in fact she battled stage fright and depression during much of her life. Gitta had been a child prodigy. My parents, who were close to the Cottles, told me a little about her early life.

Gitta's parents were itinerant actors in the Yiddish theater. Her early childhood was spent literally living in a trunk backstage while her mother and father eked out a precarious living on the stage. As soon as it became clear — maybe at age three or four — that this kid was a musical prodigy, she was sent to study piano with a well-known teacher. Her parents and relatives, realizing the economic potential of her talent, dedicated themselves to arranging bookings for their little gold mine. She may have been as young as five or six when she began playing professionally, and from then on, the whole bunch may have enjoyed the leisure of living off the proceeds of Gitta's genius. Many of them were still fixtures in the Cottle household during my childhood, when Gitta and Morry lived in a large house on Hawthorn Place. When we had dinner there, we were always engulfed in this crowd of family at the long dining room table. There was usually a sprinkling of other guests, including non-family indigents of one sort and another. This was the Depression, after all, and the Cottles were generous, gregarious, and relatively prosperous. So every night it was like a banquet from Babel: the Yiddish-speaking relatives, a few lonely (and hungry) theatrical strays, mixed in with the occasional Social Register types, music lovers and patrons of the Symphony who'd be thrown into this cacophonous cauldron to sink or swim, as multilingual chatter rolled in waves among the diners.

Gitta, a master mimic and storyteller, regaled us with tales of her life as a prodigy. In her husky voice she'd deliver a stream of Yiddish *bon mots* to embellish her narratives. Once, she recalled, she was in New York for a concert (possibly in Carnegie Hall) and decided that she had to have a new gown for this occasion. Her mother, who spoke little if any English but pretty much managed Gitta in her early years as a performer, also oversaw her wardrobe, and guarded her health with superstitious ferocity. She should be well, the family meal ticket, so she could perform in the concerts. Ma knew that Gitta had to dress elegantly, maybe even a trifle flamboyantly. But God forbid she should catch a chill.

Gitta, in her expressive, husky voice, recalled that she and her mother decided to look for an appropriate gown for her concert appearance in the exclusive salon of Jean Patou. Ma selected a spectacular, diaphanous number, suitable for a soloist to wear, though perhaps a trifle fussy for the lanky, raw-boned girl. She insisted, further, that Gitta wear long underwear (Yiddish: *gottkes*) beneath it to protect her from drafts, so prevalent onstage. However, Gitta described how, determined to do justice to her stunning gown, she rolled up the sleeves and legs of these bulky gray woolen *gottkes*, pinning them up to conceal the ugly, old-fashioned drop-seat drawers. Dressed for the performance, she was walking to the concert hall with Ma when, horror of horrors, the pins came loose and the *gottkes* rolled magisterially down to her ankles, like a lowering stage curtain. What a spectacle for passersby as she struggled feverishly to hoist them back up underneath the gown, with her ma hopping around yelling Yiddish imprecations and trying to keep the dress modestly below the girl's knees as the kid struggled with pins and the intractable gray woolen bulk. I cherish the memory of Gitta at her dinner table, regaling us with such specimens of family lore.

Gitta had a cook, an overworked woman whose flexibility was sorely tested by the unpredictable number of diners on any given night. There was the baseline crowd of relatives, but then there were such non-family "regulars" as Mischa Mischakoff. Except in the language of music, Mischa was naïve, shy, and inarticulate. Usually this lonely young innocent was at Gitta and Morry's for dinner, along with the Yiddish-speaking madcap relatives.

Gitta's cook could prepare and serve simple food, but her dessert repertoire was limited to one dish: chocolate roll. So every night that Mischa dined at Cottles' — and that was almost every night — chocolate roll was trundled out for dessert. The regulars like Mischa dealt with the monotony philosophically. After all, though it suffered from overexposure, the chocolate roll was truly delicious. One evening, when an especially eminent Social Register couple was coming to join the usual raffish diners, Gitta warned Mischa beforehand, "Now, listen, Mischa, we're having some company for dinner tonight. We're going to have chocolate roll again. So I want you to keep quiet when the dessert comes. Don't say anything, understand? Just keep quiet and eat it."

Mischa looked at her reproachfully. "Gitta, why I would say anything? Of course not I wouldn't. What you think?"

The guests arrived, and amid the characteristically animated conversation dinner was served and consumed with relish. The table was duly cleared for dessert, and in came cook, proudly bearing the platter resplendent with chocolate roll. Into the appreciative silence that greeted its appearance, Mischa blurted out, "Oh—chocolate roll!" As Gitta's basilisk eye shot him a lethal glare from the far end of the table, he added hastily, "But tonight it's good!"

Mischakoff was another of the musicians Gitta funneled to Daddy for legal help with contracts or with the endless rancorous battles with impresarios. When he came to our house for dinner, which gave Gitta's harried cook an occasional breather, he'd usually come early and play his violin. Getting home from school, I'd slip in and sit in an adjoining room and listen to the entrancing sounds. He wouldn't even be aware of my arrival. Once, when I came home at about four and walked into our living room, there stood Mischa, looking out the window that faced Lincoln Park, playing his violin with tremendous feeling and with tears running down his face.

"What's wrong, Mischa?" I asked him.

"Oh, Jeanie," he sobbed, "I have more trouble. I don't know what to do. I hope your father, dear Oskar, will fix for me so I don't go to jail and lose my work."

It seems that Mischa, who was still learning how to drive, had bought a car. Pulling into a parking space in front of the Belden (he was having dinner with us that night), he nicked the fender of the car in front of him. That car's owner, who saw the accident, flew into a rage at Mischa, yelling and threatening. Mischa was terrified. By the time I saw him, his fiddle playing had worked its soothing magic, and though he was still weeping, he was already anticipating the enveloping comfort that my father—and a good dinner without chocolate roll—would offer.

It was a special experience to be around these musicians when they were offstage. Horowitz, Volodya to us, was a clown, like Gitta, and they were devoted to each other both musically—they both had a powerful way of playing—and emotionally, both of them tormented by depression and related ills of the soul. He came to our house only a few times when he was just becoming known in the U.S., once with Gregor

Piatigorsky (Grisha). Though Piatigorsky was at our house only that one time, he was a Presence: tall, dark, slender, beautiful; waves of intensity seemed to vibrate around him. There's a story (which may be apocryphal) that Grisha, Jascha (Heifetz?), Sasha (Schneider, later the founder of the Fine Arts Quartet), Mischa (Ellmann?), and Nathan Milstein were an ensemble of child musicians who played on the streets (of Moscow? Kiev?), until they managed to escape from Russia and seek refuge in Europe between the two world wars.

30

Daddy's work as legal counsel for that bunch of mercurial and litigious artists probably gave his otherwise pedestrian profession a welcome dose of color and spontaneity, to say the least. Somewhere inside my sedate, self-effacing father lurked more than a trace of the romantic. That part of him flourished on contact with artists in all their economic, legal, and emotional turmoil, and revealed his own aesthetic sensibility.

Once, on a business trip to Europe, he took our 16mm home movie camera with him, and he simply stood on a street and shot scenes of (a now-vanished) Paris. The footage he shot was like a documentary: there were marvelous sequences where the camera simply watched, motionless, as the insane auto traffic raced around the Place de la Concorde. That film, since lost, revealed his poignant response to the city in all its dignity, grace, and turmoil, and revealed his gift for capturing the essence and mood of place and time. He had more of an artist's eye than any of us gave him credit for.

He was considerably less successful at making home movies without panning the camera at a dizzying speed in an effort to encompass the entire scene, featuring his darling daughters at play. There were reels and reels of Darl and me, of Darl when she attended the Lincoln Public School, before Parker and maybe before or just after I was born. She was filmed dancing in some sort of gauzy costume, taking her role as a Spring Sprite terribly seriously but looking shy, awkward, all knobby elbows, knees, and deeply tangled feet, earnestly working through her dance as though the future depended on her uncoordinated leaps and arabesques. There were movies of us in Lincoln Park, romping about and waving coyly at the camera, while in an occasional shot Mother, smoking the ever-present Lucky Strike, sat on a park bench looking bored; her hair, which she was still dyeing an unforgiving opaque black, made her look even harsher.

All these marvelous reels of film were lost, but I had seen them often enough to remember some of the shots vividly. We used to love seeing those family movies, all of us laughing at our awkwardness and our antics before the camera. We even enjoyed the nature shots and cityscapes that Daddy inevitably included. He must have had a sense that he was making a record, not just of us but of the world and times we inhabited: the cars, the buildings, the clothes people wore—all the men wore gray fedoras—and the feel of places.

Daddy loved to travel, revisiting the sense of freedom he'd discovered as a child on the deck of the ship to America. Any conveyance that could carry him away from daily life brought him both relaxation and a sense of adventure: auto trips to New York, sailings to Paris, train trips to California, transformed him from anxious lawyer to carefree adventurer. And fortunately his profession afforded him opportunities. He'd taken a business trip to Paris with Mr. Goldberg of the shoe company O'Connor & Goldberg in 1927—a trip that was greeted with icy disapproval by Mother. I was only three and a half, but I remember her expressing suspicions that this trip was more monkey business than business. What could the Goldbergs need *him* for? There was talk of all the loose women and racy uninhibited shows in Paris: the Folies Bergère was the one Mother harped on. In fact, Daddy *did* go there and was enchanted by all the exposed female flesh and body parts in the floor show. His diary entry for that adventure was somewhat cryptic, but he made the innocent mistake of describing it to Mother. He never heard the end of it! She would bring it up in her best accusatory manner whenever he got on the subject of the Goldbergs or Paris. But that was when he had made his little movie tribute to the city.

In the early 1930s, he booked passage on one of the earliest transcontinental airplane flights from Chicago to Los Angeles, on United Airlines. The flight made several refueling stops and took twelve hours or more, he told me. The plane had berths similar to those on Pullman trains, and all the flight attendants (called stewardesses) were registered nurses. What impressed him most of all and led to many rhapsodic descriptions at the family dinner table were the clouds that often surrounded or were beneath the plane. He enjoyed flying and was endlessly awed by the majesty and variety of cloud shapes and the play of light among them as the plane arrowed through them heading west.

Toward the end of the school year in 1932, Darl's classmate Ruth Lustgarten, who also lived at the Belden with her musical parents and brothers, invited Darl to join the family on their annual summer vacation in Garmisch-Partenkirchen, in the Bavarian Alps. Garmisch, an international ski resort in winter, in summer was a somnolent, charming refuge for the neighboring Austrians and Swiss, and the Lustgartens had continued to summer there after emigrating to Chicago, where Dr. Lustgarten, a chemist, had been invited to work.

At fifteen, Darlene was tall, awkward, with straight black hair that she wore in a sort of Dutch Boy bob. I saw the lovely, leggy colt, the gazelle, in her, and was jealous of her artistic intellect; but I was the beauty, the radiant butterfly, while she was the plain, gawky moth. She was hunched over, and Daddy, who adored her, kept after her mercilessly, it seemed to me, to "Stand up straight!" "The Hunchback of Notre Dame," he'd taunt her, much to her chagrin.

The only person who could really undermine Darl's composure, though, was Mother. She'd get on a sort of personal inquisition jag: "Why do you let X push you around? You should speak up, not be a doormat. And also, that's not a flattering outfit you're wearing. Why did you pick THAT color with your sallow complexion? And the style makes you look more flat-chested than you are. You should be more assertive, don't let people take advantage of you. You're too trusting . . ." and so on. It sounded like her manipulation of Daddy, but Darl was more vulnerable and suggestible than he was.

Sooner or later — and this always seemed to take place at

the dinner table (which was a kind of theater for Mother) —
Darl would push her chair back from the table, rush into
our (shared) bedroom, slam the door, go into our bathroom,
and slam AND lock that door. I was the one assigned to talk
her down and at least lure her out of the bathroom and into
our room, if I couldn't get her to return to the dinner table. I
remember climbing out our bedroom window onto that sooty
courtyard between the two wings of the hotel and tapping on
the frosted glass of the bathroom window, trying to get her to
relent a little. We had always loved and trusted one another —
there was never any guile or manipulation between us. (Well,
hardly ever.) So she'd often give in to my pleadings: they were
just for her, with no ulterior motives — always something to be
wary of with Mother. Looking back, I can see how Mother, our
anti-Pygmalion, had sought to keep Darl a shy, undeveloped
girl and me an eternal toddler. If we grew up, she would be
old; we'd supersede her.

Mother and Daddy discussed the political conditions in
Germany and Austria; was it safe for Americans — *Jewish*
Americans — to be in Bavaria this summer, they asked Dr.
Lustgarten, given Hitler's ominous rise? Dr. Lustgarten assured
them that Garmisch was still peaceful and secure. He would
not subject his family, and certainly not a youngster who was
a guest under his care, to a situation that he saw as perilous, or
even uncertain. He had connections that gave some authority to
his assertions, so Mother and Daddy said yes! Darl was thrilled.
She sailed gaily off on the SS *Bremen*, Third Class — that's how
Europeans traveled, not like Mother (who would never have
considered anything but First) — to several weeks of adventure
with her dearest friend.

She departed a moth and returned a resplendent butterfly.

To my dazzled eyes her transformation was so dramatic, it
seemed as though she'd been tapped by a magic wand. Darlene
had emerged from her cocoon a stunning, charming, confident,
outgoing young woman. Her whole demeanor had changed,
and with it her sense of style. No more droopy shapeless
unimaginative dresses: she was now clothed in simple but elegant

frocks or a smartly tailored skirt and jacket, all purchased with the tasteful oversight of Mrs. Lustgarten. This "fairy godmother" had seen to it that she got a flattering new hairstyle in place of that drab Dutch bob. And as a crowning glory, there were gowns and shoes suitable for the Garmisch afternoon tea dances, where Darl found herself much sought after by young German and Austrian aristocrats—all educated, charming, perfect in their courtly Old World manners, and eager to practice and improve their English. In exchange, they would teach her the subtle differences between mellifluous Bavarian and the classic German of poets and authors such as Goethe. Mr. Lustgarten had been right: Garmisch, for now, at least appeared to be what it had always been: a peaceful, hospitable, cultured haven, and an oasis of friendly locals.

"*Grüss Gott*," you said to each apple-cheeked shopkeeper as you inhaled the fragrance of fresh-baked coffeecake that perfumed the air. Darlene and Ruth explored Garmisch tirelessly; all the Lustgartens spoke German, and Darl was quickly picking it up. One day she decided to buy a pair of socks. My sister remembered that the proprietor of the shop bowed in welcome as she entered: "*Fräulein*," he said.

Darl realized she didn't know the word for socks. "*Bitte, ich wille Handschün für die Füsse*," she said, haltingly. "Please, gloves for the feet."

The proprietor bowed politely, went to his stockroom, and returned with a selection. While Darlene was mulling over her choice, he signaled neighboring merchants to come over. He asked her politely please to say again what she was looking for. It was a shared moment in which she learned the word for socks (*Strümpfe*) and felt the warm amusement of the witnesses to this gentle comedy.

When Darlene, thanks to Mrs. Lustgarten's tact, taste, and insight, returned from Europe an international glamour girl, I was awed—my sister had suddenly become a grownup, and a very stylish one. Mother, clearly impressed by this metamorphosis, treated her with new respect. All unknowingly, Mrs. Lustgarten had altered the family dynamic by seeing Darl as she really was. To Mother's credit, she changed course, transforming Darl into her boffo shopping pal. I remained an unwilling case of "arrested development" until I rebelled — at everything.

What astonishes me now is how unaware we were of the world-changing Nazi nightmare that was thundering toward us. Even the Lustgartens seemed to be complacently ignorant of the horror that was soon to engulf much of the world. The grim irony was that they had chosen to take their holiday in the cradle of anti-Semitism. Perhaps Fate protects the innocent — or the foolish — but their summer vacation was without incident.

It was, however, their last trip to Garmisch. The following year, Hitler was appointed Chancellor of Germany.

Nineteen thirty-three was also the worst year of the Great Depression, and it forced changes on us. We had been shielded by Daddy, who labored to pay down his debt to Noble Judah while supporting us in the Belden Stratford in the style to which Mother insisted on being accustomed. I was to continue my education at Francis Parker; Darlene would go to the college of her choice when she graduated the next year. In the midst of all this, Daddy proposed to take us *all* to Europe for the summer.

Something had to give, and the "something" was elegant Apartment 122, with its views of the park and the Shakespeare statue, where we had lived for as far back as I could remember. We'd have to move to someplace less expensive, surely less charming and comfortable. Daddy wouldn't have continued to pay that exorbitant rent through a summer's absence, so perhaps the trip was an excuse for the economizing that was anyway necessary — or a consolation for it. It would undoubtedly be a spirit lifter for Daddy.

Where would we go? Mother's idea of "economizing" wasn't looking for a less pricey neighborhood, or a no-frills flat. It was simply searching and haggling to find a bargain . . . *in the Belden.* Moving out of that Nirvana was unthinkable. And, miraculously, she found one, on the eleventh floor.

Apartment 1102 was within our budget, but it was a fright: a cheerless string of poorly designed spaces strung out along the west side of the hotel, as inhospitable as it was economical.

233

Instead of lush green Lincoln Park and the Shakespeare statue, it looked out on a dreary urban landscape: rundown two-flats, small factories, broken sidewalks, weedy empty lots glittering with shards of smashed whisky and beer bottles. And it had a serious drawback: it was possibly the only "apartment" in that hotel, or any hotel, that had *no real bedrooms*. That seems incredible in retrospect, but that's what it was. Daddy and Mother slept on a convertible roll-out double bed in a space adjoining the living room that by day was a sort of library/study, with three book-lined walls and a fourth one with the niche that held the sofa bed. The bed had to be pulled out and made up by the hotel Night Maid every night, and every morning the Day Maid stripped off the sheets and blankets, restored it to a sofa, and pushed it back into its niche.

The "living room" itself was really two rooms joined end to end into one long, narrow, featureless corridor, like an empty railroad car or a carpeted bowling alley. Perhaps Mother had fantasies of throwing large parties in there, but I don't remember her ever having one; the room was not at all conducive to cozy conversational groups. In an effort to compensate, she impulsively bought two very expensive antique French couches—an extravagance that must have consumed any savings the cheap rental had gained. They were eighteenth-century *récamiers*, a type of *chaise longue*: dark, fluted wood in a graceful curve, upholstered in the original beautiful grosgrain silk, a pale green, lavender, and cream or eggshell stripe. I loved them, but they were totally useless: no one wanted to sit there, and once one of us plopped down too hard on one and a leg broke. It was hard to get it repaired because they were antiques. The living room was never much lived in by us.

Darl and I shared the most awkward of all these makeshift spaces, however. What passed for our "bedroom" was a narrow oblong, like another, short corridor, just wide enough to accommodate two day beds—no headboard or footboard, just a box spring and mattress—against opposite walls. The beds took up almost all the space. The narrow passage between them would allow one slender person—not two!—to walk from the west end of the room, where there was a fire-escape window and a small desk, to the other end, where a dresser stood guard over the head of my bed and a closet over Darlene's. The second dresser, Darl's, had to be stuffed into the closet, sharply limiting precious hanging space—there was no other place for it. This caused a certain amount of tension because most of our clothes were crowded into that one closet. At least we had our own bathroom, the least problematic of any of the so-called rooms. My dresser, crammed into the tight space between the head of my bed and the bathroom, was small enough to allow the bathroom door to open. I had to be careful when I sat up in bed not to crack my head on it, but it gave me the luxury of its one side as a backrest so I could read in bed.

Glass-paned French doors, heavily painted over to give the illusion of privacy, separated our "room" from the dining room. They were adequately opaque, but not solid or soundproof, so if Mother and Daddy had loud, cheery guests, we heard every dirty joke, like it or not. The tiny dining room was the only recognizable room, pleasant and conventional, with a table, chairs, and spaces for dishes, linens, and silver. Mother, who loved to play *grande dame*, had the electrician come up and install a hidden buzzer under the carpeting at her end of the table, so that she could step on it and it would buzz in the kitchen—about five steps away— to summon Olga, when we were ready for the dinner plates to be taken out and the dessert plates brought in. That buzzer was much enjoyed by our raucous young friends, who would buzz it over and over with great hilarity. To them it was a novelty, but Darl and I thought it was a ridiculous affectation.

I was nine and my big sister was sixteen when we were wedged into the close quarters of Apartment 1102. "Discomfort" was the operative description. What were our parents thinking? I wonder now whether on some subliminal level Mother was trying to give us a taste of "slum" life as she had known it— crowded, no privacy, no chance for solitude, little comfort— incongruous as it was in the Belden Hotel. It was an insult to which we had never before been subjected, but it was the story of her whole childhood. The lack of privacy, a very strong characteristic of the slum, would have been especially damaging to the emotional stability of a young person. Respect for one's own space may only become significant in retrospect, but to be a Person with Boundaries set *by* yourself *for* yourself is essential to emotional well-being, I think. Mother could never quite shake off the traumas of the ghetto, and that was probably one of the roots (another being, perhaps, genetic) of her recurrent depression.

Fortunately, Darl and I had the kind of love for each other that had none of that intrusive "corrective" that was so much a part of Mother's affection for us — or at least for me. And Darl was a lifesaver in interpreting for me our mother's baffling moods and incomprehensible behavior.

Mother and Daddy's was not a tranquil marriage; it was punctuated by frequent spats of varying intensity. There was an occasion after we had moved to the eleventh floor when Mother and Daddy had an angry shouting match, one that introduced a new feature in their marital warfare: Mother strode out of our apartment, slamming the door behind her. Daddy was both angry and distraught. I was terrified and felt helpless (on Daddy's behalf) and abandoned, rejected by my mother. Daddy was grim, and to all my anxious questions — Where was she going? Why did she leave? Would she come back? — he could only give me what he must have felt was an honest answer: "I don't know."

Darlene, however, was totally serene. "She'll be back," Darl assured me.

"How do you know?" I blubbered.

"She's left her fur coat here. She'll be back."

That shrewd observation was very comforting, and it made complete sense to me. That was the sort of reason that would motivate Mother to come back. Sure enough, as Darl had predicted, Mother returned, and the incident shrank to just that, an incident, and passed silently into history, except that I never forgot it. Darl never forgot it, either. She confessed to me many years later that she was petrified, too, but she had to keep up the fiction of confident reassurance for me, and possibly for Daddy.

31

As we prepared for our trip to Paris for the summer, I was nine going on ten, but much to my resentment and embarrassment, my parents lied and said I was eight and a half because then I could travel at half fare. The money-saving aspect meant nothing to me compared to my shame that they'd lie, taking from me a hard-won year. I was ashamed that Daddy, this lawyer of spotless reputation, would become party to such an unethical, low-life deception. I was sure that Mother was the instigator of this misrepresentation; she may not have been the penny-pincher in our family, but she was the daughter of the initiator of *fagelach*, not averse to getting the upper hand over the French Line, part of the Compagnie Générale Transatlantique — a Goliath so big it would never notice a little harmless cheating.

We sailed to Le Havre on the *Lafayette*, one of the more modest ships in the French fleet. (However, we experienced the luxury of the French Line's crown jewel on our return trip, on the *Île de France*.) The crossing from New York started inauspiciously for me. As soon as I went below to our cabin, I was overcome with nausea. The enclosed space, the sickly-sweet odor of some sort of heavily perfumed cleaning/disinfectant fluid . . . I promptly threw up. We hadn't even left the dock and already I was seasick! Not a good start. But once I got past that first nausea, Darl and I roamed the ship and were exhilarated by the air and the sea, whose featureless vastness both bored and awed us. It was that endless ocean unspooling in our foamy wake that was a constant reminder of how far we were from either shore. To make the ocean crossing more interesting for Darl, there was some discreet flirtation. She was appreciated by the French crew, a jaunty lot in their round white hats with red pom-poms.

A French lady, a sort of recreational director for the many children on board, led us all around the ship, arranged games for us to play, and put on the classic French puppet theater, the Grand Guignol, replete with the French counterparts of Punch and Judy, only much more entrancing and naughty. The characters yelled in shrill French patois, not all of which we Americans could understand, but the French speakers among us gave us spontaneous translations. They did a lot of shrieking and battering of one another with brooms, shovels, alligators, whatever came to hand. The Guignol was definitely the high point for all the polyglot gang, whose ages ranged from toddlers to twenty-year-olds, all wildly enthusiastic about the hilarious puppets.

Daddy was transformed by being at sea. At home he suffered from digestive problems: heartburn, incipient ulcers, that whole array of stress-induced gastric complaints. They all vanished when the lines attaching our ship to the docks were cast off. Out of reach of the anxieties and demands of his work life, he positively blossomed. He loved the ocean and did a lot of walking round the decks. Mother, on the other hand, felt her last tie to terra firma gone. She had never learned to swim, she was afraid of the water, and her way of keeping her anxiety under control was never to venture out of the cramped cabin she and Daddy shared. She wouldn't even look out the porthole, panicked by the sight of endless water.

For the entire voyage, four or five days, she lay in their stateroom, pale and sickly-looking, pretty much unable to eat. Whether it was naïve enthusiasm or a touch of triumphant superiority that motivated him, Daddy would descend to their cabin after breakfast and regale Mother with descriptions of the mounds of delicacies on offer in the dining saloon. I was there once when he bounded in and described, in self-amazement, relishing sardines and raw onions for breakfast, at which poor Mother turned her face to the wall and moaned piteously. He appeared unaware of the effect the mention of any food had on her.

On this crossing to Europe, which finally got boring and

confining in spite of all the activities for the young—all that empty, endless ocean—we managed some suspense toward the end of the trip. The last day out, we became fogbound. I remember the sensation of everything being muffled. The subliminal hum of the engines dropped to a lower pitch as we crept along to the regular rhythm of the foghorn. Its intermittent moan, about every thirty seconds, reminded us that we were groping our way blindly through this mysterious nowhere. There was no horizon, the sole unchanging directions being up and down: only gravity didn't desert us. We passengers stayed off the decks. They were desolate and wet, and looking out the portholes you got the sense of how pervasive this fog was.

The day before we were to make landfall, the sound of the foghorn suddenly became more urgent, its intervals shorter. Then we heard an answering foghorn—how quickly the ear distinguishes even small contrasts in pitch—which sounded alarmingly near. Looking out a porthole I remember seeing a large blackish-brown wall—another ship! It looked close enough to touch, and we were all aghast, just gaping and frozen in our tracks. The engine noises changed—the captain must have put the engines into reverse. We avoided a collision, but there was a lot of buzz about the episode that night at dinner.

Poor Mother, who'd suffered through those days of seasickness and fear, now had our entire six-week holiday abroad in which to anticipate with dread our return transatlantic passage. She crept out of her isolation at Le Havre, pale, with dark circles under her eyes. Though the ocean crossing had been an ordeal, her spirits revived once we were on terra firma and on board the boat train to Paris.

We were booked into a cheap, unfashionable little hotel that Aunt Mayme Abbott had recommended, well located in the heart of Paris. Named the Hôtel Lincoln, it was at 24 Rue Bayard, just off the Rond-Point, the very end of the Champs-Élysées. Mother would probably have preferred to stay at the George V, the premier hotel in Paris, where Daddy had stayed with his clients the Goldbergs a few years before; or the Crillon, another elegant place. But this was the Depression and those places were out of our economic reach. In fact, by staying at the Lincoln, we really came to feel like part of the real life of the city, not tourists.

We spent six relaxed weeks in Paris, going to a lot of museums and making side trips to Fontainebleau, which impressed me with the French sense of landscape design; Malmaison, where I hung, fascinated, over a glass case displaying a bloodstained handkerchief of Napoleon's, and tried to imagine him and Josephine strolling (hand in hand?) around its grounds and rooms; and Versailles, where the hall of mirrors was Darlene's favorite. She wrote a poem, "Ghosts of Louis and Marie Antoinette walk through the hallways of Versailles."

Darl and Mother entertained themselves shopping, and the four of us enjoyed relaxed afternoons strolling the Champs-Élysées, or sitting at the little tables of sidewalk cafés, drinking something or other. No one hurried you along; you never got the sense that you were being rushed from your little table to make room for the next party. That didn't seem to be the French way. On the contrary, you were expected to sit there most of the day, watching the world go by, chatting up people, taking time to absorb both the food and drinks and the atmosphere, the ambience. It was a fascinating firsthand look at Parisians, and gave you the sense of their relaxed *politesse*. Each time you ordered, the food or drink came with a little saucer that had the price marked on it. The stack of little saucers grew gradually but inexorably, marking off the alert and contented hours. When you were ready to pay up—"*L'addition, s'il vous plaît*"—the waiter added up the numbers on the stack of saucers, an ingenious way of computing not only the cost of your refreshments, but also the duration of your stay at the café.

Once we had a lovely lunch at a restaurant with a veranda, and Daddy drank wine with his lunch, an extraordinary departure from his customary habit. He was not a daytime drinker, and at night his drinking at home was circumspect and inflexible: when dinner was announced, he would toss down a straight shot of "schnapps." Was it to fortify himself for the ordeal of dinner with mercurial, unpredictable Mother? Or to sharpen his appetite? Then he'd come directly to the table, in coat, vest, and necktie — always. I don't remember his ever eating dinner in his shirtsleeves. Even much later, when he and Mother would come to our house and eat with us and the children, Daddy always wore the coat and tie. (This was the boy who had spent weeks in steerage, coming to America with a lot of other eager but frightened, ignorant, non-English-speaking immigrants.) On this occasion in Paris, the smooth, insidious wine worked its seductive charms on him, and he became — for him — quite giddy and silly. "Shicker," Mother called it. After we left the restaurant, we sauntered up the wide boulevard toward the U.S. Embassy, very sedate behind its elegant wrought-iron fence. In a spontaneous outburst of silliness Daddy took hold of the fence and peering between its iron bars, called out, "Oh Izzy — it's Oscar! C'mon out and play!" (Isidore Straus was the U.S. Ambassador at the time.) Did Daddy know Izzy? No, of course not. But he kept calling Izzy to come on out until we worried that the embassy guards might take a notion to investigate this guy. What a sight! We had a hard time coaxing him away from there, all of us giggling at our repressed Daddy acting like a kid!

In the evenings I was often left in the care of the Hôtel Lincoln's *patrons*, a man and wife, while Daddy and Mother took Darl with them to sample Paris night life, including a couple of Folies Bergère burlesque shows and other "adult entertainments," deemed unsuitable for me. Americans would have considered it too risqué even for a sixteen-year-old, but the French were much less puritanical. Mother had been outraged when Daddy reported such activities on his business trip, but she had two sets of morals, one for her and one for everybody else, and this was her idea of fun. When I was about eight she'd even dragged me along once to a burlesque joint in Chicago, full of dirty old men with their hand in their pocket. I didn't know quite what was going on, but I hated it. In Paris I was happy to stay "home" with the *patrons*, who were unremittingly kind and hospitable. I recall having dinner in their kitchen, and they sometimes played cards with me, so I learned to play simple games *en Français*. I relished those evenings in their kitchen, and then Madame would escort me up to our little apartment and help me get to bed.

We were almost beginning to feel like Parisians ourselves, living in the cadences of a different language (Darl and I got pretty comfortable translating from French to English for our parents), when we got a long-distance phone call from Nathan Milstein, the violinist—one of Daddy's musician clients—and his (then) wife, Rita: "We're in Switzerland, in Gstaad. Come see us, it's an easy train ride!"

Now, this was the era when even a phone call from Chicago to suburban Wilmette caused something of a flurry. One had to keep the call brief because long distance was expensive. Between Nathan's Russian accent and the name of the place he was inviting us to—it sounded like a sneeze—and the fact that not only was this long distance, but also mysterious *European* long distance, Daddy was so agitated that he couldn't figure out what Nathan was saying, so he put Darl on the phone, the most talented linguist among us. She, too, was baffled, so she said, "Nathan, could you spell it for me?"

He began unpromisingly, "G – S – T – "

"Wait a minute," Mother said, taking command, "Nathan," she ordered him, "send us a telegram." Brilliant solution, and the telegram arrived: "Welcome to Chalet Pinehurst, Gstaad." Just because we'd never heard of Gstaad didn't mean there was no such place.

Daddy had a romance with mountains, Mother and Darl wanted to buy watches and handkerchiefs—why not? So we got train tickets from Paris to Lucerne. The train trip, which took several hours, revealed an example of the pervasive tension between the French and the Swiss. As soon as our train crossed the French border and entered Switzerland, it was stopped at a small railroad station and all passengers were required to disembark. First, workmen swarmed aboard and cleaned the inside of the carriages, sweeping the floors and spraying some sort of decontaminant in the air. Then the entire exterior of the train was scrubbed with soapy water and rinsed. Finally then, we were permitted to reboard, all traces of French *schmutz* having been scoured away. The industry and efficiency with which all this was accomplished made it clear that this was standard procedure for every train entering the immaculate precincts of Switzerland. The Swiss, not given to spontaneous flights of imagination, visible emotional outbursts, or innate artistry and style, were orderly, punctual, and, it seemed to me, rather deficient in humor, imagination, or any sort of goings-on "outside the box," so to speak. Between these two contrasting cultures one sensed a reciprocal contempt

From the dark and Spartan simplicity of the Hôtel Lincoln, we were catapulted into the overwhelming elegance and luxury of the Schweizerhof, a venerable, rambling hotel on the shore of Lake Lucerne. Lucerne was a cosmopolitan city, but quite a contrast to the bustle and disorder of Paris, and I remember the few days in Lucerne as a tranquil, pleasant, and mildly dull interlude. There wasn't the excitement and the "chic" of Paris, but looking out at the lake from the broad veranda of our hotel, the box-clipped plane trees and the immaculate little white sailboats gently plying the shore, was like living in a scene from a nineteenth-century watercolor.

And the mountains were glorious. We stopped in a valley, Interlaken, I think, walked through fields of edelweiss, and saw the majestic Jungfrau, an icy white immensity framed by bosomy green foothills. While we were in Lucerne, we took the funicular railway up Mt. Pilatus, at the end of Lake Lucerne, to Burgenstock, a little cluster of souvenir shops, tea rooms, and scenic overlooks. I have to hand it to Mother, who, besides being afraid of water, couldn't stand heights. She gamely came along on this mountain adventure, with the cogwheel railway's vertiginous vistas from the windows of our tiny, delicate tramcar. It crept through space, swaying and suspended in midair, toward the summit of Pilatus. Once on terra firma, Mother was diverted by the interesting hikers and tourists in the little mountaintop tearoom, and the ordinariness of their cheery conversation calmed her anxiety. The views were spectacular, and the air, crystal clear, was noticeably cooler than in the valley.

There was a train to Gstaad, so we headed for the Milsteins and the unknown. At the time, Gstaad was a sleepy little ski resort that also boasted a girls' boarding school. It was nestled picturesquely among the mountains. On the crest of a formidable hill that looked down on the center of the little village was the hotel where Nathan had reserved a suite for us. The Royal Hotel and Winter Palace was a castle-like edifice of fairytale splendor and opulence and, in the summer of 1933, quite deserted.

Just as we arrived at the hotel and were getting settled in our suite, a frightening episode occurred. The beautiful highly polished wood floors had small Oriental scatter rugs, and as Mother was rushing from one room to another, she skidded on one of those rugs and fell hard, skinning her elbow. It bled a lot, and Daddy, never good in that sort of crisis, was agitated and helpless. Darl, who didn't like the sight of blood, fled into a bathroom and hid. I coolly took charge, wiped the blood off with a towel, wiped the scrape gently, and put a gauze on it. It was not a major injury, but after everyone had calmed down, I remember going into the bathroom feeling all clammy and faint and having to sit on the toilet with my head down between my knees waiting for the spell to pass. I never told anyone what had happened to me. I paid a modest but definite price for keeping cool in that little emergency.

The resort reversed nature's pattern and hibernated in the summer. It drowsed contentedly under the deep blue Swiss sky, dreaming of winter when it was alive with ice skaters and skiers, and the school was in session. There was a little *patisserie* in the main part of the village, and every morning our family would troop down the hill—quite a steep hike—and order "boolkies," the Yiddish word for rolls. The jolly and polite Swiss *boulangère* invariably greeted us: *"Grüss Gott,"* she'd smile and dip a curtsey. I learned to reply in kind and so did Darl, but Mother and Daddy were uncomfortable around these Germans (even if they were actually Swiss).

Here in rural Gstaad the air was gloriously brilliant and clear. There were cows in the mountain meadows and some woolly sheep or goats. The Milsteins had rented a chalet across an open field (probably a skating rink in winter), and some other musicians were also staying in the village—it was really cheap living in the summer off-season. Our parents and Darl did a certain amount of nighttime merrymaking, as much as possible in this tiny place. I think they must have gone to other friends' houses. I was too young, and missed out on that revelry.

At dusk, though, we'd all walk over to the Milsteins' across that field, and I recall vividly that I developed a pathological terror of the *Fledermaus*, or bat. At that hour, just as night fell, the bats would be zigzagging back and forth, scooping up unwary insects. Whether they actually did swoop down silently around us, or whether I imagined that, I refused to go out unless I wore a large knit cap into which I stuffed all my long black hair (because I'd heard that bats could get entangled in long hair), and even then I ran shrieking crazily ahead for the safety of the Milsteins' chalet. Everyone got quite exasperated with me, but there was no coaxing, reasoning, ordering, or jollying me out of that fear. Maybe it was because of that fear, rather than my age, that I was left to myself in the hotel. Maybe it was because I was such a pestiferous attention-grabber, really too old, at almost ten, to be whining and carrying on so.

I don't know how long we stayed in Gstaad—several days? A week? My next recollection of the trip is the return voyage on the *Île de France*, the flagship liner of the French Line at that time. The *Île de France* was much more elegant than the *Lafayette*, with more-commodious staterooms and dining saloons that were lavishly decorated and boasted exquisite cuisine. It didn't calm Mother's fears, however, and on this return voyage, worse luck, we hit a day or so of very rough weather a couple of days out at sea. Darl, Daddy, and I had our sea legs, and we'd go lurching and staggering down to the dining saloon, actually giggling and enjoying ourselves. It was rough enough for the crew to have installed little fences around the edges of the tables so that the dishes wouldn't slide off as the ship pitched, rolled, and bucked up and down from bow to stern. We learned after we docked in New York that a passenger had been lost overboard during that rough part of our passage. There was never anything that we saw in the news. Was the man a suicide? Was it an accident? It was during a brief period when I think the captain ordered passengers off the decks for their safety, as the rough seas made for treacherously slippery footing. But I have often wondered why there was no news story: "Mystery Disappearance on the *Île de France*." Darlene, years later, could have written it as a sequel to *The Mystery of the Thirteenth Floor*.

Then it was time to return to the U.S. after this magic fairytale summer: Back to dismal Apartment 1102, all the worse in contrast even to the modest Hôtel Lincoln!

32

Sharing a shoebox of a room while luxuriating in a hotel with daily maid service couldn't—by any stretch of the imagination—be considered "hardship," compared with our immigrant grandparents' early lives in America, about which we knew little. But it was a test and builder of character for Darl and me both.

From her point of view, what a pest I must have been: The Kid Sister, always wanting to know what she was doing, what she was thinking, who had called her on the telephone. For my part, I worshipped her, she was of gigantic importance in my life—but even as an international glamour girl, she was still a careless slob. And as fiercely possessive as she was about her own clothes, she had a cavalier attitude toward mine.

No underwear in her drawer? She could "borrow" Jeanie's— without asking. (At ten I was chubby enough so mine already fit her.) I was supposed to be honored that she wanted something of mine, even underpants. I was outraged! The trouble was, she helped herself to them, wore them, and then *tossed them back in my dresser drawer dirty*. Disgusting! I complained to Mother, of course; Mother's rationalization was that Darl was just lazy. Well, she wasn't too lazy to rifle through my underwear, just too inconsiderate to put it in the laundry hamper after she'd worn it! I saw this as contempt for me—clearly, I was a second-class citizen in this relationship.

We never came to blows over this—a minor miracle. There were a few shouting and door-slamming episodes, but they didn't lead to any permanent reform on Darl's part. Soon she was back to her disorganized ways. This was one of the few really chronic annoyances; of such *tsuris* did our lives consist. For the most part, we put up with it.

Apartment 1102 only had windows that faced west, over Clark Street. It was a gritty neighborhood, but if you raised your eyes, there were spectacular views of sunsets and thunderstorms — which sent me almost literally under the bed — as well as good earshot of Al Capone gunshots. In front of those windows, for two or three hours almost every day when he was in Chicago, Nathan Milstein would practice the violin.

After our visit to Gstaad, the Milsteins became close family friends. For two or three years, until I was twelve or thirteen, Nathan and Rita would make the Belden, and more specifically our apartment, their informal Midwest headquarters during at least part of his U.S. concert tour. They probably had a room at the Belden, but they'd show up for breakfast every morning — their first hearty meal of the day. Uninhibited and gifted freeloaders, they loved the food prepared by Olga, our wonderful red-haired Norwegian cook. She was sorely tested by these accomplished moochers: she'd grumble under her breath as she served, "Those Gypsies, nothing but Gypsies." At regular intervals she'd threaten to quit, but she may also have been flattered by their enthusiasm for anything and everything she cooked. (And, more important, she and our Bowman milkman had become lovers — they eventually married. I was happy for them.)

Rita, a gray-haired, blue-eyed cosmopolite, combined exquisite style with shrewdness and worldly-wise experience. She was a significant influence on Mother and Darlene with her knowledge of the details of grooming, both public and intimate. She impressed me and I admired her, but as a preteen I wasn't ready for the full musky force of Rita. Too bad — a few years later she might have transformed me into a Woman of the World. Rita was somewhat older than Nathan, whom she called her "little English lord." In fact, she had transformed this former street urchin into a suave man about town. He loved the fine British made-to-order suits Rita had taught him to prefer.

Except when he was practicing. Then, he always wore a

pair of ratty purple silk pajamas, some sort of superstitious talisman, a kind of magic invocation that's typical of many performers. Ballplayers, actors, dancers, writers—they have a favorite garment they wear, possibly an adult version of the security blanket. While Rita taught Mother the finer points of international urbanity and socio-sexual intrigue, Nathan would don his purple silk pajamas, shut the door to our living room, and do at least part of his daily practice. He loved his otherwise shunned and charmless "practice room"—was it friendly to the tones of his violin?

We'd sit in Mother and Daddy's book-lined space adjoining the living room, murmuring quietly so as not to interrupt Nathan's two- or three-hour practice sessions, and we'd listen spellbound as he worked on scales, finger exercises, repetitions of tricky passages, the occasional chaconne, a little jazz improvisation or folk song, even a whole virtuoso movement of a sonata or concerto—but mostly a sort of drill, which he obviously relished. What an amazing experience for all of us! I once asked him how much he practiced. He told me seven or eight hours a day, a little less on days when he was to perform. Practicing was not drudgery but a joy for him, and he needed and looked forward to it. "It's all music," he told me.

When he wasn't practicing, Nathan would sit in our little dinette with his traveling watercolors and make small paintings. He seemed to find it relaxing to use his visual memory as well as his hands in another artistic language. He once gave me one of those little paintings (since lost, unfortunately). Sometimes he did card tricks to amuse himself and me, and his manual dexterity made him a dazzling sleight-of-hand trickster. He was remarkably sweet and patient with me. Only once did I ever feel a truly icy chill from him, and it was my tactless fault. We were all at dinner one evening and I asked him, "Nathan, have you ever forgotten the music when you were right in the middle of a performance?"

He shot me a look and gave me a clipped, monosyllabic "Yes." I knew enough to abandon that line of questioning and understood, perhaps for the first time, the *frisson* of performance anxiety that even the most poised and stage-wise artist probably suffered frequently, if not always.

There was always action, a kind of tingling excitement, with Nathan and Rita around. It was hard to tear myself away and go to school. But fifth grade at Parker demanded attention. Under the stern tutelage of Dr. Herman T. Lukens, it was a watershed year.

Over the summer families had gotten a letter warning about the philosophy that drove Dr. Lukens's curriculum and his disciplinary pedagogy, so prospective fifth graders were given the option of spending that year elsewhere and returning to the school for sixth grade. Some parents elected to remove their children for that one year, with the school's sanction. I stayed at Parker.

The change from Miss Davis to Dr. Lukens was like going from a dreamy vacation in the Mediterranean to being dunked in the Arctic Ocean. In sharp contrast to the world of humanism, art, the birth of democracy, the challenge of exploring philosophy, and the beauty and terror of Greek drama that had consumed us with Miss Davis, we were now catapulted into a meticulous and businesslike classroom. How did such a strict, formal person come to be teaching in this progressive school? Still, there were those (like me) who admired, respected, and yes, maybe even loved this impersonal-seeming man, with his white hair and neatly trimmed beard and goatee, his stiff collar and old-fashioned necktie, always dressed in a dark suit, including a vest.

The brown linoleum floor of our classroom was a map of the forty-eight United States (this was long before Alaska or Hawaii became a state), with star-shaped tacks marking each state's capital and smooth tacks indicating other principal cities. Before the year was out, we could name all the states, their capitals, and the major cities those tacks represented. Dr. Lukens believed that memorizing things was good mind exercise, so we memorized the tables of fractions; Chicago's mile streets (north-south and east-west); even the presidents of the United States. It was a rigorous year of serious learning. As it turned out, Dr. Lukens was also a great believer in "excursions," so those of us who took the hard work also had some merry times and wonderful experiences. We visited most of the city's museums and art galleries, explored the parks and zoos, and may even have gone on the occasional picnic after studying one of Chicago's obscure geographical or historical sites. These excursions always had an air of high anticipation associated with them. As our yellow school bus rolled along, we all chanted out names of the city's mile streets as we traversed them. They were Chicago's armature, the grid that unlocked the city's geography — and helped to keep you from getting lost if you were in a strange neighborhood.

Every Friday afternoon, as a reward, we had "Literary Society." Sometimes Dr. Lukens read to us — a story or poem that he particularly liked. On other occasions one of the working groups into which our class of about twenty was divided would give a program they'd prepared. I once took on the challenge of memorizing and reciting Lewis Carroll's poem "The Walrus and the Carpenter." A showoff to the end (my unfinished business with Miss Cooke and "Little Lamb, Who Made Thee?" brushed aside), I reeled off Carroll's long opus with only one memory lapse. Dr. Lukens gently prompted me but didn't make me feel that needing some memory help along the way was a disgrace. Rather, he seemed to enjoy my feat of memorization as much as I did. That episode removed the last of the residual sting of Miss Cooke's reproach five years earlier. I loved that school year and really liked Dr. Lukens and his twinkly blue eyes behind the half-moon glasses.

Either he told us this story about the great tragedy in his life, or it reached us through the school underground. He had been married and had a young son. His wife and the child, who was under ten at the time, were both killed in the notorious Iroquois Theater Fire of 1903, an inferno that took hundreds of lives. The inadequate and locked exits that caused this catastrophe in Chicago became the catalyst for better emergency procedures in public auditoriums nationwide. Once we knew that story, our hearts were softened toward that formal-seeming man.

I inveigled my parents into inviting him to dinner once, an

event I don't remember at all. I can't believe it would have been a comfy evening. My dad would've been interested in Dr. Lukens and they would have had a pleasant time talking, but Mother would have been both bored and made to feel inadequate by this elderly (probably fifty!) gent who looked like a nineteenth-century schoolmaster.

Having sailed through fifth grade with fine marks, all work completed, I was smugly confident but, it turned out, riding for a fall. Near the end of the year we would often stay around in the East Field after school and have a pickup baseball game—boys and girls, various ages. I was bringing my entire year's work home, all these neatly paperclipped groups of papers, with their slips that recorded each week's completed assignments, stored in my schoolbag. I was taking it home to look over admiringly and to marvel at my accomplishments before turning it back to Dr. Lukens for him to check over in final affirmation that I was ready to pass into sixth grade. I shoved the bulging school bag under a bench at the edge of the field and plunged into a dusty, sweaty, happy game of baseball. When the game broke up an hour or so later and I went to retrieve my school bag, it was gone. Vanished! I searched under all the benches, around the field, quartering it like a hunting dog. I asked my companions. I returned to the school building and checked the Lost and Found. No sign of it.

Worried now, I trotted home and telephoned some of my non-ballplaying friends to see whether any of them had seen my bag, or seen anyone carrying it. No luck. Well, I knew the work was complete and Dr. Lukens knew it, too, and he even had a record of it, of each and every assignment, so I'd probably be fine and he'd waive that final check-off of all the papers. I was such a responsible, exemplary student. . . .

No such luck! No exceptions were made by Dr. Lukens. I should have known that: No tickee, no washee. I was shocked. "You'll have to come into school over the summer and make up the work along with the students who have incompletes [*the dummies, I'd be with the dummies and layabouts!*]," he told me.

"Make it up?" I said, trying to keep my voice and demeanor cool. "All of it?"

"*All* of it," he replied. I was dismayed, angry — at myself mostly — miserable and heartsick. I knew how Dr. Lukens felt about rules: you obeyed them, and if you flouted them, however that came about, you took the consequences. I had been so sure that, obedient child, good student that I was — always on time with assignments — I'd be given special treatment. Because I wasn't, it was a character-building experience that I remember with chagrin. As it turned out, Dr. Lukens let me do an abridged version of the year's work and let me off after two or three weeks of all-day, every-day summer school. He also excused the other summer attendees, classmates who hadn't completed assignments the first time around, people who had flunked a test or two and had had to make up those shortfalls. He made his point unequivocally: one's work is one's responsibility. After all, that was the school word — Responsibility — and this was how you learned its full, literal meaning.

33

Darlene graduated from Francis Parker that June of 1934. I don't remember her graduation; there must've been a prom, but I don't remember anything about that, either. Mother's main interest would have been the prom dress, but none of that seemed to reach me. I might have been jealous of all the attention being focused on her.

She and Mother shopped for all the right clothes — sweater sets, saddle shoes — for her freshman year at Connecticut College for Women. Darl had chosen CC, then a WASPy Eastern girls' school surrounded by prestigious men's colleges and the U.S. Coast Guard Academy, over Smith, Vassar, or Radcliffe. She had what it took to get into any of those, and Miss Cornell, Parker's social studies teacher and college admissions counselor, would have seen to it: Darl was a favorite of hers. But Darl preferred not to go to a school that was so extremely top-of-the-line: full of Brahmins, almost no Blacks (it goes without saying), and a very few Jews, who either had money and had bought their way in, or who "knew their place" and were compliant and mannerly. Darl didn't want to be typecast either way.

Mother and I accompanied her on the train to New London. I loved that train trip, even though I was always a touch queasy at first. I loved the scenery skimming by to the rhythm of wheels on track. The cocoon of the upper bunk when the Porter zipped up those green curtains. The weight of the buildings above us as we arrowed through the tunnel — and then: NEW YORK! We changed at Grand Central Station to the train for Connecticut.

I remember a dormitory full of twittering girls unpacking,

dashing in and out of each other's rooms. Darl and her roommate had corresponded, but this was their first meeting. I, a foreigner, watched as from some distant planet.

Our goodbyes were short: we left her absorbed in her new world that would never be ours.

Having our narrow "bedroom" all to myself was a strange sensation after ten years of sharing a room with my sister. In all those years we had slept apart only once: when Darl got diphtheria, and they moved her into our parents' room. I couldn't see her until she was getting better and presumably no longer contagious. We were quarantined; I probably couldn't leave the apartment—I was quite young, maybe five, so I don't remember. I just remember her sitting up in bed in Mother and Daddy's room, finally not coughing anymore. And then we were roommates again.

Now I even missed her rifling through my underwear drawer.

I really missed her reassuring presence as a buffer between me and our parents' dynamic. I remember a fight I had with my father after Darl was gone. Mother was going out to the Drake bar every evening and having a drink or two with a "friend," a handsome guy named Al Marshall. He was married: his wife, Stella, was a hatchet face, a little skinny woman; his daughter, Alice, and I were friends. Mother would waltz in around the time Olga was ready to serve dinner and announce, "Here I am, kids—drunk again!"

Daddy was very forgiving, and I got mad at him. I started pounding on his chest and his beautiful cashmere suit coat, saying *"How can you let her do that??"* He was so gentle, sweet and kind, he didn't get mad at me for impugning his masculinity that he let his wife behave that way. He was upset; his feelings were hurt. We were both in tears. I felt terrible, but I also felt righteous. That episode, neither repeated nor resolved, lives on in my memory: Do I understand it now?

The car was a predictable battlefield. Daddy was not as good a driver as Mother, but he assumed the conventional role of family chauffeur. Mother, though competent and decisive behind the wheel, had quit driving after a minor accident (she gashed the side of our car against the wheel of a horse-drawn wagon on Clark Street), rationalizing that her superior skills were better employed as a backseat driver. So, on short Sunday drives to the suburbs to see the beauties of Nature or on our infrequent longer road trips, Daddy drove, while Mother was "copilot" (in fact, more like Generalissimo), sitting beside him, monitoring his every move, shouting, "Osc! Be careful! Osc! You're going too fast!" (The speed limit was 35 mph, and anything over that brought more shouting.)

She was witheringly contemptuous of Daddy's driving, and with some justification. His most trying—and dangerous— shortcoming was that he tended to be uncertain at intersections. He'd hesitate, with Mother yelling at him to go, just long enough to make it a real gamble. Then, at the last possible minute, he'd gun the car and shoot across, Mother screaming, "*Osc!!* Look out! Are you crazy? You could have gotten us all killed!!"—all this accompanied by the cacophony of honking horns, curses and imprecations from other motorists. There would be the inevitable breaking point, at which he'd turn to her, furious, and yell, "Bun, for Chrissakes! Then YOU drive!" and she'd subside—for a while.

But not even all Mother's nagging could spoil Daddy's love for the Open Road, the open country. I must have caught that wanderer's pleasure from him. I remember one automobile trip to New York in the 1930s, in our ritzy gray 1933 Packard, when we spent Saturday night in Lancaster, Pennsylvania, in the heart of Amish country. There was a big hotel and lots of interesting sights: horses and buggies, men who looked like pioneers in their boots and big-brimmed hats, and ladies in plain, buttonless dresses (buttons, we were told, were considered frivolous, signs of vanity). The women also wore prim little organdy caps.

Sunday morning, as we were preparing to move on, Daddy dropped his car keys. We'd heard them clink on the marble floor of the lobby, but they were nowhere to be found. It was as though they had been swallowed by a malign spirit. The hotel staff rolled back the rugs, even moved the telephone booth in case the keys had rolled underneath it. To get a locksmith on a

Sunday in Amish country was out of the question. There was a group of Amish ladies across from our hotel, all holding hands and making a barricade in front of the town's movie house, which effectively prevented it from opening on the Sabbath—a firm reminder that on the Lord's Day neither frivolity nor work was to take place. We were going to have to spend an idle Sunday in Lancaster.

Daddy went out the front door of the hotel and sat down disconsolately on the curb to get a stone out of his shoe. But Eureka! It wasn't a stone, it was the car keys! They had evidently bounced into his shoe! So with light hearts and thankful apologies to the hotel staff, we set off. Despite the frequent cries of "Osc! Look out! There's a tractor ahead! For God's sake, what are you *doing*??" and "Jesus Christ, Bun, let me alone, quit yelling! I know what I'm doing!" much of the trip was fun: reading the "Burma Shave" signs—"The Wolf is shaved so neat and trim/ Red Riding Hood is chasing him! Burma Shave"—and looking at the scenery.

Theirs were not the only unpleasant domestic situations I suffered the discomfort of witnessing. When we'd lived in our first-floor apartment, we were often unwilling eavesdroppers to terrible fights between the across-the-hall couple, Dorothy and Morrie Horwich. He was the classic henpecked ineffectual type; his wife was the witch who'd turned us in for tracing our skipping with pencils on the Belden's hallway walls. Once, there was a lot of yelling and then a door slammed. Loudly. We heard pounding on their front door and Morrie's voice pleading, "Dorothy, open up, let me in!" We peeped out and there poor Morrie was, standing in the hall in his underwear shorts (gaudy striped ones, I recall) and his black socks and garters. Darl and I were both amused by his plight and embarrassed for the poor guy.

Closer to home, it wasn't funny. My beloved Aunt Evelyn and Uncle Archie had moved out west to Beverly Hills, and we visited them and my little cousin Arlyn for several weeks the year I was eleven and again when I was twelve. In the year bracketed by those two visits, their marriage came apart.

The first and happier of those visits, I got to play with Jackie Paley, the adopted child of Archie's Uncle Jay and his wife Lil. Jay was in "the movie business," and they lived on a grand estate in Holmby Hills, a much more elegant and affluent area than Beverly Hills. Their house, a huge Spanish Colonial pile, had extensive and elaborate grounds. There was a Japanese garden with funny prickly grass, an Italian grotto, and an Olympic-size swimming pool, with pool houses for changing clothes, or perhaps even for overnight guests. The place ran like a resort, with an endless procession of guests and favor-seekers. Jay was, even to my inexperienced eyes, a conspicuous adulterer and a total cad. Lil was content because he showered her with diamond jewelry, recompense for each new chorus girl he bedded. Lil, laden with sparklers, watched mildly as the procession of bimbos and aspiring "actresses" passed through this palazzo like a dose of salts.

Jackie was a scrawny little kid, rail-thin, with dark eyebrows, dark hair, and tawny skin. Supposedly a year or so younger than me, but physically and morally precocious, she cheerfully carried on her "dad's" tradition, sleeping with the stable hands, would-be jockeys who were about her size, occasionally running off with one of them and having to be found and fetched back home. She thought nothing of parading naked around the house and grounds, and was already an accomplished smoker and drinker. Her "parents" had hired a French governess to civilize this wild animal, but the poor lady was helpless and clueless in the face of Jackie's determined debauchery: she did whatever she pleased — and that was plenty!

I remember the proper, elegant English butler, who, despite his formal attire and cultured accent and demeanor, couldn't provide even a superficial air of decorum, let alone of bliss and harmony, to this crazy household. I remember Jackie and me leaning over the balustrade upstairs and watching the parade of movie stars who came to the Paleys' lavish dinner parties. At one such affair, when someone complimented her on an especially elaborate diamond necklace, Lil was said to have remarked, "Oh, that. That's last year's diamonds." Jackie spoke pretty good

French, thanks to the governess, whom she called Mam'zelle, but her main language was dissoluteness and lechery, even at her tender age. She was a mercurial kid with a ferocious temper; still, we liked each other, and got along well most of the time. I loved all the gardens, and while I made up stories or read or played there, Jackie would vanish on her own degenerate errands. Then she'd reappear, and we'd have a swim.

The second summer, when my aunt and uncle's marriage disintegrated, I didn't see Jackie. I stayed in Evelyn and Archie's house. Why didn't I stay with my parents at their hotel? Was it because I was to function as a distraction for Arlyn from the problems her parents were having? No one seemed to think that I might have had sensibilities that would be disturbed by the emotional turmoil in that house. No one thought about the discomfort I suffered because I had to sleep on a sun porch, the only exit from which was through my aunt and uncle's bedroom. Awakening in the morning and having to go to the toilet was an agony of conflict: Do I walk through their bedroom—they were sometimes arguing, sometimes stonily silent, which was worse—or do I try to wait until after Uncle Archie leaves for work? Aunt Ev slept late, and I was less shy about tiptoeing through their room when she was alone. I remember it as a summer of agony, not only the physical misery of a distended bladder, but also the anxiety and embarrassment of being an unwilling witness to something I wasn't supposed to see or comprehend: the sad and ugly end of my aunt and uncle's marriage.

My cousin Arlyn, who must've been four or five, had an English governess, Miss Shanky, almost a dead ringer for Mary Poppins as far as appearances were concerned. There the resemblance ended, however, as she was prim and conventional. The atmosphere around the house was tense and disordered: in spite of a staff of domestics, meals seemed haphazard; Ev and Archie were remote both from each other and from us. Archie wasn't around much; he wasn't the fun uncle he used to be. Evelyn would get out of bed late in the morning and spend literally hours putting on her makeup and carefully choosing her wardrobe for some momentous appointment.

Later I found out that she was the patient of an eminent local psychoanalyst, Dr. Bertrand Frohman. In the course of her treatment they had become lovers, and in absolute contravention of the directives of the Analytic Association, the doctor did not turn her case over to another analyst. He may have been drummed out of the Association, I don't know what happened, but my parents were busy intervening, trying to salvage Ev's and Archie's marriage, trying to pry her away from Dr. Frohman (whom Daddy branded a Svengali) and to get her into the hands of another analyst. All their meddling only antagonized Ev and Archie further, disrupted the household, and opened a rift between Mother and Evelyn that effectively put an end to their frequent and intimate exchange of letters. (I was always curious about those letters, because neither of them ever saved them but always destroyed them right away. I guess they must have exchanged very intimate secrets with one another, or maybe they were just paranoid — permanent scarring from their ghetto childhood with its lies, blackmail, and dark threats about the Evil Eye.)

Though I felt very uncomfortable in the midst of this emotional maelstrom, there were brief intervals of calm, during which I played with Arlyn in their picturesque garden. It had a little pond that was full of tadpoles when I first got there, and I was enchanted watching them metamorphose into lively miniature frogs. In yet another example of Mother's complete lack of sensitivity to my early-puberty sensibilities — I was almost twelve and very much aware of, and ambivalent about, my budding breasts and sprouting wiry black underarm and pubic hair — she overrode my pleas to wear some sort of blouse or shirt when my cousin and I played outdoors in the garden. At four or five, Arlyn went shirtless, and Mother contemptuously assured me that I was "still a child, don't be ridiculous and try to act older than you are. You and Arlyn can both run under the sprinkler in just your panties." I felt terribly conspicuous and thought I saw Mother and Aunt Ev simpering behind their hands, commenting on my micro-breasts. Darlene had broken her spell, but Mother seemed to believe that as long as she could dress me like a little girl — and treat me like one — she, too, would still be young. As long as I was her little Jeanie, I would be rewarded with her love and approbation for participating in her perpetual-youth fairy tale. But everyone in that household was so tense and distracted that I was afraid of becoming the disruption that would send it over the edge. I just wanted to smooth things over.

The marital conflict affected us all, and I think both Arlyn and I tried to play at being happy "normal" children, romping to the tune of our parents' faltering fantasies that everything would go back to being the way it was at some indeterminate "before." Finally, Mother and Daddy, in a misguided effort to break Bert Frohman's hold on Evelyn, took her away for a Palm Springs weekend. That was such a resounding failure that our visit was cut short, I was whisked out of 715 North Maple Drive, Beverly Hills — formerly a paradise of security and contentment — and bundled onto the train back to Chicago with my disgruntled parents.

Jay was furious and unforgiving: how could Evelyn dare to be unfaithful to Archie? Uncle Jay's female relatives (unlike Uncle Jay himself) were forbidden to have loose morals, and divorce was a sin of Old Testament proportions. So, in spite of threats and imprecations from Jay and strenuous butting in from Mother and Daddy, Aunt Ev and Uncle Archie got divorced. The field of battle was strewn with wreckage. Except for curt exchanges about their parents, Rose and Louis — who would retire and move out to live near Evelyn a few years after Great-grandma Anna died — Evelyn and Mother didn't speak to each other at all for many years. Reconciliation, late in coming, didn't restore the joyous intimacy of yore. Archie we never saw or heard from again. The adored uncle of my childhood was gone from me, and Arlyn also vanished from my life.

34

Sixth and seventh grades were pallid after the challenge and intensity of fifth grade. Except for the arrival among us in seventh grade of a contraband copy of *Lady Chatterley's Lover*, those weren't particularly distinguished years, nor did we have distinguished teachers—adequate, but not distinguished. (All that would change with our entrance into eighth grade.)

An annual event that marked the passage of time in a memorable way was our "Old Soldiers' Day" observance (the holiday was officially called Decoration Day at that time, but is now known as Memorial Day). Each year toward the end of May the surviving members of Colonel Francis Parker's Civil War regiment, our very own "Boys in Blue," would appear at school and take the stage in the auditorium for Morning Ex, in full uniform. They were an impressive sight, these dignified old men in their spotless but antiquated uniforms: broad-brimmed hats, and double-breasted tunics with the brass buttons polished so that they shone like rows of little suns. In my first awed exposure to Old Soldiers' Day, in 1928 or '29, they had filled the stage (which in the earliest years I remember, first through third grade, may have been in what we called "the Old Gym"). There must have been twenty or thirty, sitting erect in three rows. One by one they'd stand, tell us their name and rank, and describe what they had done in the war. It gave the Civil War and the Grand Army of the Republic an immediacy that shook me.

Since Parker was a school with a strong pacifist leaning, seeing and listening to these men brought me face to face with a rush of conflicting emotions. You couldn't help but admire them, feel the glory of the victory in which they had participated, and still there was horror. In my imagination,

I heard the rolling thunder of cannon and smelled the acrid smoke and heard the shrieks and moans of wounded and dying men. It made pacifism seem the only sensible course. There was one tall, lanky, bespectacled veteran; the youngest of the group, he boasted. He'd run away from home at age twelve (lied and said he was fourteen) to join up. So they'd started him out as a drummer boy, but as the war dragged on, he was handed a gun and ended up fighting. He got shot in the neck, injuring his vocal cords and affecting his speaking voice, which was why we had to strain to hear him.

Each year we looked forward to Old Soldiers' Day—everyone's all-time favorite Morning Ex—and each year we scanned the dwindling group, searching for our favorites. The Drummer Boy was one of the first we lost. I felt a sharp jolt of grief: these men were still close enough in space and time for me to feel the breath of the Civil War, which I'd thought of as so remote—in the previous century!—that it only existed as a story entombed in history books. Yet here on Decoration Day every student in the school joined the solemn line that snaked around the gym behind the auditorium and shook the hands and thanked the men—the still-living, breathing men—who'd held guns and shot them at other men and fought to save the Union and America.

Year by year the number of our much-loved Old Soldiers dwindled. For a few years their number seemed to stabilize at five or six; then there was just one, too frail to stand and speak to us, but still loyal to the tradition of Colonel Parker, their regimental commander and comrade-in-arms. Then, the following year, Old Soldiers' Day was celebrated but the stage was empty—a poignant sight. It wasn't Old Soldiers' Day anymore. It became Memorial Day.

My first encounter with alcohol took place the year when I was twelve, and Daddy's family gathered at the Belden Hotel to celebrate the fiftieth wedding anniversary of his parents, Bubbe and Zhazh.

In their late sixties or early seventies by then, Grandma and

Grandpa Stern had a grocery store on West Gladys Avenue, way out in Garfield Park; and they had moved from their sunny proper apartment (whose carpeted stairs I remembered climbing as a small child) to a cramped living space behind their store. You couldn't call it an apartment, it was a "dwelling space": a kitchen with a gas stove, cabinets, a sink, a light bulb with a glass shade above the all-purpose kitchen table; and a tiny triangular "bedroom" filled to capacity by their double bed and one dresser. Their move must have had something to do with the Depression, and perhaps with Daddy's debt to Noble Judah and his responsibility to support Grandma Anna Silverman in yet another apartment (with browbeaten round-the-clock aides). I can only guess the reason for and timing of their move; it must have been economic. But there was a time—when I was maybe eleven or twelve—when we would make the long drive every Friday night to have (what I now know was Shabbat) dinner with them in their little back-of-the-store dwelling. (It was always just the three of us, Mother, Daddy, and me. I don't remember Darlene coming, even when she was back home.) Though the whole Stern clan—my aunts and uncles, Daddy's four sisters and their husbands, and their children, my cousins—used to gather for major family occasions at Grandma and Grandpa's apartment, now, for an event such as this golden anniversary, a first-floor party room at the Belden had to be booked, with catering.

Having spent his youth working with his father on a large rural estate in Russia—I remember Grandpa's descriptions of orchards full of peaches, and of pressing grapes, growing olives, and making cheese using huge heavy wooden machinery—Zhazh knew how to make cherry wine. It was called *vishnik*," and he made it with pitted cherries and sugar. He'd let it stand in stoneware crocks over the range in their tiny kitchen behind the grocery store—someplace consistently warm—and in due course it would ferment. It came in several strengths: for Daddy there was a powerful *vishnik*, enhanced by the addition of some brandy during the fermentation process, and with the cherries still in it. It had a kick like a mule, and Daddy relished it. Then there was a sort of medium version without cherries; and finally, served to the children on festive occasions, a feebly spiked cherry juice. I was bored by the blander vintages and intrigued by the lip-smacking, cherry-laden strong stuff that Daddy loved and hoarded. He'd bring it from Grandpa's in gallon jugs and keep it in a dark corner of his closet. As a dedicated snooper among all his personal possessions, I knew how much there was of each of the strengths.

On this anniversary occasion, I, ever the show-off, led my younger cousins Paul and Dick away from the droning conversations of the adults and up to our eleventh-floor apartment, where I headed straight for Daddy's closet and his stash of the twenty-mule-team *vishnik*. I was something of a temptress to those younger — male — cousins. There were other cousins: Harriet, Bob, Arlene, but they were older and therefore outside my sphere of influence. Marilyn, the youngest, was clearly underage for this enterprise. So I introduced the two boys to the Real Stuff, cherries and all. My, but it burned like fire all the way down the windpipe! I don't remember whether we took seconds, but if we did, they were small ones, as I didn't want to make a noticeable dent in the contents of that jug. By the time the grownups missed us and traced us to the apartment, we were a bit loopy but had put the incriminating jug back in its hiding place. Our behavior was abnormal enough to raise suspicions, and though my honorable cousins kept mum, I was quickly identified as the miscreant in chief (by Mother, of course). I guess it was a disgrace, but for me, the principal value of the experience was the discovery that I didn't like Daddy's special *vishnik*.

By the end of her freshman year at Connecticut College, Darlene had decided to come back to Chicago and transfer to Northwestern University. What had put her off Conn College? Was it too provincial? Not academically or socially challenging enough? Maybe the all-girl environment was a bore. Maybe New London wasn't urban or urbane enough for a big-city kid (and future New Yorker)?

I wondered whether economics were a factor, and Darlene's younger son, Stephen/Yaakov Geis, confirms this: "That's what I recall Mom saying. She loved Connecticut and treasured the memory of it." At Northwestern, though, she could commute to classes on campus in Evanston while living at home—and, of course, sharing an ever-shrinking bedroom with me, an arrangement that would last almost four more years.

For schoolwork we shared the one desk that was at the foot of our beds, though Darl, as a college student, had priority on its use. The bigger problem was privacy, a problem that would become acute when Darl began bringing the occasional boyfriend home. There was no place in Apartment 1102 to entertain "gentlemen callers" except our bedroom—with me in it. But that came later.

I was thrilled to have her back—and a little awed: she had matured. I could FEEL it. So a new respect, a sort of distance, had crept between us. She still drove me nuts with her conviction of entitlement to rifle through my drawers, with no reciprocity. And I still drove her nuts by talking to her when she was trying to study.

On the cusp between childhood and adulthood, sometimes I felt grown up and responsible in my head, as though I comprehended the complexities of being a human in the world; sometimes I wished I could return to being the baby in my stroller, bundled in my warm fur bunting, cuddled under the wicker canopy, where I could snuggle down and sort of hide, study the world Out There through half-closed eyes, and feel safe and protected. The mystery of social interaction, of friends, "popularity," easy relationships with peers, was a haunting void I was afraid to face. I confronted the inexorable changes in my body: budding breasts, sprouting pubic hair, more than passing interest in males—what were *they* experiencing?

There were a couple of summers when we spent several weeks at the Moraine Hotel in Highland Park. Daddy took the train into the city to work, Darl had a bunch of suburban pals, and Mother and I, who didn't have any suburban girlfriends at that time, went to the beach connected to the hotel or explored the little village of Highland Park. The hotel was an old, high-ceilinged rambling relic of the 1890s. We had a ground-floor suite with a screened porch that seemed to hang over the ravine that was between us and the beach. It was another variety of boring summer, but Mother liked it much better than Union Pier because it was a hotel, with a dining room and maid service.

They were idle, undemanding summers, shapeless and planless, until I had my first direct encounter with scary sexual "flirtation." In Chicago, there were men cruising the neighborhood now and then, exposing themselves for the benefit of the schoolkids, but I don't remember ever seeing one in Lincoln Park, and I roamed all over that park by myself. My encounter at the Moraine Hotel was of a different order, not just seeing someone at a distance whom you could cross the street to avoid.

There was a corps of bellboys, elevator operators, the usual hotel staff that hustled luggage, ran errands, delivered things to the guests, and stood at attention in various locations around the lobby. They wore a quasi-military-looking uniform, brass-buttoned jacket, dark trousers with a gold stripe down the side, white cotton gloves. Staying at the Moraine Hotel for several weeks, I had little to occupy me, so I struck up idle conversation with several of the bellboys, talk like "Have you got sisters or brothers? What's your last name? Where do you go to school?" It was probably against regulations for them to "fraternize" with the guests, but neither they nor I took that seriously. Most of them were townies from Highland Park and Highwood, just working for the summer. They were an undistinguished lot, all just past the pimply adolescent stage, and (though I was blissfully unaware of it) chronically horny. I was this friendly pubescent girl with long black hair, wandering the hotel and the grounds, wearing shorts, unaware of how I might have looked to these young fellows. It seemed to me that I had an easy, though slightly distant, kind of relationship with them—I was a guest, they were the Help.

And then one evening when I was alone in our apartment—Mother and Daddy had gone to Ravinia, maybe—there comes this knock at the door and it's one of the bellboys. He stands there with some book or package that he's bringing, and he steps into the living room. He's talking innocuously all the time — about the weather, or about how he's working toward buying a car, or that the chef had some delicious cookies in the kitchen and he could have a few — would I like one? We are standing in the middle of the living room facing one another and he says, "Mind if I sit down and stay a moment? It's been a busy day."

"Sure," I say, not sure whether this is OK, guests and help mingling like this, but it seems the polite and friendly thing to do. He sits on the couch. I sit on a chair. We talk trivia some more. I wonder if I should offer him a glass of water. I decide not to. He's not exactly an invited guest, he's an employee, isn't he? Of course he's just a young guy with a summer job, but — then he moves to the end of the couch near the chair I'm sitting on.

"Why don't you come here and sit next to me?" he asks.

Well, I'm not sure about this but I don't want to appear snooty or hostile. And then he puts his hand on my knee. He starts moving it up my thigh. He says something about that feels nice, doesn't it? His hand is gliding up my inner thigh. If he thought this would set me on fire, he couldn't have been more mistaken. I turn to ice. I realize this is not right at all. I'm scared and I don't want him to touch me anymore. I stop worrying about seeming uppity. I stand and move toward the front door to get away from him.

"I think my parents will be home any minute. You'd better leave," I tell him.

He turns just a shade ugly. "Aw, I'm just being friendly. Wattsa matter, I'm not good enough for you?" I am at the front door by now, and I have opened it — wide. Either he leaves or I run down the long corridor to the relative safety of the lobby. He follows me to the door and tries to get close to me. "Are you scared or what?" I sense a menacing tone in his voice. "I won't hurt you."

I shove him out, shut and lock the door.

I realize I'm shaking all over, in a cold sweat. I keep the door locked. I close and lock the door to the screened porch. I shut and lock the windows. When Mother and Daddy return, I make sure it's them before I unbolt the door. I'd been afraid this guy might get a passkey and come back.

I told Mother and Daddy the story. They didn't say much, except Mother said that you shouldn't ever let an employee come in and sit down. That bellboy was gone the next day, never to return, but I was afraid for the rest of that summer that he'd be after me, to get revenge for having been fired. I didn't want to walk to the little town anymore, or through the leafy ravine to the beach. I didn't tell Mother or Daddy why, I just kind of moped around the apartment, and I never got into conversations with any of the other bellboys. We avoided each other, as though by common agreement. The manager had probably lectured them about social distance and appropriate conduct; they undoubtedly learned what had caused the summary disappearance of their comrade.

35

Eighth grade was a watershed year, when our recognition that we'd crossed into pre-adulthood was reinforced by a superb teacher and extraordinary human being, Sarah Greenebaum. In Miss Greenebaum we encountered a woman who understood us, enjoyed us, knew how to teach us, made us laugh at grown-up things and feel grown-up compassion, anger, sympathy, and delight at the world's marvels and foibles.

I've always believed that age thirteen and fourteen are a threshold: awkward, difficult, scary, exhilarating, and a confusion of child and almost-adult. The mind is ready to grasp subtleties and complexities in the world of ideas, but the emotional component of thinking — and living — is still immature. Miss Greenebaum understood this disjunction and honored it, even took it as a welcome sign that we were sentient humans and were growing up and developing just as she figured we would. This was often in sharp contrast to life with our families, parents especially (at least mine), who seemed only to notice the chasms, the discontinuities in our behavior and the way our minds and bodies, minds and hearts, seemed always to be at cross-purposes — to our parents, definitely an inconvenience or worse. They made us feel "abnormal"; Miss Greenebaum took it in stride: that's how people learn to be comfortable with themselves and understand thinking and feeling on many levels and in many situations.

She was also an unabashed leftist who believed in exposing her students to the full spectrum of world politics and culture. The result was a year of wide-ranging inquiry, an invigorating experience. We studied China, from its long history of art, warfare, discovery, and technology to its twentieth-century transformation into a communist effort at utopia. We studied Chicago's prehistoric shorelines, witnessing traces still discernible along preternaturally hilly streets, and picking out ancient bluffs and valleys whose hinted-at shadows could be lifted away from the urban jumble if you were alert to them. We had a Current Events segment every morning and were encouraged to share timely news with the class. On one memorable occasion, a student, reporting the latest bulletin on Pope Pius XI's mortal illness, announced, "Today the Pope feels good." Miss Greenebaum's raspy voice boomed out from the back of the room, "I should hope so," reminding us, with delighted sarcasm, of the difference between feeling good and feeling well, showing us the pungency of grammatical precision, and sending us into gales of laughter.

Lawrence Spitz, a smart, mild-mannered, good-natured boy, was her runaway favorite student. She probably had a favorite in each class, and she didn't make any effort to hide her partiality. So, mornings, as she called the class to order, she'd announce, "All right, sit down, everyone, even Lawrence." We *all* liked Lawrence, and we were perfectly comfortable in the knowledge that he was special to Miss Greenebaum. You couldn't resent him or be envious when she never pretended about much of anything, least of all that everyone had equal favor in her eyes, when it was plain to see how partial she was to Lawrence, and how richly he deserved it.

Miss Greenebaum was nearly six feet tall, an albino, with a tiny cannonball head on top of a pair of football player's shoulders. She had the pale myopic eyes of an albino and a cap-like bob of white-gold hair. Her assistant, Miss Jean Friedberg, was almost ludicrously the exact visual opposite of this husky six-footer: a small, dark-haired young woman, newly graduated from some Eastern college, with a dry, sharp wit and quick intelligence that complemented Miss Greenebaum's and contributed to the classroom ambience. (Much later, when Harry and I were married, I would be reintroduced to her as the daughter of Aline Friedberg, one of Harry's mother's close friends; we both remembered that delightful eighth-grade year.

271

In later years she and her husband, Sam Block, would become friends and neighbors in Hyde Park.)

We could never figure out how Miss Greenebaum managed to read our papers or read much of anything, as she had to hold her nose against the page to see it. She seated us in alphabetical order so that she could quickly memorize our names. There were two of us named Jean in this class; I was Jean Stern and my name-mate was Jean Fihe, so we were at opposite ends of the room. This should have made it easy to know which one of us she was addressing, but her pale eyes wandered like fish in a tank behind the thick lenses of her glasses, and we were never sure which way she was looking. So when she called on "Jean," Jean Fihe and I would look at each other quizzically, shrug, and take a guess. Sometimes we were right and sometimes not.

Mother had taken one look at Sarah Greenebaum and pronounced her one of the homeliest creatures she'd ever seen — and a lesbian to boot. I resented her snap, superficial appraisal of a teacher I respected and admired. I decided that I wanted to be an eighth-grade teacher like Miss Greenebaum when I grew up; I wanted to communicate to other thirteen-year-olds the sense of self-respect, the confidence, and the social conscience that she had instilled in me. I wanted to be like her and make other poor misfit children of that age feel approved of: understood and valued and respected as People.

That was the year that Mayme Abbott got me some modeling jobs. She had put Mother and me into walk-on parts in a vaudeville act at the Chicago Theater when I was little — maybe five. Then, when I was twelve or thirteen, she arranged some clothing catalogue shoots. I also modeled in a few fashion shows in the Walnut Room on the seventh floor at Marshall Field's. One of several elegant tearoom-type restaurants, this one boasted glossy dark wood paneling, and waitresses in prim black uniforms with starched white caps and matching aprons. It was especially popular with prosperous matrons who met there for lunch while watching the latest fashions for their little girls and boys be paraded before them. I had to be excused from school — often for the whole afternoon — for rehearsals and fittings, and then the actual show. So Mother would sashay into the classroom and archly announce to Miss Greenebaum that I had to be excused from class that afternoon to rehearse and have fittings for my modeling job.

I loved the modeling. I loved wearing all those stylish, smart-looking clothes, being made up, having rehearsals that laid out the winding route among the tables where the audience could get a good close look at the garments. Then I'd mince up the steps to the little platform, where I twirled around so that everyone could see each of my stylish ensembles from all sides. But Sarah Greenebaum made her stern disapproval very clear—to me, at least. What kind of values did someone live by who'd put the frivolity and narcissism of modeling ahead of schoolwork? I felt the chill of Miss Greenebaum's censure. I wondered whether Mother was seen as the culprit who thought so little of education that she'd yank me out of school for this frippery, or whether I was judged a willing participant in the rejection of the world of Ideas in favor of Vanity.

I couldn't imagine a resolution to this conflict between higher learning and prancing down the runway in the Walnut Room. I felt uncomfortable leaving school for what could be dismissed as a superficial activity, but was, in its own way, quite an education. There were my fellow models, many of them professionals, very accomplished and businesslike. Most of them were from the city's public schools; many of them knew one another. There was the exposure to (more like reinforcement of) appearances, style, how you *looked*, rather than who you *were* or what you thought about people and events in the world—more substantial stuff, more like what Darl and Daddy thought about and discussed.

Being the kind of person she was, Miss Greenebaum never "punished" me for participating in an activity for which she had little respect. And in the long run, the lasting stimulation and challenge of that school year trumped modeling. Though it fed my adolescent narcissism, that wasn't who I wanted to be. I wanted to be as good an eighth-grade teacher as Miss Greenebaum.

The angst of early adolescence, however—romantic fantasies

273

and the importance of boys and crushes—was an emotional drama she left to other sympathetic counselors to deal with. It wasn't that she didn't know or countenance that aspect of growing up; her big-heartedness and tolerance simply followed another path. Sarah was not the woman in whom an adolescent girl would have confided her romantic preoccupations.

My Aunt Evelyn was.

In eighth grade at Parker, my female classmates were all talking about their boyfriends. Some had boyfriends to whom they wrote letters, some had boyfriends closer to home. I don't think my classmates had parental consent to go out on dates very much yet, if at all, but there must've been a lot of flirting and a lot of comparing notes about the mysteries of boys. I felt dumpy and left out. No boy was writing to *me* or telephoning *me*.

I wrote to Aunt Evelyn and confided to her my feelings of terrible inadequacy, something I could never have done with Mother, who would have ridiculed the whole thing. Not long after, I got a letter from "Jack Roberts" in California. Inside the envelope there were two letters, one from "Jack Roberts" and another, addressed "To Jeanie—the other is for the cats." In that one, Aunt Evelyn counseled me to be of good cheer: boyfriends would come. And don't let these girls put you down—they're probably doing a lot of empty, wishful bragging. Just show 'em the accompanying letter from the fictional Jack Roberts, you'll knock their eyes out.

So I took the letter from "Jack" to school. In it he reminisced about the good times we'd had together when I visited the previous summer, how we'd enjoyed that orange juice and all the trips to the beach, etc., etc., with a few sly references to a possible almost romantic feeling—something about the way I wrinkled my nose when I laughed. The "cats" were impressed but skeptical: it didn't sound like the girl *they* knew. I gloated— just let 'em wonder—but it was a turning point for me. Aunt Evelyn had calmed my anxiety about being attractive. Even though "Jack Roberts" was a fiction, he seemed plausible enough for me to believe in him and to realize that there might be a *real* admirer someday. More importantly, I had an adult ally who understood the tortures of adolescence and took the time to act on that understanding.

It reassured me not only about growing up, but also about adults and how you could really connect with some of them, confide in them, be respected and taken seriously by them. Evelyn was just a wonder — funny and full of empathy. Even that sleeping-porch summer, when her marriage was ending and she was so preoccupied with Bert, her analyst-lover, she'd radiated this good-humored skepticism and an embracing warmth. There was something about her wry perspective that reminded me of Sarah Greenebaum, actually. Like Sarah, she treated me as an equal — in comprehension, at least, if not in experience.

With her astringent wit, outspokenness, and progressive politics, Miss Greenebaum jarred us out of our self-involved preadolescent torpor and awakened social and political consciousness in many of us. More, she invited young members of her own family, our generation, to model and explain to us how we could get involved right now. Her nephew Peter Kuh, probably a sixteen- or seventeen-year-old high school student at that time (1936–'37), was a member of the American Student Union, a liberal-left group of students. He spoke to our class about student participation in the political events of our nation. As eighth graders, we should be thinking about our responsibility as future citizens, and the ASU was organizing high school students to learn about breaking world events and America's role in them. This was going to be *our* world, Peter reminded us, so we had better start understanding and learning about it.

I was impressed with Peter's grasp of world and national politics — and with him. Afterwards I went up to him to ask about this group, which at that time was still urging the U.S. not to meddle in all that trouble in Europe, about which I knew very little. I liked being part of the effort to keep the U.S. from making a foolish mistake. (Not long after this, as World War II rumbled into our lives, that position would be exactly reversed.)

Another young ASU activist from Sarah's extended family also came to Parker that year: Peter's first cousin Alan Gottlieb, then a freshman at Harvard. Handsome, charming, and personable, he, too, spoke to us like we were equals, not little kids. It was quite refreshing. By freshman year this "rich girl from the Belden Hotel" had joined the ASU. I spent some time volunteering in the organization's downtown office, a small, untidy place, spattered with purple ink from the ditto machine, crowded with desks and stacks of leaflets and papers. I was one of those "rich peons" who stuffed envelopes and performed similar low-level jobs. There I once crossed paths with Alan Gottlieb again: I rode down in the building's elevator, all unknowing, with my future brother-in-law, and was impressed that he didn't talk down to this ink-spattered fourteen-year-old.

I liked meeting earnest, idealistic contemporaries whose orientation was nothing like mine. Certainly none of my hotel friends—not Pauline Marks, not Lolly Lurie, not Lois Fried— joined the ASU; not Mary Ann Burgoon, either. I liked the feeling of comradeship with people from other schools, mostly an array of Chicago public schools. They were the sons and daughters of dedicated intellectual radicals, many of whom were either associated with the labor movement or were academics. It was my first exposure to my public-school contemporaries, one of whom, Jessie Polachek, a lifelong political radical, became an acquaintance all over again when she married activist Dr. Quentin Young and we were neighbors in Hyde Park-Kenwood, both herding our children to the local public school.

Though she may have had inner doubts about the sincerity or permanence of my commitment to liberal and radical causes, Sarah Greenebaum encouraged and supported my efforts. She was positive, not skeptical, affirmative, warm, and humane, full of zest for life. During that time Peter and I dated sporadically. We were mostly just friends, but that friendship not only introduced me to the ASU, it also brought me to his sister, Esther.

At the end of the school year Miss Greenebaum gave her summer address to any of us who wanted to write to her: Menemsha, Martha's Vineyard, Massachusetts. I had never heard of Martha's Vineyard, and "Menemsha" seemed such an odd, exotic name for a place, an Indian name, no doubt. Little did I know that Menemsha would play a profoundly life-changing role in my world—or that Miss Sarah Greenebaum would become my cherished relative through marriage. Her sister, Charlotte, was married to Harry's maternal uncle, Edwin Kuh.

36

The transition from grade school to high school at Francis Parker was not a major event: you just went from eighth grade to ninth grade, no parties, no diplomas like our public school age-mates. Academically, high school was almost an anticlimax. A few teachers stand out, a few subjects: Miss Lura T. Smith taught Latin in a workmanlike and practical way. I quit after second year (up to and including Julius Caesar) and have always been sorry I didn't listen to Miss Smith, who urged me to continue, holding out Virgil as the gift I'd get if I stuck it out.

(Much later in my life, even that scant two years helped me through a challenging project at the Newberry Library, where I assembled a checklist of the library's holdings in science books printed before 1750. That project was an extension of my graduate-school work in bibliography, but it was also an archaeological dig, because I had to delve into the library's card catalog [no longer in use, but still an active research resource when I began this effort]—and most of the volumes I examined were written in Latin. The books I was interested in were classified as something other than astronomy or medicine or the biological sciences—printing history or travel or astrology— so my searching had many pathways, and even my scant and superficial memory of freshman and sophomore Latin [and a good Latin-English dictionary] helped me to figure out what some of the more obscure and indirect books were really about.)

I loved the French classes taught by Mme. Helene Richard, an imaginative, exacting teacher, a Viennese Jewish refugee, who spoke and taught impeccable French—and made us speak it as it should be spoken. Proper pronunciation was not a frivolous matter. It was the soul of the language and the culture it illuminated. Mme. Richard gave us an appreciation of all the arts, history, poetry, philosophy, and the people who made them. She brought them, vividly alive, into our schoolroom.

Chauncey Griffith, music teacher *extraordinaire* and director of the high school chorus, was another memorable personality, a revered teacher who awakened our sensory appetites for listening to—and participating in—all kinds of music. Even though I never learned to read music (having rejected piano lessons at age four or five), he let me join the chorus because I was a quick study when it came to remembering a melody, and I could carry a tune. Miss Cornish and my second-grade shame almost vanished; Mr. Griffith's music classes gave us the thrilling experience of singing Mozart, Handel, and many others. We performed *Ballad for Americans* at Orchestra Hall (with other high school choruses); sang opera selections from *The Flying Dutchman*; Christmas music of all kinds; psalms that had been set to music, popular and folk tunes, and Mr. Griffith even tried to get me interested in opera, though that didn't take until later in my life. He was unfailingly good-natured, even with the tenors, boys who, as a group, were the most capricious (probably hapless victims of rioting hormones).

English class taught by young Mr. Ellison was enjoyable but too easy. I wrote a glowing report on Thackeray's *Vanity Fair* without ever having read it. I sort of skimmed it and wasn't too interested, but I wrote a coherent paper. Mr. Ellison gave me an A for that piece of crookedness, and then—I guess it was adolescent egotism, tinged with hostility?—I told him what I'd done. He was angry and insulted, I think; he was much too nice a person and too good a teacher for me to have pulled such a stunt. He never really trusted me after that. We talked about it more than fifty years later (he was living in a retirement complex in Hyde Park), and I apologized for my smart-aleck behavior. I promised him that I would now read that book, not as penance but as the proper thing to do. This wasn't going to be Miss Cooke and "Little Lamb, Who Made Thee?" all over again. I did read *Vanity Fair*, and I think reading it late in my life, through the prism of my ancient cocky and foolish deception, I found it more interesting than it would have been in high school. I regret, however, that I never got to tell him that I'd finally done right by that half-century-old assignment; he died shortly after that final (cordial and forgiving—he was that sort of person) meeting.

I once had an unpleasant episode in an after-school biology lab, about which I never told anyone. Mr. Wallace Worthley, our biology teacher, a pasty man with patent-leather hair and a wee pencil moustache, tried to lay hold of me for purposes that instinct told me were prurient at the least. He pursued me around the big square slate-topped lab tables with their Bunsen burners and glass retorts, saying something unintelligible, until I got to the door of the lab and escaped. I was frightened, angry, ashamed: angry at him for not being the respected teacher I thought he was, ashamed wondering if I had done something, acted in some way to bring this on—which I learned later is a common response to sexual harassment. I stayed away from after-school labs from then on, and lost interest in biology until I got to college. Mr. Worthley joined Miss Cooke in that exclusive group of teachers assiduously to be avoided.

There was one other.

Miss Hazel Cornell, teacher of social studies (statuesque, commanding, elegant), stands out as the sourest memory of my student-teacher relationships at Parker. Several episodes contributed to our mutual antagonism. We got off on the wrong foot when, in our introductory class freshman year, she read my name as she took attendance and asked, "Are you Darlene's sister?"

"Yes," I replied. Perhaps things would've gone better if I'd said, "Yes, Miss Cornell." Did that curt response seem rude, boorish?

"I hope you will be as fine as student as she was," our teacher effused.

That was It. I thought to myself, "You're Out, lady." Miss Cornell's remark had fired my competitive rebelliousness, the Kid Sister syndrome from which I had always suffered at Parker, trailing in the starry wake of Darl: poet, conscientious pupil, brilliant student, A-1 cooperator and participator. I'd *never* be as insightful and articulate, as accomplished in all things academic as she was. So I was resentful right off the bat.

I remember only snatches of what we studied under Miss Cornell's cold, watchful, blue-eyed gaze. I know we studied American history, but I was totally bored by the pieties of the Founding Fathers according to Miss Cornell. My mind tended to wander; I fidgeted a lot. I paid only perfunctory attention to classroom protocol, and didn't participate in class discussions (out of character for me, the perpetual showoff), passing the time by doodling in the margins of my textbooks and notebooks.

It was in her social studies class that I nursed my first infant hangover. I had gone on an after-school date with George Rothschild, a witty and entertaining person I had met through Peter Kuh. And although I was certainly under legal drinking age, we drank champagne (to celebrate? What?). It was dangerously pleasant to drink. I'd left my schoolbooks in George's car, and when our revels were ended and George drove me home, he must have slipped a little note into my history book. In Social Studies class the next morning I found the following bit of wisdom: "He whose thirst is never sated wakes the morrow dehydrated." How apt! I had been suffering all morning from a persistent thirst. Now I knew why. That bit of doggerel wisdom made me laugh out loud, a breach of classroom etiquette, especially in righteous Miss Cornell's classroom. Earning an icily disapproving look from her, I reinforced her unambiguous conviction that I was both academically and morally inferior to the lovely Darlene.

At least I did our writing assignments (I wasn't completely self-destructive), but I sidestepped Miss Cornell's meticulously prepared list of topics, coming up with ones of my own that were offbeat but relevant enough that she'd have to accept them. My persistent defiance evidently wore her down. (No thanks to Miss Cornell, I eventually discovered the challenge and importance of American history, and came to admire those of our friends, lawyers, politicians, and academics who always carried a much-thumbed copy of the Declaration of Independence and the U. S. Constitution in their pocket.)

Any possibility of a rehabilitation in my standing with Miss Cornell received the *coup de grâce* when her sister overheard Lawrence (yes, dear, good Lawrence) and me gossiping about Parker on a public bus. We were returning from a Friday afternoon concert at Orchestra Hall on a late, already-dark winter afternoon, and though it was rush hour, we were sitting together chatting amiably about boring school, tiresome teachers — by name! — and similar confidential topics. When Margo Faust, an older schoolmate, turned up on the bus and stood beside us, Lawrence offered her his seat, which she declined. The three of us continued our critical assessment of the school, details of which I no longer remember.

The following Monday's Social Studies class began with Miss Cornell announcing, "I regret to tell you that a terrible breach of propriety, good manners, and common sense occurred last week. My sister overheard two students who are in this classroom . . . " My blood ran cold, my palms got sweaty: it was like being nailed by the Inquisition. I didn't dare look at Lawrence because I was sure he would be terribly upset, too, and I was afraid that my composure would crumble. My face felt pale and bloodless, my lips icy cold. "I hope that the miscreants will come forward and confess publicly, before this class, their regrettable performance. I know who they are, and they have disgraced not only themselves but our school."

She then described the conversation between Lawrence and me in considerable detail: "Two Parker students, seated in a public conveyance, were talking loudly about our school in unflattering and very specific terms. They discussed people — *by name* — and didn't hesitate to criticize, in the most personal way, some faculty members as well as other students. My sister was sitting right behind them and heard every word." Miss Cornell continued her bill of particulars. "As if that weren't shameful enough, another schoolmate came and stood beside them. Though she was older, no attempt was made to show her the common courtesy of offering her a seat." I was really angry at that; this snoop of a sister didn't have the right to accuse Lawrence of a lapse of which he wasn't guilty. I, however, deserved her accusations, having dragged our school's name through the mud in public, bad-mouthing people by name. All of that was my terrible burden of sin, but Lawrence was innocent as a lamb. He was also much more nonchalant than I about the whole thing.

Miss Cornell concluded her scalding account—finally, "As a matter of honor and to demonstrate contrition, the guilty pair should come to my office and confess. I cannot devise a punishment more painful than the anguish of their own consciences, but they must make a clean breast of this as a way of assuring me that such a serious breach of respect for their school and its members will never be repeated." I sat through the class in fear and misery, bowels twisting, heart pounding. All those blithe unguarded remarks we'd made, which seemed so amusing and harmless then, weren't intended to be overheard by a spy and then paraded before our scandalized classmates.

I dashed up to Lawrence as soon as the class ended. "We've got to go right to her office and confess," I urged in a shaky, terrified voice.

"Oh, I don't know," he replied calmly, "It wasn't a capital offense, and she already knows it was us, so why bother going there to be scolded for something as trivial as this? Calm down, her sister had no business being such a busybody." Lawrence obviously had an easygoing, rational temperament and a better sense of proportion than I did. In the end, however, I prevailed, and the two of us faced the music with Miss Cornell, who turned the psychological thumbscrews as tightly as possible. But Lawrence's good-natured and steadying influence enabled me to be composed, polite, and monosyllabic, not one of those emotional Jews. I'd already branded myself a Loud Jew by being overheard on the bus. In spite of her partiality to Darlene (a *good* Jew), I felt that Miss Cornell was an anti-Semite—an impression that would be confirmed by my final experience with her in senior year.

37

At the end of freshman year of high school, I was at loose ends; a long, empty summer stretched out before me. My friend Jackie Sherman gave me the hard sell about how much I'd love Camp Meenagha, in Fish Creek, Wisconsin. She said she was my pal and she'd introduce me to people. Though I was probably too old to be a first-time camper, Jackie made it sound like she'd be my mentor and we'd have a great time. So I signed on.

Mother and Daddy were probably relieved that I wouldn't be hanging around the hotel all summer, not having much of anything to do. (It never occurred to them—or me—to look for some sort of volunteer work, or to take a summer art class.) Jackie and I took the train to Fish Creek, and as soon as we got there, she ran off to greet all her pals from the previous summer, ditching me as though I didn't exist. I scarcely saw her for the rest of the summer. Someone must have taken me in hand and shown me around. I was jolted by the primitive conditions. The cabins were cramped, made of raw wood, and smelled of mildew. The toilets were semi-public, a long row of outhouse-type holes: no private little stalls. I was appalled. The showers were also open to the world—it was all women, after all—but nothing like my bathroom at the Belden Hotel! The camp was run by Mrs. Clark, a Christian Scientist, which meant you didn't get sick.

I was miserable, wouldn't comb my wild hair, didn't want to have anything to do with anyone. We were not allowed to telephone home; we were allowed one phone call a month, or some such impossibly long interval, and then we were forbidden to complain about any infirmities, especially homesickness. It was my first away-from-home experience and showed every sign of being a spectacular failure. But my parents, who had had to sign me up for two irrevocable months, managed to make it necessary for me to come back to Chicago to see the orthodontist (!) and have the braces on my teeth adjusted. This was something of a put-up job, but it was the only way to get me away from the incarceration of picturesque Door County. I'd been bombarding my parents with letters pleading desperately to get me out of this hellhole of a camp. I was crashing, going down in flames! But they were advised by Mother's shrink—she had begun treatment with a well-known Chicago psychoanalyst—to make me stick it out. Character-building, he said.

So my plan to revolt once I got home flopped; I was bundled onto the train and sent back to camp. I actually had a better time that second month, felt less like an alien, began to enjoy it, even developed a sort of fondness for those toilets that didn't flush— their silence seemed appropriately bucolic. The loud snorting of city toilets seemed vulgar and exhibitionistic by contrast. I even quit hating the guy who played the bagpipes as our morning wake-up. He also taught sailing, and I loved that, even before I knew Martha's Vineyard, or Harry. Though I knew camp life was not for me, the overnight canoe trip was another marvelous experience for this city girl whose parents' notion of the Great Outdoors was suburban Glencoe. Lying on the cool damp earth and being drowned in stars, feeling the silky water sliding under the canoe as we paddled silently around the lake, and hiking in the woods, eating over a campfire, were all new to me. I don't think I saw my erstwhile mentor Jackie twice the entire summer, but the way things turned out, I made other friends and Jackie didn't matter to me anymore. It ended our close friendship, however.

Not a high point in my life. But I had unlocked the emotional handcuffs that had kept me at the Belden Hotel, Lincoln Park, and the zoo through some earlier summers of solitude and boredom, opening the door for my first, fateful trip to Martha's Vineyard the following summer.

Meanwhile, I endured the most inappropriate aspect of sharing a small—really intimate—space with my older sister.

Naturally, as a twenty-year-old college student, Darlene attracted a coterie of boyfriends. I knew the roster of her swains—who was preferred, who were "one-time Charlies." Although she wasn't a confiding kind of person, she'd come back from a date and tell me about the guy she'd gone out with, and I knew what she thought of each of them, which ones she found attractive, which ones were duds, like poor hapless Edgar Greenebaum, who had nothing much to recommend him besides his impeccable German-Jewish pedigree and his ritzy address on Lakeview Avenue. Joe Wolfson was a handsome dog, but dumb as a stone. Chuck Levy was good-looking but irredeemably wild. There were many others whose names, fortunately for them, I have forgotten.

In our mistake of an "apartment," her only place for entertaining callers, if she didn't want to traverse Mother and Daddy's "bedroom-library" to get to the dismal and unfriendly "living room," was our bedroom, which was not designed for sitting and chatting. The only "sitting" space in it was the bed. So, not to be deterred, Darl entertained her most select swains on—or in?—her bed, across the narrow aisle from mine, while I tried to sleep four feet away.

I didn't like being an uncomfortable, though transfixed, witness to this part of her "romantic" life. I'd pull the covers over my head in a vain effort to muffle the rustlings, whisperings, gigglings, sighs, bursts of laughter, occasional whoops—the whole orchestration from flirtation to courtship, which both embarrassed and enticed me, and gave me uncharacteristic insomnia. If I couldn't sleep, I tried to avoid paying attention.

Only a favored few were admitted to the "sanctum sanctorum" of our bedroom. Irv Soboroff, a tall, handsome fellow, kind and mannerly but dull, was one who spent a good deal of time there in the dark with her. There was also Chuck Levy; maybe one or two others I don't remember; and then, somewhat later, along came Berney Geis, who became the runaway favorite.

The trouble was that Berney had a close bachelor friend

and workmate, Abe Blinder, who trailed him like Mary's Little Lamb. While Berney and Darl whispered, giggled, cooed, kissed, and otherwise disported themselves on her bed, Abe wandered, lonely as a cloud, with nothing to do. I tried or pretended to sleep, but once when he noticed that I was awake, he sat on the edge of my bed and started talking to me. I was a little uncomfortable about him sitting on my bed, and then he tried to stroke my hand and take hold of it. Next thing I knew, he just climbed into my bed with me!

At fourteen, I was both furious and frightened. I knew I had to act decisively. I remembered the bellboy at the Moraine. Berney and Darl were oblivious as I kicked, scratched, and pushed Abe, got him out of the bed, and hissed to him to clear out of our room or I'd make big trouble. When I told Darl about it the next day, I asked her to keep Abe out of our room and out of my bed. I had some leverage: I wasn't going to tell Mother anything about what was going on at night in our room, unless . . . unless Darl didn't intercede for me and get rid of him. She couldn't think I wanted him as my sexual tutor, this "older man," could she? To give her the benefit of the doubt, considering how nuts she was about Berney, I think she was so wrapped up in him that she had no idea where Abe was or what he was up to. At any rate, Abe was not invited back, and I must have become a more determined sleeper, because I neither heard nor interfered with the lovebirds after that.

Another sometime client of my father's was Léonide Massine, principal dancer and a choreographer for the Ballets Russes de Monte Carlo. He never came to our house, wasn't a familiar like Nathan or even Volodya, but Daddy's role made our family insiders of a sort, and the four of us went regularly to the ballet. Darl and I would abandon ourselves to the multisensory magic of this art form: the sinuous bodies, captivating music, and fairy-tale narrative. Spellbound, we'd grip the armrests of the theater seats and be carried away to an exotic, perfumed world of unearthly beauty. I was always transported by a well-executed ballet: the romance of the stories and the interaction of music and movement, of drama, lavish costumes, and the painterly beauty of stage sets created by such luminaries as Picasso and Jean Cocteau.

But all my years of dance training left me with no illusions about the unseen parts. I understood Degas's pastels from the toes of my sympathetically aching feet to the arch of the neck and the winglike extension of arms, hands, and fingers. I was still taking ballet and other kinds of dance from Mayme Abbott. Though I was modestly proficient, I lacked (among other qualities) the motivation and obsessive dedication that life as a dance professional demands. But knowing the technical aspects of dance, the steps and positions, intensified my respect for dancers whose mechanics were seamlessly welded to their emotional and musical insight.

Daddy would take me backstage at the Auditorium Theater, and there, watching Massine prowl the shadows of this fiefdom of his like an alpha male black panther, I developed a scalding, overwhelming crush on him. I don't think I ever spoke a word to him—I was overcome by his animal presence. He had a silky dark smoothness, so lithe and compact and muscular, his feline power and grace quite undid me.

Protected by the bustle backstage, transfixed and gluttonously feeding my fantasies, I'd watch parts of various ballets—*Les Sylphides*; *Petrouchka*; *Choreartium* (set to the music of Brahms's Fourth Symphony); *Swan Lake*; *La Boutique Fantasque*; *L'Après-Midi d'une Faune*; *Firebird*, *The Rite of Spring*—and all the impressions and sensations I absorbed were folded into watching the performance as part of the theater audience. I'd observe the dancers waiting in the wings for their cues, scratching themselves, grunting like oxen; I'd marvel at how these flat-footed workers could be transformed into lighter-than-air, glittering butterflies or birds as soon as they stepped (or leapt) across the dividing line between the dark, cavernous backstage and the brilliance and high-tension glory of the footlights. It seemed that the music, the lights, the audience, banished all but the affinity of their bodies for the ballet; the music shot through them like an arrow, lifting them, seemingly weightless, skyward. The excruciatingly demanding physical work they sweated and panted through was never visible— until they came offstage.

I'd watch ballerinas, so graceful onstage, swathed in their tulle skirts, every gorgeous mannered gesture speaking of perfect beauty; then offstage they'd clump heavily into the wings on their flatfooted toe shoes, sweaty and exhausted, as though they'd been scrubbing floors. Mayme Abbott referred to some of those women as "cows," as hard to get unglued from the floor as a block of stone, but you never saw that from in front of the footlights. I shamelessly ogled the male dancers, as, like steel springs uncoiling, they flew in impossibly high arcs into the air, or lifted one of those ballerinas as though she were a feather. Then I'd watch the men slump offstage, as drenched and weary as day laborers.

I don't remember Massine ever looking like that, however. He seemed to my dazzled eyes to be tireless, to have an almost unearthly power, both physical and emotional. I'd hold my breath as his body shot into one of those prodigious leaps, his muscles moving like pistons beneath the taut sheen of his skin; I'd melt into rapture watching him radiate erotic power as he lifted one of his ballerina partners into an effortless airborne arabesque. His controlled power, ferocity, and sensuality were hypnotic. Being backstage was a rich source of raw material for my fantasy life, with Massine the principal hero, deliverer, partner, and—dared I imagine it?—lover.

Besides bringing musicians and dancers into his professional life, Oscar Stern was also one of the legal counsels for the Arts Club of Chicago while Mrs. Rue Winterbotham Shaw, wife of Alfred Shaw, an eminent Chicago architect, was its president. The Club had been founded in 1916 to promote and support contemporary art and artists; its members included connoisseurs, collectors, and patrons of most aspects of the arts and literature, as well as painters and sculptors, architects, musicians, composers, actors, and writers. My father respected and admired Mrs. Shaw; they had a collegial relationship, working together on legal matters for the club, such as negotiating the lease when the Arts Club moved from the Wrigley Building to Ontario Street.

Both of my parents loved the Arts Club: Daddy for its wonderful collection of artworks, its musical and cultural programs, its cultivated atmosphere; Mother appreciated the elegance and discriminating taste exhibited throughout, and the club gave her the opportunity to get dolled up—understatedly, of course, like a true aristocrat—and to impress her nonmember friends with its elegance, its old-money clubbiness, its discreet snobbery. She loved having lunch there, served in the early days by a corps of Scandinavian men in black tie (still the "uniform" of the waitstaff, who are now multiracial and both male and female). Meticulous attention to all aspects of presentation, menu selection, and service was, and still is, an Arts Club "tradition."

Though she relished its air of intimate self-assurance, Mother never felt really at home in the club's milieu. Daddy, on the other hand, basked in its ambience as though he'd been born to it. After all, he practiced law in a highly respected, predominantly Gentile law firm, and his clients included a few Chicago socialites, many of whom were fellow Arts Club members, and some of whom became close personal friends. One I remember warmly for his hospitality—and his daughters (about my age: we had pleasant times as playmates)—was Elmer Stevens, a member of the aristocratic dynasty that owned and operated Charles A. Stevens Department Store on State Street, and a dear close friend and client. We visited them at least once at his summer home in Lake Delavan, Wisconsin, over Mother's protests. And there was Mrs. Charles Goodspeed ("Bobbsey" to her friends), a high-society philanthropist and member of the city's cultural elite for whom Daddy did legal work.

At the age of fourteen or fifteen, when I was old enough to go to the Arts Club, I delighted in the whole experience: the art, the general ambience, the delicious food. An Alexander Calder mobile, a fanciful tree, stands at the foot of the staircase (designed by Mies Van der Rohe and moved from the Club's previous location to the present structure). At the entrance to the second-floor dining room, seated on pedestals, three Ming goddesses gaze down on the lunchtime activity, casting a spell of serenity over the diners. Across from the dining room is the salon, where objects and paintings from the Club's collection are on view. For many years (until it was sold to the Art Institute) an Isamu Noguchi sculpture stood sentinel near the salon entrance. Darl and I both loved the Arts Club, for lunch and for its variety of programs and exhibits.

Mother never lived down the taint of her ghetto childhood, however. The gracious milieu that now surrounded her was only a flimsy curtain: the West Side ghetto kid with dirty fingernails who ate at a newspaper-covered kitchen table was still there, ready to make an unscripted appearance. I had to remind myself that when she was growing up, their Gentile customers and neighbors had remained "the other," to be charmed and cheated; as for the charitable matrons of Hull House, her mother had done her level best to instill mistrust. As an adolescent, despite her dreams of college, Anne had been most comfortable with her "own kind," a bunch of happy-go-lucky "wild" boys and flirtatious, provocative girls who pretended to be demure. Like my mother, many of those girls had settled into a married life whose pursuits, as she described them to me, seemed aimless and superficial. They formed a closed social circle of Jewish women whose sole ambition was to be ornaments for their tough, opportunistic husbands, who'd clawed their way out of ghetto poverty to become extraordinary financial successes. These women enjoyed a work-free existence of stunning triviality and idleness which, even as she shopped, gossiped, and played mah jongg with them, left my mother dissatisfied, bored, restless, and depressed.

It was always the college-educated who made her especially insecure, and if they happened to be *goyim* as well, her charm and animation deserted her and she became silent, almost sullen. She envied their suave self-assurance, their air of being "to the manor born," and it seemed to her that no amount of money gave you totally welcoming and uncritical entrée into that exclusive group. Being a Jew exposed you to prejudice, no matter how adroitly you aped the Gentile lifestyle and mannerisms. You could change your name, get your nose "fixed," give money in the "right" places; that Jew identity was as indelible as your blood type. In the grip of such an attitude, she imprisoned her imagination within a self-imposed emotional ghetto whose constraints hobbled the inner artist, the rebel, the impetuous explorer who fought, but failed, to find expression in her life.

Darl and I both knew (Mother told us) about Francis Parker's Jewish quota. Darl, ever the protective big sister, hadn't seemed to notice much anti-Semitism in the school, and she ignored Mother's morbid fixation on it. Perhaps Darl didn't experience it (which I doubt). It's likelier that she had assumed our father's equanimity on the subject, while I may have been more exposed to Mother's lurid stories about episodes of anti-Jewish prejudice. She saw it all around us, asserting that her second sight enabled her to sniff it out no matter how smoothly disguised or craftily concealed it was. You always had to be on your guard, watching for that telltale slip that, she told me, even your best (Gentile) "friend" might inadvertently make, and which revealed to you their REAL attitude. So I went around feeling not only vulnerable for myself, but also as though I had to defend and protect Mother from her own mistrust of so much of the human race. I wanted to convince her that she had a distorted and mistaken belief that any sniffy turndown (for instance, if you couldn't get a table in an elegant restaurant) had its roots in the rampant anti-Semitism that surrounded us.

Still, she reminded me, overtly as well as by heavy innuendo, that I was different from my schoolmates because I was Jewish. Any slight, real or imagined, happened because I was Jewish. I half believed this—there were always little snippets of circumstantial evidence that you couldn't overlook. I didn't go to the debut parties, to the Fortnightly Club, didn't spend lazy summer Saturdays at the Saddle and Cycle Club. I never visited most of my schoolmates at their vacation homes, and we didn't go to the same summer camps. I wasn't—and would never be—just like Sally Mitchell, Mary Cornelia Aldis, George Goddard, Frank Simpson, and the rest of my classmates.

A boy named Fred Heuchling had entered Parker freshman

year who, not immediately, not suddenly, but gradually, beginning in sophomore year, became a full-blown crush. When I confided my swooning fixation on Fred to Mother I got a predictable response: "No Gentile is going to look at you," she announced. Peter Kuh might have been more her speed—a German Jew from the North Shore. I liked Peter, and was flattered that this "older" boy had asked me to go out with him, but he inspired little more than pleasantly friendly feelings in me. His blueblood bona fides, however, would help sway Mother to let me visit him on Martha's Vineyard the summer after junior year, 1940—a life-changing stroke of fate that, unknown to me then, would set the entire course of my future.

38

In 1939, we finally decamped from the Belden Hotel, and for the first time since I was born, Darlene and I had our own bedrooms. I found it lonesome: no more giggling at night in our beds. On the other hand, no more pretending to sleep through the goings-on in the other bed.

Darl had graduated from Northwestern, Magna cum Laude in English. She was now twenty-two, with old maid-hood closing in, and Mother may still have been hoping that someone more "aristocratic" would appear on the scene to sweep her off her feet and away from her favorite swain, Bernard Geis. Berney seemed shy and uncommunicative—though not with Darl—and I now realize it was because he was uncomfortable around Mother, who had immediately sensed a romantic liaison of which she didn't approve, to put it mildly. What did Darl see in him, a nobody with no pedigree, an undistinguished putz, whose father was a bartender or a bookie or some sort of low-life?

Since appearances were everything, if not the only thing, it was determined that we should move into a more imposing apartment. Not in a hotel, but a "regular apartment," which meant Mother would have to "go into housekeeping," which meant having to have her own linens, and someone to launder them; having responsibility for all the little details of life in a *home*: changing the light bulbs, finding a handyman when things break, having someone to clean and scrub floors, having a completely furnished (by you, not the hotel) kitchen, having your own beds, tables, chairs, etc., not hotel stuff that you chivvied them into upholstering and maintaining for you. It was going to be Durance Vile for Mother, but if it got Darl a good match, it would all be worth it.

We moved into an elegant penthouse apartment at 70 East Cedar Street, in a lovely building with liveried staff, wood-paneled elevators and lobby, an attached garage, and, of course, a doorman. What it lacked in the hotel amenities we had grown up with, it compensated for in quiet elegance. Mother got an interior decorator, Dorothy Goldsmith, to help her create a veritable stage set of a dwelling—for all of us, but especially for Darlene, so she could find and marry a rising Jewish star, preferably one who had already shown his stuff by making big money. Mother fought every stick of furniture, every fabric, every placement of everything, from bookshelves to end tables, every color scheme, with Dorothy. Why that poor woman put up with it I cannot fathom. When the dust settled and we moved in, it was a really glamorous apartment, a tour de force. It was a duplex, with wood-paneled study, two-story living room whose French doors opened onto a narrow terrace, and dining room downstairs, three bedrooms and three baths upstairs. Such an establishment required a maid and butler, and there were servants' quarters behind the kitchen where our new help—a live-in maid, Edna, and a "houseman," her husband, William—lived.

Once we'd moved to 70 East Cedar, I missed the enforced contact with Darl that our tiny space at the Belden had imposed on us. The way it was now, days could pass without my even seeing her. She was a working girl, with a paying job as a "dress pirate" for Harry Sherman, who had a very successful string of dress shops that sold stylish cotton dresses for under $3. He and his wife Mae were our parents' close friends, and their son, Bill, and Darlene were classmates at Parker; that was how the job had come about.

It involved cruising department stores and dress shops, looking through the racks for dresses that were well-cut and flattering and that could be easily and inexpensively copied. Then she'd surreptitiously sketch the dress, noting its design and construction so that Harry's pattern makers could create the cheap knock-offs that became big sellers in the late 1930s.

She had to avoid being spotted by the store detectives or even the salespeople, because no one appreciates having their stylish designs purloined to resurface as Everywoman's housedress. Darl had a sharp eye for the dressmaker details, a good visual memory, and a quick pencil for creating accurate and readable sketches. She enjoyed the work, and the piquancy of this style-stealing was bracing and challenging. It was not a philosophical blow for social justice—the working poor were entitled to look stylish—it was business acumen: steal someone's idea and then undersell the so-and-so.

Mother was critical of Darl's job even though friends of hers and Daddy's had arranged it. She had prided herself on never having to work—a girlhood spent helping in the grocery store had hardened her resolve never to be a wage slave—and she couldn't understand why her daughters didn't want to spend our leisure days shopping or having lunch with the girls, idling up and down Michigan Avenue, checking out the latest fashions in all the department stores on State Street, maybe seeing a play or a movie. But for Darl and me there was a sort of romance in being part of the work force, swimming in the great stream of working-class America.

Her evenings Darl spent dating what seemed like regiments of suitors, who, as Mother had foreseen, were attracted almost as much to the fabulous apartment as to attractive Darlene. Mother never hesitated to express her opinion about all these boyfriends, which was generally negative. None of them was the Crown Prince of German-Jewish society, the scion of some rich, well-connected North Shore family, that Mother was hoping for. Darlene had already decisively nixed Edgar Greenebaum, who had the pedigree, but no pizzazz. Berney remained the undeniable front-runner; in fact, she had set her heart on marrying him, Mother's stratagems notwithstanding.

Now that I was compelled to observe all this scheming from the remoteness of my own room, I was no longer as involved in all the dramatic details. Those nights when Darl would come back to our room and tell me about her dates had pretty much ended. Now, I no longer even knew how late it was when she got home from a date. I missed those fascinating and educational post-mortems.

Once Darl and Berney had a serious enough fight that my future brother-in-law took me to a fancy French restaurant for lunch and plied me with wine in an effort to learn why my sister was giving him such a hard time. It had something to do with a satin Easter egg that he'd given her, about which she apparently had very negative feelings. He picked me up at school (in those days there were no restrictions on high school students leaving the campus with undocumented individuals for frivolous social reasons). So there I was in my prim navy blue serge school uniform, sashaying into Emile's, this elegant Gold Coast restaurant on Delaware Place, with this guy in a business suit who worked for *Esquire* magazine. The restaurant people, who knew Berney, probably figured it was an assignation — or so I self-importantly imagined. He didn't try to get me drunk, just wanted to loosen my tongue and ease my conscience in case I had any scruples about divulging privileged information that would reveal why their hot romance had gone off the rails. So I cheerily violated the confidentiality injunction and told him about the Easter egg: she'd expected something more — um — significant, like a bracelet, a pin . . . a ring?

The romance, which I knew had never really been in danger, was restored, no thanks to me, the only hitch being that Darl was furious with him when she learned that he had pried information out of me. I don't remember any reprisals for my lapse — maybe I really did expedite the romance, and she just couldn't admit it to Berney. In any event, the desired ring was soon forthcoming, and they began planning for a small wedding in the apartment in the spring of 1940.

Now that Darl and I were separated, I spent a lot of time alone in my pretty room. This genteel (and probably Gentile) building was inhabited by staid, patrician people, none of whom appeared to have children — a disheartening change after all those rollicking years with my confederates at the Belden. One day, out of sheer boredom, I sat on the window ledge of my

room, dangling my legs out of that fifteenth-floor window—
"to get a tan," I explained to Mother when she burst into my
room, nearly hysterical with fright. Someone in some nearby
building had seen me, and had managed in some way to alert
our building maintenance people, who then came to our door
and discreetly warned Mother. It didn't seem so terrible to me;
I don't think I had any intention of committing suicide, though
there was some kind of fascination in letting my legs go farther
and farther out into that empty sunlit space. Mother's arrival
jerked me back to reality and also to the guilty recognition that
I was flirting with danger—because I sought attention? Wanted
to make a spectacle? Was it a more adult manifestation of the
running-away-from-home impulse?

Be that as it may, I announced that *I* was going to get a summer
job at Marshall Field's. Darl was the pioneer who had shouldered
all of Mother's criticism and contempt about working, so she
put up only token resistance. Neither Mother nor I had thought
of my modeling stints at Field's as "work" in the conventional
sense. Though I'd had to get a Social Security card, I doubt I was
paid for those modeling appearances. Besides, I had no interest
in resuming that career. I yearned to be a *real* working girl—
anonymous, not a glamorous show-off. So I applied, and was
hired to be a bus girl in Marshall Field's Men's Grill, obviously
one of the least desirable jobs, and probably one with high
turnover. It required little training: "Just clear the tables, honey,
and keep the water glasses filled." I had to wear a white smock-
like uniform and a cap that covered my hair.

As someone who had never cleared the table or washed
dishes or done any of that "menial" work, I quickly realized
that dirty dishes were quite disgusting, but worse than the low-
end drudgery of the job was discovering that the uniform you
wear announces what level of treatment you are to receive from
the public. In the Men's Grill, the waitresses in their perky little
uniforms were spoken to deprecatingly but politely, maybe
discreetly flirted with, but they were serving the hungry patron
and he wanted his businessman's lunch to be promptly delivered,
so you were brisk, slyly condescending, and subtly deferential.

The bus girl was another story. She was like a conscript from the Gulag, she was a peasant, a know-nothing, a menial of the lowest order. This meant that these old lechers could reach out and grab you as you went by, carrying a tray heavy with dirty dishes, or try to put an arm around you as you reached over to fill their water glasses, or make unseemly personal remarks for the general amusement of their tablemates.

I quit at the end of that first and only day, but it is indelibly imprinted on my memory: the smug dark woodsy masculine look of the dining room—for men only. That should have been a tipoff, but this was 1939, and "for men only" was a commonplace. The manager hadn't warned me what to expect. Why should he? He didn't know that I lived at 70 East Cedar Street. He didn't know I went to the Francis Parker School. Doing that sort of job means you are doing it for the money, nothing else, and that means that you don't have a lot of choice about what sort of work will be available to you, with no training, no experience. You fend for yourself. So I did. I went back to the Marshall Field's employment office and said, "Find me something else."

I got three days' training (paid) to learn how to be a salesgirl, to write out sales checks, which, in those days, were elaborate four- or five-part documents interleaved with limp carbon paper. I had a somewhat shaky start as a salesperson. My first day on the job there was a sale in the blouse department. Mostly I went around and kept the blouses that customers had mushed around neatly refolded and stacked in orderly fashion. Just watch how shoppers will unfold something, not even look at it, and walk away; or they'll manhandle a stack of merchandise and get it all disarranged. So I was always straightening and folding; it was like Basic Training either for working in a laundry or becoming mother of a hectic brood of children who seldom folded their clothes (until they became parents themselves; there *is* justice in life, after all).

A customer approached asking me to direct her to the fitting rooms, as she wanted to try on a blouse, a treasure she'd excavated from one of the piles I kept having to refold. She was a size 44 at least, and she'd found probably the only sequin-covered size

44 blouse in our entire stock—doubtless a buyer's mistake. She emerged from the dressing room in the blouse: "How do I look, dear?" she asks me.

I have never been on the seller's side of a transaction. I am young, I go to a school that encourages integrity. I say, "Well, you might do better with something more subdued," or words to that effect.

The woman became outraged. She waddled over to the floor manager. "This little snip was impertinent to me," she announced, describing how I had talked back to her. Talked back? I'd thought she wanted an objective opinion on the suitability of her choice. I thought that was one way I was supposed to help customers. The manager fixes me with a stern, reproving glare. He apologizes profusely to the customer, explaining that I am new on the job, have no fashion know-how, that I will be appropriately disciplined for being fresh. Then he turns to me. "I'll speak to you later."

I slink off and he turns his floorwalker's charm on the lady, soothes her with "a man's opinion: the blouse looks dashing on you," and makes the sale. The satisfied customer departs. Then he gives me Lesson 1 in customer relations: If they've picked it out, they want it; if they want it, it looks fabulous on them. The customer can look in the mirror to see the whole objective truth. She's asking you for reinforcement of a position already taken, a decision already made, not a piece of fashion savvy from a sixteen-year-old.

Despite that start, I kind of liked the salesgirl job. I earned enough money to buy a record player/radio combination that closed up to become a somewhat cumbersome suitcase-size portable. I don't remember what it cost, but the 20 percent employee's discount was part of my motivation to stick with the salesgirl job. I probably pumped more money back into Marshall Field's than they ever paid me. The record player traveled with Harry and me to our first "home" in a Long Branch, New Jersey, rooming house, and we had many hours of wonderful music from that durable purchase.

39

When school resumed, I now had to be driven there, no more walking through the alley. William sometimes drove me, and sometimes I got a ride from my pal Barney Rosset (later the publisher of Grove Press). Ours was more affectionate friendship than flirtation, but I did find him bright and interesting—an affluent radical, hence very compatible. He had a flashy gray touring car convertible whose horn played "Boys and Girls Together," an apt description of the uses to which the car's back seat was often put, though not with me. His big romance was classmate Nancy Ashenhurst, and the rumor was that they were sleeping together.

Barney's father owned the Maryland Hotel, one of many modest single-room-occupancy buildings in the area, which was populated then by simple, hard-working people, with only a few raffish musicians, undercover call girls, and small-time hoodlums. Barney's dad set him up with an apartment there, where Barney could entertain his numerous girlfriends without disturbing his parents. His close friend, classmate, and fellow radical, cinematographer-to-be Haskell Wexler, was also his principal rival for Nancy's affections, and in the end Haskell triumphed and married her. Not long after, Barney had a well-publicized and stormy marriage to Joan Mitchell, who became a renowned painter. A few years younger than Barney, she was also a Parker student, younger sister of Sally, who'd been my classmate at Parker until high school, when she left to go to the less progressive but more patrician (and non-Jewish) Latin School.

Dinner with my parents at 70 East Cedar was usually just the three of us, served by William in his starched white butler's jacket in the dining room. Daddy, always impeccable in coat and tie, regaled a visibly disinterested Mother with tales of his day: Rue Shaw this and Bobbsey Goodspeed that, and Elmer Stevens and his wife Harriet up at their summer place in Lake Delavan. These college-educated *goyim* aggravated her sense of inadequacy and made her uncomfortable and insecure. Mother managed to muffle the tedium of Daddy's recitations of his workday with the aid of a few pre-dinner drinks, while Daddy adhered to his habit of downing one straight schnapps just before we sat down at table. He generally listened politely as Mother described the trivialities of her lunch with Sylvia Lurie, the envy-producing shopping trip with Blanche Greene, whose extravagance was legendary; Mayme Abbott's horror stories about her adopted son Frankie (who was a gifted liar and opportunist). The whole dinner scene with just us three seemed overplayed and boring, the conversation dull, mostly clichés and platitudes. Edna cooked, but lacked the magic touch of dear Olga, who had left us when we moved (and was finally happily married to her milkman). There was also an underlying tension: Mother waiting for Daddy to say the "wrong" thing so that she could turn on him and snarl mean and demeaning things at him, poor innocent guy.

My parents had continued the tradition of driving out to Gladys Avenue for Shabbat dinner with my Stern grandparents—a concession Mother made for Daddy's sake—but since age thirteen or so, I had balked at going there every week. Not that I had anything better to do. But I was set on boycotting the Friday dinners as often as I possibly could, which was most of the time

I have poignant memories of those Friday nights. To reach my grandparents' warm, bright rooms, we had to walk through the darkened grocery store, closed at sundown for the Sabbath, and negotiate the storeroom stacked with their grocery stocks. I remember how cold and dark and spooky that no-man's-land of a storeroom was, with the silhouettes of all the boxes and crates looking like a fallen city. The toilet was in that dark, unheated space between the store and their living quarters.

Was there a bathtub? I don't remember seeing one. Finally we'd be welcomed into the light and warmth and fragrance of their kitchen. Grandma would've worked in the store with Grandpa all day, but both of them were unfailingly cheerful when we arrived. The table, which dominated the room, was set with a white tablecloth that Grandma had ironed, two brass candlesticks, and small glasses for the Sabbath wine. Everything was immaculate and breathed order and tranquility. No wonder Daddy's dresser drawers were so tidy: this household was his neatness training. The room radiated warmth and intimacy, the happiness of having reached this Sabbath of rest, and the anticipation of breaking bread together.

Of the Sabbath itself, the prayers, the candles, I knew nothing. Bubbe and Zhazh were impressively devout, but Rose and Louis Preaskil had long since abandoned religious observance. And Oscar had left *cheder* far behind for the Standard Club. For many immigrants, becoming American also meant becoming secularized. So I didn't know that my grandparents kept a kosher house. I never understood why I couldn't have butter on my bread when we had delicious beef or chicken as a main course. No one explained. They'd just shake their heads and murmur something unintelligible. All I knew was that that little kitchen was suffused with a contented pleasure.

The contrast with 70 East Cedar provoked considerable conflict within me. Our house was elegant, our food was served with a flourish by an appropriately formal butler on gorgeous china plates; we used sparkling silverware and crystal drinking glasses. But the meals were flat: they lacked the painstaking care lavished on each dish that made Grandma's cooking—even the weird things she made, like kishkes, that I could hardly bring myself to taste—a deeply satisfying experience. (Olga's cuisine, though totally different, had had that same aura of creative attentiveness.) Grandma prepared everything with loving care that gave the food an emotional as well as a physical flavor.

Why, then, did I reject those Friday nights?

I suspect that, as my mother's puppet, I acted out a negative signal she was sending. I sensed her resentment that Oscar was treated with such loving deference, especially by Grandma, who served him first, seeing that he got all his favorites, prepared especially for him. That was not the American way, where ladies were deferred to and served before the gentlemen. Sensing Mother's boredom with this whole Old World scene, I performed what I assumed was her preference — to reject the whole Shabbat shebang out of hand. In one of Daddy's rare victories, they gave up on changing my stubborn, misguided mind. Forcing compliance from your children wasn't the American way, either.

Now I regret that I turned my back on my grandparents, two loving people who told stories about their past, and who had many more to tell.

At home, I took to eating in my room, playing folk songs (John Jacob Niles, Paul Robeson) or classical music on that record player bought and paid for with the money I'd earned on my summer job. I preferred my own company to dinner with my parents.

My memories of Darlene and Berney's small but glamorous wedding in our Cedar Street apartment, March 28, 1940, are partially eclipsed by an eruption of trauma. In the middle of the wedding, Grandpa Preaskil had some kind of psychotic episode. He suddenly got very agitated and wouldn't sit down or be quiet or hold still. Instead, he was stalking around the apartment yelling, "I am the king!" Everyone at the wedding sort of shrank back into the corners, away from him, and pretended not to notice. And so I took charge. Darl had always been Grandma's favorite, but Grandpa was my kind of person, a melancholic who loved to make things and tinker with stuff. I followed him around, trying to take his hand or get hold of his sleeve, saying to him, "Sure, your majesty, you are the king," hoping to tranquilize him a little. I remember how scared I was, but how sure that he'd listen to me and that I could help him — though I really couldn't.

I don't remember the details of how Mother handled this crisis; I think they left right away, in the midst of the wedding reception. She must have bundled him and Grandma into a cab or an ambulance and somehow gotten them packed up and onto a California-bound train, sending them back to Los Angeles, where they were living, and where they'd continue to be Aunt Evelyn's responsibility. I don't recall that Evelyn was at the wedding. It may have been one of those periods when she and Mother were on the outs. Probably the breach that occurred when Evelyn married Bert Frohman hadn't healed. Of course, Evelyn was furious because Grandpa should probably have been hospitalized in Chicago. I think he must've had a stroke or some sort of seizure; it was known that he had high blood pressure. He may have been hospitalized after they arrived in California. Just two months after that episode, in May 1940, he died. I don't think Mother went out west to help with him or with Grandma. She just dropped the responsibility.

Grandma Rose continued to live in Los Angeles under Evelyn's watchful eye until her death in 1953. To the end, she was a dynamo who enjoyed life. She played poker like a demon, and would cheerfully attempt a little small-time cheating if the opportunity presented itself. When we visited her, Harry played with her at her little kitchen table, and he caught her out. She shrugged good-naturedly and backed off the cheating. Some catch you, some don't: that's how it goes.

40

Barney Rossett graduated a year before me, in 1940, and when he was gone, life was pretty lonely.

So when Peter Kuh tossed off a possibly casual "You should come and visit me at the Vineyard sometime," I quickly took him up on it. Whether my "forwardness" unnerved him, I don't know. I just know that I had begun to find home more confinement than haven. My parents had feet of clay up to their necks. They didn't know who I was; they just had an inflexible preconception that didn't fit me anymore: Little Jeanie, the beauty with raven hair and a gorgeous smile (even though I wore braces on my teeth until just before I got married!). I wasn't programmed or perceived to be "smart"; that was Darlene's territory. The turning point for me, the year that had helped me separate from home—and especially from Mother—was that unhappy summer in Wisconsin at Camp Meenagha. After that, I felt quite grown up, and quite capable of going to Martha's Vineyard by myself as Peter's guest. My parents, I think, felt that such an aristocratic family would offer all the protection I'd need.

I traveled alone on the train, getting myself to Woods Hole and onto the ferry to Vineyard Haven, where someone from the Kuh family—not Peter, my alleged host—met me to take me to Menemsha at the other end of the island: probably Edwin (Skipper), Peter's jolly, pleasant dad, who had earned his nickname by expertly captaining a succession of sloops and catboats that had names and quirks of their own. Many years later I learned that Charlotte and Skipper were taken aback that my parents had allowed me to travel alone to visit their son, all unchaperoned, and that some of the Kuhs' friends, Buddy (Mrs.

Paul) McGhee especially, disapproved of me as an aggressive, flirtatious little nobody. In any event, no sooner had I arrived than Peter basically ditched me. He had gotten a summer job at the local gas station, and he really had little time for or romantic interest in me. In fact, he confided in me that he was seriously in love—with Frederica, whom he later married.

Why was I cocky enough to think I could spend a couple of weeks in this strange place with people I hardly knew, while the person who had more or less invited me to be his guest simply dumped me? Why wasn't I upset? Rejected? Lonely? I didn't feel self-conscious or uncomfortable, the way I'd felt at Camp Meenagha when I was ditched by Jackie Sherman. Was I, perhaps, relieved? Peter and I were really more like pals, so when he sort of evaporated, it wasn't a heartbreak situation. In fact, it was the best thing that happened to me, because it threw Peter's kid sister, Betsy (Esther), and me together. Her brother probably told her to look after me while he was at work.

Betsy and I were the same age, and we were soulmates from the very start. We loved jazz; we loved reading; we loved talking; I think there was nothing we dared not discuss. She had a fine quick wit, was gentle and unassuming, but had more iron in her backbone than was visible to the casual observer. I loved her dearly and tenderly, and she loved me. She would be my cherished and intimate friend for the rest of her too-short life.

The Kuhs had a wonderful house, really a sort of compound, at Menemsha. Lodestone was the "dormitory" in which we all slept: Kuh children and their rowdy and variegated guests. It was where we brushed our teeth, showered (cold water only in those days), and it was only casually screened from the driveway where guests and delivery people came and went. Lodestone was two stories, with male and female occupants rather casually separated (in the best Progressive School tradition): there may have been males at one end of the second floor, females at the other. And there may have been some additional sleeping space on the first floor. Beetlebung was where Skipper and Charlotte slept; it was also the living room, dining room, and kitchen for all the rest of us visitors or family members. Betsy and I would lie out on the prickly grass between Lodestone and Beetlebung and talk half the moonlit night away. We talked about everything and anything and nothing in particular: deep talk, as we watched the star-dusted sky wheel majestically over our heads.

Peter and I did make occasional trips to the beach together, including one to a private beach called Windy Gates. There the rule was "no bathing suits." Nudity was not exactly enforced, but if you wore a suit, you felt as exposed as you would have if you'd been naked at a "conventional" beach. I was sort of taken aback at first, but Peter explained that this custom had originated with the owners of this vast swath of private beach, enjoying the freedom it offered their friends and guests to swim, frolic, or sunbathe *au naturel*. Actually, it was a delicious sensation, that silky water gliding over one's skin and the all-over warmth of the sun. It didn't seem to encourage lascivious public conduct, but it satisfied some of my curiosity about human anatomy (especially male), what other people looked like in the altogether. I hadn't seen that many — or any? — naked boys or young men in my life, so this was definitely enlightening and interesting. (Seeing Peter without any clothes on did nothing to transform our friendship.) Betsy and I also made a trip or two to Windy Gates during my brief stay. You really got spoiled by the natural beauty of the place, its grass-fringed sandy cliffs that walled off this terrestrial heaven from the rest of the world.

By the time I returned to Chicago, Esther and I had shared all kinds of interests and confidences and established a rapport (or a "rappaport," as she fondly called it) that endured — a soul-nourishing friendship the memory of which sustains me still. Over that fall and winter we'd exchange overnight visits with each other on alternating weekends. One weekend she'd come into Chicago and stay with me, and we'd be up talking until all hours — I don't know about what, but it was Important! — and listening to the all-night call-in jazz program on radio station WIND. My mother was pretty relaxed about "lights out" or any of that kid stuff; she figured we weren't in trouble if we were just gabbing and listening to the radio. Then the next weekend I'd go to Highland Park and stay with Betsy. There we had to be a bit more circumspect: no giggling, and we'd have to listen to the jazz program with the sound almost muted so as not to—ahem—disturb the sleepers. We'd still manage to call in our regular requests to the disc jockey for arcane numbers by Muggsy Spanier, Sidney Bechet, Louis Armstrong, Jack Teagarden, Earl (Fatha) Hines, and other jazz luminaries, to be played in honor of "the Chilmark Mob"—which was just the two of us.

Out in Indiana Harbor (I later learned), where he was then working at Inland Steel, or from his rented room at the Hyde Park Y on 53rd Street, Harry Gottlieb, listening to the same show, would hear "the Chilmark Mob" and wonder if it was his cousin Betsy.

During the week between visits, Betsy and I would continue our long, dreamy, stream-of-consciousness talks on the phone between Highland Park and Chicago. Long distance was expensive, and Betsy's mother—and mine, to a lesser extent—got exercised over our thoughtless extravagance; Charlotte Kuh phoned Mother and suggested firmly that calls be limited to five or ten minutes, ample time to transact whatever matters Betsy and I had to discuss.

I think I made more visits to Highland Park than Betsy did to Chicago. Was there hesitation on Charlotte's part because we lived in the city, not in the suburbs? Or was it that I seemed altogether too flighty and spontaneous, not properly controlled by my parents, whose "breeding" and familiarity with etiquette may also have been open to question? (My mother was ready to haul out the old Eastern European vs. German Jew refrain.) It took Charlotte a while to warm up to me. Even after she and Eddie realized that I wasn't a complete, headstrong nut case, she wasn't so sure about my family and whether we'd be adequately "supervised." But our behavior was exemplary . . . with one exception.

While my folks took their annual two- or three-week winter vacation to Palm Springs, William and Edna provided easygoing oversight—a kind of surveillance-free holiday that was a vacation for me, too. That winter, while Mother and Daddy enjoyed their Palm Springs holiday, Betsy was allowed to spend the night even though my parents were away. Charlotte, arbiter of decorum, was assured that William and Edna were the souls of propriety, and there would be adequate—and sustained—supervision of the two of us. Betsy and I dutifully presented the Kuhs with our agenda, a much-anticipated and worthy one: we were going downtown to see Walt Disney's *Fantasia*, which had just opened. Then we'd dine at home and spend a quiet evening together. With an approving nod to our new status as autonomous adults, the Kuhs invited us to lunch at the Tavern Club (an understatedly elite Chicago dining and cultural club) the next day.

We headed for the Loop on that sunny winter afternoon to see the much-heralded Disney full-length animated movie. Set to assorted pieces of classical music ("The Sorcerer's Apprentice" and "The Rite of Spring," among others), it was an exciting experience, the music and animation mostly a harmonious pairing. Edna had prepared the dinner of my choice (lamb chops, spinach, baked potato), and we were to dine in high style, just the two of us, with all the silver, crystal, and formal accoutrements that were our usual family dinner style, and to which Betsy was no stranger.

William helped us off with our coats when we got home, pink-cheeked and frost-nipped, and asked us whether we wanted anything to drink. Now, Mother had warned me, "If you want to drink, don't do it in public or outside of this house." Would I have thought about drinking at all if she hadn't brought it up? She'd evidently given William (a teetotaling ex-bartender) the OK to serve me on request.

What got into me? Showing off for Betsy, whose parents drank socially but abstemiously and would never have offered alcohol to underage kids like us? "How about a martini for each of us, please, William?" He never cracked a smile, just went off to start us on the road to perdition. I figured we'd get the real Mc Coy from good old William, though I had no basis for comparison as I'd never had a martini.

He mixed us a very potent frosted shaker full, pouring it with a flourish over the olive that seemed to eye us balefully from the bottom of each glass. At first it tasted awful, sort of like perfume, but after the first few sips had numbed our taste buds, it became mellower. We got quite overwhelmingly drunk; we must have felt it incumbent on us to consume that whole wicked shaker full. We never made it.

We got kind of blurrily tired of martinis after a while and made our way in to dinner. Trying to focus on the food as it rose and fell in waves on the plate or to spear either the spinach or the lamb chop with my fork as it kept greasily undulating before me suddenly made eating dinner seem like a bad idea. We repaired to the cozy little wood-paneled library, a more congenial place to try to sober up than our cavernous formal living room—and besides, it had an adjacent bathroom. Betsy tried hard to be dignified, sit up straight, and not keel over and pass out. She actually made it back to the kitchen and asked Edna for coffee. Perhaps that would sober us up enough to make it upstairs to bed. We yearned to lie down on the cool comfort of crisp sheets where maybe everything would stop spinning and bucking and weaving.

Next thing I know, Betsy is leaning over me with a cup of steaming coffee, but, her balance being precarious, she accidentally slopped the scalding liquid on my arm. That pain gave me a brief moment of sobriety, during which I realized that we'd better get upstairs to bed in my parents' twin-bedded room, where we were sleeping in their absence. I wasn't able to stand up, the room wouldn't hold still, my legs were like rubbery logs; I felt far away from everything, including myself. There was a dim rippled sighting of William and Edna standing in the shadow of the entrance foyer, and they appeared to be giggling discreetly. Betsy evidently made a heroic effort, got herself upstairs, and simply tumbled into bed, fully clothed. Somehow William and Edna got me to my feet, but my legs buckled. So William picked me up and proceeded to carry me upstairs. I kept insisting, "Put me down, put me down, I can walk," so at the landing halfway up, he did indeed put me down, and I crumpled into a helpless, boneless heap. I remember saying to him as he picked me up again to get me into our room, "I declare, you're just like Rhett

Butler," which was neither accurate nor tactful. He and Edna had just given us a lesson — in the safety of home and in their care — about Demon Rum. They were very discreet, never mentioning this episode to my parents — or to me.

I awoke a few times in the night to hear poor Betsy retching and gagging in the bathroom. I don't remember throwing up, though I wished I could. But it didn't seem to relieve Betsy, who was up and vomiting every couple of hours all night.

Luncheon at the Tavern Club was looming; we daren't be late, we must look fresh and well-groomed even if we felt sour and bloodshot. So we dressed gingerly, and, fortified with a few sips of coffee, we crept out into the painfully bright day. I felt as though we'd both aged visibly. Eddie and Charlotte greeted us, commenting approvingly on how grown up we seemed, grown up enough, in fact, for them to ask us if we'd like a drink. The very mention engulfed Betsy in another wave of nausea — I could see the grayish-green pallor spread over her face — as she murmured some excuse and bolted for the ladies' room. I followed at a more measured pace, as mine was more of a sympathetic reaction. We splashed, cold water on our faces and strode resolutely back into the world of trying to act ordinary. The rest of the luncheon was so pleasant that I began to feel more comfortable with these two warm and interesting people, who only *seemed* formidable — especially Charlotte.

Much later, in Charlotte's very old age, long after Eddie had died and Betsy had succumbed to cancer and both young Eddie and Peter were also gone, I'd drive out to the large, lonely apartment in Wilmette in which Charlotte spent her last years. Our real, natural affection for each other blossomed, and we'd sit and talk and hold hands. Her memory was mercifully clouded by then, but we cherished each other because we both loved Betsy. So much death and sorrow in that family: Peter married his Freddie, a brilliant, charismatic, and troubled soul. She died as a result of burns she suffered bending over a gas stove to light a cigarette, leaving two half-grown daughters, Charlotte and Audrey. Peter met and fell in love with Margaret, converted to Roman Catholicism, and went on to have many more children.

Eddie, a distinguished professor of economics at MIT who had more than one wife, was felled by cancer in the midst of his distinguished academic career.

41

In the late fall or winter of senior year, each of us had a conference about college choices with Miss Cornell and Mr. Smith, the principal who had succeeded Miss Cooke. I was commended for my excellent academic record, my participation in school events, my Parker spirit. All this, I felt, was to get me to let my guard down. I neither liked nor trusted these two, and I suspected them of collusion and unsavory motives. "With your record," they continued, "you can get admitted to whatever college you choose." I listened skeptically: What's the hook? What plan do they have for me? "However," they continued, "We recommend that you sever your connection with the American Student Union. After all, you don't want to be stereotyped as one of those Radicals."

The word *Jewish* hovered unspoken in the air between us. I felt my face flush, my heart race. I kept quiet. I had a mother who had sensitized me exquisitely to the merest hint of prejudice. I was both furious and frightened. What kind of counsel were these two going to offer me that I would trust? Miss Cornell leveled her chilly, blue-eyed gaze on me. "You could be a fine student, Jean, but you are far too interested in boys. I'd recommend an Eastern girls' school for you. Bryn Mawr would be an excellent choice, and you'd be a credit to our school, especially if, as a non-Christian student, you avoid the bad name that radical political organizations can burden you with."

I'm thinking to myself, "I hate you both, you smug, patronizing 'Christians'! What's become of our School Motto, **Everything to help and nothing to hinder,** that dear Miss Cooke (who seems like an angel compared to Mr. Smith) had us repeat every morning, along with the School Word, **Responsibility**? We don't hear either of those anymore. It's more like 'Dog Eat Dog.' So I'll be a credit to 'our' school—that's how I pick a college, which is going to have a life-shaping influence on my future? And what's wrong with being distracted by boys? Why does Miss Cornell dress like a fashion plate all the time? To stand at the blackboard before a bunch of pimply, randy adolescents and get chalk dust all over herself?" I thanked them for their "counsel" and left.

After that interview, I was disillusioned and bitter. Did these educators have any insight into their students' needs and dreams, any understanding of how to foster the development of thinking citizens? It reinforced my mother's assertion that this progressive school, with its mottoes and social conscience, was just as snobbish, narrow, and anti-Semitic as plenty of other American Protestant institutions at that time. It also undermined my already shaken self-confidence and left me without any possible choices for a college education that would be meaningful to me. This was the outcome of a meeting that was supposed to "help me decide on my future."

Being defiant and opinionated was my cover-up for bruised self-confidence. So, conspicuously ignoring their "advice," which seemed self-serving and not remotely related to my intellectual or emotional development, I chose a women's college—but not out of deference to them. I went West, as far west as I could go without falling off the edge of the Pacific coast. It was probably a disappointment to them that I didn't burnish Parker's reputation as a reliable purveyor of top students by choosing Vassar or Smith. Instead, I picked a relatively obscure school on the "wrong" coast. Actually, Scripps College in Claremont, California, had a fine humanities-oriented program, and it turned out to suit me well. It was less a reflection on the college than on the times that I left Scripps after freshman year, never to return.

This combination of passionate adolescent defiance and an effort to stand against prejudice had two positive outcomes during my last year at Parker: remaining a member of the

American Student Union and becoming friends with Timmy Osato, the school's first and (at that time) only nonwhite student. It was a friendship rather than a romance: we went to movies together and talked about the plots and the actors. He looked beyond the banal superficialities of the popular output of Hollywood and had a critical aesthetic unlike any I'd ever encountered. His family (his mother was Irish, I think, and his dad was Japanese) must have been deeply committed to the arts: they operated the Japanese Tea Garden in Jackson Park on Chicago's South Side. It exposed us Midwesterners to the subtlety and elegance of Japanese art and lifestyle, but was ahead of its time: World War II forced them to close it.

For me, at least part of Timmy's attraction was his exotic upbringing (or so it seemed to conventional me). I got a certain perverse pleasure out of defying my mother's racial prejudices and scandalizing her friends by being seen in public with this kid who not only wasn't Jewish but was also Asian. And, at that time, shorter than me. Our friendship lasted until I graduated in 1941, a few months before Pearl Harbor and America's entry into World War II. Later, I heard that Timmy served with the 442nd Infantry Regiment, the famous Japanese American regiment in WW II, and fought heroically in Italy at the Anzio Beachhead, one of several ferocious encounters in the Italian campaign.

The progressive-school atmosphere of Parker was determinedly secular and nondenominational, so any religious observance that took place at school was mostly sort of generic. Our annual Christmas "tableau," for example, illustrated the story of the birth of Jesus in a pretty toned-down bible story kind of way, not as a call to religious devotion of any particular brand. The tableau consisted of a series of scenes from the Nativity story, portrayed by students. Juniors or seniors were selected to represent the Holy Family, and the more tractable lower-school children, in diminishing order of grade level, were cast as the Three Kings and the shepherds.

As a school Big Shot, I thought surely I'd be in the

Christmas tableau either junior or senior year, even perhaps in the coveted role of the Virgin Mary. After all, I would have been THE perfect Mary—a Jewish virgin! However, I was counseled by the school's director of this production that it would be "inappropriate" for me to appear in a depiction of the Nativity. Mother's conviction that we were surrounded by anti-Semitism, implied if not overt, seemed to be vindicated once again. But why on earth would I even have *wanted* to be in that tableau? Hunger for the limelight, no matter its source or its social significance, as I see it now. At that time I was resentful of Mother and her narrow-minded attitude, though it infiltrated and infected my innermost adolescent insecurities.

Then, in senior year, when I was one of the three candidates nominated by my classmates to be voted on by the entire school for the fairy-tale role of May Queen—probably one of the loveliest honors that could be bestowed on a senior girl—I was shaken but not taken unawares by her reaction. They *had* to pick me, she maintained, despite my being a Jew, because I had no real competitors among my classmates. There were only ten or twelve girls in our class of twenty-three, but the candidates had to be pretty, have a good academic record, be involved in school activities, and generally embody the Parker spirit. Then the winning candidate was crowned on May Day, and honored by all 300 students from kindergarten through twelfth grade. May Day was an all-day romp of games, music, poetry, a picnic, and more. Mary Ann Burgoon was a candidate, and I think Mary Waller was, too. Mary Ann and I were still close chums, but Mary W. was a late arrival at the school, not entering our class until high school, which made her sort of second-rate. Besides, she was something of a slut (she was rumored to be sleeping with one of our classmates—and she *smoked!* In the spirit of full disclosure, so did I—smoke, that is). Though she was only a mediocre student, she was a knockout voluptuous blonde, which may have had something to do with her being one of the nominees.

I was elected May Queen, which both stunned and thrilled me, after eleven years of dazzled heroine worship of each spring's lovely magical May Queen. I was almost afraid to bask in the pride and pleasure that welled up in me. It didn't feel real — or legitimate, somehow — that I, a Jew, should be chosen May Queen by the whole school. I remembered my May Queen predecessors, all goddesses to be adored.

A whole collection of traditions accompanied the celebration of May Day. Mr. Merrill, our much loved (and flagrantly effeminate) English teacher — he taught all twelve grades and started us early listening to him read Shakespeare's poetry — had cobbled together a sort of verbal pastiche consisting of snippets from the Bard: "Foot it featly here and there"; "Our revels now are ended"; "Merrily, merrily shall I live now/ Under the blossom that hangs on the bough." Mother made a big to-do about "this pansy," which angered and embarrassed me. Most of the teachers and students respected and admired our dapper little Englishman whose imagination made Shakespeare's poetry part of our lives, its cadences and imagery familiar to us. With his encouragement (and occasional prodding) we'd memorize whole chunks of the plays and poetry. Mr. Merrill showed us that by memorizing passages we loved we made them ours. He had a wonderful sonorous actor's baritone, and we appreciated that he continued to read aloud to us, with his impeccable diction, even when we were grown-up seniors. He gave us a lasting gift: love, appreciation, and understanding of poetry. And his enthusiasm for the traditional Englishness of May Day, as he presented it to us, hovered over the day and its events.

The tradition included a Lord of the May (it was Bob Wright in our class) who acted as Master of Ceremonies. The Lord of the May, as it turned out, had lots more responsibilities than the queen. She just sat there smiling benignly at all the honors being showered on her. He recited most of the wonderful poetry that accompanied the activities, and at the prescribed moment, he crowned the queen. Then he called on each grade to perform whatever ceremonial presentation they'd prepared to honor her. When this portion of the program was over, he led the entire school in procession out to the East Field, where the maypole had been set up. The third graders performed the traditional maypole dance, with the participants prancing around the maypole with ribbons that their dance braided into a rainbow of colors down the pole. When all the outdoor games and performances ended, the school's bagpiper, in full regalia, led the entire school, with the Queen and Lord of the May right behind him, into Lincoln Park for a great informal picnic.

Mother's intimations about anti-Semitism didn't detract from the magic of my May Queen experience. But times were changing: I was the first Jewish May Queen. And I was also the last May Queen. That lovely little springtime tradition was abandoned after my senior year. Was it the war (World War II) that caused such frivolity to be dispensed with? Of course Mother's opinion was that rather than have another Jew walk off with that honor, they'd just throw out the whole tradition. I still wonder whether she might have been right, though reason tells me no, it *was* the war. (Furthermore, Mr. Merrill left the school not long after our class graduated.) But the May Queen ceremony was never reinstated, as far as I know. My memories of that sunny May Day are still suffused with a dreamlike quality: did this really happen to ME? Was I really the May Queen, worshipped by the school's little girls, and treated — all that fairy-tale day — with the deference and affection reserved for royalty?

Mr. Merrill also directed our senior class play, Thornton Wilder's *Our Town*. I had one of the leads, and Fred Heuchling, the classmate on whom I'd been incubating an increasingly desperate crush for the last three years, played opposite me. I had moved beyond solitary fantasies of knights on horseback coming to sweep me up and carry me away in their tender but powerful arms; I'd moved beyond the erotic daydreams featuring Massine. I was being ineluctably propelled into a flesh-and-blood contemporaneous "love." And to my dazzled eyes, Fred was a gorgeous hunk. With his shock of silky dark brown hair, high coloring (or was it just that he was always blushing when he was around me? Didn't I wish!), he looked like the comic strip character Li'l Abner, a handsome hillbilly.

I sketched him endlessly — but surreptitiously, I hoped. I wrote his initials in every shape, form, color in my schoolbooks and notebooks. Was this a magical invocation of the person? An incantatory spell I was casting? I tried, with elaborate casualness and dissimulation, to be wherever I thought he'd be — but I hoped I was inconspicuous. My obsession even inspired an early piece of biographical research, as thorough, though not as informative, as the research I'd done for my senior paper on Henri Christophe, the Black ruler of Haiti at the turn of the nineteenth century. I did learn that Fred was a Roman Catholic, which made him the epitome of the unattainable. (I wasn't aware of the religious affiliations of any of my other classmates, perhaps because they were all some variety of pallid Protestantism. I think Bob Wright's dad was a reverend of some sort, but no one made much of that — I didn't even know what denomination he belonged to.)

This had all started sophomore year, but it was when I was a senior that the obsession really possessed me. I knew that once we graduated, he'd be forever gone from my life, so there was a distinct increase in the level of desperate anxiety I suffered.

At home I'd follow Mother around, asking her over and over, "Do you think Fred likes me?" How the hell would *she* know? Besides, she had her own problems. With both her daughters growing up, conspicuously attractive and enticing (thanks to her artistry), she was now suffering a kind of Pygmalion's Regret: she'd made us stylish and we were beautiful, but worst of all we were YOUNG, just ripening sexually at the moment that she was approaching fifty and suffering the first evidence of desiccation that foreshadows "middle age." Always prone to depression, never able to accept loss — looks, money, admiration from others, sexuality (and here menopause dealt her some body blows) — she sought the help that psychoanalysis was said to provide. A treatment that she should have begun earlier in her life — some eminent German analyst had once offered to take her to Vienna to be treated (in the Freudian orbit, it was hinted), but she suspected his motives were more ulterior than altruistic, and she refused — she had finally begun, with a well-known Chicago analyst (nothing but the best), before we moved out of the Belden Hotel. So while I mooned around after her, pestering her to assure me that this high school boy who probably didn't know — and didn't want to know — that I existed, did, in fact, like me, she showed great patience and forbearance, advised, I suspect, by her analyst. She was honest, not dismissive, and said he probably liked me but I shouldn't pin my hopes on him — that Jewish-Gentile thing again. At least after her initial salvo she was less harsh and cynical, and miraculously willing to listen to my endlessly repeated litany.

That winter of senior year, when I'd just turned seventeen, desperation had made me bold. My parents were away in Palm Springs, and I had their season tickets to the Thursday night Chicago Symphony Orchestra concerts. I don't remember how I managed to invite Fred to come with me — did I ask him at school? Write him a note? Telephone him? I don't remember how we got there — did William drive us downtown? Did we take the bus? What I *do* remember is sitting beside him at that concert, arms touching (I felt the heat of him through the sleeve of his wool jacket), knees touching. In my fevered state I was oblivious to the music; my intense focus was on those electrical contact points that sent molten waves through me.

I don't remember how we got home, but he escorted me up to our apartment. William and Edna, true to form, were discreetly out of sight. Fred stepped inside the door, murmured "Thanks," and then leaned down and *kissed* me! It wasn't a long-drawn-out sort of passionate, searching kiss with a message, but it was more than a perfunctory peck. I think we embraced for an impulsive, scared but fascinated moment, but I was so overwhelmed by sex and fear of the unknown that I am not sure about the embrace. An avalanche of powerful sensations engulfed me. Then he was gone in a rush.

For weeks afterward I scarcely caught a glimpse of him. What sort of terrible Catholic guilt gripped him? I just longed to see him, something that wouldn't seem too difficult to do in a small school and a small class. But I swear, he was as elusive as a wild deer, so sightings were scarce, and when I did spot him he'd look away. No words passed between us. When my parents returned from Palm Springs a week or so after this episode, I told Mother the whole story of my delirious joy followed by dashed hopes. She pronounced it a case of anti-Semitism overwhelming his undeniable attraction to me.

But then Destiny took a hand.

42

I went to Highland Park to spend the night with my dearest friend, Betsy. It was the end of May 1941. I arrived on the North Shore Electric interurban train from Chicago, and someone from the large Kuh family, probably Peter, must have met me at the station. I walked into the Kuhs' dining room, making a conspicuous, mildly contrite entrance—I was a trifle late for dinner.

The usual weekend assemblage of eight or ten people was already seated at the long table: Betsy's mother, Charlotte, queenly and formidable at one end, and her father, twinkly Edwin, at the other; the three Kuh kids; cousins, and friends, possibly George Rothschild. It looked like a lively occasion, the festive board decked out with a centerpiece of fresh flowers, and candles in the silver candlesticks. Thomas, the dignified Black houseman, wore his starched white jacket to serve Charlotte's signature tiny canned peas, which looked woefully out of place nestled in their aristocratic silver tureen. (It always struck me as hilariously inappropriate that Charlotte would serve CANNED peas in this elegant vessel when all the rest of the food was exquisitely fresh-cooked to a turn by Thomas's wife.)

I murmured an apology and tried to slip into my seat as inconspicuously as my late arrival would allow, but the men at the table had gotten to their feet as I walked in. It wasn't a formal dinner, but this was the custom in Skipper and Charlotte's house. That's how it used to be done in those days—and men took their hats off indoors and in elevators, and you only wore a baseball cap if you were playing baseball. They'd even stand up for a seventeen-year-old girl! Well, all but one of them stood to greet me. This one young man did not stand. I was introduced to that one, the only person I hadn't known before. He was Edwin and Charlotte's beloved nephew, Betsy's adored cousin, Harry Gottlieb. He was a good-looking young man, but I was quite put off because he didn't show me the requisite deference by getting to his feet like the rest of the male diners. Such a lapse of manners seemed quite out of place.

I'd heard about Harry Gottlieb *ad nauseam*: everyone said he was wonderful, special, and on and on. So I look at him and am challenged. Mother had shown us what you do: you seduce, you flirt, you charm, you provoke—whatever it takes—but you definitely "put yourself on the map," no man gets away—unless you aren't interested in him, and even then, maybe you lasso him just to stay in practice. So I'm going to make Harry Gottlieb notice and admire me and show him that I am Someone he should stand up to greet, I'm not just some kid pal of his kid cousin, who was very dear to him.

I got sort of smart-alecky and wisecracky. Not having Mother's talent, I didn't impress Harry—"pretty girl, but young," was his assessment (I was seventeen)—and I was not particularly impressed with him, either. After all the accolades I'd heard, he was sort of quiet. To be honest, it wasn't that he didn't make much of an impression on me—it was more that I was aware I didn't make much of an impression on him.

After dinner, Betsy told me that he had just gotten out of the hospital, and was convalescing from an appendectomy. He'd sought sanctuary with his Aunt Charlotte and Uncle Eddie to avoid having to stand around at a large party his parents were having that night. So that was why he didn't stand up! I was chagrined.

Well, we're not quite through with Fred yet.

Senior year was nearly over. Nostalgia was in the air, especially for those of us who'd been classmates for twelve years. I'd loved that school, anti-Semitism or no; I'd gotten a superb education: challenging, thought-provoking, it had endowed me with lifelong curiosity, love of learning and thinking, and I'd had superb teachers. But there was still the Senior Prom, the social climax of school life, and then graduation.

Out of the blue, it seemed to me, Fred invited me to the Prom.

It was a dream come true, the fairy-tale realization of all my fantasies. Mother said it was probably just paying me back for that concert I'd invited him to. Even if it was nothing more than discharging a social obligation, how often does such a miracle happen — except in movies and romance novels? Though she'd never understood my hopeless yearnings, the pursuit of what she saw as throwing myself away on the unattainable, she understood that it was vitally important to me — the glorious culmination of years of longing for Fred. That wasn't Mother's style: she didn't pursue the impossible dream in relationships, she vamped and put out vibes and as the bright-eyed boys flocked to her provocative, musky signals, she'd look over the field and choose from among the eager supplicants: the handsomest, the cutest, the one who'd take her places. She loved to dance, to rub up against these guys until she'd feel what she described as something like a bunch of keys rubbing up against her; that was the fun she was after. Still, she understood that in my lexicon, the realization of what had appeared insubstantial, *fantasy*, was my miracle, all I'd ever desired.

A major assault would have to be made on the department stores and dress shops to find THE prom dress: not your ordinary, prissy little white thing with puffed sleeves and demure ruffles, not your tastelessly daring slinky satin, but something that would announce, "Here I Am!" Mother had undeniable style, incontestable taste, and the prom gown she found was gorgeous, not at all conventional, but it made the perfect statement: not brash, just confident. After all, she had always been my "dresser" from before I could walk on my fat little feet, and she knew her customer. The dress had a full red dotted Swiss skirt with a jaunty white piqué top, little cap sleeves, square neck, and this crisp little top set off that full skirt just perfectly. It was a classic and would still be in style today, would still turn heads. I loved it and knew I'd be the standout at the prom. (In fact, I saved that dress, and it had a second life some twelve years later, when it found its way into the box of cast-off garments that our daughters used for playing dress-up.)

So the great day of the prom finally comes. I am out in the East Field at school playing one of those pickup baseball games where you could have twelve people on a side if that many wanted to play, or only six if it was a small group, and everyone sort of rotated positions, and it was boys and girls all mixed together — the diametrical opposite of Little League. I am out in the outfield, filled with happy anticipation and trying to keep my mind on my fielding position, when Fred comes up to me.

"I can't take you to the prom tonight," he says, eyes downcast, "My sister is getting married and I have to be an usher at the wedding."

The chill of death descended on me, the sun was extinguished, the world went silent. "Oh, OK," I said. He would never, ever know how traumatized, how crushed I was.

I think he said, "I'm sorry," but I'm not sure. None of my senses seemed to be working properly. As quickly and unobtrusively as I could, I picked up my schoolbooks, left the game, and headed home. Why didn't I yell at him? Hit him? Ask him why? Say, "How COULD you?" Not in character. Did I weep? I must have, but I was mostly numb.

Mother was wonderfully compassionate and consoling. Tactfully, she didn't allude to anti-Semitism. She didn't have to. What other explanation was there? His family had put its foot down and prohibited him from taking this Jew to the prom — they'd been arguing over it for weeks, and finally the family won by exerting that final force: economic. No money for the prom, the flowers, the car, whatever. That was the scenario I invented to salve the wound. But as a practical precaution, I phoned Jackie Sherman, a junior, who I knew was going to the prom with one of my other classmates. As I told her the whole terrible story, I felt anger beginning to rise in me, and I charged her to keep an eye out for Fred and let me know if that so and so had the temerity to turn up at the prom either alone or with someone else, someone like Mary Waller, some Gentile. If he did, if he showed up, even alone, if that wedding story was just that—a story, Hell would be too good for his Catholic self. (He didn't.)

It was unreal—that whole episode. Had I dreamed that he had asked me to the prom and then abruptly (and clumsily) dumped me? Much later in my life, during the time when Harry was a mortgage banker with the real estate firm of Draper and Kramer, Fred came in to apply for a mortgage. Harry, of course, knew the story of my senior prom that never was, and as he sized up this applicant (supplicant?), he mentioned that he was married to Jean Stern, a former classmate from Francis Parker, what a coincidence, right? With characteristic tact and restraint, he never brought up the prom issue, he just thought about hiking up the interest rate on this guy's mortgage—a fantasy of sweet revenge.

Then, even later in our lives, Fred's and my paths crossed several times. There was our fiftieth high school reunion, and at least a couple of occasions when two or three classmates came to our house on Fort Myers Beach; one occasion when we met a few of them on Boca Grande, at a lovely old house one of them had rented. It must have been about 2005 when Fred and his wife Mardy retired and were living in Naples, Florida, just a few miles from us. We four had dinner together a couple of times and talked politely. The burning question about the prom seemed to swim before my eyes, but I couldn't think of a tactful, playfully casual, or Just-In-the-Interest-of History way to ask him what the hell happened, short of a medical emergency, that caused him to back out of that long-standing date. Then later I heard that his memory had gone—there were foreshadowings of that at our last encounter—and Mardy had some sort of terrible chronic ailment. So we will never see each other again, and the mystery of the prom will remain a mystery.

43

Sometime early that summer, in June or July, Peter invited me to go to a White Sox baseball game with him, on a double date with Harry Gottlieb and his date, Madge Friedman, a girl I knew from Parker, though she was older than me. I had always liked baseball — I used to listen to the radio broadcasts — but I'd never been to Comiskey Park. I was a Cubs fan, being from the North Side of the city, and Comiskey was *terra incognita*. The old Comiskey Park was a kind of industrial strength ballpark (since replaced by a bigger, less engaging one). Harry and I would both remember approximately where we sat in the stands that night: in the lower deck, on the right-field side, about halfway back. Harry even remembered who pitched and what the final score was. (Or he thought he did. Decades later, when there was an internet, he looked it up and discovered *there was no such game* — another enduring mystery.) I just remember really liking him.

That was the night when I really *saw* Harry: the quick, gently funny wit, his easiness with people, not all awkward edges like my high school classmates — like Fred. His was a welcoming personality, and he wasn't a show-off. Of course, I'd met Harry's younger brother Alan at the ASU a year or two before; he was a charmer, warm and outgoing. This one had a kind of reserve. You didn't get to know all about him right away, you just got glimpses, snapshots, which was enticing. He made you want to know him better, to find out what other ideas and thoughts were inside him. He had, among other intriguing talents, an encyclopedic knowledge of baseball. It turned out he'd been impressed that I knew, understood, and enjoyed baseball, too.

As we made our way out of the ballpark, he said something

to the effect that he'd call me some time, "look after" me over the summer while all the Kuhs were at the Vineyard, "Sure," I said.

To my pleasant surprise, he did.

So it began. Harry was working at Inland Steel in Indiana Harbor and living in the YMCA on 53rd Street. (Ah, how life goes in circles! Later, after we were married and had Annie and Sara, we moved from the Near North Side to that neighborhood in about 1950, and that YMCA was where they learned to swim.) He would drive from the Y, or directly in from work at the steel mill, to our ritzy apartment on Cedar Street. He'd pick me up at this fancy building, and we'd walk along the shore of the Oak Street Beach, or go to Lincoln Park and rent a rowboat in one of the lagoons and row around. Once he asked me, would I like to go sailing? "Sure!" I said. But it turned out you had to take a swimming test—jump off the boat into the water, remove your shoes (in the water), and then swim to shore. It wasn't an endurance swim by any means, but I realized that I was not THAT kind of swimmer, and so, although Harry took—and passed—that test, I was a wimp and backed out.

We liked walking along the lower level of the Michigan Avenue Bridge, which led you to a plain sandy shore along the Chicago River; then you'd come to the shore of Lake Michigan. It was, as I remember it, just natural; there were no skyscrapers lining the riverbank, and there was some sort of magic about that lower level of Michigan Avenue: it was a paved street, but there weren't buildings as there are now. There WAS no Outer Drive, no development around Navy Pier at that time. We'd buy a Good Humor ice cream bar and just walk along the lakefront and talk. It was wonderful! I just liked being with him: he was easy to talk with and to, thoughtful, interesting, relaxed.

Of course, Daddy liked Harry, but even fault-finding Mother was quite captivated by him: good-looking, nice pedigree. But why didn't he ever get dolled up and take me dancing? What kind of a date was it to just walk around eating an ice cream bar and TALKING?? Finally, after a lot of "Why don't you two go dancing or something?" from Mother, I asked Harry if he'd like that. He was noncommittal about the dancing, but said, "Sure, we could do that."

So we went to the Edgewater Beach Hotel, a big pink building right on the lakefront a few miles north of downtown. There was an outdoor dance floor and a band and some tables right at the edge of the beach, the lake maybe fifty yards away. It was not very interesting: the band was banal. Both of us were jazz lovers, but that meant *musicians* like Jack Teagarden, Muggsy Spanier, Benny Goodman, Louis Armstrong. And, I discovered, Harry was not a dancer by nature. He had many intriguing and wonderful characteristics and talents: dancing was not one of them. So we got sort of bored with the pallid music and the expensive beverages (I was still not old enough to drink legally, and didn't care). So Harry discovered that you could get a speedboat ride, with a driver, and have a tour around part of the beachfront: a thirty- or forty-minute ride for a modest fee.

It was a starlit, mild night, and we climbed aboard the speedboat, strapped on our life vests, and the "captain" shot out into the velvet darkness. It was lovely: the city looks quite small but bright from half a mile out, surrounded by the black water, hearing the waves slapping against the sides of the boat. You get out there half a mile or so—and there are just the stars and silence, except for watery sounds of the little waves, and the big city is just a strip of light punctuated by the Palmolive Beacon sweeping the sky and the occasional floodlit skyscraper. (There weren't that many in 1941.) You'd hear a faint siren sound drift across the water now and then, but most of the city noises disappeared in the "laughing waters" of the waves in the black lake. We returned from that little ride refreshed and happy.

When I told Mother that we'd gone for a speedboat ride, she was horrified: "What! Didn't you dance? What's the point of going someplace where they have a band and you don't DANCE??" Well, there was no explaining to her. I loved to dance, but not as much as I loved the experience of Lake Michigan at night in a speedboat with Harry. Now I think of all the different kinds of boat rides he and I shared across the years: ferryboats; a riverboat cruise in France; various types of fishing boats: bonefishing with guides; tarpon fishing, with and without guides, day and night; a boat cruise with the whole family on the Rhine; glass-bottom boats in Florida; whale-watching boat in San Diego Harbor; boats in Guatemala, Mexico, San Blas. And I have probably forgotten some.

Later that summer, Betsy asked me to come to the Vineyard to visit her, and I said I'd love to. Harry said he'd come, too, and we could travel together: on the train to Boston, then a bus, I think, from Boston to Woods Hole, then the ferry to Martha's Vineyard. One of the Kuhs would drive in from Menemsha to Woods Hole to pick us up.

I didn't ask my parents, I *told* them I was going. But they liked this boy, and I don't recall any problem, though some of the Kuhs' friends were scandalized that my parents would allow me to travel on an *overnight* train, unchaperoned, with Harry. Lodestone, the "dormitory," had boys on the third floor, girls on the second, and a sort of code of honor with respect to conduct. Betsy and I shared a room and had a wonderful reunion, lots of talk. Harry was there for only a few days; then he was going to visit his parents at their place in Vermont.

I have an indelible recollection of being outside, in the moonlight, embracing and kissing him, and I knew something very different had entered my life: real love. I don't know whether this was a message that passed through both of us; I never asked him. But when he got to Vermont, he phoned me at the Vineyard to ask me whether I'd like to come to Randolph Center — just for a very short visit, because he had to go to a recruitment center, as he was trying to get into the Navy (rather than be drafted). Of course I accepted *immediately*.

The Kuhs raised a collective eyebrow: What would my parents say? I was a guest at their house; and they felt a responsibility. Oh, sure, I said, I would "ask" my mother and father. There was NO WAY they could stop me, but I didn't say that to Skipper and Charlotte! Instead of my parents, I called my beloved sister, who was living in New York with her new husband, Berney Geis. I *told* her I was going to Randolph Center, Vermont, to see Harry and his parents (whom I had already met, though I don't recall the details). I swore her to secrecy. I told her that I would make my way back and would see her on the way. I'd call her when I got on the train that would bring me to New York, where I'd visit her and Berney and then head for Chicago. I was going to be leaving for my freshman year at Scripps College in the fall, and it would be time to prepare for that. Darlene, bless her heart, kept this plot confidential. Sort of.

Harry met me at White River Junction, and we drove to Randolph Center and his parents' house. I don't remember much about that visit, except that it was short. I was already wondering when (or if) I would ever see Harry again: I'd go off to school, he'd enlist or get drafted—and *then* what??

After the Kuhs returned to Chicago from the Vineyard in early September, Betsy came to stay overnight with me. We were sunning ourselves on the little patio, just chatting and catching up. She wanted to hear all about my brief foray to Vermont. The words that came out of my mouth shocked her, and they surprised me, too:

"You know, I think I could spend the rest of my life with that guy."

PART THREE

44

braham Gottlieb, Harry's grandfather, was born June 17, 1837, in Domažlice, Bohemia (German name Taus), a town in what was then part of the Austrian (later Austro-Hungarian) Empire, and is now in the Czech Republic. His father was a prominent merchant. Only three Jewish families were permitted to live within the city; Abraham Gottlieb's family was one. Domažlice was an ancient settlement, founded in the tenth century, and was probably a walled city.[1] Numerous restrictions were imposed on Jews, mandating not only where they were allowed to live, but also in what businesses or professions they were permitted to work. So Abraham went to Prague and began his studies when he was about ten years old (he may already have been betrothed to a suitable girl, an arrangement traditionally made through the marriage broker while they were still children).

How did he decide which of the professions open to a Jew he wanted to apply for? Did his father make the choice for him? History is silent on these subjects. We know that he attended the University of Prague and the Polytechnic Institute, completing his studies in engineering and receiving a diploma or degree (whatever the requisite certification was) around 1857.

He was hired immediately by the Francis Joseph Railroad, in the capacity of Construction Engineer. The railroad was still under construction at that time. In his final two years there, he was given the title of Assistant Engineer of the railroad (ca.

---

[1]Harry and I visited Domažlice in the 1970s or '80s; we took snapshots of the massive stone masonry arch at the entrance to the town's center, one of the gates of the original wall. A plaque on the wall stated that the town had been liberated from the Nazis by American armed forces in 1945.

1863), and when he left in 1865, he received a commendation from Emperor Franz Josef, according to one account. Returning to Domažlice, he married Rose Pollack (1844–1925), and in 1866 Abraham and Rose, accompanied by Rose's mother, Amalia, emigrated to the United States and settled in Chicago.

Did Abraham (or Rose) speak English? Had he studied English at university in Prague? The only clue we have is that one of his first employers in Chicago was August Bauer, an architect and probably a fellow German speaker, who may have helped Abraham adjust to doing most of his business in English. For a time Abraham called himself "Albert"; when or why he dispensed with this gesture of assimilation is unknown. Was it a sign of growing confidence? Maybe it just didn't fit.

Abraham next became associated with the A. B. Boomer Bridge Works (later called the American Bridge Company). He was named Chief Engineer of American Bridge, which he left in 1872 to become Engineer of the Keystone Bridge Company in Pittsburgh. The growing family moved to Pittsburgh, remaining there for more than a decade. A book of photographs, "Examples of Structures Built by the Keystone Bridge Co., Pittsburgh, PA" (n.d.), has "A. Gottlieb, President" on the title page. There are twenty-one photographs (with captions annotated in German in Gottlieb's hand!) of structures he built. Among them were railroad bridges over the Mississippi River at St. Louis (1874); the Ohio River at Cincinnati; and the Monongahela River at Pittsburgh (no legible dates on these last two). He also built a lighthouse in Tampico for the Mexican government. The family lived in Pittsburgh until 1885, then moved back to Chicago permanently.

Abraham was clearly a "larger-than-life" person: ambitious, proud, meticulous, gregarious, with friends and associates from all walks of life. Considerate of his working crews, he was evidently a fair-minded employer, who expected—and got—high performance from his men. His employment history suggests restlessness, perfectionism, a quick temper, or some combination of these. His abrupt departure from the Keystone Bridge Company came about in response to a letter in which, Gottlieb charged, the owner (who had hired him) made derogatory remarks about him. (Was anti-Semitism involved?) He immediately resigned his position, left the company, and moved the family back to Chicago, where he established the firm of A. Gottlieb and Company and continued to build bridges and other structures all over the United States and elsewhere.

Gottlieb was structural and architectural engineer for the Chicago Stock Exchange Building, the Rand McNally Building, and the Medinah Temple (since designated a historic landmark). He is probably most famously remembered, however, for his brief but creative association with Daniel Burnham and the World's Columbian Exposition of 1893, when Burnham named him its first Chief Engineer. In addition to designing the Administration Building and the Fine Arts Building (still standing—it is now the Museum of Science and Industry), Gottlieb did much of the construction planning for the Fair. Both men of strongly held opinions, both experts in their fields, their differences ultimately swamped continued harmonious cooperation, and Gottlieb resigned under pressure, an incident documented briefly in the best seller *The Devil in the White City*. (According to the author, Erik Larson, the fault was Gottlieb's: he had admitted to "a potentially catastrophic error," a failure "to calculate wind loads for the fair's main buildings." Gottlieb protested that "even without an explicit calculation . . . the buildings were strong enough"; Burnham said he couldn't take that risk. He was later criticized for directing Gottlieb's replacement to make the buildings excessively sturdy.)

The Gottliebs lived in a house at 3424 Vernon Avenue. Abraham was said to have been a loving and attentive father. How did he manage a demanding career, involvement in religious life and institutions (he served two terms as president of the reform Zion Congregation on the near South Side, one of Chicago's first synagogues), membership in a number of professional and social organizations (among them Engineering Brotherhoods and at least one German-American society), and have time to devote to his family of nine children? And what of his wife? Rosie must have been a consummate—and long-suffering—home-management expert.

Abraham's sudden and dramatic death on February 9, 1894, was front-page news. I quote from *The Inter Ocean* of Saturday, February 10: "Abraham Gottlieb, well known as an expert civil engineer, died suddenly in the Rookery Building yesterday afternoon. He entered . . . through the Adams Street entrance. . . . He was observed to stagger, then, tottering, made his way to the stairway and sunk [*sic*] down upon the steps. . . ." [The elevator starter] went to bring him some water, and returned to find him "gasping for breath convulsively . . . and several [people], who by this time had assembled about the suffering man, hurried away for a physician . . . and before medical assistance could reach him [in less than 15 minutes], he died."

One of Gottlieb's employees went immediately to fetch Richard, his oldest son, who was in the courthouse nearby, serving as a juror in a murder trial. Since the jury was about to begin deliberations, the Judge did not interrupt the case to inform Richard. Though deliberations were brief and the verdict reached quickly, it was still a good three hours after his father's death before the judge could impart the shocking news to young Richard. Visibly distraught, he fled the building. The news story ends with Richard's departure. Had anyone gone to tell Rose? Such details are lost.

As oldest son of Abraham and Rose, Richard faced a chaotic period in his family's life. At twenty-four, already a civil engineer (whether by his father's mandate or his own choice), he was appointed administrator of his father's estate and designated his family's representative in the long process of unraveling and settling Abraham's disordered affairs. It must have been a "learn-on-the-job" effort. Richard was sworn in and performed the requisite duties under oath.

Abraham had not left a will. He was only fifty-six. The unfortunate man had been plucked from the tree of life, with apparently no warning, in the prime of his career. Every outstanding project—and there must have been quite a few, including one Abraham had closed on just a couple of days before his death—had to be analyzed. It had to be determined how much work in drafting and preliminary design had been done, how much new material had been stockpiled against the actual performance of the work itself. All of this is summarized in the documents to which the Court and Richard and the various clients (and creditors) contributed.

As these contracts were painstakingly examined, it became ironically, tragically clear that Abraham Gottlieb, brilliant, perfectionistic structural engineer, was hopelessly bankrupt, mired in debt.

It seems that Abraham would contract to do the structural engineering work on a project (a bridge, a building), and when the agreement was signed, he would be expected to purchase the materials himself before a structure could be built. The party with whom he'd signed the contract may not have been obligated to reimburse Abraham for raw materials before there was something to "show" for the iron, steel, and so on. So he'd be ready to begin a bridge or building, but not able to start until he had money for materials. He was dependent on payment for a previous project for cash to pay for the material for the next project. Rather than incur delays that would have hurt his professional reputation, he'd sometimes arrange to pay the supplier on a sort of "installment plan" — which meant that he was always "behind": owing money for materials in a completed structure that he also had to disburse to a supplier for the next project, which only got under way when he was paid for the finished structure.

Was this a common practice? It seems to be both treacherous and cumbersome, not a good business model. Was it Abraham's character to be eager to move ahead with work, for which he was apparently much in demand, but possibly indifferent to (or unknowing about) the intricacies of credit, of timing, of how to prepare a contract that satisfied both client and builder? Abraham left monuments of his ingenuity and perfectionism, but he had not known how — or had time — to lay an economic groundwork for his family's security.

Nonetheless, the family had to find a way to survive. There are unanswerable questions: How did they manage? It would take a number of years and much negotiating to satisfy creditors at least partially—or to have them forgive the indebtedness. Some simply wrote off uncollectable bills. Rosie elected to keep Abraham's desk, office equipment, and tools (valued at $955.50), while relinquishing household items: beds, sewing machine, books, and "two milch cows and calves, ten sheep and fleece, a horse, saddle and bridle," for which she was paid $2,000 in cash. Having been thrust into the role of "the man of the family," for which he may or may not have been either suited or prepared, Richard remained in Chicago until 1906, twelve years after Abraham's death.

Mother Rose, the new widow, was ordered to appear in court to supply, under oath, the names and dates of each child born to her and Abraham, whether living or dead. Her testimony revealed for the first (and only) time the full number of Gottlieb children: nine. Two did not survive infancy. The firstborn child, Annie (1868-1869), was about fourteen months old when she died. No cause of death was given. Did the sisters and brothers born after Annie know about their sister? There is no mention of her anywhere, to the best of my knowledge. Edward, the last Gottlieb child, was born around 1881 and lived only six months. All of the children were probably born at home; there do not appear to be any family records of their births, nor birth certificates issued by the city.

The children, in birth order, are:
Annie, 1868–1869
Richard, 1870–1932
Caroline, 1871–1939
Minnie, 1872– 1868
Ida, 1874– (no death date given)
William, 1877–1945
Harry, 1879–1948
Florence, 1881–1979
Edward, 1881–1881

45

D id Richard feel that he had adequately discharged a first son's obligations after twelve years? In 1906 he married Pearl Bartholomei (born in Missouri in 1880); their marriage license was issued in Indiana, conceivably as they left Chicago for their new life in Texas. Pearl was a *shiksa* (a gentile), and the couple had evidently had a long, clandestine relationship. At least some of the children knew about Pearl but kept the liaison from Mother Rose, who was a devout and observant Jew. She died in 1925 never knowing that Richard was married, and had a daughter. His sister Minnie kept in touch with him. I am not sure whether he ever returned to Chicago. Harry Jr. remembered going to Texas with his dad at least once to visit the estranged family — his Uncle Richard, Aunt Pearl, and cousin "Toni" — in Houston. He never had much to say about those trips. His most vivid recollection was of meeting a Texas politician, Jesse H. Jones (later Franklin Roosevelt's Secretary of Commerce in the 1940s).

Richard, a successful architectural engineer, built a palace for the Emperor of Japan that was said to be the only building left standing after the devastating Tokyo-Yokohama earthquake of 1923. Richard and Pearl adopted a daughter, Catherine Dorothy, born in 1901 (whom they must have adopted when they settled in Houston, when she was five or six). Harry remembered that she was called "Toni." There was nothing good to be said about this child, according to family gossip. Was that girl a secret "love child," raised out of sight of the righteous Gottliebs, and finally reclaimed when Richard and Pearl moved to Texas? History is silent on this. In 1979, lawyers for the family tried to locate all possible heirs still living, each of whom was entitled to a portion of the estate of the next-to-youngest Gottlieb child, Florence (of whom more later). The exhaustive search for all heirs turned up no trace of Catherine Dorothy, or "Toni."

Abraham and Rose's third child, Carolyn ("Carrie") Gottlieb (1871–1939), was called "the most beautiful girl in Chicago." She had her portrait done in pastels by a local artist. The young face gazed blandly at us for many years from the hallway of our Chicago apartment. If the portrait was a good likeness, either it didn't do her justice, or Chicago was shockingly deficient in beautiful women. However, according to her niece Clara she was a "knockout," a very good bridge player, and an excellent golfer. She married handsome—though never very successful—Sigmund Woolner. She had a long affair with a local doctor, and wanted to divorce Woolner and marry him, but Abraham, the lawgiver-father, counseled against it, and she obeyed him.

Carrie and Sigmund had two daughters, Edith and Louise. Niece Clara, a self-proclaimed arbiter of tastes, characterized Edith as "crude" and Louise as "tall and wild." Edith married a "crude" man named Wieder; had two children, Carolyn and a boy whose name I forget. The Wieders divorced and Edith took back her maiden name of Woolner. She and her two children lived in Chicago. A bachelor Woolner uncle left $500,000, a respectable fortune, to Edith and Louise (who was married to movie actor Dewey Robinson and lived in L.A.; they were childless). Louise hung onto her share of the money and lived comfortably until she died in 1982. Edith ran through her share, gambling with reckless abandon as her retail women's dress business spiraled into bankruptcy. Destitute and on welfare, she was helped by her cousin Harry Jr. to get an apartment in a public housing development, where she lived out the rest of her life in cheery contentment.

Her daughter, Carolyn, moved to Fort Lauderdale when she retired. Harry and I visited her during our winter sojourns in Florida. Carolyn was upbeat but soft-spoken, unlike her noisy, ebullient mother. Carolyn enjoyed the just rewards of a happy and serene retirement, sharing an apartment with a colleague. Still, I always liked loud, tobacco-reeking Edith: a big horse of a woman with a foghorn voice from her heavy smoking habit. Spontaneous, jocular, easygoing, she had none of the cultivated refinement of the previous generation of Gottliebs. I guess Minnie's daughter, Cousin Clara, was right: Edith *was* "crude."

Minnie, the fourth child, was born in 1872, a year or so after Carrie; she was only twenty when she married Benedict J. Greenhut of Peoria in a storybook wedding at the Standard Club, Chicago's premier Jewish business and social club. The *Chicago Tribune* reported that the ceremony was performed by "The Reverend Doctor Stolz and the Reverend Doctor Felsenthal" under an arch of flowers (was this the chuppah?). *The Inter Ocean* more accurately referred to the celebrants as "Rabbi." The *Tribune* listed many of the 200 guests, while *The Inter Ocean* rhapsodized about the flowers, the furnishings, and, not least, the bridal party's attire. The bride's gown: "an exquisite Paris robe of glistening crystal silk with a long, sweeping train . . . [and] "a veil of illusion [that] fell in soft profusion, confined to the hair by a diamond pin."

The newlyweds lived in Peoria, and Clara, the first of their three children, was born there in 1893. She died in 1984. Rose (1901–1974) married Ernst Kauffman, and Joseph Benedict (1903–1989) married Ruth Humphrey. B. J. "Joe" Greenhut died in 1932, at only 61; Minnie outlived him by 37 years, reaching her late nineties.

But let's step back a generation to look at B. J.'s father, Joseph Greenhut (b. 1843), the immigrant whose dynamism, vision, resourcefulness, and courage set their stamp on his descendants. He was also born in Bohemia; his Greenhut family, like the Abraham Gottliebs, were probably prosperous, if not wealthy, German-speaking Jews. Joseph immigrated from Bohemia to Chicago with his mother and sister when he was about ten years old; then he quit school at the age of thirteen, possibly assuming the life of an itinerant peddler. He is known to have traveled through the Southern states, perhaps making a living peddling needles, thread, dress goods, pots and pans, and trinkets, as well as being a purveyor of news and gossip to farmers in the isolated hamlets of the region.

By 1861, the threat of war between the North and South brought him back to Illinois, and at about age eighteen, he joined the 82nd Illinois Regiment, among the first Jews in Chicago to become one of the "Boys in Blue." The 82nd was a German-speaking regiment, officers and men, with enough bilingual men among them to convey orders to all. Though this might seem discriminatory to a twenty-first–century sensibility, it enabled these nineteenth-century immigrant patriots to participate in the great Cause of preserving the Union. Greenhut served with distinction at Gettysburg, in the bloody fight to hold Cemetery Hill. It may have been as a consequence of that heroic defense that he was made a captain, given a battlefield commission (by General Grant himself?). He was called "Captain" for the rest of his life. Wounded more than once, he served for about three years, after which (ca. 1864) he resigned from the Army and returned to civilian life. In 1866 he married Clara Wolfner. They had three children, Benedict Joseph (B. J.) (b. 1870), who married Minnie Gottlieb; Fanny; and Nelson.

Captain Joe Greenhut moved his family to Peoria after the Great Chicago Fire of 1871. He established a distilling and corn products business in Peoria, later moving to New York, where he went into the "big store" retail business. The "big store" was the granddaddy of the department store, which reigned supreme over most of twentieth-century retail, but is currently being starved out of existence by the computerized, do-it-all presence of online commerce. Siegel-Cooper, the dry-goods retailer Captain Greenhut purchased from its financially overextended founder for half a million dollars, ruled New York City shopping from a grandiose emporium on Sixth Avenue until Macy's ate its lunch.

In keeping with his exuberant, larger-than-life personality, Captain Greenhut purchased Shadow Lawn, in Long Branch, New Jersey, as a summer "cottage" (of fifty-two rooms!), a gathering place for his family and guests. An estate of magnificent proportions, it was the scene of many elaborate balls, feasts, and entertainments from about 1910 to 1918. It became the "Summer White House," "rented" to President Woodrow Wilson in 1916 (for $1). Minnie Greenhut, poor efficient and orderly soul, had been tasked with running this hotel-size establishment for the pleasure and relaxation of family and friends. The summer that the President was in residence, she had a well-earned respite from that responsibility. Shadow Lawn was a lustrous, if brief, interval in family life, inspiring fond memories among the Captain's many descendants. Clara Greenhut, daughter of Minnie and B. J., was close to that grandfather, the vibrant and energetic Civil War veteran, Captain Joe Greenhut. His death in 1918 marked the end of an era.

Though born in the Midwest, Clara Greenhut always saw herself as a New Yorker. She grew up in a house on West 72nd Street. She did not attend college, an activity still regarded in her day with suspicion and even disapprobation for young women of her social class by socially conservative parents. She regretted that omission, but compensated for it by pursuing work in the fields of social justice, women's suffrage, and endeavors related to her husband's interests in real estate and politics. She married Aaron Rabinowitz (1884–1973) in 1921. Theirs was a marriage that flouted the convention that discouraged (if not outright prohibited) marriage between German and Eastern European Jews (which still raised a few highbrow eyebrows when Harry and I married two decades later). In general, German Jews were better educated, more affluent and "cosmopolitan" than the Jews of Russia, Ukraine, and Eastern Europe. The latter's reputation for ignorance, illiteracy, superstition, unscrupulousness, and all manner of low-life characteristics — the stigma my mother could never quite shake — distanced them from their cultured, gently reared German Jewish "cousins." There were exceptions, of course; Aaron Rabinowitz was one.

Astute and a quick study, Aaron understood that the health of a complex urban giant like New York City depended on providing for its poorest citizens if the whole urban organism was to flourish. He became a developer of various areas of Manhattan; the concept of apartments for low- and middle-income families became an important component of urban life in the nation's biggest city. Rabinowitz was one of its influential innovators. The Rabinowitzes had three children: Betty (1922–1977), Susan (1924–2015), and Alan (1927–2017).

Ida Gottlieb was born in 1873, about a year after Minnie, and the year the family moved to Pittsburgh. Those two girls were close all their lives. Ida married Philip Mayer in 1904, when she was a "mature" 31-year-old. By 1905 they were living in New York, where both of their daughters were born: Elsa (1905–1995), and Phyllis (1911–2004). Elsa married Henry Baer; Phyllis married Thomas Sternau.

The sixth child born into the household of Abraham and Rose Gottlieb, William (1877–1945), was kind, gentle, and very shy. He was born with a port wine "birthmark," which covered almost half his face and part of his neck. It was disfiguring. There was no way known at that time to erase or conceal this conspicuous blemish, and it had a profound effect on Bill's entire life. He never married, tended to be shy, withdrawn, appearing antisocial — until you penetrated his defense against stares and comments (or his embarrassed fear of ridicule or disgust).

For his nephews Harry Jr. and Alan, Bill was *the* runaway favorite Gottlieb relative of that generation. They loved him and he loved them. When they were young boys, they would ride the North Shore Electric (a quaint streetcar-like interurban), change to the El when they got into the city, and meet Uncle Bill at Wrigley Field, where the three of them would have a merry time at the Cubs ballgame. With them he was relaxed, animated, funny, and those memories lingered on long after they were grown up and away at school. They'd still always manage to see Uncle Bill.

When Harry and I were married, I entered that loving circle: Bill wasn't shy with me because I wasn't shy about him — really forgot about that disfigurement that made him feel such an outsider. He had a neat small apartment on the North Side, not far from the ballpark (by coincidence), and even if we didn't go to a ballgame, we'd visit him and walk around the neighborhood or have lunch somewhere. He was fun to be with: had a wry, twinkly sense of humor, knew a lot of interesting things, as he was a reader. He worked in some low-level job in a local real estate firm, where he didn't have to meet the "public." Harry always felt that he was grossly underpaid and taken advantage of because of his perceived need to be inconspicuous. What a loss to people whose lives he'd have enriched, to his own open-heartedness that never could fully express itself!

Harry and I were the ones who went to his apartment after he died, to go through his modest "things": maybe a souvenir ash tray from someplace, neatly folded shirts and underwear, no letters or personal stuff like that. But Harry was heartened to find a box of condoms in Uncle Bill's dresser. So maybe he wasn't so lonely all the time.

Bill's younger brother, seventh-born Harry N. Gottlieb (Sr.), was born in Pittsburgh on January 7, 1879, and died in Chicago on April 13, 1948. He was about six years old when Abraham resigned from the Keystone Bridge Company and moved the family back to Chicago in 1885. He was fifteen, attending South Division High School, when his father suddenly died, intestate and insolvent. It must have been a formative experience for Abraham's brilliant and ambitious seventh child to observe the catastrophic consequences of his father's inadequate economic planning and lack of preparedness for contingencies. It was apparently a lesson not lost on Harry, who took it seriously to heart. He was determined to do better, making his own way.

In 1896, two years after his father's untimely death, Harry won a scholarship to the University of Chicago. There he was a relentlessly competitive and articulate member of the often-victorious debate team, as well as captain of the varsity tennis team, which won the Big Ten Championship in 1900—a major, prestigious triumph. (Our family treasured a large woolen blanket with "1900" emblazoned across it that must have been the trophy awarded to each of the team members. Until it fell apart from overuse and old age, that blanket accompanied us on auto trips to and from Florida; it was also the favored cover for the children and the dog when everyone sat snuggled under it on the couch, watching *The Howdy Doody Show* or *The Lone Ranger* or *The Mickey Mouse Club* on TV.) Harry graduated from the University of Chicago, Phi Beta Kappa, that year. Already in college he had known what he wanted to do with his future: he would become a lawyer, perhaps with a leaning toward public affairs.

Abraham's unintended legacy to Harry, more than to most of his other children (Richard being similarly endowed), was tireless alertness to all kinds of monetary details—teaching his children the merits of clear, careful account keeping. (Harry Jr. passed this along.) He was both meticulous and foresighted, a fastidious record-keeper, a scrupulous watchdog of loose ends and of ambiguous, foggy thinking. This is a skill that also has its place in creative thinking and work.

Florence, the eighth and penultimate child born to Abraham and Rose, but the one who lived the longest (1881–1979), was also the one who suffered some unspecified behavioral or psychological abnormalities that were neither discussed nor described but that evidently demanded vigilance, surveillance, and provision for her lifelong support and care. Two of her nieces, Clara Rabinowitz and Elsa Baer, offered some insights into her character and behavior.

Clara: "Florence never married—did teach school many years in Chicago . . . and always urged all to introduce her to the right man—and she dragged Grandma Gottlieb to summer resorts."

Elsa: "Florence lived with her mother for a long time—then moved to California. Wacky—always going to make her fortune in real estate—mostly mines—thought the FBI was after her. . . . Florence was mad at all of us because when she visited Mom [Ida Gottlieb Mayer] in the [19]50s [an ill-fated trip to New York described below], I think she disappeared one night—we called the police — when she reappeared we took her to Bellevue. After her discharge, she went to a home in Westchester near Phyllis [Elsa's sister]. She was pretty but wacky."

That visit to New York was probably the same trip that brought Florence into Harry's and my life and gave us a glimpse into her chaotic personality. Her sisters Minnie and Ida evidently decided it was time to bring Florence back East where they could watch over her. She was put on the train in California, and Harry Jr. was informed that *he was to meet that train* at its stopover in Chicago — and *not to let her out of his sight until he got her back on board* for the final leg of her transcontinental trip. He was to tip the porter generously and tell him NOT to let her leave her railroad car until the train pulled into Penn Station, where her sisters would be waiting for her.

So Harry went to Dearborn Station to meet Aunt Florence, whom he may have seen once or twice in his life, many years earlier. The Pullman Porter had been a conscientious custodian: Aunt Florence was duly handed over to Harry along with two very heavy suitcases. They took a cab to our apartment on Cedar Street, where he could keep track of her and she could rest (ha! she was not the resting type, as we found out immediately) until it was time for the return to the railroad station and the final leg of her trip.

So I got to meet Aunt Florence, whom I only dimly remember as having dark hair and being very physically active. She talked about her valuable but secret cargo, telling us that she wanted to deliver it to the Government to help in our defense system. It was very important but very secret. She wanted to go "out," so Harry took her for a short walk, which involved him making sure she didn't slip away from him. I don't remember that she showed any interest at all in her great-niece: Annie was three or four years old when Florence visited us.

She was talkative. She confided to us that she was transporting some radium-laced rocks to New York — that was why the suitcases were so heavy. She had radium on her property in California, she claimed, and she knew that it would be very useful to the Government and that it was valuable, what's more. She didn't seem to be worried about getting radium poisoning herself, and we realized that the greatest health hazard was back strain from the weight of her luggage. Poor Harry!

As they left to get a cab to return to the railroad station, Florence almost got away from him as he tried to wave down a taxi. She was fast as a jackrabbit: he was lugging the suitcases, which slowed him down, but he dropped the valises and tore after her, caught up with her, and cautioned that they had to hurry back so no one would steal her bags. That got her attention (though no one could—or would—make off with those staggeringly heavy things). She made one more attempt to escape in the railroad station: said she had to go to the ladies' room, but by this time Harry was onto her: parking himself beside the washroom door, he grabbed her as she attempted to sail past him. I remember that she was good-natured. And talkative! Don't recall what she talked about: Was it rambling? Did it make sense?? This was a long time ago, but I think it was mostly sort of a verbal torrent.

Aunt Florence was put on the train with her two "radioactive" valises, the porter was duly paid off, and that was the end of OUR part of this saga. In New York, Minnie and Ida decided to have electroshock therapy administered to her in hopes that she might have a miraculous "cure"; their hopes were promptly dashed: though strapped down to the table on which she was to receive the treatment, she apparently broke the restraints, fell off the table, and fractured an arm or shoulder. That was enough for Minnie and Ida: as soon as her injury was sufficiently healed for her to travel, they shipped her back to Hermosa Beach. Neighbors apparently looked after her for the rest of her long life.

Florence died in a nursing home in California in 1979. There are a few letters between lawyers in the 1980s indicating confusion or dispute about ownership rights to some barren desert property. After four or five years of desultory communication between attorney Irv Askow in Chicago and the Los Angeles Public Administrator, the issue was allowed to fade away, the ownership of the property never firmly established, and the whole thing not worth pursuing.

Edward was the last of the Gottlieb children; the ninth child born to Rose and Abraham (ca. 1881), he died at about six months of age. Neither he nor Annie, the firstborn, is mentioned anywhere or by anyone, excepting only in widow Rose's deposition under oath when the estate was being examined and recorded.

46

After his triumphant graduation from the University of Chicago in 1900, Harry Gottlieb entered Columbia University Law School in New York (Chicago did not have a law school until 1903). Columbia was not far from the residences of his two married sisters, Ida Mayer and Minnie Greenhut. They kept a watchful eye on their brother, which probably saved his life. I don't know how or when they learned that he was not well, but they came — or were summoned — to his dormitory room and found him writhing on the floor in acute pain. He was rushed to the hospital, where surgeons operated immediately and removed his ruptured appendix. He developed peritonitis, a virulent, often fatal infection at that time. (Antibiotics were at least twenty-five to thirty years in the future.) The only hope was that his youth and strong constitution would save him. The doctors made stringent efforts to keep the area as "sterile" as possible by repeatedly flushing it with water (the only "treatment" in use at that time to help his body defend itself). Miraculously, he survived, and he graduated — with his classmates — from Columbia University Law School, Bachelor of Law, in 1903. He returned to Chicago, where he passed the Illinois Bar Examination and was admitted to the Illinois Bar.

By 1904, he had met young Dorothy Kuh, and though neither of them knew it then, "Destiny" stepped in and took a hand.

I traced Dorothy's lineage back to 1802, when Salomon Kupfer was born in Burgkunstadt, in northern Bavaria. In 1833 he married Amalia (or Amalie) Iglauer, born in the same town in 1812. Salomon was a clothmaker and a tailor.

"I am not only an ordinary clothmaker, but I sew all

kinds of specially fine worksuits, silk scarfs and dresses."
(From a letter "to the High Honored Government of the Ober
Main County," n.d.) Salomon asks permission to change his
name to a less Jewish-sounding one: "In countries where the
governments are not as tolerant as in Bavaria, there the people
are not tolerant either, . . . and I am exposed to the worst and
cruelsome prosecutions, when I am known to be a jew. And
that happened to be known just by my name. . . . because I got
letters from my home addressed to Salomon Kupfer and it was
just the name which made the Master realize that I am a jew.
What kind of disagreeable situations I had I will not mention,
but only complain that during the 4 years I had to wander about,
the shame I felt." (from translated documents and letters in my
possession) It wasn't "Kupfer" that sounded Jewish to him,
however: it was "Salomon," and he was asking permission to
be called either "Sebastian Kupfer" or "John Salomon." There
is no evidence that he ever got a reply from the government, so
Salomon's name remained unchanged.

Salomon and Amalia Kupfer had twelve children, and
Mathilda, the second-born, married Isaac Kuh (see the family
tree for details). Isaac and Mathilda had three sons: Edwin
(1858–1940), Sidney (1866–1934), and Henry (no information
about him). In 1886, when he was twenty-eight, Edwin married
twenty-year-old Jennie Cahn. They had three children: Dorothy
(1887–1955), Edwin Jr. (1889–1972), and Frederick (1895–1978).
Edwin Sr. and Sidney (a bachelor) were both physicians.

Jennie's mother, Ida Cäcilie Lorie (1837–1923), was the third
of four children born to Herz Samuel Lorie (1803–1885) and
Sara Schwarzschild (b. 1808). (The Lorie surname is said to be
Sephardic: descended from Jews who fled the Inquisition in Spain
in the fifteenth century rather than convert to Christianity.) In
1844, when Ida was seven, her mother died, age 36, after months
as an invalid following the birth of Fannie Esperanza. "They
took us to her coffin, a simple wooden box," Ida remembered,
"and we saw her face for the last time; never will I forget that
impression." Perhaps as a consequence an independent young
woman, Ida left Frankfurt in 1859 to go to her older sister Lena,

who was living in New York, homesick and married to tyrannical Herman Jacoby. Ida met Aaron Cahn, Jacoby's charming cousin, and the two promptly fell in love. Jacoby forbade them to marry, citing the looming prospect of the Civil War. They were married, nonetheless, in the Jacoby apartment in New York City, in 1861.

Ida later wrote a memoir (in German) at the request of Beatrice (Beatie), her youngest child. The bound copy I have has an English translation as well as a photocopy of her original--in German "Gothic" script. The story of their wedding is told in Ida's memoir (along with descriptions of a gun battle on their street in Frankfurt during the turbulent Revolution of 1848); of her brother, Victor Salomon Libertus Lorie, an artist who may have been one of the first "war correspondents," illustrating his dispatches with on-site sketches of battles in the Middle East. [See Appendix A for excerpts from the English translation of Ida's memoir about the revolt in Frankfurt and a fuller biographical sketch of Victor.]

The prettiest of the Cahn sisters, Jennie was self-centered and needy, woefully unready for marriage at age twenty, especially to someone as urbane as twenty-eight-year-old Dr. Edwin Kuh. Though theirs was a socially "appropriate" union and they had three children (Dorothy, Edwin Jr., and Frederick), the marriage never became a genuine partnership. They apparently lived together for ten or twelve years. But Edwin's philandering finally tripped him up: a scene exploded, with shouting and hysterics. The children, Dorothy recalled, were hustled upstairs, where, clinging to the banister, wide-eyed and frightened, they watched their life as a family disintegrate before their eyes. Edwin had been caught once too often diddling a housemaid, and was summarily banished from home and family. Dorothy remembered comforting little Freddie, while Edwin Jr. defiantly assumed a devil-may-care attitude. It was a melodramatic ending to this once-promising union.

Packing up Dorothy and little Frederick, "ailing" Jennie left for Europe. Young Eddie remained in Chicago, under the more relaxed supervision of his father, Edwin Sr., and his bachelor uncle, Sidney, a psychiatrist on the staff of Michael Reese

Hospital (who used hypnosis as anesthetic for minor surgeries). Their philosophy of child-rearing was to let the boy learn his way around; what he doesn't know he can either ask us (we are doctors!) or discover for himself: they would make a "man" of him, not allow him to become a simpering pantywaist, his certain fate if he remained under the fluttering wings of overprotective women.

Jennie, Dorothy, and Frederick took shelter with Jennie's sister Sarah, in Vitznau, Switzerland, on the shores of Lake Lucerne. Sarah and her husband, Alfred Strasser, occupied a house with a walled garden, and Jennie and the two children settled into one nearby. (I remember Sarah and Uncle Alfred: by that time, in the 1940s or early '50s, he was a dirty old man. He was dapper, looked dignified, but—WATCH OUT! You had to stay out of reach, which wasn't easy--he'd try to corner you. I may be making this up, but I think he drooled, too! I had a few skirmishes with him, but learned a lot of broken-field running, and he WAS old. But it was a drag. Aunt Sarah was contrastingly prim—that may explain Uncle Alfred's endless hunger for soft young flesh.) There was also a young Strasser cousin, Joszi, probably a few years older than Dorothy, and their "comradeship" involved one of them climbing the wall into the other's garden. It was an idyllic summer for Dorothy and Joszi. (Did it have a hint of "assignation" about it?) Joszi was handsome, tractable, charming; he later became a cavalry officer in the (notoriously anti-Semitic) Hungarian Army; he looked like a million bucks in those knee-high cavalry boots and the exquisitely tailored jacket with its double row of brass buttons. (I once had Dot's dashing photo of him—now lost, alas!)

Europe, despite its squabbles and upheavals, had a long history and settled traditions; it offered Jennie the comfort and security she yearned for. Enfolded within her family community there, she felt protected, cossetted, in contrast to what seems to have been an unsettled existence after she and Edwin separated (date uncertain; I estimate 1898). I don't think they ever divorced, but they had nothing to do with one another. There is no record of a "permanent" Chicago address for the family after they returned from Europe. The first of the few surviving letters from Harry Gottlieb is dated 1904 and was addressed to Dorothy Kuh at 4330 Drexel Boulevard; that was the house Dot remembered living in as a child, when Jennie and Edwin were still together. (In the early 1950s, we Junior Gottliebs made a trip down "Memory Lane" with Dot, driving past that nineteenth-century brownstone.) Where did they live from 1905 to 1910? There was a period when Jennie, maybe with Dot, lived in the Moraine Hotel. The 1910 census shows Jennie Cahn living with her mother, Ida Cahn, and with her children Dorothy and Frederick Kuh. Addresses on envelopes of the sparse and reticent "courtship letters" from Harry to Dot during the intervening years were to six or more addresses, all probably South Side. But most were addressed to her at out-of-town summer resorts.

Dorothy, an independent spirit by age sixteen or seventeen, and apparently not burdened with a chaperone's surveillance, had joined the group of young people who spent convivial summer vacations in Charlevoix, Michigan, a favorite gathering place for Chicagoans. Swimming, sailing, tennis, hiking, producing and acting in impromptu dramas, and, of course, dancing were among their activities in that pre–movie-radio-TV era. Dot and Harry may well have met there. The first of the few surviving letters he wrote to her is a short note dated Charlevoix, December 20, 1904. She was seventeen, he was twenty-five. He writes (somewhat stiltedly), "May I employ Charlevoix parlance and say simply, 'All right, lady I'll let you determine, at the time, if you can, which of the two roles you offer I have chosen to play.' Sincerely Harry N. Gottlieb." Not much of a come-on, but a spark of mutual attraction flickered, though Harry was reserved and Dorothy expressive. (When I knew them forty years later, those traits had not been much altered by Time.)

Though he had graduated from Columbia Law School with his classmates in 1903, apparently recovered from his traumatic ruptured appendix, Harry was still struggling to overcome the weakness and debilitating fatigue that seemed to consume him. Was this related to his near-death experience with peritonitis? Tuberculosis is not mentioned by name anywhere in Harry's few surviving letters. However, present-day research has uncovered evidence of a connection between peritonitis and TB that could have afflicted him with this persistent and profound fatigue. After his graduation from law school, Harry may have had contact with the Sanitarium at Saranac Lake in upstate New York. Dr. Edward Baldwin at the famed Adirondacks sanitarium advised him to live in a high-altitude region of the American West — Wyoming, Colorado, Arizona, New Mexico, California — for its "salubrious air." He had also consulted a Dr. Laks in New York City, who advised him to get married.

There are no surviving letters from Dorothy to Harry, though they apparently wrote each other with considerable regularity. Harry's early letters reveal few signs of outspoken affection; his tone is newsy, friendly. By 1905, though, this formal tone was cautiously becoming relaxed and familiar, even, to some extent, confiding. In August 1905 he had written, in a rare moment of self-revelation, that he must "be careful not to do too much. I have played about enough [tennis] to get my hand in." (This from the captain of the University of Chicago tennis team in 1900, the year they won the Big Ten Championship. Now he was a convalescent.) It is noteworthy that this reticent young man confided to Dorothy that he was concerned about his unrelenting fatigue, his most insidious and stubborn enemy.

He also began to assume a condescending, avuncular tone toward her, encouraging her to apply for admission to the University of Chicago, which she did. When he stopped by to visit her in September, he was surprised to find that she had left the country to accompany her ailing mother to Europe. He chided her gently, "Gee, but you're a truant: but I shan't regard your present desertion of the University as anything more than a temporary absence and shall still hope to see you get your degree on some bright day at a U of C convocation."

When she began her studies, Dorothy was taken aback by the University's medieval emphasis on memorization as both teaching method and learning tool; she bristled and despaired by turns. Harry, on the other hand, had been an active member of the Debate Team and used his prodigious memory and formidable skills in argumentation in debate competitions. He participated in national competitions and continued to write articles for University publications long after he had graduated. He enjoyed the act of memorizing; it was both an essential and a pleasure for him. Dorothy, meanwhile, despaired; she confessed to him that she'd failed the class in Political Economy (why on earth did this literary humanist take THAT course?) and was considering transferring into the School of Nursing! Was she thinking that she might have an invalid spouse to look after, given Harry's frail health?

Fortunately, Dorothy abandoned that thought, and Harry offered to be a sort of informal tutor, to help her with her studies — and possibly even get her to enjoy committing to memory a favorite poem or song. He assured her that the Political Econ. class wasn't worth bothering about anyhow. Though he'd initially told her not to bother about getting the degree — proclaiming that it was just a piece of paper of little worth — later, as he came to recognize and value her strong intelligence AND retentive memory (for subjects that interested her), he urged her to stay the course and graduate, which she did, in 1909.

In the years 1905–'09, while Dorothy was enrolled at the University of Chicago, Harry spent at least two winters in Santa Barbara, California, with Wormser, a friend who probably functioned as a companion-caretaker; then, perhaps some time in Arizona and New Mexico, and possibly one interval at a working ranch (as guest or participant?) in Clermont, Wyoming, in 1909. At first too fatigued to do much more than read and rest, he found the energy to maintain an active correspondence with Dorothy. It seems possible that much of their courtship was conducted by mail. Only fifteen or so letters survive, dated from 1905 to 1910, the year they were married.

The letters reveal a slowly developing closeness. In 1907 Harry describes the passive, idle life of a convalescent: "How quickly a week slips by when you are doing nothing." A year later he writes, "Idleness becomes more irksome with returning strength." He waited for Dorothy's letters, and when there was an interruption in what seems to have been a pretty steady twice-a-week exchange, he expressed anxiety. By 1907, he writes to her: "I am sorry that you find me reserved, lady. May be some day all will be plain sailing & you won't think me so. But you must not disparage yourself as you do. Just remain 'always the same Dorothy' and that will be most pleasing to those who know and love you best, including Harry."

During the summers, when he returned to Chicago, Harry practiced law independently [possibly part-time?] with the firm of Judah, Willard & Wolf (where young Oscar Stern would later work), and also in partnership with his friend Alvin Wise: "Wise and Gottlieb/ Lawyers/ 906 Association Building, 153 LaSalle St./ CHICAGO/ Telephone Randolph 3008/ Alvin W. Wise H. N. Gottlieb." In 1909 he wrote Dorothy on the firm's letterhead, expressing relief at Wise's return to share the burden of the firm's affairs; he may not have been well enough yet to practice law full-time. Addressing her as "Sweetheart," he mused, "Love is wondrous strange, isn't it, the way it both goes and abides."

Dorothy was quite smitten with this Adonis, six feet tall, brilliant, convivial, not aggressive, but goal-driven. With no correspondence from Dorothy to Harry, one can only guess at how she determined that this handsome, ambitious young man was the one for her above all others. But she knew by 1906, when she wrote to an unidentified "Matchmaker-in-Chief": "Don't worry about me, I found my affinity two years ago and am waiting for him to realize the fact." (Clairvoyant? Or persistent?) Forthright and expressive, Dorothy had probably confessed her feelings unhesitatingly and early. She was not repressed!

The relationship gradually intensified. Finally, in 1910, the year of their marriage, Harry outspokenly expressed his love for Dorothy, in response, apparently, to a letter from her. "Sweetheart, I fear that this letter does not convey to you all that I would have it carry. Oh, if I could take you in my arms and tell you as I wish the meaning to me of such a message from you. I sometimes feel that my nature must seem rather passive, but I think you know the fire that lies beneath the surface, burning with an intensity of love for you. Ever lovingly yours, Harry."

47

Chicago Daily News, Tuesday, October 18, 1910:
The marriage of Miss Dorothy Kuh to Harry Gottlieb will take place this evening at the home of Mr. and Mrs. Frederick D. Silber, 5632 Washinton avenue. [*sic*.]

The Inter Ocean, Wednesday, October 19, 1910:
The marriage is announced of Miss Dorothy Kuh to Harry Gottlieb. The ceremony was performed last evening at the residence of Mr. and Mrs. Frederick D. Silber, 5632 Washinton Avenue [now Blackstone Avenue in Hyde Park].

In fact, Harry and Dorothy were married on October 17. I haven't found any mention of who officiated, who attended—NOTHING. The Chicago newspapers printed brief announcements (but not more detailed accounts) of Jewish weddings. Social events and weddings of prominent (Gentile?) citizens appeared on the Society pages.

Mr. and Mrs. Silber were Dorothy's Aunt Beatie (her mother's youngest sister) and Beatie's husband, Fred. (Beatie, whom I knew in later years, was a calm, no-nonsense woman. She and Fred had four children, one of whom, Elizabeth, was divorced and left her daughter, Marie Worth, with grandparents Beatie and Fred. They were living at the Belden Hotel at that time, as we were, and Marie and I were classmates at the Francis Parker School during the few years that she lived with the Silbers. Aunt Beatie and Uncle Fred were pleasant, hospitable, calm, and welcoming. Through Marie I met the third Cahn sister, Aunt Susie, a maiden lady and an uninhibited live wire, who entertained Marie and me with tales of her free-wheeling youth in pre–World War I Europe, with lots of "beaux" who'd take

her for sleigh rides in the winter, covered with blankets which —
ahem — gave them a certain privacy. She was irreverent and fun,
unlike prim Aunt Sarah, or Jennie, who was temperamental,
anxious, bitter, and full of psychosomatic complaints. Life had
dealt Jennie a bad hand, she always seemed to feel.)

Newlyweds Dot and Harry made their way to Sheridan,
Wyoming — their first home — accompanied by Mama Jennie (!)
and Dorothy's closest friend, Helen Becker. (There was a snapshot
of Harry on this "honeymoon trip," as well as a sentimental one
of Dot and Helen Becker, with "Goodbye, Darling" written at
the bottom.) Harry, who had evidently explored various places
out West in an effort to find one that suited him and that would
accelerate his recovery from whatever his undisclosed health
problem was, had chosen Sheridan.

"I think you know the fire that lies beneath the surface," Harry
had written in his loving letter to Dorothy. The words may
well be construed as referring not only to their full-flowering
romance, but also to the fire of ambition to become a force in the
political life of his chosen home. He wasted no time.

A paragraph in the *Sheridan Post* of December 20, 1910 noted
that "Attorney H. N. Gottlieb, who attended the oil convention
in Cheyenne the past week, has returned home much elated
because of the attention given by the people from every quarter
to one of the most promising industries of the state. A complete
organization was formed, and the industry will be properly
exploited."

On December 27, 1910, this announcement appeared in the
Sheridan Post:

H. N. Gottlieb Attorney-at-Law
Admitted to Practice in New York and Illinois
R. S., First National Bank Bldg. telephone 194.

In 1911, "upon the recommendation of the [State] Supreme
Court," Harry was admitted to the Sheridan County Bar, making
him eligible to run for public office and also qualifying him to

practice in the Sheridan County District Court. Harry's regular attendance at Criminal Court hearings (most involving the illicit sale of liquor) also got him a mention in at least one of Sheridan's newspapers. He was already becoming a public figure, and one is impressed by his energy as described in these newspaper accounts. The convalescent has vanished, supplanted by a man of seemingly boundless vitality and formidable acumen.

His involvement in the affairs of Sheridan extended beyond city politics and into another of his enthusiasms: debating. The *Sheridan Post* and the *Sheridan Daily Enterprise* announced in January 1911 that Attorney Gottlieb was coaching Sheridan High School's debate team, preparing it for the contest with Billings. I can imagine his pleasure advising these high schoolers as he had been trained at the University of Chicago: showing them the fine points of constructing an argument and turning them into skilled debaters.

The trajectory that propelled Harry into public life in Sheridan (where, by 1914, he was City Attorney) was based on his character and intelligence; his education; his skills in negotiation and problem-solving; and his personality: mild but with integrity and high standards of performance for himself and his associates. He was scrupulously honest, an astute judge of people, and, in his soft-spoken way, most convivial! (His namesake son had many of those same traits, but spiced with some of the pepper that sparked his mother's personality.)

The only story that Dorothy told me (with considerable relish) about her early married years in Wyoming had to do with her effort to instruct the young girl she had hired as maid-housekeeper on how to serve dinner guests as she'd seen it done in her childhood home: you served the seated dinner guests from the left and cleared the dishes from the right. At one of the first dinner parties, everything went quite nicely, as her "maid" served the main course properly, from the left. Then, as she began clearing the dishes after the main course, she announced, "Keep yer forks, we're havin' pie!"

What kind of life did the Gottlieb newlyweds live in Sheridan? Local newspapers reported that Dorothy played afternoon bridge with wives of other political, business, or professional men of the city. She and Harry must have entertained prominent citizens at dinners in their home. Did she volunteer in any of the traditional local organizations? Maybe she took up horseback riding, an activity she loved in later life when I knew her. She owned a horse then—but all of that comes later in her story.

Harry, in addition to practicing law and presumably still coaching the high school debate club, became active in the town's Roosevelt Club and promoted "certificates of charter membership" in the State Progressive Party, of which he was State Chairman in 1912. This fund-raising activity was part of the effort to reelect Theodore Roosevelt to a second term as U.S. President, this time under the banner of the Progressives (or Bull Moose Party).

In 1914 he was named City Attorney and moved his office into City Hall (into space vacated by the County Assessor). The *Sheridan Post* reported that he was "very busy." He was described as "being in almost constant attendance at council meetings." Was his meticulous professional work ethic a novelty to the journalists of Sheridan (who reported on it faithfully and in some detail)?

Meanwhile, Dorothy became pregnant, probably around June or July of 1914. At that time, "blessed events" were never even hinted at in the newspapers until after the infant was born. Secrecy? Discretion? Superstition? It just "wasn't done." A birth record indicates that Jane was born in Chicago on March 2, 1915. There was also a photograph of her, in an elaborate christening-type gown, in Grandmother Jennie's arms, with Dorothy standing beside her mother. No one is smiling. Jane looks frail and ill; a chill comes over you, looking at this sickly (nay, mortally ill) infant. She would have been called a "blue baby": a tiny child born with a damaged heart and circulatory system. (Now, in the twenty-first century, such babies can often be restored to normal health.) In those sorrowful days, did they know how sick little Jane was? Had they been warned that hers would be a short life, with much suffering?

Heavily pregnant Dorothy (accompanied by City Attorney Harry?) had made the arduous two- or three-day transcontinental train trip back to Chicago to give birth at Michael Reese Hospital, where the baby was probably delivered by one of Chicago's eminent obstetricians. This is speculation, as all that exists is the photo of infant Jane and the Chicago birth record. Knowing Dot's mother Jennie (a dedicated hypochondriac), it is highly unlikely that she would have made the trip to Sheridan to accompany her pregnant daughter back to Chicago. And Harry, a man of ardent sensibilities and love for Dorothy, would almost certainly have taken at least a brief leave from his duties as City Attorney to be at her side for the birth of their first child. I am fairly certain that, in those days of no ultrasound (or of any device more advanced than the stethoscope), there would not have been any way to know that Jane was doomed. Perhaps the doctors believed that the pure air of Sheridan might have a positive effect on this pathetic little creature, since the "salubrious air" had wrought such wonders for her father. So the little family returned to Sheridan. Jane withstood the noisy, jolting two- or three-day train trip, but she died in Sheridan on July 7, 1915, at the age of about four months. Her death was recorded in the files of the Champion Funeral Home in Sheridan.

By June 1915, Harry was back at work, heading a committee that was investigating expansion of the Merchant Marine, with the Government acquiring vessels, then leasing them to private shipping companies to operate. (Perhaps this was indirectly related to the Great War, already raging in Europe.)

On September 28, 1915, a short announcement in the *Sheridan Post* stated that "Mr. and Mrs. H. N. Gottlieb went out to Horton's [Ranch} Saturday. Mr. Gottlieb returned today, but Mrs. Gottlieb will make an extended stay." A fuller account appeared in the *Post* on October 5: "City Attorney a Real Pioneer. H. N. Gottlieb spends anxious hours on road. Caught by Storm and Darkness Midway Between Horton's and Sheridan." He got "a little sample of pioneering on his own hook which he enjoyed Monday afternoon and night of last week":

Mr. and Mrs. Gottlieb . . . were caught in the snowstorm of Sunday. . . . It was necessary for Mr. Gottlieb to return to Sheridan . . . and, since the roads were impassable for automobiles, he engaged passage on a freight wagon coming from the ranch with a load of baggage. The wagon was drawn by four husky horses but the going was so bad that next to 20 miles per hour were made. In consequence, night and black night at that, caught the freight outfit before half the distance had been traversed. With the darkness came rain, steady, cold rain. Mr. Gottlieb and the driver were wet and chilled through. They could not see the road in front of them, even with the driver riding one of the lead horses. To make matters worse, the horses were unused to that particular road and, even before darkness came, evinced a propensity to turn from the beaten track into the wilds. After darkness really came the men were in momentary fear of landing, wrong side up or under the heavy wagon in some lonely ravine or at the foot of an embankment.

To go on was next to impossible: to stop was an even less desirable alternative, for they had neither shelter, food, nor horse feed. So they kept on. Massacre Hill was navigated in safety, though at the cost of several gray hairs and, after interminable hours, they reached Banner.

There they secured food and shelter for the horses and the privilege of occupying a haymow for themselves. Daylight brought new confidence, and upon looking themselves over and finding nothing missing they proceeded toward Sheridan, arriving in time for lunch and a meeting of the city council in the afternoon.

Mr. Gottlieb frankly acknowledges that he was "nervous" while his unwieldy vehicle was negotiating the sharp curves and skirting the high banks of the Massacre Hill road, and it was not the associations which cling round that old battleground that made him nervous, either.

48

The next chapter in this story finds Dorothy and Harry in Winnetka, where their first home was on Cherry Street. Harry practiced law in Chicago, part of the generation that commuted to work in the City from the leafy, sylvan world of the suburbs.

The suburbs were really "sub" in significant ways in their earliest beginnings. They were outposts of calm, quasi-rural life. (My father referred to a drive to Glencoe as "a trip to the country.") The point had been to get away from the noise and clutter (the unmanageable diversity?), the hurly-burly; the scrum of workers, the noise and dirt of the economic engines of urban life. Screened by silent pristine snow in winter, by the rustling fragrance of trees and gardens in summer, the suburb would be peace and calm, a function of its separation from the cacophonous city.

The citizens of this new frontier were fashioning an "ideal society" with excellent public and private schools, houses of worship that supported and enriched the lives of these "pioneers"; the wives, by and large, managed the household, had domestic help, volunteered in (and sometimes founded) various public and social service organizations to accommodate the small but growing group of workers who made this suburban Elysium viable. Chicago's arts and cultural institutions were enthusiastically supported by the suburbanites, who contributed time, money, and expertise to keep the Art Institute, the Symphony, the Opera, the museums, the Planetarium, and similar major urban landmarks vigorous and relevant. Libraries, however, were able to replicate themselves (in a modest way) and so were among the suburban amenities, which also included specialty shops, groceries, and even art galleries in some places.

Harry Gottlieb was one of a small group who founded the first Reform Jewish temple in the suburbs, the North Shore Congregation of Israel. It was important to that generation to acknowledge the spiritual significance of their religion (as godlessness seemed to run rampant after World War I). Harry Jr. and (presumably) Alan were confirmed there (in those days the Reform movement did not "do" Bar Mitzvahs).

Harry Gottlieb Sr., founding member of the Temple in Winnetka, also became President of Michael Reese Hospital on Chicago's Near South Side, at 2929 Ellis Ave. One of Chicago's premier hospitals, it was a renowned teaching and research institution. Founded in 1881, it closed in 2009. Although the Gottliebs lived in Winnetka, twenty-five miles north of Michael Reese, it was "their" hospital, loyally patronized by many of their fellow (German Jewish, upper-middle-class) North Shore residents. It attracted a staff of distinguished physicians, and during its heyday, it educated scores of medical researchers.

Thus it was that as the birth of Harry and Dorothy's second child approached, their hospital was twenty-five miles away. I don't know whether there even WAS a hospital closer to them near Winnetka in 1918! Anyhow, Harry Sr. was President of Michael Reese, and Michael Reese was where Dorothy's doctor, Lester Frankenthal, who was also a friend (and who also lived in Winnetka), delivered babies. Both a train line and roads already linked commuters to the city, so at the first signs of labor there should have been time to make a reasonably comfortable trip.

Except that the baby chose to announce its arrival in the midst of the great blizzard of January 6–7, 1918, the worst in Chicago's recorded history up to that time.

As Dorothy went into labor, winds of up to sixty miles per hour were piling drifts six to seven feet high. Trains weren't running because tracks were buried in snow; roads were also snow-blanketed. Harry Sr. hired a sleigh and some strong horses — as they'd done in Wyoming winters — and took along a couple of strong young men with shovels. Dot remembered driving the horses across open fields (a lot of the area was still farmland). Luckily, she was in the early stages of labor; it took them a number of hours to get from Winnetka to 29th and Ellis. It was almost dusk when they arrived!

Her labor became more intense, and she was weary from the long, jolting ride. She asked the doctor if he couldn't speed things up. He said she was doing fine, it was not necessary to accelerate the process. She was desperate, after ten or twelve hours, much of it pretty bumpy, and, she told me, she (uncharacteristically) abjectly begged the doctor to do something. "It's almost midnight—and today is Harry's birthday. I was hoping I could give him a baby for his birthday!"

"Oh," says the doctor, "Great idea! In that case, let's try for it!!" Harry was a baby with a big head, so the doctor may have used forceps.

In any case, Harry Jr., a healthy baby boy, was born shortly before midnight, January 7— his father's thirty-ninth birthday.

A mystery (minor) is that Harry's birth certificate was signed not by Lester Frankenthal but by a Dr. Margolis. I had thought from Dorothy's account that Frankenthal was there, but given the conditions, perhaps he did not make it in from Winnetka (not everyone had Harry Sr.'s frontier qualifications); or, seeing that Dorothy was proceeding toward a normal delivery, he chose not to spend the night in the hospital in a blizzard.

Harry and his brother Alan were only two years apart: Harry, born in January 1918, and Alan in April 1920. They always shared a room. In about 1920, Harry and Dorothy moved from 982 Cherry Street to 1137 Laurel Avenue in Winnetka, their home until 1942 or '43, when they moved into an apartment in the City, at 190 E. Chestnut Street. Harry (Jr.) fondly remembered life in the house on Laurel Avenue, an anchor in his world from the age of two or three until he went off to war in 1941. He spent happy summers at Camp Wanaki, loved his four years at Williams College, but Laurel Avenue was the Rock of Gibraltar in his life.

He and I would drive slowly past it when we visited friends

in the suburbs, and at least once, we got up the nerve to knock on the door and be welcomed into the house that sat, unchanged, at the end of a gravel path set into the emerald green of a summer lawn. He found the crack in the wall where the steps descended to the basement. Finding that "landmark" delighted him: the owners were amused at his pleasure in it: he said he used to run his fingers over that crack when he and Alan would be flying down those stairs, chasing each other through the house, laughing, and Marta Dagestad, the cook-housekeeper, maintainer of order, would be shaking her head (and smiling, I suspect) as she fixed dinner in the kitchen.

They had two nicknames for Marta: "Dame" and "Shoes," the latter because she was always after them to pick up their shoes and put them away. I've no idea how she got the name "Dame." She had come to America from Norway with two of her sisters, all young girls, and Marta worked for the Gottliebs all during the boys' childhood, staying on not only after they were grown and out of the house, but also with Dorothy after Harry Sr. died. Marta threaded her way even into Harry's and my household when we needed her, and it was hilarious to hear her order Harry around just as she had when he was ten or eleven, in the good old days.

Harry (and, I think, Alan as well) attended the Hubbard Woods School, a short walk from their house. Harry's oldest and closest friend was Ned Rosenheim, son of Fannie and Edward, the Gottliebs' friends and neighbors (and, I learned while researching this account, possibly distant relatives through the Cahn side). Harry and Ned celebrated birthdays together from their very first ones: Harry's on January 7 and Ned's on May 15. There was also Mickey Mayer, third member of the triumvirate, Ned, Harry, and Mickey, notorious for (among other things) their cheery performance in a piano recital. Their long-suffering piano teacher, Miss Sophie Seligman (God rest her tortured soul), managed to get the three of them to sit at the same keyboard and perform a piece whose title is lost to history and which was referred to irreverently (probably by Ned) as the "Concerto for Six Dirty Hands."

Mickey was the subject of a little jingle made up either by Lilly, his mother, or his dad, Arthur: "Daddy's Ford Machine/ Was never very clean;/ It was dirty as heck/ Around the neck/ Was Daddy's Ford Machine." (Explanation: Lilly and Arthur had to choose between buying a car and having a baby. They decided on the baby, so Mickey's middle name was Ford: Michael Ford Mayer.) That little jingle was a great favorite among the Six Dirty Hands Triumvirate. The Mayers broke up the trio by moving to New York (where Arthur Mayer opened the first art-house cinema and became something of an eminence in the early movie theater business). We kept up with Mickey, who became a lawyer, and his brother Peter. We faithfully and enthusiastically sent campaign donations to his daughter Shelley, whose political efforts we supported for several years. She ran for—and finally won—a seat in the New York State Assembly. Harry supported her efforts before he died and we agreed to continue doing so. I mailed her a check a week after his death.

The Gottliebs had a wide circle of friends, both suburbanites and city folk: the Franks, Betty and John; Mr. and Mrs. Herb Weil, whose son Bud was a fine athlete and Harry Jr.'s friend (Bud's sister Marge was Harry's first "girlfriend," about whom more later in this narrative); Min and Herb Spiesberger, whom I only knew as city folk; and Dolph Rosenthal, who is immortalized in "The Elijah Episode," as follows: The Gottliebs hosted the Passover holiday Seder, and on one such occasion, when he was quite young, Harry was tapped to open the door for Elijah at the Seder dinner. He dutifully got up and opened the door—and there stood—*Dolph Rosenthal!* Everyone gasped; real Drama at the Passover Table!

Harry Sr., who seemed a quiet person, was a magnet for friends: some were associated with his professional life as a lawyer, some knew him as an affable citizen, golfer, legal scholar, Master in Chancery, much interested in the challenges of our judicial system; but he did not want to be a judge. In 1921, he and Ulysses Schwartz founded the law firm of Gottlieb and Schwartz. U.S., as he was called, did become a judge, and the firm, prominent and respected, enjoyed both business and political connections. Harry Gottlieb was associated with the transformation of the Chicago Surface Lines into a unified transit system for the city, which became the Chicago Transit Authority, the CTA.

49

The Gottliebs had a dog, Judy, some sort of collie mix, an affable creature, except toward people who delivered packages or mail. Then she snarled menacingly, and I think actually bit the mailman once. The boys were fond of her, playing "fetch" with her and taking her along on rambles down to the beach. In those days dogs did not have to be on a leash, and Judy loved those walks. According to Harry, she'd be on her best behavior, not chasing birds or barking at other canines. There was only one occasion on which (with only the flimsiest of circumstantial evidence) she was accused of killing (a duck).

Harry had gone to Riverview, a much-loved amusement park on the North Side of Chicago. Besides the exciting roller coaster and the merry-go-round, there was a test-of-strength device where you hit a metal plate with a mallet and if you could put enough muscle behind your swing, the metal plate would cause a ball to rise up and ring a bell at the top of this device. (You had to have the power of an experienced lumberjack to win THAT contest!)

Harry's favorite of these games of strength or skill was the "ring toss": in a spacious cage, several birds, mostly geese and ducks, milled about sociably. You'd purchase three plastic rings about the size of a dinner plate. The object was to toss the ring so that it went over the bird's head and settled round its neck. The proprietor took the ring back and you would have the bird as a prize. It was trickier than it sounds: the birds seemed to know that for them the object was NOT to get "ringed," so they'd weave and duck at just the right moment and the plastic ring would sail past them. Harry loved that game best of all: a test of skill, timing, and luck.

Once, when he was at the ring-toss place, there was a big, plump, succulent goose in the enclosure, along with the bunch of mallards, small and fast-moving compared to the majestic goose. Harry wanted that goose, he told me. He had visions of it roasted to a crisp golden brown, fragrant and big enough to be a real feast. On his third or fourth set of rings—that goose was smarter than he'd imagined it would be—he finally positioned himself and waited for the goose to be in just the right spot. With a flick of the wrist, he sent the ring flying to its target. However, at the very last moment, that goose lowered its long neck—but lo and behold, cowering behind it was a modest little duck, poor innocent!

Bingo! The ring settles over the poor little duck's neck, the proprietor reaches into the cage expertly, slips the ring off Ducky's neck, ties his webbed feet together, and pops him into a paper bag. "Here you are, son, good job!" And there is Harry, clutching this squirming, terrified, squawking creature, all his! The frightened duck is also peeing and pooping copiously. And Harry has to take the train back to Winnetka with his prize! He said it was quite a ride; the paper bag sort of dissolved, it seemed, and it was a tussle keeping the terrified bird tucked under his arm.

It must have been dark when he got home, and no one was around to help him, but he finally decided to tie Ducky to a tree with some string. The bird was probably exhausted but also comforted by the quiet and the out-of-doors of the Gottlieb yard. So Harry went off to bed, leaving his exhausted prize tethered to a bush. Awakened some-time in the night by some loud squawking, he was too tired to get up and investigate. Until morning, when he went out to find the duck gone without a trace. No feathers, no telltale evidence of murder. Why did Judy the dog get blamed? Had she liberated Ducky? Or did a fox come out of the Forest Preserve and carry Ducky off? Harry loved that story, especially the part about the horrific ride on the train.

Harry and Alan were very attached to each other, but nonetheless—I once asked him whether they ever fought. "Only once," he recalled, did they have a fierce, boil-over battle. It started over some trivial matter, with jabbing and shoving each other first, as the two of them headed toward the bluff that led to the beach. By the time they got down to the sandy shore, the jabbing became punching, their anger flamed up, and Alan, fleet of foot and sensing defeat, turned back toward home, scrambling up the bluff and stairs from the beach, just ahead of Harry. As they got up to the level grass near their house, Harry caught up with Alan and was pushing him and trying to get in position to land a serious punch.

At that moment the towering figure of their father appeared, striding toward them, sleeves rolled up, his stern gaze moving from one to the other. The boys, engrossed in drumming on one another, were brought up short as their father stepped into the melée of flailing arms and kicking feet and separated the pair. Holding them, one with each hand, he spoke sternly to Harry: "Don't you ever do that again. He's smaller than you. That is no way to settle an argument." Still holding them apart, he marched them back to the house, into the living room, sat each one in a chair, and stood, facing them. Harry didn't remember what his dad said, but he did remember the feeling: the air fairly shimmered and trembled with Harry Sr.'s aversion to brute force as a negotiating tool.

Both boys suddenly felt their fury shrivel: What had all this been about, anyhow? Harry Senior stood over them as they sat very still in their chairs, pale and subdued. Harry didn't remember a lecture, just that his dad looked from one to the other, and quietly said something like, "Don't ever try to settle a conflict of ownership that way again." Then he put one of his big gnarled hands (with all the crooked baseball fingers from his youthful athletics) on each boy's shoulder, and giving each one a very light squeeze, urged them to their feet, and the three of them went out into the yard and played some catch.

The episode was so vivid in Harry's memory that he imprinted it on mine, and knowing Harry Sr., I could picture that whole scene. The man was truly a wonder: twinkly, soft-spoken, with a wry sense of humor and the absurd — partisan of baseball, lover of numbers, meticulous thinker, keen analytical mind, deep reader of American history and other "serious" books. In his quiet way, he was an imposing yet humane presence. Harry Jr. remembered that most mornings his dad would come down to breakfast (prepared by Marta Dagestad, who lived with the family), invariably a tad behind schedule, and Harry and Alan would watch him pour his hot coffee, with cream and sugar in it, out of his coffee cup and into the saucer so that it would cool enough for him to get a few fast sips before he ran for the train to the city.

And Dot: What was her life like?

She had many friends: Betty Frank, Fannie Rosenheim, Min Spiesberger, Helen Sulzberger (née Becker, probably her oldest and most intimate friend, the one who, along with Mama Jennie, had "chaperoned" Dot and Harry's wedding trip to Wyoming), and others whose names I can no longer recall. Dorothy knew that she wasn't a "homemaker" in the traditional mold, but professional aspirations for young women were still the exception. Perhaps, thinking of future work opportunities, she had taken a secretarial course during or after college. In any event, she became secretary to Anna Willmarth Ickes, wife of Harold Ickes, who would serve as Secretary of the Interior during Franklin Roosevelt's presidency.

Mrs. Ickes was a politician in her own right: she served three terms in the Illinois House of Representatives. She also studied the Navajo and Pueblo Indians of New Mexico and Arizona; her account of tribal life in that region, *Mesa Land: The History and Romance of the American Southwest*, was published in 1933–'35. Dot's job with Mrs. Ickes started her on a career path that served her well. Sometime while or after providing her services to Mrs. Ickes, she branded herself "Secretaries, Inc." She also began selling personalized stationery on the side. (Though the stationery business outlasted her employment with Mrs. Ickes, they remained good friends.) At some point she added a book rental library to her stationery business and eventually opened a bookshop in Winnetka, in partnership with Fannie Rosenheim, another avid and eclectic reader.

Dot loved the book business; at some point, she decided to

open a bookstore in Chicago. Fannie became sole proprietor of the Winnetka shop, and Dot moved into a little ground-floor space in an old brownstone on Oak Street, calling it "Secretaries Inc., Bookshop." It became something of a pathbreaker, with its book rental component and stationery business as well as its brisk retail book sales. She had a personal touch, suggesting titles to her regular customers that were just what they were looking for; there was also brisk street traffic into the shop: tourists and walk-ins who often turned into habitués.

In those days, publishers sent representatives out into "the field" to sell their clients on forthcoming titles that would appeal to their particular clientele. Dot was a voracious and wide-spectrum reader, and she enjoyed consulting with these young (male) publishers' representatives. Many deals were made over convivial lunches in the neighborhood, which still had a sort of small-town feel in those years of the 1940s and '50s. She added a few book-related knick-knacks, which added to the informal, homey atmosphere. She loved going to trade shows and finding unusual and original items to enhance the shop's personality. She took me with her once or twice; I loved those outings: she was lively and fun to be with; she treated me like the equal I wasn't, and we got a lot of pleasure out of palling around together.

By 1945, the shop had moved from Oak Street to a space in an unused lobby of the Churchill Hotel (on Goethe Street, across from the Ambassador East Hotel). It was now "The Bookstore in the Churchill—Secretaries, Inc." The space was large and airy but not very bookish. Sometime later, she moved the shop again, this time into the basement of the Ambassador West Hotel, a smaller but livelier and more convivial environment: there were a couple of other commercial tenants (one may have been the barber shop); it was a cheery, though more cramped, space.

This vibrant, literary woman suffered a fatal stroke while at work in her bookstore in 1955—a shocking, sudden loss to Harry Jr., several years after his father's death.

50

arry loved to repeat the following story about his brother.

The Coles (probably née Cohen) were invited to dinner one night, and in keeping with the family's usual habit if it wasn't a major dinner party, Alan and Harry and the guests ate together informally. So the Coles came to dinner and the meal went along in chatty fashion. Harry might have noticed that his brother was becoming fidgety and flushed — in any case, as the main course was being cleared by Marta Dagestad, Alan jumped to his feet, quite red in the face, and blurted out, "Nobody likes Bobby Cole!" and ran out of the dining room. (It was true: *nobody* liked Bobby Cole, but still . . .) Harry told that little anecdote to our family more than once: I think he wanted us to get a sense of Alan's temperament (and the consternation — and hilarity — it could inspire).

For a number of summers, from age seven or so to age fourteen, Harry went to Camp Wanaki in Minnesota. He loved camp life. It was the right place for him: he swam, fished, played baseball and possibly tennis, did a lot of canoeing, and had seven or eight happy summers in the woodsy out-of-doors: a time to place himself in Nature as he grew from childhood into adolescence. Alan went to Gaysville, in Vermont, a camp that had some traditional camp features but also included more out-of-the-ordinary activities. It was founded and run by Wanda and Letty, a lesbian couple, who were significant and influential members of the Winnetka community. They espoused the philosophy of Progressive Education, as practiced in private schools such as North Shore Country Day School in Winnetka, and Francis W. Parker School in Chicago. They ran a pre-kindergarten and kindergarten in the winter season for the children in their Winnetka circle. Harry and Alan both attended that school, as did many of the children in the Gottliebs' circle of friends.

The summer camp in Gaysville, Vermont (which I think may have been coed, a departure from camping conventions in those days) was wonderful for Alan. It gave little children hands-on experience among many plants and animals, encouraging them to be young naturalists. By the time they were eleven or so, they got introduced to the physical work of land maintenance as well as animal husbandry. There were still the campfires and the more conventional aspects of camp life. But the work these boys and girls did, digging post holes and grading roads, was public service work, and it was a formative experience for Alan, the earliest stage of his focus on government's reciprocal role in both directing and being a servant of its citizens. Alan continued visiting Gaysville long after he'd "graduated," returning, when he was in college, to help with the endless infrastructure needs of Vermont, a state that suffered harsh and sustained rural poverty.

I think it was when Harry was about fifteen years old (and ready for more-adult activity than being a camper) that his Uncle Edwin Kuh invited him to spend the summer looking after his three young Kuh cousins on Martha's Vineyard Island in Massachusetts, where the Kuhs had a summer home. Harry was very close to his Aunt Charlotte and Uncle Edwin (a.k.a. Skipper), and they respected and admired his responsible character, his independence and resourcefulness, his consistently affable good nature, as well as his tact, high intelligence, and self-discipline. At fifteen, he was a licensed driver, which was important on the Vineyard, as beaches and other attractions required driving around on the island. He would be living with Skipper and Charlotte, and they would go to sea on the *Gertie*, Skipper's beloved sailing craft (of irregular temper). A strong and willing extra pair of hands, an instinct for the ways of wind and water made Harry the perfect choice for a summer of independence, responsibility, and many spontaneous and unscripted pleasures.

The Kuh children: Peter, probably 12, Esther, 10, and Eddie,

8, knew their cousin Harry well, and the summer arrangement turned out to be a bonanza for all: Skipper had an able-bodied seaman to help hoist the sails and keep the *Gertie*'s temperamental engine compliant; the three children had a companion who could not only drive them around the island, but also think up fun stuff to do. But he was no pushover, which meant that Skipper and Charlotte could pursue their active and interesting social life at full throttle, knowing that Harry had good judgment, was a dependable and resourceful companion as well as conscientious watchdog of his charges.

He often told me about that summer and how, looking back on it, he realized it had started him on the path to adulthood — in the pleasantest possible way: he got to know many of the Kuhs' high-profile friends: the Gudes (Jap was head of CBS); the McGhees (Paul was an academic at one of New York's prestigious universities; his wife, Buddy, was the friend of theirs who didn't approve of me at first because she thought I was shamelessly chasing after Harry — either a social climber or a gold-digger — but we eventually became good friends); various writers, painters, musicians, all drawn to the beauty of the (at that time) undiscovered Nirvana that was Martha's Vineyard in the 1930s.

After that first idyllic summer, Harry managed to return and spend as much time as he could at the Vineyard. He was regarded as a family member by the Kuhs' circle of luminaries and was encouraged to join some of their informal get-togethers. There was always sailing, swimming, and playing in the Sunday morning community baseball game, an exuberant mix of "off-islanders" and locals of all ages. Once, Harry took S. J. Perelman out on the *Gertie* for a bit of late-afternoon fishing. They caught fish, drank beer, laughed and talked until it was almost dark. Returning — quite late, but triumphant — with their catch, what were they to do with the fish? The Perelmans had a fish-loving Norwegian nanny who expressed enthusiasm at this bonanza — until she discovered that they were not pan-ready but had to be scaled, gutted, and fileted: not part of her M.O. She suggested that they prepare the fish for cooking, then leave them in their bucket on top of the refrigerator; she'd get the two children to bed and THEN she'd cook these succulent little critters. The fishermen were absolutely NOT to dispose of them out of pure sloth. If they did, she'd quit.

This elevated their predicament to a whole new level: If she quit, the Perelmans' summer idyll would be *kaput*! A surreptitious midnight burial was out of the question. So, showing great ingenuity, they got one of Harry's local professional fisherman pals to clean the fish and duly leave them in the kitchen, as ordered. It happened, however, that the nursemaid either forgot about them or got a better offer. Next morning the rank smell of decomposing fish forced Harry (the conscientious fishing guide) to take them out back and at least give them a decent burial. (No further mention of the nursemaid.) Of such epic adventures did the prewar summers of happy memory consist.

There was the oft-recounted tale of Harry's first and only swordfishing venture with his pal Eric Cottle. Eric and his dad Roy were both professional swordfishermen, an occupation that, along with "lobstering," was an economic mainstay of the Island in those days. Mrs. Cottle (Polly to most of us but always called Pauline by her husband) was a rabid Boston Red Sox fan and the Kuhs' cook, housekeeper, purveyor of all Island news and gossip, and Charlotte's trusted friend and confidante.

Here is Harry's story of swordfishing in Vineyard Sound, a story he loved to tell on himself:

The day dawned hot and still, with slick seas and only a mild, heaving swell: great for swordfishing, Eric proclaimed. The way these sleek, streamlined creatures were fished in those days was time-tested but not exactly automated: you searched for them by sight. To get a longer view, you climbed the mast to the crow's nest (seventy-five feet above the deck) and scanned the sea with your binoculars for signs of basking fish: a telltale fin or broad tail, or a swirl in the still water.

By the time the boat cleared the harbor for open water, and was moving slowly across the oily swells of Vineyard Sound, Harry began to feel a bit queasy. There was no shade in which to hide from the merciless sun; he felt more and more miserable.

Eric, the helmsman, ran the boat while his experienced helper readied the harpoon, fastened to a coil of rope attached to a barrel that they'd use as a marker. There was no harpoon "gun" in those days; you had to have a powerful arm, flawless aim, and good eyesight. When a fish is harpooned, the crewman flings the barrel overboard, lowers a dory into the water, jumps into the little boat, and rows in furious pursuit of the barrel marker with the harpooned fish at the other end. It can take a while for the fish to tire enough for the dory to catch up with it and secure it.

Eric suggested Harry make himself useful and take his mind off his nausea by climbing the mast to the crow's nest with the glasses to look for signs of fish. Concentrating on climbing the sketchy footholds of the rope ladder did help temporarily, but it didn't take long for Harry to feel seriously nauseous up there, where the sea's gentle swells were magnified into a rolling and heaving misery by the height of the mast. It wasn't even ten minutes before he warned Eric that he HAD to descend — quickly — or deck cleanup would be needed. Slithering recklessly down from the crow's nest, he staggered into what little shade he could find and lay on the deck, as close as he could get to a rail.

Harry spent much of the rest of that endless day prostrate on the deck. The vibrating engines, the smell of fuel, the lack of a breeze, the blazing sun were misery enough, but he felt ashamed to be so useless. He never got seasick on the sailboat *Gertie*, neither in the calm, rocking at anchor, nor in rough seas. But then the sun began to glide down from its zenith, and after what seemed like an eternity, they finally spotted a fish! Harry mustered an effort of sheer will to watch the drama of the chase as it had been conducted ever since the days of sailing ships.

The crewman readies the harpoon; Eric throttles down the engine and the boat glides up as close as possible to the basking fish; Eric moves forward to grasp the harpoon as the crewman hands it to him. He hurls it skillfully: straight and true. The fish is hooked! Rope starts leaping off the coil. Immediately the crewman pitches the barrel into the water, lowers the little dory that's at the ready, jumps into it as it hits the water, and begins rowing furiously in pursuit of the harpooned fish, which is moving smartly away. The captain, at the wheel, is following that barrel marker on the heels of his frantically rowing crewman. Harry, momentarily roused from his misery by the excitement, is once again prone.

They'd probably left Menemsha Harbor around 6:30 or 7:00 A.M.; their fish was harpooned around 3:00 P.M. (and is, of course, bleeding—which can attract sharks!). The man in the dory is finally catching up with his prey. The skipper approaches the harpooned fish and dory and must position the boat so that he and his crewman can haul the exhausted fish out of the water (and away from sharks). Rope and barrel are piled into the dory and Harry has perked up, now that the sun is low and the trip soon to be over. He watches as the dying fish, a piece of stout line made fast to its tail, is hauled onto the deck. The dory, with its barrel marker and pile of rope, is made fast astern where it is out of the way until they are done with the weigh-in of their catch and can wash down the boat. They make for home, where the fish's length and weight are recorded. [Now it's all done electronically, including, I believe, locating fish.]

There are still fish out there. I don't know whether there's any catch or size limit imposed now (in the twenty-first century); but the technique of hunting and hooking swordfish had probably been pretty much the same ever since the first Native American fishermen took up the chase—and until mechanical power and electronic instruments supplanted (to some extent) craft, instinct, and muscle. That was Harry's first and only swordfishing experience: just another day's work for Eric, but for Harry, an indelible recollection of misery and drama. The two of them recalled it with wry pleasure whenever they got together.

51

Dot and Harry Gottlieb Sr. had a summer place in Vermont, where Dot spent convivial summer vacations, socializing with locals and also with Chicago friends she'd invite to visit and enjoy the relaxed quiet of rural, hospitable (but impoverished) Randolph Center. Alan spent at least part of his summer vacations there and, while he was a student at Harvard, he'd sometimes open the house during the winter holidays to ski and relax, often with friends: a break from the academic down-East atmosphere of Harvard. Harry Sr. spent summer intervals there (as did Harry Jr., though he preferred Martha's Vineyard).

My parents were invited but made only one visit to Randolph Center. It was not my mother's kind of place. She didn't take to rural isolation, to the informal "communal cooking" that produced simple country meals of baked beans or stew, with the visitors peeling potatoes, creating salads, and washing up afterward. Her chronic sense of inadequacy among college-educated German Jews failed to diminish despite the relaxing effects of Dot's hospitably heavy hand with liquor. Oscar, lover of all things rural and sylvan, enjoyed it. That one visit to the Gottlieb summer home was their only one. Of course, I made my own visit there my first summer with Harry.

Dorothy Gottlieb wasn't a mah-jongg player or a golfer or a tennis player; she loved horseback riding and owned a horse (whose name I forget). He was stabled in Highland Park, and she rode nearly every weekend with Bob Trier, a horse-owning neighbor. Bob was a refugee whose strong German accent never faded, although he spoke fluent English. He was an Alpha male: firm stride, deep bass voice, thick neck, military bearing, he radiated confident masculinity. Dot's friends, the Ladies of Highland Park, did a certain amount of discreet "tut-tutting" about this unconventional—and rather public—"liaison": poor Harry, they whispered, it seemed somehow "improper"; it didn't LOOK right, etc. Alan seemed to encourage his mother in whatever this relationship was; Harry Jr. made no comment, was cordial to Trier, but that was that. Alan struck up a sort of friendship with Bob, and made jokey comments about him in one or two of his letters to Dot. Harry Sr. was quite unperturbed: he was comfortable with Bob.

It seemed as though Dot had energy to burn; Harry, whether never completely "recovered" from that terrible long-ago peritonitis, or just quieter, more reflective, was articulate but deliberate: he thought before he spoke—few, but wondrously well-chosen words. I am further convinced that he and Dot loved one another deeply, to the very end. Dot just needed action and talk; Harry was comfortable with his pellucid clarity of thought, his astuteness, all so unassuming and quiet, while Dot was all-out social—an extrovert. She was made whole, however, by Harry's strong logic and judiciousness, and by his surprisingly fey sense of humor. How I wish I had spent more time with them! But I was young and preoccupied with growing up.

I got to know Bob Trier after Harry and I were married. I remember going to his house in Highland Park: dark wood, sort of masculine-looking furniture, horse paintings on the walls, large fireplace—there was a Nordic air about it. Two chairs flanked that fireplace: low to the floor, but proportioned for adults, each had a heavy leather back fastened with brass studs to two uprights, and brown velvet cushions on the seats. Although low to the ground, they were remarkably comfortable, just right for thawing out before a Viking-style fire blazing in the cavernous fireplace. Bob would hand you a hot toddy, welcome after the snowy ride. Those two chairs are now in our family: Dot must have "inherited" them from Bob. Though the brown velvet finally wore out (replaced by less-Nordic tweed and needlepoint), their indelible Viking-ness endures.

Harry and Dot had enrolled Harry Jr. at North Shore Country Day School, *the* prestigious progressive private day school, for high school—in preference to New Trier, the local (and highly regarded) public high school. They wanted top-of-the-line college prep for their son. One prerequisite was a student interview with the Principal of Country Day. Harry obediently met with the Principal (who might have been Perry Dunlap Smith, an eminent educator, but I am not sure). The Principal's opening question to Harry was, "So, why do you want to come to Country Day?"

Harry replied, "I don't want to come to Country Day, but my folks want me to."

The Principal stood up, patted Harry on the shoulder, and, smiling, said, "Don't worry, son, I'll fix it for you." So Harry attended New Trier. Most of his schoolmates also went there, it turned out. Among them was Bud Weil, whose sister Marge became Harry's High School Romance.

Mandatory ballroom dance classes imposed coed sociality on the youngsters; it was an awkward beginning, but it served to initiate the relationship between Harry and Marge that lasted almost all the way through high school. He took her to dances; he felt comfortable with her; he liked her. Bud, her kid brother (a superb athlete), was his sports pal. Harry and Marge were a twosome until the end of junior year in high school. Then they just sort of drifted apart. They didn't even go to the Senior Prom together. (Harry didn't seem to remember how that drama might have played out.) In any event, for the Grand Procession at graduation, students were paired off by height--and who should be Harry's partner in that final high school event but Marge!

Whatever chill had fallen over their relationship dissipated after that final pairing-off, and they remained friends ever after. I got to know Marge and her husband Bob Oppenheimer; we visited each other in Chicago and later, after Bob died and Marge moved into a retirement facility in Florida, we saw her there. And we attended her funeral—at Lake Shore Country Club (in Glencoe, Illinois), which had been the center of her social life for so many years: golf, luncheons, card games, and in earlier years dances and parties.

Harry had applied to Swarthmore College — its Quaker viewpoint appealed to him. He was not accepted, however, and his Uncle Edwin, a graduate of Williams College, suggested that he might like it. He was accepted, and it was a fortuitous outcome: he spent four stimulating years at Williams, enjoying a rich academic and social experience. He joined the Garfield Club (an independent local alternative to nationally connected "Greek" fraternities). He forged lifelong friendships. We attended reunions at Williams as often as we could; we remained in touch with his closest student friends and their wives; convivial reunions took place not only at Williams but also in Florida when we had a home there, and, on at least one occasion, at the home of Alex and Marilyn Carroll, in Indianapolis.

There was also David Simonds (a few years ahead of me at Francis Parker School), who was Harry's college roommate, and who restored the pleasure in music that his Grandmother Jennie had pretty much stamped out: she'd shush him loudly and demand absolute silence during the New York Philharmonic's Sunday radio broadcasts of classical music, inspiring a smoldering resentment in him. Then, along came David, with his beautiful baritone voice, good nature, and ardent love of music of all kinds. He reawakened Harry's innate affinity for music: jazz, classical, and folk. Further, David was a skilled carpenter and handyman, who could unravel the mysteries of the internal combustion engine as well.

Thus, in sophomore year, when they were permitted to have cars, he and a couple of his pals bought Model A and Model T Ford Roadsters — freeing them to roam the beautiful Berkshires. They went to concerts, dated girls, attended dances, explored the small, quiet towns and the ski slopes of the region. Various adventures became legend: people getting stuck in snowdrifts in some of the perilous winter adventures they engaged in. There was a lot of visiting back and forth with the local women's colleges in the vicinity: Smith, Wellesley, Mount Holyoke, Vassar, Bryn Mawr, and others. There was a good deal of driving over the mountainous roads from Williams to other snowbound northeastern locations to attend dances and various social events.

On one harrowing occasion Harry had to drive José Iturbi, a renowned conductor, to Albany, where he was to conduct a concert. A ferocious blizzard had stranded him near Williamstown, and his orchestra was snowbound in Troy. The driving was nightmarish, and Iturbi, near tears, kept yelling, "Mine Orchestra! Mine Orchesra! She is in Troy!" Harry dutifully got Iturbi to Albany; whether the concert happened or not is lost to History, but he remembered the horrors of negotiating icy mountainous roads in the dark in a driving blizzard.

Harry had a couple of other less terrifying recollections: one was sleeping in the boiler room of one of the nearby women's colleges after a dance, when roads were impassable. The Housemother made up a cozy temporary bed for him there. He remembered that fondly. He would have recalled his date's name, but I don't. At another formal, possibly at Smith or Wellesley, Harry had to seek help from the Housemother, a formidable-looking woman: he was quite helpless to tie the bow tie required for the occasion. The Housemother turned out to be not only dexterous but also quite warm and friendly. She must have been charmed by this good-looking young man, so friendly and open, and so helpless when it came to the simplest of sartorial procedures. (Interesting that he was very good at tying rope line on boats, mastering the various knots; and later, when I knew him, he was an expert at tying lures onto fishing line; the bow tie was his nemesis, however, an inscrutable mystery whose impenetrability he sidestepped by never wearing a tuxedo – or never going to formal events at all, just to be on the safe side.) He loved to tell the story about getting help with the necktie, and also the boiler room one.

Harry and three or four other entrepreneurs got this brilliant idea: they'd buy a piece of land off campus and build a cabin, a sort of retreat, away from college restrictions. At least one of the group had a girlfriend, but the others just thought it was a great idea and they'd work out a sharing plan. (Such free-wheeling entrepreneurship is unthinkable in the twenty-first century! College Regulations would forbid unsupervised living; but these young men didn't ask, and discreetly didn't tell, and, as far as I know, the College never knew about the cabin and its owners.) David Simonds was evidently a good enough carpenter for the group to be confident that they could build a sturdy little shack with him as principal contractor. Rocky Rothschild (a Winnetka chum whose parents, Ike and Bea, were close friends of Dot and Harry Sr.'s) had a few mechanical skills, too, so all they had to do was to find some scenic land and an owner willing to sell off a small piece.

They scouted the area and found a hillside with a stunning view. A little negotiating with the farmer and they became owners of this little site. In due course, the cabin got built and furnished (consisting, as I recall, of a bed, a chair, a table, and a lamp—probably an oil lamp). I don't recall an outhouse or any running water, but I only visited it once. The group of boys who were the original owners and builders left it to David Simonds, who'd been the principal "architect," lived in Williamstown after college, and had become caretaker by default. He built a lovely home on the outskirts of Williamstown that had the conventional amenities of a house—heat, plumbing, water, and electricity—and he and his wife Kirby, their dog, and some chickens lived there all their lives. He farmed the land in modest fashion (grew corn, had a grape arbor, made wine), and had a job as a chemist or something at the Sprague plant nearby. Before his death, he gave the land back to its original farmer owner's descendants. The cabin had been a well-used and much enjoyed retreat. Others besides David, Harry, Rocky Rothschild, and possibly Max Berking probably used it.

Rocky fell in love with Mary, a "Townie," later married her, and when he retired, after a long career in Chicago—in the clothing business—he took up the work that was his lifelong heart's desire: he bought and ran a gas station, on the outskirts of Williamstown. We visited him there and saw him "at work": ear-to-ear grin, grease-spattered coveralls, gas pump in hand: a life fulfilled!

One of Harry's undergraduate summers was spent working at an asphalt plant in Lawrenceville, Illinois, doing unskilled roofing work—and, incidentally, playing on the company baseball team. He ruefully recalled that his skills in both baseball and asphalt spreading were less than superior, but he held onto the job, *and* the place on the ball team. There was a shrill fan who heckled him mercilessly; she'd let him have it—and she came to just about every game. Then, at the end of the season, she came up to him, complimented him on his performance, and wished him luck. He never forgot both being razzed all season by that woman—and then getting a pat on the back from her.

He had never done "hard labor": he may have shoveled snow at home now and then, but he was not a user of tools, a fixer of anything except the occasional flat tire on Genevieve or Emmeline, the two Ford roadsters he'd owned during his college years. He was not a "Mr. Fix-it" handyman type. So labor was a new experience. It may have been the summer before his senior year at Williams that his father's friend had a work opportunity for Harry, this time in Texas. So Harry drove the little Ford Roadster from Chicago to Texas, and, that was an Adventure.

He may not have been aware that Texas law gives herds of cattle right of way when it comes to crossing highways. The sheer mass of a herd blocked the road at first, but as the final few stragglers were crossing, Harry accidentally hit one straight on. It flew up over the hood of the little roadster and rolled off to the side of the road, quite dead. The car had a couple of dents, no more. But he had to get to his new job, so leaving cow at roadside where she fell, he steamed on to his destination. The following day, however, he drove back to the scene of the accident. The cow was gone, but the evidence of her demise was unmistakable. He located the rancher's house, and made his apologies. The rancher said he'd settle for $100. Harry got the money to him somehow, and all was settled amicably.

His job in this remote, dusty area of Texas involved putting up fencing, and he was to be helper to the man who ran a post-hole digging vehicle. Harry, the unskilled member of the team, followed along, inserting and setting the posts securely. This was during the Great Depression of the '30s, and men were lined up along the road, watching the workers and hurling insults as they waited (hopelessly) in line for a job. The working men had only this flimsy fence separating them from the "petitioners." Harry said he felt nervous and apologetic; he was just getting "experience" while the men in line had hungry families to support. How could he look as though he needed the job? His work pants were brand new, his shirt was pressed, and some of the bitter unemployed hurled insults at him: "Git yore n------- outta here!" Harry's boss on this job, the guy driving the post-hole digging tractor, was Black. Harry felt like he was running the gauntlet. This was Texas in the mid- to late 1930s.

The rooming house he lived in was run by Mrs. Geneva Cribley. (Her husband Fred worked for the company, but he had a desk job of some sort.) Room and board was something like 60 cents per day, payable every week on payday. It included breakfast (an egg, toast, and coffee) and a bag lunch: an apple and a sandwich. The Cribleys were very good to Harry, occasionally inviting him to have dinner with them. When he left at summer's end, Geneva Cribley gave him her pineapple upside-down cake recipe. It was a special favorite of his. Somehow, Harry hung onto that recipe, and after we were married, he gave it to me. I made the cake now and then, and it would set off a torrent of recollections of that dry, dusty Texas summer. And it *was* a "dry" county, which meant you had to drive as far as fifty miles to buy beer!

He may have checked in with his folks, at home in Winnetka, but he probably also spent a few days at the Vineyard, just as the Kuhs were packing up at the end of another idyllic summer. Then it was back to Williams for senior year.

A major in Labor Economics at Williams, Harry had a much-admired mentor, Professor Robert Romano Ravi Brooks (known as "Triple R"). He ignited the young man's interest in labor unions and the businesses that encouraged, tolerated, or tried to stifle them. Improving the workingman's lot—and his productivity—through employer-supported unionization seemed an exciting prospect to Harry. Professors Frederick

Schuman and Max Lerner brought to life the challenging theory, philosophy, and history of the labor movements spawned in Western Europe's venerable universities. The historical and philosophical literature in the curriculum challenged not only Harry's thinking but also his reading: he explored history and economics — and fiction and poetry from a new perspective: the miracle of Inquiry. It became woven into his outlook, colored his writing, his capacity to explore the poetry of baseball, and the economic challenges of racial and religious discrimination in our society. He delighted in these seeming anomalies.

After he graduated from Williams in June 1939, Harry (again with "connections" his father had with the officers of the company) was employed by the Inland Steel Co. He was hired as an unskilled worker, a "hooker." His job was to fasten some sort of device around bars of red-hot steel so that they could be transported from the furnaces (whence they emerged as rough glowing bars) to further stages in the production process. (The company probably saw this graduate of a prestigious Eastern college as a future executive, an "idealist" who wanted to know all aspects of this immense and complicated corporation.) As a "hooker" at Inland Steel he worked indoors, moving steel ingots from the white-hot furnace to other locations in the cavernous plant. At least he was not exposed to the lines of haggard men waiting outside for a chance to get hired. He had to wear two layers of heavy woolen underwear (even in summertime!) under his work clothes to insulate him from the terrible heat of the steel as it emerged from the furnaces. Harry worked an eight-hour shift, and since the plant was operating at full capacity, it ran twenty-four hours and the men rotated through two weeks on each shift: 7:00 a.m.–3:00 p.m.; 3:00 p.m.–11:00 p.m.; 11:00 p.m.–7:00 a.m.

How did this gently reared, college-educated boy get into this line of work? He wanted to learn about Labor from the ground up; the gritty work itself; he wanted to get to know and understand the workers, said to be the pride and backbone of America: their sweat made us the industrial giant of the world at that time. This was steady, skilled, well-paid work; many of the workers were originally from Mexico; how did they get into this line of work? They were Union men, and there didn't seem to be friction because their native language was Spanish.

Harry soon was offered the occasional sample of their "native" food, which they'd heat up by putting it on one of the (still very hot) ingots. Those samples of the tortilla, the enchilada, internationalized his eating habits: the restaurants near the mill had that same delicious food. When he worked the night shift and got off work at 7:00 a.m., he'd step into one of them, have a shot and a beer, then order "dinner": tortillas or enchiladas, then go home (to the YMCA on 53rd Street) and tumble into bed.

When he was working a day shift, he liked to listen to late-night jazz on radio station WIND: Sidney Bechet, Louis Armstrong, Earl (Fatha) Hines. . . . He'd hear requests from "The Chilmark Mob," and wonder if it was his cousin Betsy.

One day he didn't feel so well: nausea, belly pain. Thinking maybe he'd eaten an enchilada that was past its prime, he went to work anyway. The illness didn't subside, and within a couple of days he took a day off from work to see if a rest would improve matters. He really was feeling ill. He called his father in Winnetka for advice.

Harry Sr. listened and then said, "Get in a cab. I'll meet you at Michael Reese Hospital."

Harry said, "But—but—" but his father, the survivor of a ruptured appendix at about the same age, had hung up, brooking no argument.

The next morning Harry Jr.'s inflamed appendix was safely removed, and he began the convalescence that led him—unready to stand around at his parents' cocktail party—to dinner at the Kuhs,' where he notably did not rise to greet me, his future wife of seventy-three years.

Abraham Gottlieb

Rose Pollak Gottlieb

Aaron and Ida Cahn

A page of Ida Cahn's memoir

Dorothy and Edwin Kuh

Harry N. Gottlieb Sr. on the
UChicago tennis team

Harry and Dorothy Gottlieb on their wedding day

Harry Sr. on his wedding day

Harry Gottlieb Jr.

Harry Gottlieb Sr. in 1922

Harry and Alan Gottlieb

Harry Gottlieb Jr

Harry and "Skipper" Kuh playing horseshoes on the Vineyard

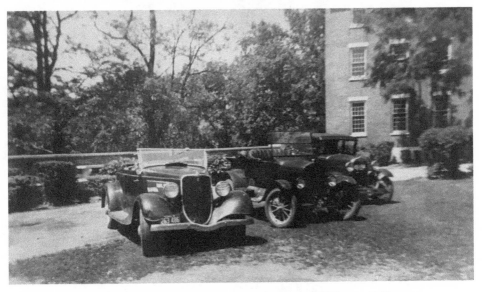

Model A and Model T Ford roadsters at Williams College

Aunt Evelyn with Grandma Rose and Arlyn, L.A.

Lieutenant Gottlieb at the train station

Just married: Lt. and Mrs. Harry Gottlieb, Jr.

Harry

Jean

Happy in Tampa

Pensacola, Christmas 1942

CAH165 56 2 EXTRA GOVT=NAS VEROBEACH FLO 28 400P

MRS H M GOTTLIEB=

REPORT DELIVERY 22 EAST ELM ST=

DEEPLY REGRET TO INFORM YOU THAT YOUR SON, ENSIGN ALAN
GOTTLIEB AV(N) USNR FAILED TO SURVIVE INJURIES SUSTAINED IN
AIRPLANE CRASH DIED 2:20 PM THIS DATE. ALAN DID NOT SUFFER
PAIN AS DEATH WAS INSTANTANEOUS. HIS FATHER MR H N GOTTLIEB
HAS BEEN NOTIFIED. SINCERE SYMPATHY IS EXTENDED TO YOU IN
YOUR GREAT LOSS=

COMMANDING OFFICER NAVAL AIR STATION,

AV (N) USNR 2:20 PM.

Ale

Headed north with Cassie Greider (Georgie on board)

My "war wife" apartment

New Guinea: Encampment at "Station Secret"

School and church (village houses were built over water)

A ride to the feast

A friend of Willie

LST (Landing Ship, Tank) from Hollandia to Leyte—1,250 miles!

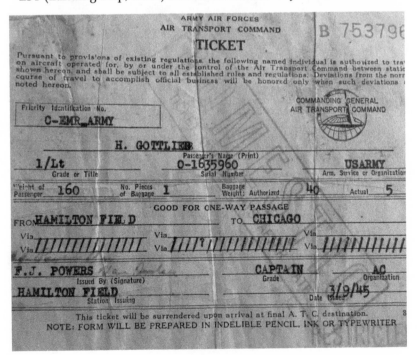

Harry's ticket home

PART FOUR

52

As I prepared to leave for freshman year at Scripps College, in Claremont, California, I was distracted from thoughts of a college career by my feelings for Harry. I was falling in love with him — or was already a goner. But, preoccupied as I was with the bustle of getting ready for college, there wasn't much time to see him.

He, meanwhile, was trying to find a branch of military service that he'd prefer to being a "dogface" (one of the many terms of opprobrium slapped on lowly privates). Harry and his brother had already made an abortive attempt to enlist. The U.S.'s first peacetime draft had been signed into law by President Roosevelt in September 1940, and all men between the ages of 21 and 64 had been required to register. Though the United States was not at war, the handwriting was on the wall; men began to be drafted and trained. Harry, 22 at the time, had duly registered, but had not yet been called up. Alan was a 20-year-old senior at Harvard. "Still hoping for a peaceful future," Harry wrote much later in a biographical tribute to his brother, "he was thinking about becoming a lawyer, and in March 1941 he had received acceptance of his preliminary application to Yale Law School."

On Alan's twenty-first birthday, April 28, 1941, the Gottlieb family convened, the four of them, in Detroit, of all places — a scheme crafted by the two brothers. They had a merry, celebratory lunch, and then the boys put their folks on the train back to Chicago and walked across the bridge from the U.S. to Windsor, Ontario, and the nearest Canadian recruiting station.

Our country was still not convinced that this war in Europe was a World Problem. "There was much sentiment at the outset

in the United States to avoid entering the war," Harry wrote —
and Alan, at first, had partly shared that sentiment.

As the German forces overran France and seriously
threatened to defeat Great Britain, the country became very
divided on the issue. Through 1940, Alan had taken a position
in favor of maximum aid to England but in opposition to a
United States entry into the war. In a December 1940 letter
he wrote, "I finally got so mad at the pro-war taunts to the
peace picketers of 'damned pacifist' and 'yellow' that I
briefly joined a group of pickets myself."

But if Alan doubted that our country should get into the war,
he and Harry had no such doubts about themselves. As Jews,
the brothers were acutely aware of Hitler's evil; as liberals,
they had no illusions that his murderous intent would stop at
the Jews. So they announced to the recruiter behind the desk
in Windsor that they had come to volunteer for the Canadian
Air Force.

The soldier asked if they knew how to fly a plane. When
they said, well . . . no, but they were quick learners, he shook
their hands, thanked them (did he keep a straight face?), and
said they should go back home to the U.S.A. and learn how
to fly — THEN they'd be welcomed into the Canadian military.
Did they ever confess that naïve plot to their parents? Probably.
They'd all have had a good laugh over the innocence of the two
naïve patriots.

Harry went back to Inland Steel; Alan returned to Harvard.
He graduated that June, *magna cum laude*, Phi Beta Kappa, class
of 1941. Harry recounts that "during the summer following
his graduation . . . [Alan] was director of the Grafton, New
Hampshire work camp . . . sponsored by the International
Student Service," whose participants spent the summer
working with farmers to rebuild a washed-out flood control
dam.

Meanwhile, Harry and I sauntered along the Chicago
lakefront, talking, falling in love.

After our end-of-summer visit to the Vineyard and to his

parents in Randolph Center, I rode the bus back with him as far as New Jersey, where he had an interview to see if he could get into some branch of the service other than the U.S. Army. In the course of this effort he discovered that he was red-green colorblind, which (supposedly) limited his options — and certainly, together with his flat feet, kept him out of the Navy. He'd never been able to pick strawberries because the contrast between berries and leaves was indistinguishable to him, but he didn't think about it — until he failed the "yarn test" so spectacularly that later, in basic training at Fort Riley, Kansas, he would become the exemplar of classic red-green colorblindness before groups of medic trainees.

Just as I headed west on the two-day, two-night transcontinental train ride to California, Harry got his draft call in Winnetka. But he had begun to complain of an itchy face. By the time he was supposed to report for his physical, his entire face had broken out in a virulent case of poison ivy: his eyes swelled shut, and he had to put off the physical. He was staying with his folks, and they got a trained nurse to come in and bathe his face with boric acid solution. He wrote me one letter with a description of how miserable it was. He was sensitive to poison ivy; he always managed to pick up a little of it at the Vineyard, but he usually got it on his legs from walking in the woods. This flare-up happened too long after our return from the Vineyard, and it was just on his face. He'd gone bowling with Joanie MacArthur, the wife of his Williams college friend Jack Whiting, and he thought he must have gotten poison ivy from the bowling ball he used, though I don't see how that would be possible.

It only lasted a week or so; then he went for his physical, passed it, and waited to find out what would happen next. But it was the hand of fate. The draftees who were called up on that first date all went to Europe. If not for that ghastly case of poison ivy, none of us might be here.

In September 1941, I began the 2,000-mile train trip to Southern California and Scripps College for Women, the school I had chosen sight unseen. There was just one other

Scripps-bound freshman from Chicago on board: Jane Loeb, a suburban friend I'd met a year or so before, during another summer when my parents and I (and possibly Darlene) stayed at the Moraine Hotel in Highland Park, that leafy suburban retreat far removed from city life. It had brought me and Jane and Patsy Frank (later Spitz, and still later Baldauf) together.

Janie's very wealthy family had been shattered by the murder of a fourteen-year-old boy by her uncle Dickie Loeb and Nathan Leopold in 1924, when Janie was a baby. The Loeb family had fled their mansion in Kenwood (across from where the Obamas would later live) to their estate in Charlevoix, Michigan, the same lakeside resort—a favorite of affluent German Jews— where Dorothy Kuh and Harry Gottlieb Sr. may have met. Janie's earliest memories were of Charlevoix; only after the notoriety of the murder had faded did some of the family return to the Chicago area. Dickie's brother Ernie occupied an elegant house in Highland Park. Janie was one of only two girls I knew—Jackie Paley was the other—who had a French governess. Jane's was called "Zellie," short for Mam'selle.

We liked each other, and had exchanged occasional overnight visits, but our close friendship began on that train to college—and lasted until her death. Her life was shadowed by tragedy: the murder that darkened its beginning, then Dickie Loeb's murder by a fellow prisoner; the death of her seven- or eight-year-old daughter Cathy from cancer or something equally terrible, and Dave Silberman, the father, battling with Jane over which treatment protocol to follow while the kid was dying. It was horrible. Dave was a boor. In her grief, a paralysis of both legs afflicted her. The doctors never were able to describe it except as a "hysterical response to emotional shock"; it never abated. She and Dave divorced. For a couple of years she lived in a huge round penthouse overlooking Lake Michigan, unable to walk. She got remarried to a man, Bob Sooy—tall, dark, quiet, kind—who also had a disability of some sort, and they eventually left Chicago and retreated to the peace of Charlevoix, the place she loved most. Janie and I continued to write to one another as long as she lived.

But back to the beginning: talking, reading, and eating together made the monotonous two-night, two-day transcontinental trip interesting and diverting—and let Janie and me half-forget this epic change we were about to experience.

53

Stepping off the train at the insignificant siding in an open field that was Claremont, California—brilliant sun, the smell of dry grass and eucalyptus, the silent emptiness— shocked me into a kind of clammy apprehension. What had I done? Two thousand miles from home—strange country with mountains in the distance; so few people—nothing like the lunatic bustle of Union Station in Chicago. I felt quite lost and scared. At least Janie and I had each other to get us through those first homesick days.

A few Scripps people were waiting to greet us: dorm "Mothers," some administrators, and a group of girls, each designated as "big sister" to one of us arriving freshmen: a junior or senior who'd be advisor, friend, helpmeet, to indoctrinate or familiarize us with the campus and its environs: to show us where our classrooms were, and the library; where to buy toothpaste, how to learn about campus amenities, and how to get to "downtown" Claremont, home of the World's Most Delicious Hot Fudge Sundaes. The "big sister" assigned to me was Jan Fuller, a junior from Arizona: calm, self-assured, open. Luckily, we liked each other immediately. And she showed me the ropes, all right! Sexually a free spirit (and bright, and a very good student), she was, in my sheltered way of life, more than a breath of fresh air—a veritable hurricane.

Scripps, which had some subtle religious affiliation, had particularly strict regulations about "morals." It was all girls, surrounded by a wall. Its two nearby sister schools, Pomona College and Claremont Graduate School, were coed, so there was no shortage of opportunities for men and women to mingle. But the regulations at Scripps were like those in a cloister, forbidding any but the most innocent and public "contact" between the sexes. Male visitors were prohibited from all areas of the dorm except for the first-floor parlor. The dorm "Mothers" were basically watchdogs, according to Jan, who—she freely shared with me—carried on a brisk program of sexual activity. She and her various swains spent a lot of time outdoors, since renting a room somewhere was too expensive, and conspicuous. She had at least one boyfriend with whom she had regular trysts somewhere up in the mountains.

Jan offered to arrange a partner for me for some "partying." I told her about Harry and me. There was no "commitment," but I felt that this was the love of my life, and he seemed, on paper as it had to be now, as much in love as I was. So my heart—and all the rest—belonged to Harry; and scholarship, not dating, would be my primary focus in college.

Jan listened respectfully—and immediately saw in me a perfect cover for her illicit shenanigans. I could be HER protector: a safe haven for her contraceptives! They were forbidden on campus, she told me; possession could get you expelled. Since no one would ever suspect *me*, this innocent, of nefarious fornication, my room would never be searched for sexual contraband. (After all those years of having my sister as roommate, I was now in a place where single rooms were the rule.)

I was delighted to oblige. For the rest of the school year Jan kept her contraceptives, whatever they were, hidden in the dresser drawer in my room. Though it made me a bit uncomfortable to be privy to the frequency of her sexual escapades, I felt honored to be the "Keeper of the Device," and at least she was discreet. She never got caught.

I'd fallen crazy in love with Harry, and it *was* crazy: there I was, starting my College Career, with my heart elsewhere and my ability to CARE about scholarship seriously compromised. Part of that was induced by homesickness, however. And as Jane and I made friends, and got challenged by the interesting courses and stimulating faculty, we were both seduced by the varied attractions of college life, and the homesickness abated.

I have vivid memories of the articulate, imaginative biology professor (whose name I've forgotten), who restored my love of that discipline and finally exorcised the prurient ghost of Wallace Worthley; and Dr. Edgar Goodspeed, an authority on ancient Egypt and the Near East, fluent in Assyrian, both ancient and modern Hebrew, and numerous other languages of the region. He was an eminent scholar—a retired professor of Egyptology and Biblical Studies from the University of Chicago, author of numerous scholarly books and articles — and an enthusiastic teller of stories: about himself and archaeological digs he'd participated in, and mysterious, beautiful, mystical, and cruel stories and fables of the vast empire of the Pharaohs. Both Janie and I were entranced by his detailed knowledge of the Ancient Near East and Egypt, his ability to transmit both that knowledge and his enthusiasm to us, bringing the past to life before us. Jane and I briefly attempted to learn Hebrew from Dr. Goodspeed, but (no fault of his) we gave it up.

Another life-changer was the art class taught by Millard Sheets, a watercolorist of some renown, who taught us how not just to look, but to look hard, really to *see*: to experience the discipline of intense looking, then to transmit the result of that looking (which might include admiration, boredom, wonder) onto paper. A spare, simple vase stood on a pedestal in the Art Studio. Art class met for three or four hours a day, three days a week. Every class, for the entire first semester, we drew that same vase: with charcoal, pencil, crayon, watercolor, pen and ink. After the first couple of weeks we stopped being bored and resentful and became curious (and surprised) about what was happening to eye-hand coordination, to emotion, to ways of looking, seeing, thinking, feeling. The same vase, the same pedestal, the same draped cloth. You *did* get sensitized, in ways you'd never have imagined: little shadings and shadows became disproportionately significant, changing all sorts of relationships between line and form. And space. It was enthralling: a profound education of the emotions, and the senses — the entry to a mind-expanding year.

When I got to Scripps I had gotten in touch with my Aunt Evelyn, who lived in Los Angeles, now Mrs. Bertrand Frohman. You may remember that she had had a love affair with her psychoanalyst, and then divorced Uncle Archie and married him. Daddy never got over his conviction that "that Svengali" actually held her captive, emotionally if not physically. I didn't see it that way. Maybe my admiration and love got in the way of a more impersonal judgment. But Evelyn and Bert seemed to me to have a congenial and comfortable marriage. Though I never got to know Bert well, he was always polite and friendly. And he won my respect because he had saved Evelyn and understood her.

I spent my Thanksgiving holiday of 1941 at the Frohman house. Bert was only marginally in evidence; he considerately let us have a marathon time together—something truly unforgettable, even though I can't remember what we talked about. I do know we did not discuss Mother or the rupture in the relationship between these two formerly deeply attached sisters.

Evelyn was an especially imaginative, sensitive, and tender person. She seemed to me to have an enormous reservoir of unconditional love for me and also for Darlene. It was much more accessible—to me, at any rate—than Mother's mercurial, often jealous ambivalence. Aunt Evelyn got and gave us unequivocal pleasure. We knew she loved us. She knew we adored her. And Darl and I had the kind of love for each other that both of us also had for Evelyn.

Mother, however, had this volcanic center that, paradoxically, made her icily inaccessible just when I needed her. She could be charming, fascinating, funny, but she didn't offer me that open enthusiasm that Evelyn did. She withheld some essential connection, I felt. Evelyn never made me feel that her caring about me was conditional on some intangible characteristic of mine being displayed in the right way. Loving Evelyn was fun, loving Mother was work. Maybe that's the blessed contrast between a mother, who's got the burden of making you turn out right, and this aunt, who's just in it for the joy of the ride.

Once, after she and Bert were married but during a detente when she and Mother were on speaking terms, we met Bert's mother, a tiny, wizened aristocrat, a native Californian, Francesca Plaut. She lived in a glorious penthouse apartment on Russian Hill, with views of the city and the bridge. Her wealthy second husband, Mr. Plaut, had left her comfortably off, and her apartment was crammed with lace pillows, spindly antique tables, and a gallimaufry of knick-knacks and expensive kitsch from all over the world. I was especially impressed with her bed, a double king-size affair (she was about four feet tall) with a lurid satin spread. The bed was literally paved with dolls—all sizes, all descriptions. They overflowed the bed and were arranged on chairs, in corners, on shelves; there must have been hundreds of dolls. I was awestruck.

Mother was certain that Bert, who hadn't married until Evelyn came along, was really a mama's boy. This little pixie of a lady looked as though she wielded considerable influence. She had a presence, a formidable bearing for such a tiny wisp of a thing. She impressed me. It was a tribute to Aunt Evelyn that Mrs. Plaut recognized and tolerated her as Bert's wife in spite of her domestic deficiencies and lack of pedigree.

After Bert Frohman died, Evelyn had what must have been the most satisfying relationship of her life. A man named Matt came on the scene, to become her long-time live-in boyfriend. He and Evelyn and her two boxer dogs had a loving life together, based on the one or two visits we had with them. Matt loved her and seemed to supply the emotional haven she had never had. She and Mother managed to negotiate a sort of shaky truce: they resumed writing wonderful gossipy letters to each other, sprinkled with recipes and trivia, but the intimacy of their earlier years was irrevocably gone.

The *coup de grâce* was that Evelyn died of pancreatic cancer in 1982, some years after their tepid truce, and Mother only learned of it after Ev's death, when Matt finally got around to phoning, weeks after the fact, to tell her. It was a blow from which Mother didn't recover. Her own death came six years later.

420

By the beginning of December 1941, I was settling into life in the San Gabriel Valley, a lovely mountain-ringed area of lush vegetation. The homesickness I'd felt in those first days at Scripps fell away like an insect's discarded carapace. I was stimulated by the classes I took and by the friends with whom I shared new delights: avocado sandwiches, the world's best hot fudge sundaes, talk, and companionship. My "big sister" Jan and I enjoyed sitting around and talking; or we'd walk the fragrant, leafy Scripps campus, talking, talking; we always had a lot to say to each other. Sometimes we went to plays or movies. We might even double date: Jan would introduce me to some attractive and personable young man, whom she would have "briefed" in advance on my unavailability, and the evening's event would be followed by lively, interesting conversation.

I also had my first encounter with lesbian sexuality. Tweege Rocky (how's that for a name?), a big, rangy, redheaded upperclassman and art major, was an accomplished sculptor: she'd had a show or two at the school, and I admired her work. We got to be acquaintances, and she asked me if I'd like to model for her. The old modeling instincts reasserted themselves, and I, an innocent in the world of the sexual come-on, said, "Yes, I'd like to." It was to be an evening session, because of classes, et cetera, she explained.

I go to her studio and it's to be upper torso, so I strip down. Then I realize that this is NOT about sculpture at all. She is being amorous and I tell her I am there to model only, and she tries to argue me out of that narrow-mindedness. She was a lot bigger than me but didn't make an athletic contest out of my refusal, thank God. So I said no, thanks, I do not wish to partake, put my blouse back on, and left. And that was the end of any possibility of just friendship with Tweege.

Though homesickness was gone, lovesickness was not. I found myself writing to Harry every day. For both of us, it was a new life: I was "on my own," and Dogface Harry, the draftee, was in Basic Training in Fort Riley, Kansas, in a cavalry unit, driving two-and-a-half-ton trucks (not horses) with fancy gears, like nothing he'd ever driven before. With his Ivy League-ish education (Williams is considered one of the "Little Ivies") and cultured background, Harry had the option to enter Officer Candidate School after Basic Training, but he was resisting (though he would later reconsider), preferring the democratic camaraderie of the enlisted personnel. He relished being part of that Great American Melting Pot, the U.S. Army, its population more diverse than the bunch of skilled Mexican steelworkers who had been his *compadres* at Inland Steel.

His activist brother, Alan, meanwhile, had taken a more unabashedly elite track—and the first steps in what might become a political career, as Harry noted in 1993:

> In the fall of 1941 Alan was selected to serve as a public service intern in Washington, DC. . . . During the several months he worked in Washington, the idea of government service as a career seemed to grow on him. He was encouraged in this thought by the friendship he developed with Eleanor Roosevelt, wife of President Franklin Delano Roosevelt. She was such a wonderful human being, who had the good sense to know the importance of young leaders like Alan to the future of the United States and to the quality of the world in which we live. With just a few others, he had several lunches and dinners with Mrs. Roosevelt in the White House.

Though Harry and I were writing to each other with considerable regularity, he never said much about what sorts of things he was learning, and I can't imagine what I wrote about. We wrote more about how we felt than what we were doing. When I skimmed over our letters to each other, now sorted into packets by date, the "courtship" ones are much more intense than I'd remembered. We expressed feelings in writing that we'd probably never have spoken face to face.

And then, our feelings—and everyone's—were shaken to the depths.

54

On the night of December 6, 1941, there was a dance at Scripps, somewhere on campus. A long-forgotten date and I attended; the dancing was wonderful; we must have had a sparkling time. I'm sure there was a dance orchestra (no alcohol on the Scripps Campus — ever — that I recall). I remember what I wore: a form-fitting, flame-colored lace gown that had belonged to Darlene, a floor-length formal, glamorous and dramatic. It made me feel like a femme fatale. I came back to the dorm at the midnight curfew, tossed the dress over a chair, collapsed, happy, into bed, and fell asleep.

I awoke in time to listen to the New York Philharmonic Orchestra broadcast from Carnegie Hall, a Sunday ritual. I don't remember the program, but it's easy to look up: Shostakovich's Symphony no. 1 in F minor, Artur Rodzinski conducting. It was almost noon, and I was lounging in bed, half asleep, listening to the music, when the sonorous voice of the announcer broke in.

"We interrupt this broadcast to bring you a special bulletin."

The bombing of Pearl Harbor by the Japanese was being beamed all over the world. I don't remember the precise wording, but I remember the sensation, as if the earth had shifted its orbit. My blood ran cold; the bottom dropped out of my world.

There are occasions, like that one, that are seared into memory: you remember where you were, how you felt. The infamous 9/11 was another such; perhaps the day we dropped the bomb on Hiroshima; the day Franklin Roosevelt died; the day John F. Kennedy was assassinated.

Harry! This would mean War! Harry — what did this mean for him? For me? for Us?

Harry wrote: "I remember clearly thinking of you ... wishing you weren't so near the action. ... I wondered where you were and what you were thinking. ... I knew it was one of those moments ever marked in one's lifetime."

I would not know it till his letter arrived days later, but Harry, oddly, had also been at a dance the night before. Some of the Jewish families of Kansas City, Missouri, sent invitations to the Jewish soldiers at Fort Riley, Kansas, to celebrate the Sabbath with them. That weekend, Harry had taken advantage of this opportunity, and had dragooned his pal Murray Stedman (not Jewish, but his name could "pass") into accompanying him. The two young soldiers were met at the railroad station in Kansas City and taken to the home of the family Bernstein, where they partook of the festivities with the Bernsteins, their daughter, a couple of her girlfriends, and Grandmother Bernstein, who, Harry confided to me, was by far the most animated and interesting member of the family. Harry and Murray and the gaggle of girls went to a dance Saturday night, and both the young soldiers found it pleasant to return, if only briefly, to civilian life.

The next day the thunderclap of the attack on Pearl Harbor struck, and they were ordered back to base immediately. All over the United States, all military personnel were ordered to report in uniform Monday morning.

I scrambled into some clothes and went to see what there was to do. At Scripps College, the first order of business was to make the campus invisible at night in case there were planes or ships that might spot a telltale light. So we spent the afternoon and early evening making the campus a blackout area. This meant creating makeshift lightproof hangings to cover all dormitory windows and doors; turning off all outdoor lighting, including traffic lights, streetlights, the lights over dorm entryways; and shielding the headlights and taillights on cars by painting the top half with black paint, so that lights shone only dimly downward and wouldn't be visible (to an attacking airplane?) from above. We were to notify our families that we were safe, but avoid any frivolous or unnecessary telephone communication to keep lines free for official use. There were rumors (unsubstantiated) that Japanese submarines had been seen prowling off the California coast near Santa Barbara: near us? We were too busy to be panicked. It felt like a slightly dangerous lark as we scurried around helping to put up blackout curtains, organize ourselves into groups of watchers and wardens, prepare to live under a kind of ominous uncertainty. We listened somberly to President Roosevelt proclaim December 7, 1941 "a date which will live in infamy."

That Sunday night—it might have been the dark of the moon—the full impact of that world-changing day was brought home to me. How inky black it was outside! We were suddenly back in the Middle Ages. The night outdoors was totally, unrelievedly black: no car headlights, no streetlights, no flashlights, and an eerie silence that seemed to be induced by the darkness. The world had gone blind.

We were encouraged, but not ordered, to stay in or at least close to our dorms. Dinner in our dining room was subdued, none of the usual chatter and peals of laughter. Some of our fellow students were children of military personnel; they sat through dinner pale-lipped and mostly silent. We were all trying to assimilate this unthinkable happening.

Photos of burning U.S. Navy warships in Pearl Harbor appeared in Monday's papers (there was no TV; instant contact was only by radio): horrifying photos of black smoke billowing from burning ships. In Kansas, Harry was anxious about his dear childhood friend and Williams classmate, Bob "Rocky" Rothschild: "The other [person I thought about] was Rock, the newly married friend who is God knows where in the Pacific on a destroyer." (He was OK, Harry later learned.)

A string quartet had been scheduled to give a concert on campus that evening, and the school administration, demonstrating both resourcefulness and insight, agreed that the show should go on, which raised our trembly morale. We were in a bewildered, unsettled, anxious state, and the prospect of the music program was something "normal" to experience. The concert was moved into a small chapel whose windows could easily be blacked out, instead of the large auditorium, which would require retrofitting to keep it from leaking light. That sharply reduced the size of the audience.

We all walked the night-black silent pathway and crowded into the dim space of the chapel, with its makeshift window coverings, the candles on the performers' music stands the only source of light. Hushed by the darkness, the place had a sort of medieval feeling about it. The rustling of people settling into their seats, the sound of breathing, all came forward out of the deep gold glow of the candlelit room. The candlelight seemed to enfold us, sheltering us from the deep darkness outside.

It was one of the most profoundly emotional experiences of my life. The musicians must have played several selections, but it is the Hindemith String Quartet that is unforgettable. Pensive, spare, and articulate, it fit the time and the place uncannily, as though it had been written for this portentous night. It had a lot of emotion in it, but it was rather like Finnish furniture: devoid of ornament, long on lovely line, full of open spaces. The darkness enhanced the sensory and emotional intensity of the music; our nerve ends trembled to meet the sounds that seemed to enter into us, soul to soul, with no impediments to separate us from their wordless beauty. We were a single organism, taking in this beauty that sang to us of hope and consolation. There *would* be tomorrow, and we'd live in it and in all the tomorrows to come, drawing strength and insight from having shared this most intensely mysterious, intimate interlude that lifted us out of—and away from—Real Time. All of us, performers and audience alike, were deeply moved. For us, living in our first night of wartime, it was especially poignant to have the sense of tender, contemplative peace that Hindemith's music gave us.

Then, silent and full of wonder—and a little fear—we filed out of the chapel into the utter blackness of a moonless night. Picking our way along the gravelly street to the crunching sound of our steps and the murmur of voices, we groped our way back to our dorms with their shrouded windows. The air was very still and the earth seemed to exhale a wisp of perfume into the night. Nothing had changed, but everything, *everything,* had changed.

From Harry's letter to me, Fort Riley, Kansas, December 8, 1941:

> I think when the news broke that Japan had attacked Hawaii, every soldier listening was moved in a way he'll never forget. I know it happened in camp, in the beer joints of Junction City, in cities anywhere people were listening, I can only tell you this about the way I felt. I came near to crying, and I became a soldier too. Why I wanted to cry I can't explain. . . . [Then President Roosevelt gave a radio address and concluded by expressing "confidence in our armed forces."] That's us, and now, for the first time we think as soldiers--not in terms of when do we go home, Xmas furloughs, when can I see my girl again. Now one thing stands topmost, above all. We are at war, and each one of us is wholeheartedly at war.

From Alan Gottlieb's journal, December 9, 1941:

> The stunning blow of Japan's attack has led to the rapid abandonment of hope for a "secure" life or an easy war. From now on — for ten years with any luck — War supersedes education and even living.

In the wake of Pearl Harbor, Alan, who had passed his physical for the draft in November ("Another A-1 son," he wrote to their parents), decided "not to wait for the draft," Harry wrote years later. "He quit his job and concentrated on choosing a branch of service."

55

The portentous outbreak of war catapulted me into authentic adulthood. College, much as I enjoyed it, in the foothills with the wonderful hot fudge sundaes and interesting classes, seemed like a dalliance. What were my priorities? Not Harry, not now: he belonged to the U.S. Army! Never one to be a Stoic, I yearned to see him. But the die was cast: in his own words, he had become a soldier; he was thinking as a soldier. What was going to happen to him?

As his six weeks of Basic Training drew to a close, the Army in its infinite wisdom assigned Harry to . . . *the Signal Corps*! His difficulty distinguishing red from green should have immediately disqualified him from that branch of the Service. All those flags of different colors . . . So much for military logic! Nonetheless, off he went, to the Signal Corps at McChord Field in Tacoma, Washington State, to be trained for the next stage of his Army career.

Within a week Scripps College closed for the Christmas holidays; only a skeleton crew of maintenance people remained, my friends had scattered to their various holiday destinations, and I was on the *El Capitan*, the Santa Fe Railroad's cross-country train, racing across the Great Plains of the West toward my city. It was a long trip: two nights and two and a half days in a sit-up car. The train had been converted to blackout status; at night, all the window shades had to be drawn all the way down—no peeking out the sides or the bottom!—and the exterior lights painted black on their upper sides, the train's enormous brilliant headlight also blacked out at the top like a half-closed eye.

Back in Chicago, I moped. My heart was elsewhere. Harry and I were still exchanging letters. Shaken by Pearl Harbor, our mutual longing was so intense that I came up with a nervy and outlandish idea. I suggested to him that maybe I could come out West to Tacoma after Christmas and see him, if he was still at McChord Field. Harry responded with delight. He asked his commanding officer whether he could be granted a short leave—a couple of hours, maybe—to see his girl, who wanted to come all the way from Chicago to visit him. The Captain said yes! Just give him the date she'd be visiting, and he'd take care of it.

I bulldozed my mother, who forbade me to make such a trip unchaperoned, to accompany me. Perhaps it would be only a few hours with Harry: but who knew when I'd get to see him again, if ever? I also insisted that we travel sit-up coach because the berths were needed for sick or injured military. That was totally against Mother's (acquired) preference for First Class Luxury in all matters of personal comfort. But I think she may have liked the whole crazy romantic adventure aspect of this preposterous plan. She had a romantic streak, and she liked Harry: he was attractive, and so guileless; he wasn't after anything. Of course, she found reasons to be critical: he wasn't stylish, his pants hung off his backside . . . But mostly she was wonderful. Her better side came out on this trip.

The train pulled into Tacoma, and there stood Pvt. Gottlieb, resplendent in a GI overcoat about two sizes too big (Supply was not yet perfect in all respects, but at least he was warm), a rifle slung over one shoulder and a gas mask over the other. It turned out the Captain had managed this plot successfully by designating my visit an "emergency"; maybe that accounted for the appearance of combat readiness. What a moment! (Sometime later, Harry wrote a poem: "My Rifle, My Gas Mask, and Me." The poem is now probably lost, but the title, which lives on, brings back the whole scene.) Of course there were MPs on guard duty in the station, but they just looked at us, expressionless, and didn't ask for Harry's ID.

As soon as we got out of their sight, Harry fished in his overcoat pocket and brought out an unmarked envelope. Tucked inside it, he showed me—*four six-hour passes!*

He told me that a few days before my arrival, he had gone to his CO's office and, saluting smartly, handed him a sheet of paper with the inclusive dates of my planned trip. The Captain told him to come back on the day of my arrival, and he could pick up the pass. So when the day came, Harry appeared and, saluting smartly, said, "I'm here to pick up the—"

"Yes, yes," the CO interrupted, handed him the envelope, and cautioned him, "Carry only the pass for the current hours on your person, soldier. Let your girlfriend keep the others out of sight in her purse. If you get caught with the wrong one, it's your neck." And he saluted smartly: "Dismissed!"

Harry handed the envelope to me, and I quickly stuffed it into my purse. A totally unanticipated gift: twenty-four hours! I don't remember the CO's name—Harry never forgot it—but he's enshrined in our memory, and now in this account.

We had twenty-four blissful hours! We went to the harbor in Tacoma and sat by the sea, a link to Martha's Vineyard, the faraway other seacoast. We idled along the streets, looking in shop windows, holding hands, mine nestled in his big square warm one. In a letter he wrote not long after that day together, he mentioned holding my hand with its cool, slender little fingers. Every detail was illuminated with joy, tinged with the sorrow of how short a moment this was and how the unknowable future loomed over us.

We went in search of a birthday present for Harry's dad: the two Harrys were both born on January 7, Harry Sr. in 1879, Harry Jr. in 1918. The gift he selected for his pipe-smoking father was perfectly awful, I thought. It was a marble ashtray with a little bronze golf bag propped up on one side. The little golf clubs were removable toothpicks! Tasteless, I thought. "Are you *sure* he'll like that?"

"Oh, he'll love it," Harry said confidently. And he was right! It stood proudly (and permanently) on his father's desk at the office. Aping my mother's snobbish (read "expensive") tastes obviously didn't carry the day everywhere!

I think Harry had a few beers, but I was so conspicuously underage (he was almost twenty-four, I was just eighteen) that, even though I was with a soldier, and it was wartime, it wasn't offered to me, and I didn't ask. I was high on love! I was so crazy in love with this guy I was oblivious to everything else. We went bowling, we ate waffles, we looked at each other, trying to store up eternal memories to hold onto for however long it would be before we'd meet again. We necked a little bit, shyly. We talked — I cannot remember about what, but I don't think it was about what we'd do after the War. Who knew when that would be? Harry's brother, in his journal entry, had estimated at least ten years!

My mother rented a room for Harry — on the same floor of the hotel we were staying in. Bless her, she set no ground rules, other than "Don't stay together ALL night." She got herself a stack of fashion magazines and left us to ourselves. The specter of a long separation hung over us, but it didn't damage those few hours because we had a chance to confirm our reciprocal love. Our love, we now knew, was real and permanent — no matter what.

I crept back to the room I shared with Mother to sleep. Early the next morning, as our twenty-four hours ticked down, I rode the bus out to McChord Field with Harry. We sat on the bus, as I recall, not talking much, holding hands, both of us in our own private hurricanes of emotion. Mostly I wasn't aware of the weather: was it misty (characteristic of the region) or sunny? But the bus turned on the road, the mist lifted, and there was a stunning panorama: the mountain — a volcanic one — naked with snow on its peak, pinkish in the light of the rising sun, white tents — thousands, it seemed — tiny at its feet. The mountain's final showing of itself in all its big-shouldered power was overwhelming. I wonder now whether this is an actual visual memory, or whether I've blended it with a postcard photo. The memory has been so *schmeared* with wistfulness that I find it hard at this time and distance to be confident. I know I saw Mount Rainier, though, because I did ride out to McChord with Harry for one more "Goodbye, sweetheart."

We kissed — a last kiss? I might never see him again.

It was the end of the Christmas–New Year's holiday. Mother and I had a long train ride ahead of us, down the West Coast from Tacoma to Los Angeles; Daddy was coming to join her in Palm Springs for their annual winter holiday. I was to stay with them for a couple of days, until Scripps was back in session. Mother and I were both sunk. She was shook up too, because she could see how Harry and I felt about each other, and I was no help to her. Trying to "cheer me up," she played some game of chance at the cigarette counter in the railroad station, and she won the prize! It was a sticky fruitcake, which neither of us wanted, so she sold it to the girl at the counter for ten dollars.

On the train, Mother gave up on me. She had the porter make up the berth (no more of this flim-flam about saving the sleeper cars for the military). I lay down in the berth, and she threw her mink coat over me and headed to the Club Car for a good stiff drink, and maybe some conviviality.

I was numb. It wasn't grief, exactly, because it had been like a whole lifetime of delight, but it was done; it was over; I couldn't even *think* about a week in Palm Springs with Mother and Daddy. I remember how I felt: dead, even with the lovely mink coat for a blanket. I just wanted to sleep—like those fairy-tale princesses who sleep until the prince comes to release them from their deathlike trance. I didn't want to feel anything if I couldn't feel my hand in Harry's or the wordless thrill of his kiss.

The train was mostly empty; revelers had gone back to work or back to the base—except for one gang of very drunk soldiers who came roaring into the sleeper car with bags full of booze and beer. They were randy and ready for one last night of partying. And they see this girl—under an (expensive) fur coat—and they are ready for a little alcohol-fueled revelry: "Hey, honey, let's have some fun—"

"Go away," I say, and ring for the porter, who, happily, appeared right away, as though he knew this might be trouble.

"C'mon, boys," he says. "I'll find you some folks that wanna play. Leave this poor kid alone." And he buttoned up those heavy green curtains that closed me and Mother's fur coat securely into that berth. I slept; the soldiers never returned.

I don't know how long I slept, but by the time I awoke—and we were only several hours out of Los Angeles—Mother had made up her mind: she was having a nervous breakdown and had to return to Chicago and her analyst, Roy Grinker, immediately! Palm Springs would be out of the question this winter. She had exhausted her selfless mature calm, or whatever it was, and Dr. Grinker would prescribe a couple of weeks of inpatient therapy for her.

I don't know whether they got to Palm Springs later that winter. I only know that I got to Claremont somehow, only to find that the school was still closed for the Christmas break. There were a few maintenance people around, however, and they put me up in a vacant dorm room temporarily. There were signs of life, and that helped me over the grief, depression, and despair.

Harry and I resumed writing letters to each other, the idyll in Tacoma painfully fresh in our senses. He confessed that he'd entertained thoughts of staying on the bus with me and going AWOL—an impulse he knew he'd stifle. The next phase of his life as a soldier was taking shape. Up for a promotion, he had shed his "thing" about officers and taken the test for Signal Corps Officer Candidate School. Second Lieutenant wasn't such an exalted rise in rank, after all—and he'd realized that he wouldn't have to be on KP and peel potatoes if he became an officer. Signal Corps OCS was in Fort Monmouth, New Jersey, so if he passed the test (a foregone conclusion), that was where he would be stationed next.

He wrote, "If you weren't so young, I'd ask you to marry me."

It made superb sense to me. (Had the notion of not waiting until "after the war" already insinuated itself into my thinking?) What ELSE would I want to do with myself except be where *he* was? That was the best thing in the world! I'd finish my education some other time. Being with Harry was A-1 priority! It depended, of course, on where he got stationed—or did it? In my current frame of mind, I realized that I would go anywhere—in the U.S.A.—to be where he was.

So when a telegram from him arrived saying, "DISREGARD CONTENTS OF LAST LETTER. EXPLANATION FOLLOWS" (to become a family legend), I fired back my own impulsive telegram: I was NOT disregarding contents of last letter: I accepted his proposal.

I don't remember my exact words. I didn't keep a copy. At that fraught and hurried time I wasn't thinking of this as an exchange of historic documents; you might say I wasn't thinking at all. Harry, who tended to think BEFORE he acted, had the sense that I was too young, there was a war on, life was uncertain. The prudent thing to do would have been to wait. My way was, "Life is uncertain. So what?" I just had to make sure that I wasn't shoving Harry into anything. After all, he had a serious commitment to the U.S. Army.

I thought up a plan, which I imparted to him: we could get married at the end of my freshman year, while he was still an officer-in-training in New Jersey! He liked the idea, and the very prospect did wonders for our morale. Blinded by love? Yearning to be together—even if only for a little while—that would fill our lives and spirits with transcendent purpose beyond the preoccupations of war and separation. We agreed, against prudence and common sense, that this was our path.

After that, it wasn't "if," but "when."

56

W e set a date: May 23, before the Memorial Day holiday, after I'd finished freshman year at Scripps and would have had time to pack up and travel east, to New York. Darlene and Berney, now permanently settled in New York City, would help keep us all calm, and, as sophisticated urbanites, could advise about the details of what would be a small and simple wedding. My parents didn't oppose this scheme: it would've been like trying to turn off Niagara Falls to stop me. Only Harry and the U.S. Army could say "HALT!"

Alan would be Harry's best man, of course. Wherever he was going to be in training by then, he would secure leave well in advance. On January 6, 1942, on the verge of doubling down on their premature Canadian Air Force fantasy, he wrote to his brother:

> The more guys I talked to about Naval Air, the more it seemed like a damn good way to serve if I could pass the physical exam. I got more and more convinced . . . that although it's dangerous, guys like me to whom the world has been pretty damn good shouldn't start thinking of pleasant personally advantageous ways to serve.

In his diary, Alan's tone was less jaunty: "Joining the Naval Air Corps does not insure a long or a prosperous future."

Before departing for OCS, Harry got transferred for a short interval to Fort George Wright in Spokane. Unbeknownst to me, a plot was hatched between the Gottlieb parents and Harry. Harry Sr. visited his son in Spokane, and then Pop Gottlieb, assuming the uncharacteristic role of Cupid, met me in the bar at the Biltmore Hotel in Los Angeles—and presented me with an engagement ring: a circle of diamonds that had been Dot's engagement ring.

Both Pop Gottlieb and I were as nervous as though it was *our* betrothal! I recall that, uncharacteristically, he ordered a double brandy (he was not given to strong drink, I knew that about him); I, not yet of drinking age, ordered jasmine tea, hoping to settle a very fluttery physical condition. But he was comfortable to be with: kind, amusing, courtly; we had a lovely, happy time. Did we hug goodbye? I think we did: both of us a little shy, but with a thrill of happiness. He then went to visit his California sister, Florence (the crazy one), and I went back to Scripps wearing Dot's engagement ring—now mine.

Back at Scripps College I promised myself to REALLY focus on scholarship and self-motivation, and to make this year meaningful to me. I flung myself into that final semester of academic life—a kind of swan song—and made the most of it. I loved the biology classes, the art classes. The literature classes broadened and deepened the experience of painting thought, illusion, emotion through words. I was enthralled with French class: we studied—and then gave at least one performance of— Moliere's *Tartuffe: or, The Hypocrite*. It was hilarious and well-received. My friendship with Jan endured and was a lively source of enlightenment about sex. Her amorous pursuits intrigued me: a form of expression (among other things) that I could appreciate but not emulate. The mystery of sex and love: both were good, and you could vary the proportions.

In March, Harry, now in OCS at Fort Monmouth, New Jersey, was cheered by a surprise visit from his brother, about to become a Naval Air Cadet. "Ale" just showed up. There was an unoccupied bunk in Harry's tent, and, still more big brother than soldier, he invited his brother to stay overnight with him in the tent. Alan was delighted, and all was fine until the following morning, when Harry had to appear at Reveille. Alan was happily sprawled in the bunk, reading, when an inspecting officer put his head in the tent.

The Officer stepped in and yelled at Alan, "What the Goddamn Hell are you doing here, soldier?"

Alan coolly replied, "Can't you see? I'm reading Louis Fischer's *Men and Politics*."

Well, there was hell to pay for that breach of regulations — "hell" being extra KP ("kitchen police") duty. Harry loved telling that story, and told it often in the years to come: typical of Ale not to get rattled; typical of Harry to take the rap. Within days, both brothers would belong to the military:

> On March 26, [Alan] reported to the Navy at Anacostia. His first day of actual flying was on his 22nd birthday, April 28.

I left Scripps as soon as final exams were over to go East and marry Harry . . . and never looked back. But I still have very positive feelings about that cloistered-looking place. It had broadened my love of reading and thinking; of exploring and dreaming. I owe it more than a debt of gratitude — which I would like, someday, to acknowledge in a meaningful way.

I did not know till later that I had won that year's Freshman Prize for writing at Scripps. At some point after the school year ended, Jan made a trip to Chicago and delivered that prize (an anthology of some sort) to me during the whirlwind of events before I left for New York to marry Harry.

One of the New Yorkers — either someone from the Gottlieb family or Darlene and Berney — found us Rabbi Hyman Judah Schachtel, at the West End Temple. (Reform Jews in those days avoided the word "synagogue.") May 23 was a Saturday, and we arranged the ceremony for before sundown (another liberty of Reform, which, among other things, soft-pedaled the observances that set Jews firmly apart). Rabbi Schachtel, who told us he had been married, divorced, and then married again, questioned us gently but closely: Did we know what we were *doing*? Our youth, a war on . . . I think he wanted to be sure — delicately — that I wasn't knocked up, or some dumb thing like that. He was kind, but penetrating in his examination of our motives. Just love, we told him — this is for keeps. We wanted to be with each other for however long our "forever" would be. We were ready, we assured him. He believed us.

My mother and dad, Harry's mother and dad and Alan, Berney and Darlene, and Eddie and Charlotte Kuh composed the wedding party. The ceremony was set for 3:00 p.m. Harry had to march in the parade exercises at Fort Monmouth that morning at 10:00 or 11:00 a.m. As the formation of soldiers circled the grounds, the sergeant gave him a prearranged signal: "As the men turn the corner, you go straight out of the parade ground and don't slow down or look back. I'm covering for you and you have the order to proceed elsewhere." And so it was. Harry took off, got the train to Manhattan, and showed up around 1:00 p.m.

Lunch was ordered. I was way too nervous to eat; Harry was not quite ravenous. I think we just had sandwiches. Then—suddenly, it seemed to me—Harry said he wanted to get a shoeshine. A SHOESHINE?? Hadn't he had to polish his shoes before that morning's parade? Off he went. I had a momentary panic that he'd decided to slip the noose. . . . Alan didn't seem apprehensive about his brother's need for a shoeshine, but then, he was thinking about another wedding: Janet Thompson, whom Alan was nuts about but had "lost" to Harry's classmate Jim Burns, an up-and-coming professor—was getting married this selfsame day! So Ale was sort of mopey—and he, too, may have wondered how prudent it was to marry at this time.

Harry came back. We all stood around some more. I could see why, in the Old Days, bride and groom didn't lay eyes on one another on the wedding day until it was time for the ceremony itself.

Around three o'clock the Rabbi called us to order, and we arranged ourselves in a semicircle in his study, a pleasant, spacious room, lined with lots of crowded bookshelves. We could hear music wafting up from one of the lower floors and through the open windows of the building. Rabbi Schachtel explained that the Confirmation Class was having its dance in a downstairs ballroom, with recordings of popular bands supplying the music for their party. Glenn Miller's band was playing "Moonlight Cocktail," one of the then-popular jazz standards, during our ceremony. (Ever after, Harry and I regarded it as *our* "Wedding March," and whenever some nostalgia-driven jazz band played it, we'd grasp hands and smile into each other's eyes.)

The prayers and the ceremony were mercifully brief: we had our first man-and-wife kiss: it felt . . . different! We signed some papers or documents. Someone gave the Rabbi a check. We thanked him. Had he made any sort of extempore speech? I don't think so. Things got sort of blurry for the new Mrs. Gottlieb. Harry and I got into a horse-drawn carriage and had a leisurely ride through Central Park and the lovely, fragrant May evening. Blissful and dazed, we didn't talk much—or even kiss much, as I recall; we held hands, we looked at each other: Married! We were trying to understand how the world had changed, how *we* had changed, crossing this major threshold of life together.

The carriage delivered us to the reception, already under way in a space like a banquet room, near (or in?) the Hampshire House, an upscale hotel facing Central Park where the "Bridal Suite" had been reserved for us. The Gottliebs arranged and hosted the reception, I think. We arrived to a wave of cheers and hugs and crowds of happy people, some of whom I recognized, some of whom introduced themselves as new relatives. A dizzying array, all enthusiastically exchanging greetings and hugs with Harry. He knew all of them and was delighted, transported a zillion miles from Fort Monmouth, in this happy swirl of family. Aunt Minnie and Aunt Ida were a formidable pair, and I immediately got myself into trouble trying to keep straight which was Minnie and which Ida: not that they looked alike—they didn't—but they were inevitably spoken of together that way. Unfortunately, the little mnemonic device I made up for myself somehow got into family circulation and pretty much got Harry and me cut off from those two venerable ladies. It was a simple little *aide-memoire*: "Aunt Minnie is skinny, Aunt Ida is widah." I don't think I was ever forgiven for that! But they both had lots of descendants who were more open-minded—even amused.

There were cocktails. I don't remember sit-down dinner. It was a blur. Harry couldn't wait to get out of there and start the REAL business of being married. I was very tired, and in a haze of anticipation and apprehensiveness about the Wedding Night. My mother had not been a good instructor or pathbreaker or truth-teller—except she said, "It hurt." Eager and scared, both neophytes, we escaped the reception as soon as we decently could. Was there a wedding cake? I don't remember. I just remember that Pvt. Gottlieb took a handful of my long black hair and steered me out into the May evening.

The details don't merit publication, except to say that out of sheer terror, I think, I got my period, so all bets were off for a day or two. Maybe a good thing—for ME: time to get used to sleeping with, caressing, exploring a man—maybe less good for Harry. We were both uninstructed virgins; within a week we'd come a long way. I don't remember giving my four daughters much factual instruction, but times were changing: there seemed to be more opportunities for sexual exploration and discovery, without the Armageddon fear of pregnancy instilled in nubile females by the likes of my mother, who I wish had educated me with a more three-dimensional view of sex and sexuality. But Harry and I were two intrepid—and not bashful—explorers; we got the hang of "it," and respected the resourcefulness of Nature, which takes a hand when it's needed.

Sunday, the morning after this long-anticipated Paradise of Love fulfilled, Harry and I were on the sooty little train to the rooming house in Long Branch, New Jersey, that was to be our first "home." Harry was the picture of blissful exhaustion. We are on this little interurban train, with the woven straw seats; he is sound asleep, head on my shoulder. I look out at the scrappy, dusty backsides of little suburban towns: "Is this marriage?" I ask myself.

57

When Harry had told the landlady of the rooming house in Long Branch, Mrs. Kate Regan, that he wanted to bring his bride there while he was in OCS at Fort Monmouth, she'd given him the best room in the house. Of course she was smitten by him! Our "bridal suite" was large and sunny, with a lovely, if rickety, double bed (which broke down once—mildly embarrassing: it wasn't US, honest!). When Mother and Daddy came to inspect our place, she was horrified: there was a CRUCIFIX over the bed!

The Regans had six kids. Francis was the oldest—my age—and he helped me cook the first dinner I ever made for Harry: lamb chops, spinach, and baked potato. It turned out fine, except I slipped up and the potato wasn't done until we'd finished everything else, so it was sort of dessert. Kate's husband, Jim, was a milkman, and he was about to lose his job, displaced by automation: the dairy company was retiring the horses that pulled the milk wagons in favor of mechanized trucks, and Jim Regan didn't know how to drive anything but a horse. But he was a merry man. He had a brogue thicker than tar, and very few teeth, so you really couldn't understand a word he said, but he and Harry would sit and drink beer, and Jim would talk up a storm in his densely incomprehensible brogue, and there was lots of laughter. Sometimes one of the kids would translate a sentence or two for us.

We quickly discovered a few memorable features about Long Branch. Just on the other side of the tracks from our rooming house at 254 Westwood Ave. was a little shack where a man made pizza. We'd never had pizza; it wasn't that well known at that time—there wasn't yet a pizza joint on every corner.

This guy kept the dough, which he made by hand, on top of his refrigerator, where the warmth from the motor was perfect for making it rise. You'd go in, order a pizza, and he'd rustle it up in no time, pop it in the oven, and it was heavenly — the best pizza I've ever had in my life.

Our big, sunny room had a tiny little alcove, the size of a closet, just big enough for a cot, and shortly after our no-honeymoon-yet marriage, we invited Betsy Kuh to come visit us — Harry's and my first "houseguest." (My mother was scandalized.) Betsy was at college — I can't remember where she went: Was it Bennington, cradle of depressives? Or Vassar? Bennington, I think. But whatever school she went to, it wasn't a good fit. I remember going to visit her there earlier in the spring. It hadn't been a good year, and when she came to visit us she was visibly depressed. What was it about? Maybe, in part, Harry getting married: they loved each other — they'd had that summer when he was fifteen and "took care" of the three kids, and he always had a soft spot for her and she for him. It was very sweet.

Betsy spent a couple of happy days and nights with us newlyweds. What did the three of us do? We had my portable record player with records — I'm sure Harry had some good jazz — and there was a little beer joint down the street. Did we take her to our pizza joint across the tracks? Almost certainly. I think we sat around and talked, and maybe went for walks, and you could see that after a day or so, she brightened up. Her visiting us was important for the three of us, because Harry loved her and so did I. And that helped her, I think. By the time she left, a couple of days later, to go to the Vineyard, she seemed much cheerier. (We wouldn't be going to the Vineyard that summer: Harry wouldn't finish OCS until September.)

What a woman Betsy was! What a gentle heart and rigorous mind! For all her rapier-sharp wit, she couldn't pull it off to be stern like her mother, but she was strong: no pushover: kind, vivid, funny, whimsical, astute, and very brave. I wish she could have found someone who loved and understood her as Harry did. I may have been needlessly harsh toward Irv, whom she later married, but I didn't feel that he did her justice. And then life battered her—the lupus diagnosis and death of her oldest child, Susie, then the breast cancer that would eventually kill her. Through it all she was brave, bewildered: How did this all happen? Born a month and a day after me, she died the day before her fifty-fifth birthday. Well—she lives in me! I will always love her.

It was after Betsy left that the rickety double bed we slept in collapsed one night with a terrible clatter that brought the Regans to our rescue. They looked at us like—"Jaysus, Mary, and Joseph, what was you doin' in here?" But then they realized that the bed was really on its last legs, and they kind of wired it back together.

Harry was required to live and sleep at Fort Monmouth while he was in Officer Candidate School, but he was allowed to leave the base two or three times a week for what they called "laundry privileges"—as long as he was present and accounted for at midnight, not a minute later. Midnight was the witching hour, when officers roamed around inspecting the tents. If Harry was still on his way back to his tent when midnight struck, they'd stop him and say, "Where are you going, soldier?"

"To my tent."

"What have you been doing?"

"Just walking around." Harry was a straight arrow and didn't like to lie, but he didn't volunteer the information that he'd been off base. I don't remember ever going to the base to visit him, either. It may not have been permitted. You didn't have the kind of personal freedom people were used to.

So on "laundry days" I'd make dinner for Harry; he'd spend a few hours in bed with me, sleeping or not, and then get up around eleven to make sure he got back to base in time. He'd pedal off on his second-hand bicycle, which he'd bought with Alan's wedding gift, a check designated expressly for that purpose ("a fourth-rate bicycle . . . if I have overestimated the cost of the vehicle, which seems unlikely, use the excess to purchase rubber handle-bar covers"). Harry named the bicycle "April Murphy," for reasons known only to him. He was a whimsical guy.

443

While Harry attended OCS, I got a job at Greenstone-Stern, a factory that was manufacturing Army pants for the war. Wool fabric was rationed, and the only way you could obtain any was if you did manufacturing for the U.S. Army; then you were entitled to a ration of non-khaki goods, so you could make civilian garments as well. I was hired as an inspector to make sure the garments that were uniforms met U.S. Army specs for quality of tailoring and to discard any pants that didn't. The finished pants were packed 500 to a (wooden) crate. If, on receipt and inspection by Quartermaster, more than a certain percentage of the shipment was rejected by QM, the entire shipment would be returned to the manufacturer (at his expense), he would be penalized, and if it happened too often, he'd lose his chance to get woolen goods under Military OK.

Mr. Greenstone had given me some cursory instructions, then left me to do my job. Well, Mr. Greenstone had a tiger by the tail. I was an eighteen-year-old idealist. I would be an eagle eye and see that the seams were tight, and so on. A few skipped stiches, a missing bar tack, loose buttons: any pants that didn't meet Quartermaster's—and my—exacting standards, I'd toss 'em in the "reject" pile.

It didn't take more than a day or two for Mr. Greenstone and me to lock horns. He didn't fire me—why didn't he??—but at day's end, he'd evidently inspect the findings of his overzealous inspectress and calmly restore most of my rejects. When he had 200 crates of inspected and passed (by him) garments (500 pairs to a crate: that's a LOT of pants!), they were duly shipped off to QM in Philadelphia. I felt pretty smug about my work, never knowing about Greenstone's Night Stealth. And he seemed to be satisfied with my work. I was paid 35 or 40 cents an hour for an eight-hour day: 16 bucks a week for a forty-hour week, which was not below average for unskilled work in those days. Greenstone was feeling smug too: he'd patriotically hired a cute young Army wife; she was conscientious (TOO conscientious, but he'd arrived at a satisfactory solution to *that* little problem), on time, and we got on fine—me flinging rejects, he sneaking them back in the piles of "OKs" by night.

Ah, but then there came a day of reckoning. QM had done their routine inspection: a certain number of pieces from each crate, pulled out at random. So there were 200 crates of 500 pr. of pants each—and QM rejected the entire lot, noting that the percentage of rejects was above the Army's tolerance. Greenstone could fix the rejects and re-ship the entire 200 crates, paying all freight, but not receiving a penalty charge. If, however, this or any future shipments were still over the permitted limit for faulty workmanship, the factory would be penalized and no longer eligible to produce garments for Our Boys.

I left before the next shipment of 200 crates was ready to ship, so I never found out what happened. What I *did* learn, sometime later, was that Mr. Greenstone died of a heart attack some months after Harry and I were settled in Tampa, Florida. I was sorry about that. I rather liked Mr. Greenstone. I seem to remember that I saved (and, I think, *framed*) my last, uncashed paycheck as a souvenir—which eventually vanished.

And then, in September 1942, Harry graduated from Officer Candidate School at Fort Monmouth, and got his first assignment. As a newly commissioned Second Lieutenant, he was ordered to report to Tampa, where neither of us had ever been, to serve in the 583rd Signal Aircraft Warning Battalion at Drew Field.

But the army gave him ten days of leave between his graduation and the start of his assignment in Florida, an interval designated as "travel time." And that was when we got what we never really thought of as a honeymoon. We hadn't had one, it being wartime, but the Kuhs gave us the use of their Vineyard house, a place both of us loved. It was a ten-day suspension of the Real World that we had in that late summer of 1942: the gift of *ten days* when Harry didn't have to be a Soldier and Officer, two roles he'd never imagined for himself.

So, for this glorious brief interlude on Martha's Vineyard, he and I just wrapped ourselves in New England's mellow beauty. We swam, we walked the beaches and the sea-smelling scrub whose paths ran through the woods and down to the beach. We basked in the golden autumn, remote from the looming unknown of military life. The summer people had left, and it was just locals like Polly Cottle — a crisp, no-nonsense New Englander — us, and a few hard-headed New Yorkers who liked the autumn peace. Polly was a fiercely loyal and informed Boston Red Sox fan. She also made an exceptionally delicious clam chowder. During the summer, she worked as cook-housekeeper, as well as helpmeet and general overseer, for Edwin and Charlotte. She and her lobsterman husband, Eric — who had taken Harry on that memorable seasick swordfishing expedition — had a compact little cabin in the woods. We'd dodge the poison ivy that formed a luxuriant border to the sketchy track between her house and the Kuhs' place up the hill, and we'd sit on the little screened porch, and Polly and Harry would argue the failings and virtues of this player or that, and the managerial missteps that seemed to bedevil her beloved Red Sox.

Harry and I walked the paths through the woods; we sat on the dock in Menemsha Harbor and looked at the boats bobbing contentedly at anchor; we explored the Kuhs' bookshelves and read aloud to each other part of the time, and part of the time to ourselves. Would we ever experience such bliss again?

And then it was time to pack up and head to — *oh no!*

Harry had to get a Military Haircut before presenting himself to Battalion HQ at Drew Field! Where to do that? Sleepy Menemsha didn't seem to have a post-season barber shop. Harry didn't want to appear in his uniform looking like some shameful civilian longhair, and certainly he didn't DARE show up for duty with his hair brushing the back of his shirt collar.

"Oh," says I jauntily, "Fear not, Sweetheart! I can cut your hair. I've watched barbers with the comb and scissors — nothin' to it!" So we pull a chair out into the middle of the living room floor, lay down some newspapers so we won't have too much of a mess to clean up, put a chair in the middle, get a couple of towels to drape over the Innocent's shoulders — and Barber Jean goes to work.

Well, it's much more complicated and subtle than I'd thought: Harry's curly hair was sort of slippery, and it began to look quite uneven at the edges--and all over, as a matter of fact. The more I tried to snip a little here and a tad there, the more motheaten and irregular it looked. When I finally stepped back to look at my handiwork, I burst into tears of shame and chagrin. There sat my darling in the midst of a pile of curls and shards of hair, his noble head looking as though it had been attacked by a lawnmower run amok and a flight of voracious moths. I handed a mirror to Harry. He had to face the awful Truth: normally not ruffled by small things like appearances, he gasped in dismay: "Oh, my God! I *can't* go to Drew Field looking like THIS!"

So we figured, OK: he could "disguise" himself in civilian clothes, blue jeans or something, and when we got to Woods Hole or Boston, he could let a professional clean up the damage. I realized now, ruefully and too late, why there were such things as "barber colleges": no kidding, this was a Profession, no place for the untrained! The barber we found looked amused: "What happened to him?" he asked. He probably imagined that in some drunken orgy we'd been playing a kind of Samson and Delilah game. Neither of us felt like telling this barber the story of my cocky ignorance and final disgrace. I never laid a scissor on any of our children, never tried to be a barber again. And Harry, in his infinite tolerance and sweet nature, forgave me. He did not get court-martialed for improper grooming, that was all that mattered!

58

We stood at the screen door of a rooming house in Tampa, a modest Florida bungalow, and watched as Mary Selvey, a lanky, good-lookin' gal with short curly brown hair, sashayed toward us, barefoot, wearing a pink satin slip and not much else.

Harry claimed not to remember this vision inside the screen door, but it made an indelible impression on me. I saw, and I became immediately vigilant. Florida in September was stiflingly sultry, but still! . . . Well, it's the South, I told myself. (As it turned out, Mary was more interested in officers of higher rank, but she had a friend, Lois Buck, of whom more later.)

This was our introduction to Florida. It was NOT love at first sight — at least, not for me.

Mary greeted us in a slow-talkin' Southern drawl. Yes, we were answering the ad, we said. We'd come to inquire about the room to rent. (As an officer now, Harry had the privilege of living off base.) She led us back to a small triangular space just off the living room, pretty much filled by a tall double bed buried under heaps of dolls, pillows, and stuffed animals. There were also a couple of very small dressers, and the bathroom was just across the way. Mary explained that there was pretty active turnover among the occupants, and she expected that a larger, more hospitable space would open up soon — if we were looking for more than a few days' stay.

We took the room, and stowed most of our luggage in the ample space under the bed. Mary informed us that we could use the kitchen, sit around in the living room if she wasn't entertaining, and so on. While this initial arrangement seemed cramped, to say the least, the location was convenient to the bus downtown and to Drew Field.

I was now an "Army Wife," living with Harry, the newly minted Second Lieutenant, in Tampa. He was Army, attached to the Air Corps, stationed at Drew Field (which, after the War, became—and still is—Tampa International Airport). We had an address, 214 S. Westland Ave., and our "landlady" was kind and hospitable. Mary's husband, Master Sgt. Eston Selvey, was in North Africa on a long tour of duty. She had a little boy, Jimmy, who was six or seven years old and well on the way to becoming homicidal. At first Harry tried to make friends with him, figuring the kid must miss his dad, but Jimmy was hostile and uncommunicative, preferring his own diversion of small animal torture to any of the wholesome pastimes (playing catch, flying a kite) Harry suggested. Mary told us that she kept a rifle (loaded) under her bed for "protection," and given Jimmy's proclivities, we were sort of anxious about that firearm, but tried not to think about the lethal mix of Jimmy and the rifle.

The greatest peril we faced, however, was none of these. It was in the person of Mary's closest chum and confidante, Lois Buck—my first experience of jealousy, envy, fear, fury, loathing, and raw hatred.

Lois, probably about twenty-two, was gorgeous, sexy, curvaceous, flirtatious, blonde, and totally devoid of conscience. She wasn't exactly conniving; she was just outright predatory: seductive, alluring, provocative—AND she went for Harry! I knew it the moment I saw her: big baby-blue eyes, luscious blonde curls, generous handfuls of bosom: my blood rival! She'd come to see Mary, sashay around the house with her, evaluating new arrivals, wriggling those fulsome hips and looking back over her shoulder to be sure she had admiring eyes fastened on her. And Harry!—eyes bright, lips parted in surprise, delight, and appreciation—was taking the bait! Oooh, how I hated her!

Now, she was a perfectly cordial, animated person, and under other circumstances, I'd have been watching to learn from her—there was plenty to learn! But she was out to get My Man and she had all the weapons: a dazzling, openly friendly (with a whiff of sexy) smile that whispered, "C'mon, honey, don't be bashful." And mostly her friendship with Mary included "entertaining" the Military (not including Harry and me). Officers only—no enlisted men—came to Mary's house, and Harry and I would be snugged down in our funny little triangular room. But I was uneasy on the occasions when Lois and Mary "double dated" at Mary's house. There was this one night . . .

Harry and I had just turned off the lights when the door at the foot of our bed banged open, and there was Lois. "Hi, just thought I'd say hello!" or something like that. This was definitely against Mary's house rules, but Lois may have had more of a package on than usual, or maybe her date was a loser. Harry tried to pretend he was asleep or wasn't there.

I sat bolt upright and, clutching the covers to my chest, shouted, "Get OUT!!!!"

"Aww," says Lois, "I was jus' comin' to say hello. How are y'all?"

"GET OUT," I shriek again.

She plops herself down on the edge of the bed—on Harry's side, of course. "I jus' wanted to see how y'all are doin'—Mary treatin' y'all OK?'

"Get OUT!" I yell, baring my teeth. I knew what it must feel like to have your hackles rise and bristle.

"How are ya, Harry?" she says.

"Get OUT!" I hiss through clenched teeth, "OUT!" I start to make a move to go for her, to shove, kick, bite, whatever it takes. She's acting like she might try to get in BED with us. "Get OUT!" I shout—"OUT!" And I am getting out of bed. Harry gets up on one elbow—watchful. "OUT!" I snarl again. Lois finally slithers off the bed and backs out. No further exchange of words.

Harry lies back down—turns toward me. I wriggle up close to him. He's still MINE. But it takes a while for my heart to stop pounding. I don't remember Lois ever bothering us—me—again. Mary continued being the easygoing, kind one.

One evening shortly after Harry started his assignment, we decided to go out for a celebratory drink and dinner at the

Hillsborough Hotel in downtown Tampa. The cocktail lounge of the hotel was on the ground floor and opened onto the street. It had been the tearoom in gentler Southern times, and the pastel color scheme and delicate tearoom ambience remained unchanged. The simple expedient of serving liquor and snacks, scrapping the tea cakes and lace doilies, converted the space into a serviceable bar that accommodated the hordes of military crowding into the city.

It was a hot late September afternoon, and the room was filled with soldiers: some with women, many in raucous all-male groups. The only vacant table was in the center of the room, where my newly minted lieutenant and I were plainly visible. Many of the soldiers were from Harry's battalion, a convivial mix of enlisted men and officers—though not fraternizing by drinking at the same table, of course. Harry gallantly asked if I'd like a martini. I had an instantaneous flashback to William carrying me upstairs at 70 East Cedar and me saying, "Put me down, put me down, I can walk, I can walk," and the insidious perfumy smell of gin and vermouth. I should have known better, but I wanted this man I loved and had married to see how self-possessed and mature I was, how sophisticated.

"Sure, thanks," I replied.

The smell and taste catapulted me back to that drunken evening with Betsy as though I'd been sucked into a space-time vacuum tube. And just as purposefully as that earlier time, I sipped those first awful sips until both my taste buds and my judgment succumbed to that evil numbness. Once again, my senses duped me: that martini actually tasted pretty good. Then I became aware that the walls seemed to be breathing: things that my common sense told me were solid and stationary seemed to be sort of viscous, they acquired a rolling seasick sort of motion. So I laid off the sipping for a while and everything settled back to normal.

We must have carried on some sort of conversation, and I must have finished that martini, and Harry must have asked me if I wanted another. I guess I thought we were having an animated and sensible conversation—oh you fool, you! Were the lessons of the past lost on you? Why didn't I quit while I was ahead? — "Yes, thanks," I replied. But as soon as that second martini appeared in front of me, wafting its noxious fumes in my face, I knew it was a serious mistake. "I don't feel well," I murmured to Harry. I could feel ominous lurchings in my stomach.

He looked around apprehensively and sized up the distance from our table to the door. "OK," he said, "wait here; I'll go get the car."

"No, no," I gulped, "I think I want to be outside in the fresh air." We were all smokers in those days, and the rank cigarette smoke that hung in the un–air-conditioned room aggravated my rapidly growing nausea.

"OK," Harry said briskly, "Let's go."

"I can't walk," I whispered hoarsely. I had no confidence in my legs, my balance, or my digestive tract.

"I'll help you," he said, looking around with mounting panic at the sea of faces, most of which seemed to have turned, like flowers to the sun, toward this little spectacle.

"I can't . . . jus' wait a minnit."

Now he was in a positive fever to get me out of there, "C'mon, Jeanie, you'll feel better out in the air. Just try. C'mon, I'll hold onto you." By this time I was swallowing convulsively and had quite lost track of my legs. In my nauseous haze I felt sorry for my poor husband, the new 2nd Looey whose whole military career was probably teetering on the brink with this booze-soaked babe hanging onto him. Even in my blurry state I could see the panic in his eyes as his gaze, darting from face to face (hoping these weren't his men), swept desperately among the tables, searching for the quickest way out of that room.

The audience for this little drama soon lost interest — it wasn't a novelty to see drunks in Tampa. So, holding me firmly by the elbow, he steered me through the maze of tables, trying to appear confident and purposeful — but nonchalant — while propelling me toward the door. My knees turned rubbery when they should have been stiff and stiff when they should have been nice and flexible; the entire world was swaying sickeningly. If we could just stand still for a moment, I'd regain my equilibrium. But Harry was desperate to get me out of there.

He propped me against the cool stone wall outside the entrance to the building and, watching me apprehensively, announced with false heartiness, "Just stay right there, I'll be back in a sec." He dove off to get the car. By this time I had glazed over pretty thoroughly, and everything was undulating like a lava lamp's gluey innards. I had to keep my eyes open for minimal sensory orientation, and I had to concentrate on not letting my legs buckle.

I remember the ride back to Mary Selvey's house, car windows open to the blessed if sultry breeze. Somehow Harry bundled me into the house, out of my clothes, and into bed. The next morning, miraculously, I felt like myself again.

And that was my last martini. Ever.

59

We are more or less settled: Soldier and Wife, living in that funny triangular bedroom in Mary Selvey's house. I feel a little more like "Mrs. Gottlieb" now, doing the domestic commonplaces of Married Life: I must have done the laundry (I cannot remember how or where I did that: Did I hang it in the yard?); cooking (Mary was generous about "kitchen privileges"), making breakfast and dinner for "my Harry," and keeping our space orderly and serene. We'd get up in the morning when Harry had to go to work at Drew Field; I'd make his breakfast. The living room was often a scene: littered with empty booze bottles, overflowing ashtrays, the occasional spilled drink—the rumpled sofa. Sometimes Jimmy would be there playing with toy Army trucks in the bombed-out debris of the previous night's revelry.

Harry went off to work at Drew Field: Battalion Adjutant of the 583rd Signal Aircraft Warning Battalion. He'd been promoted to 1st Lieutenant at some point, despite demonstrating his native lack of mechanical aptitude in electronics training. You took a radio apart and put it all back together again. He got it apart all right, but when he put it back together, there were a lot of pieces left over. He proudly brought it home, and when he plugged it in, it blew up. They realized he was not going to be a radio mechanic, but he was smart and educated, and steady.

Being the one with native mechanical aptitude, I had signed up for a course in machine shop operation. After breakfast, after he'd left and I'd cleaned up our dishes, I'd take the bus or streetcar to machine shop school, and I'd learn how to run an engine lathe, a drill press, and a milling machine. I learned how to use calipers to make measurements that were accurate but not precise; for those, I learned to use a micrometer, which gave you more refined accuracy. I learned how to machine small engine parts from cast bronze gears, to shave off their rough-cast surfaces so that the operational parts were as smooth as glass. Upon completion of 500 hours of instruction and practice, satisfactory performance would earn me a certificate stating that I was qualified to perform those operations in a machine shop— to machine small gears and other engine parts to a tolerance of one thousandth of an inch, the acceptable standard of precision.

I'd get home in time to fix dinner for us.

One time we were out of lemons, and I asked Harry to run down to the corner fruit stand and get a couple of lemons for his iced tea while I finished cooking his favorite meal: hamburger! He trotted cheerily out the front door.

When, fifteen minutes later, he hadn't returned, I became alarmed. The little fruit stand was only half a block away, it was deepening dusk: What could have happened? We lived near a busy intersection, but I hadn't heard sounds of squealing brakes or shattering glass or police sirens. The hamburgers were already overcooked.

I trotted down to the fruit stand. Yeah, the Lieutenant had bought a couple lemons and left—a while back—and the vendor hadn't seen or heard anything unusual. Where could Harry have gone? BEFORE dinner? It was almost dark now. Across the broad intersection I could see the winking red neon sign: "Beer." A little restaurant and bar across the highway.

I make my way across and peer into the window, into the golden glow: a table, four or five military, merrily talking and sipping beer. There's a pinball game in use. That was always a favorite diversion of Harry's, along with convivial beer-drinking. I peer into the window—There he is! In the middle of this group of four or five soldiers laughing and talking. He looks up, his expression freezes—he is momentarily shocked expressionless. I am glaring at him. I am relieved (he's not missing or injured), hut also outraged (how COULD he?).

He looks slightly drunk and also conscience-stricken: "Oops!" He comes over to the door of the bar and says with forced heartiness, "C'mon in and join us, Jeanie!" Trying to sound casual and cheery: "C'mon in and have a beer—or just have a sip of mine." I give him a Look—the basilisk eye—and he freezes. As he would later tell it: he just made a harmless, impulsive (across this broad intersection??) stop at this little bar to play just ONE game of pinball, and these soldiers offered him a seat and a beer; how could he refuse? So there they were, joking around—and then, Harry said, he looked up, "and here's this cloud of black hair and these two dark eyes flashing fire, glaring at me through the window: my heart froze!"

"C'mon in and meet the boys," he says.

"No, thanks," I repeat. Hell would freeze over before I would set foot in that dump. I turn to start for home. It's quite dark by now.

"Come on in just for a minute. They want to meet you, and then we'll walk home together."

The dark, the wide intersection with crazy traffic—you'd think that with gas being rationed there'd be fewer cars—He opened the door and took my hand.

I think we must've eaten the cold hamburgers, but I don't remember.

Notwithstanding that early (and indelible) lesson for both of us about what it means to be married, for the most part we were feeling settled in this life of happy domesticity—beneath the cloud of a terrifying war: Harry, a soldier; still, the routine seems quite banal on the surface: he goes to work every morning, comes home every evening; I keep house in a desultory way, still going to machine shop school a few hours a day.

The holiday is approaching—our first Thanksgiving—and, secure in our little "love nest" that staves off loneliness and nostalgia for family, Harry proposes: "Why don't we have a Thanksgiving dinner and invite a few of my buddies who are single and homesick?" There was George Greider, Frank Gannon, Joe Gorgoglione—all enlisted men, by the way. Harry never even gave "that rank business" a second thought: they had all served together since the days in Tacoma, before he went to OCS and became an officer. Just be discreet! So he invited Joe and Frank and George and a couple of others. They were thrilled! Harry delighted in hospitality, and maybe there was just a touch of showing off his new wife's prowess—or was that all in my mind?

I was cocky, a big mistake: I had NEVER cooked a Thanksgiving dinner. But I figured the local butcher could instruct me. So I went over to the butcher's shop and ordered the main course ahead of time (a prudent move—my ONLY prudent move): I told him there were going to be six or eight of us and I wanted to make roast duck, because duck was Harry's all-time favorite.

"Ma'am," he cautions me, "You better get at least two ducks, maybe three, for four or five hungry men. These here are young tender ducks, they ain't so big—"

"Oh, nonsense," I thought, for some unfathomable reason, "What does HE know?" So I said, "No, I think we'll be fine with one duck. Just get me a nice plump bird, as big as you can." So he shrugged, put in the order, and the die was cast. Duck it would be!

It was so exciting! I'd be cooking a feast for these five poor hungry, lonesome soldiers, all of whom I knew. I set about getting apples to make applesauce; and sweet potatoes, I think, and a salad, and I may even have attempted stuffing—really puttin' on the Ritz for our boys in uniform! I know I bought cranberry sauce. I was a little uncertain about how long you cooked the duck, so I asked Mary's neighbor, an older lady and obviously an experienced cook, how to cook it.

"Well," she said, "you really ought to parboil it. A duck can be tough and stringy." (She must've been talking about *wild* duck, the kind your husband shoots if he is a hunter; but this would be a a plump, tender, and juicy *domestic* bird, succulent, not all stringy and muscular.)

"Really?" I said, "How do you do that?"

The neighbor lady shows me a deep-well cooker on Mary's stove and says, "You put some water and onions and seasonings in there, and then put in the duck and just steam it, sort of, for A LONG TIME AND IT'LL BE AS TENDER AS BUTTER!"

With some misgivings, I put this hapless little duck into the "slow cooker" on Mary's stove and began the preparations for the rest of our feast, all to be served on the following day—Thanksgiving! I made the applesauce, assembled salad, and bought dessert (pumpkin pie, and ice cream to go with it). Poor soldier guests, I put them to work: I remember them gaily peeling sweet potatoes, kidding about being on KP for their own party! But this was definitely different—very non-military: neckties came off, sleeves got rolled up; they seemed happy, my "kitchen police," and Harry was beaming and handing the beer around.

At last we sat down at the Festive Board, eyes glistening in anticipation, and Harry marched proudly out of the kitchen with this little bird, surrounded by a generous bed of parsley I'd prepared for it. It looked more like a sparrow than a duck. I hadn't just miscalculated, I'd been catastrophically deaf to the Wisdom of the Butcher!

I was wondering how Harry was going to be able to give each hungry soldier even one mouthful of this wretched little critter. But he did! One mouthful was about all anyone had of the Centerpiece of the Feast, but all pronounced it delicious, and they ate heartily of sweet potatoes, applesauce, salad, and pie. The duck was but a wraith, a lingering gustatory ghost, ephemeral memory on the taste buds. So after a convivial half hour of digesting the pie, we agreed it'd be a great idea to put a little more meat into the Thanksgiving mix. And so this merry crew all trooped out for big, succulent Cuban sandwiches, with thick, juicy sliced turkey, in honor of the holiday, slipped in between the salami and the onion.

60

Christmas 1942 we celebrated in Pensacola, with Navy Flight Cadet Alan and Dot and Harry Sr., who'd come from Chicago. Ale was in Navy Flight Cadet uniform, Harry in U.S. Army 1st Lieutenant, Signal Corps uniform. The parents were both proud and anxious. Lots of animated talk: gossip from home, world and national politics, books, sports, the economy, world events. Lots of laughter. We had a lively and animated time, a delicious restaurant dinner. It was the last time his parents would see Alan.

On February 3, 1943, Alan confided in a letter to his mother, in a lighthearted tone, some misgivings about the dive bomber he was testing:

> The Brewster Buccaneer . . . has proved a wonderfully promising ship, but a woeful menace in its present form. . . . We make high-speed dives up to and above 450 mph. However, when we try it there are some disconcerting noises and almost inevitably a piece of wing, tail, or engine goes drifting back into space . . . enough pieces come off to be very nerve-wracking. Also, the engines are temperamental and the emergency landings made last week were too frequent for comfort.

On February 11, Flight Cadet Alan Gottlieb was granted a 24-hour pass to visit his brother in Tampa. Again, much animated talk and laughter. The brothers traded stories about military life. They discussed sports, of course, and other non-military topics. Their delight in being together almost overshadowed the sinister distant thunder of war.

To us, Alan characterized the Buccaneer as a marvelous

machine with a few troublesome flaws that had caused a few accidents, but that were being addressed. We sat around and talked, and I made up the living room couch for Ale. In the morning we had breakfast, and then he drove off in his little maroon Chevy roadster. We never saw him alive again.

Sunday morning, February 28, 1943. Harry had a couple of hours of duty at Drew Field, then the rest of the day was ours! Maybe we'd see a movie or go fishing in a skiff in Tampa Bay (we never did see a fish there). Or go for a walk and then read the Sunday *Tampa Tribune*.

I am bustling around the house, emptying ash trays and straightening up. The phone rang.

"Hello?"

A man's voice: "I am the Commander of the Flight Training Base in Vero Beach. Ensign Alan Gottlieb was killed in a training accident this morning."

Everything went dark, like an eclipse of my eyes. The bird sounds and children's shouts silenced . . . Everything stopped, silent. The man was still talking . . . "We'll make arrangements for you to be met at the railroad station in Vero Beach and brought to the field — you will stay with me and my family tonight and we will arrange the requisite transportation to Chicago for you and Ensign Gottlieb's body. Will you advise Lt. Gottlieb . . ."

My voice came to life at last — "NO!" It leapt out: "You must phone him. I'll give you the number." He didn't protest. I gave him the number and hung up. And began the wait for Harry to get home.

It would take him half an hour or so. I sat on the sofa — the one Ale had slept on. I waited. An eternity. I dreaded seeing Harry — broken-hearted. But when he walked in, we fell into each other's arms and cried and cried. He said the Commander had told him Alan hadn't suffered (no, that was for us, for the rest of our lives); there was an injury to the back of his head that may have knocked him unconscious. And then he was underwater — until they could extract him from the plane.

As we waited for it to be time to get the train to Pensacola, Harry and I played cribbage, game after game—sort of "automaton cribbage." We packed warm clothes for Chicago. I think we were picked up and taken to the Tampa railroad station.

It was a long trip to Pensacola, up in the Florida Panhandle, some 500 miles. We must have left Tampa early in the evening. I remember hardly anything about our stay in Pensacola. The commandant's wife was named Helen Husted. She had written a children's book about the Navy and gave me a copy. I think she had one or two young children. Both Harry and I were not in the world, it seemed: we were nowhere. I don't think there was any forensic report. None of us has made any effort to obtain the record of the accident[2] or of any subsequent issues with that plane. Harry had to identify the body; I wasn't allowed to go into the room with him. I sat in an anteroom where Alan's uniform, still soaking wet, hung over a radiator, dripping water.

Harry never talked about it. He talked about the life of his brother but never the death. Fifty years after Alan's death Harry wrote a reminiscence about their growing up together in Winnetka, about his brother's hopes and aspirations, about the closeness, the mutual affection, the understanding. Somehow, I think he left the death part to me. It hit me hard, and I was young but I loved my man and he was cruelly injured by this death, all the more cruel because it could and should have been avoided. I am pretty sure, knowing Harry—and loving him as I did—and do—that never a day passed—NEVER—that he didn't think of Ale. That's just how it was with Harry.

On the train to Chicago we had seats as close as possible to the baggage car, where Alan in the plain wooden box was lashed down among the trunks and freight. They'd put Alan in a little cleared space, and Harry sat sentinel beside Alan's box, with a bottle of bourbon. He stayed there for the whole trip, with only infrequent short breaks. He may have gotten a refill on the bourbon. I knew he needed just to be there alone with Ale. I

---

[2]Our daughter Annie Gottlieb was able to obtain Alan's naval records from a private search firm in 2019. Excerpts from the file, including the official accident report, are in Appendix B.

knew that he'd be together, no matter how much booze he'd taken in, when we got to Chicago. It was chilly in the baggage car. Maybe he took a blanket from the porter. We looked after him—just left him alone with his brother and gathering strength to help his parents when we got home.

We stayed with Dot and Harry in their apartment on Chestnut Street; they'd moved out of Winnetka once the boys had left childhood—and the house—behind. Alan was cremated, and his funeral was held on March 3. Judge Ulysses S. Schwartz, an old friend and law partner of Harry Sr., spoke of his death:

> He had returned with his plane to the landing field, where he found some difficulty in the working of the landing mechanism, and that a safe landing would be impossible. For one hour and a half, this boy hovered in the air over the field, keeping in communication with the ground force, constantly, carefully, without fear, seeking to adjust the mechanism, and when he thought he had finally succeeded, he landed on the field, but in the process something had happened to the brakes, and he could not stop the plane. Still, he might have saved his life if he had not tried to save his plane by making a ground loop.

After about a week Lt. Gottlieb had to return to Tampa and Drew Field and the military life. He'd been granted a week's leave, but that was done. We decided that I'd stay on with his folks for a week or two, and that was a comfort for all of us, though I missed him terribly.

One footnote that both of us remembered, marveled at, and were a little rueful about: on the morning of Alan's funeral Harry and I made passionate love. We were not ashamed. We weren't guilty; we recalled it more than once; our defiant answer to death. We'd talked about maybe trying for me to get pregnant—that was after I'd gone back to Tampa a week or two later. Neither of us liked the idea: the baby should have a father from the get-go; and I didn't relish the idea of being tied down to a sort of "one-armed" domestic life when I could go to work or to school while Harry was away. And so it was: family meant both of us.

Harry's most haunting dread had always been that he'd be the last of his family, the last one left—alone. Was it a premonition? He had been born in the shadow of infant Jane's death; the loss of ardent, promising Ensign Alan in 1943 was a blow from which their parents would never fully recover. It may have been a factor in their relatively early deaths, each at 67: Harry Sr.'s in Michael Reese Hospital after a second stroke in 1948, and Dorothy's in 1955, struck down by a cerebral hemorrhage in her bookstore. And so it came to pass. Although ours was a house resonant with the shouts and laughter and thundering feet of our six offspring, I think Harry lived with an inescapable aloneness. And yet . . .

On his 95th birthday, his son Alan filmed him at a lively four-generation birthday party on the Gulf of Mexico side of our house in Fort Myers Beach. On camera, Harry confessed his ancient dread of being left all alone; then, looking around at the boisterous swarm of children, grandchildren, great-grandchildren, and friends, he said, "That should have been the least of my worries."

After I had left to return to Harry, Dot and Harry Sr. received a phone call from Mrs. Roosevelt. She was in Chicago, and she said she would like to pay a visit. She came all by herself—no bodyguard, nothing. I don't know how long she stayed, half an hour perhaps, but because of the compassionate, gracious person she was, she knew naturally how to confront such terrible blows and comfort those who had suffered them. She had written to Dot on hearing the news of Alan's death, "I feel it very deeply and can not refrain from telling you what a loss it is for his whole generation."

Sometime in those next bleak months, Harry and I moved out of Mary Selvey's place and into a house on Nebraska Avenue that we shared with Sgt. George Greider, Harry's indispensable top enlisted man and good friend since Tacoma, and his wife, Cassie. This was a blatant violation of Army regulations, which prohibited "fraternization" between officers and enlisted personnel—an antique class distinction the Army held to be vital for preserving discipline. Harry, the great leveler, had no use for this; it made no sense to him. He'd initially resisted going to OCS because he detested the thought of buddies he'd served with since Basic Training having to salute him and say "yessir" and "nosir." But eventually he'd realized he could be more useful as an officer with common sense, and he kept his enlisted buddies with him through the formation of the 583rd at Drew Field and its deployment to the Pacific. Besides George, there are many whose names I can't remember, but here are a few: Allen Atwell; Art Tatman; Buck Croyle; John Solon; Cass Walker; Laycock; Willie Steckman; Frank Gannon; Joe Gorgolione. A number of them would serve together in the 583rd for the duration of the war.

The four of us—George and Cassie and Harry and I—quietly flouted the regulations. The house was a modest one, with a spacious yard and an endless supply of hot water, thanks to solar heat, a feature that was ahead of its time. We were careful: George and Harry never left the house together. George must have traveled by bus to and from the base; Harry might have driven Alan's little maroon Chevy roadster. It was a convivial arrangement: Cassie and I cooked together, and the four of us shared meals in the little dining room. I graduated from machine shop school, and received a certificate stating that I had completed 500 hours of instruction and was competent to perform certain types of operations, to within precise tolerances, on the engine lathe, the drill press, and the milling machine.

Harry and I made only one (unproductive) effort to fish while we were in Tampa: we rented a skiff and rowed out alongside the causeway that bisected part of Tampa Bay. It was a beautiful, sunny day, but not a fish was to be found, and when I managed to make a cast that twirled my line around and around the overhead power line, I cut the line, left the lure dangling overhead, and thus ended our premature Florida Gulf Coast fishing effort (to be continued).

Though the Army's Sole Survivor Policy was only made official after World War II, in 1948—exempting from combat the last living sibling of a family that had lost one or more to the service—such exemptions were granted on a case-by-case basis during the war, and Harry might have qualified. He unequivocally rejected that path. He had made it clear to his parents right after Alan was killed. His brother had chosen the most dangerous branch of the service as his way of expressing his feelings about this war, and Harry felt the same. To win the war you had to face down the enemy, not look for a safe job— even knowing that your parents were terrified of losing you, too.

So that summer, when thousands of young soldiers were sent by troop train to California, from there by ship to Australia, and then into the Pacific Theater, Harry N. Gottlieb Jr., Adjutant of the 583rd Signal Aircraft Warning Battalion, would be among them.

61

From an embankment high above the tracks, Cassie Greider and I watched the long troop train snake its way out of the Tampa rail yard. It was July 14, 1943. Harry and I had said our last goodbyes; then he had merged into the hundreds of other young soldiers boarding the train that would take them to San Francisco, their embarkation point for service in the South Pacific.

Cassie and I went back to the house on Nebraska Avenue, packed up the little maroon Chevy roadster that had been Alan's, and drove north for Chicago. Cassie drove, that is; I had never learned to drive, city girl that I was. We made it pretty stress-free, not hurrying. In a piquant addition to the adventure of the motor trip, Cassie revealed to me that she was pregnant! I'm not sure now whether George knew before the troops left, or whether Cassie broke the news to him after the soldiers reached Australia. She was adjusting to pregnancy and to the prospect of a radically altered life: raising that baby—alone—until George came home in the far-away future.

That first dazed night, we stopped at a tacky little roadside motel in Lake City, Florida. In the middle of the night I was awakened by a terrible, painful noise in my ear. I turned on the bedside lamp and saw a single-file procession of ants marching across my pillow! One must have strayed into my ear! In a panic, I phoned the night desk clerk: "You just pour a little water in your ear, Miss, and he'll either drown right quick or swim out. Either way, you'll be rid of him." It worked like a charm. I fell back into bed and an exhausted sleep.

The rest of our drive—we took a leisurely three days— was pleasant and uneventful. I remember it as an interval that helped us make the stupendous transition from domestic bliss to the lonely anxiety of a soldier's wife: always waiting for letters, wondering, where would they be? How long would it take for our letters to reach one another? Would we be able to have an exchange of thoughts and topics, like a conversation?

My parents had rented a room for the two of us in the Drake Hotel, where they were living. Cassie and I, still sort of in emotional "neutral," planned a couple of days of relaxation and rest before she took the train home to Newark, Ohio. Cassie was calm; I reverted to my most obnoxiously immature behavior now that I was back with Mommy and Daddy. Poor Cassie: well, we did a day or two of desultory sightseeing and shopping, but I made only a limp-wristed effort to be a "hostess" and an adult.

Meanwhile, the 583rd Signal Aircraft Warning Battalion departed from San Francisco, sailing — with a thousand other troops — on the USAT *Maui*, a former Matson Line luxury liner shorn of its elegant décor and converted to a working troop carrier (it had also served as a troop ship late in World War I). Stripped down to basics and wearing camouflage paint, it zigzagged a deliberate, torpedo-evading path across the vast Pacific toward Brisbane, Australia.

The voyage of a few weeks was probably the last — and only — government-paid holiday for these soldiers, save for brief and infrequent leaves; they made the most of it, having received their last stateside pay just before embarking. There was ample beer, plenty of chow, and leisure. The men thought up all sorts of amusements, mostly drinking and gambling — shooting craps, playing gin rummy, blackjack, and poker — but also volleyball, shooting baskets, whatever entertainments they could cobble together. There were a few contests: Harry and Chaplain Depkowicz squared off in a boxing match, which attracted quite an audience and considerable wagering and amusement. It was called and declared a draw at the end of the second round, however, as neither contestant could raise his arms high enough in the heavy boxing gloves to throw a punch, being unaccustomed to the weight of anything heavier than a glass of beer.

In mid-ocean, the Maui crossed the Equator, and the soldiers participated in the time-honored ceremony that accompanies that epic experience. Any man on board could become a member of "King Neptune's Court" and receive a suitably inscribed certificate. Harry treasured that souvenir [a photo of his certificate is included in the illustrations]: the celebrant had to be doused with water from the Pacific. I think the original initiation had required the individual to jump into the sea, but as there were so many candidates, and possibly not only enemy military but also predatory sharks, a dousing from a bucket seemed the prudent alternative.

Harry cherished memories of that long Government Issue Bacchanal. It was a free-wheeling good time, and the men were suntanned, well fed, and rested. Then the ship docked in Brisbane and the War became real again.

After Cassie left, I was in Limbo: living at the Drake with my parents felt all wrong for a "grown-up War Wife." But it was Mother (possibly advised by Dr. Grinker) who encouraged me to move out and be on my own: get a job, go to school, whatever I decided I wanted to do—but be autonomous. She was skillful in helping me to realize that I wasn't being thrown out, that I needed help learning to be a grown-up, that was all. So we set about finding an apartment.

Chicago's population was growing exponentially, and to find modestly priced housing was a challenge. But we lucked into a one-room place with a "Pullman kitchen" AND a working fireplace!! It was a third-floor walk-up in a nineteenth-century graystone row house at 33 East Division Street, just a few blocks from the Drake, and handy to public transportation. Rent: $60 a month. Originally single-family homes, these row houses had been repurposed into apartments sometime after World War I, when the boom of the 1920s and the inevitable bust of the Great Depression compelled homeowners to become landlords in order to cover tax increases and other costs of home ownership in the Central City. Each floor in these three-story buildings could be converted into one or two apartments. The City's licensing officials seemed indifferent to fire safety in these structures: most of these buildings did not have mandated fire escapes, as was the case with my third-floor walkup. Harry Sr., ever the planner-ahead, got me an escape ladder that could be hooked over the windowsill and would allow me to climb out of the building and at least partway down the three stories. Fortunately, I never had to use it.

There was one episode, however, quite frightening, that occurred after I'd been living there a while. There was an explosion forceful enough to blow open the transom (that had been permanently painted shut) at the top of my apartment door. My across-the-hall neighbor and I opened our doors cautiously and looked at one another. What WAS it?

What looked like smoke was boiling up the stairwell, our only exit. Cautiously, we began descending the stairs, knocking on people's doors to alert them and warn them of possible danger. There were no flames, no smell of smoke. When we reached the ground floor, still no flames, but we see our landlord, Mr. Barnett, swaying slightly, standing beneath a gaping hole in the ceiling, surrounded by chunks of fallen plaster and wearing little mounds of plaster dust on his head and shoulders. He was quite wobbly—probably more from alcohol than shock—but appeared not to be injured. Then we heard the sirens. Someone had called in a fire alarm. The police also pulled up and began taking statements from us. More of the tenants in the building crept out of their apartments, but no one was hurt.

It seems that Mr. Barnett had decided to weld a leaking pipe which, we learned later, was the gas line! Why he didn't bring down the entire structure will never be known. Considerable credit is due to the sturdy construction of these Victorian buildings.

Well, the easy part had been finding the place that was to be my home until Harry came back. The hard part was working with my mother on furnishing and "decorating" it! We fought over every lamp, every piece of furniture, every picture on the wall, I think because I had no clue about how to fix it up and make it a home. Mother had that innate gift, and perhaps I was jealous of her eye for interior decoration. It turned out so well that a magazine did an illustrated article about "War Wife" having this nest waiting to welcome her soldier back to a real "home" when the war was over! [The article is reproduced in the illustrations.]

It was a cozy apartment and Mother really did a wonderful job, in spite of all the battles we had. It had a little Victorian fireplace, perhaps the only heat available in the early days of this building. It was designed to accommodate cannel coal, a kind of oily, chunky soft coal that burned rapidly and readily and radiated considerable heat. Mr. Barnett supplied the coal, an amenity that came with the fireplace, I guess. I loved having a fire in the fireplace: it was so homey in the winter, and also warm.

I learned to be careful about letting Mr. Barnett build a fire for me, however. Once, before I knew better, he offered to set the coal and start the fire for me. Of course he wasn't sober, so that should have been warning enough for me, but this may have been early in my tenancy, before the explosion and before my across-the-hall neighbor warned me to watch out for him. So he piled an awful lot of those chunks of coal into the little fireplace, lit it with copious gobs of newspaper, and left.

Rather soon, I realized that this was much too much coal and much too much fire. I tried throwing water on it, but the water just hissed and turned to steam, and the coal burned merrily and stubbornly. Finally, as I began to be really alarmed that it might set the chimney or the building on fire, I got the biggest soup pots I had, a roasting pan and a stew pot, put some water in them, and gingerly manhandled a couple of these flaming chunks into the pots. At last, after considerable hissing and spitting, they stopped burning and were just sort of smoldering, but looked as though they might start up again. So I took the pots of coal and dumped them, still smoking, into the bathtub, which I filled with water. That worked! It took quite a few trips and I had a bathtub full of hissing oily coal! Finally, I got down to the smaller pieces and wrapped them in wet newspaper; they were not going to flare up, I was certain. I left a couple of chunks in the fireplace; as those burned down, I could add my little newspaper-wrapped pieces, but I never again let Mr. Barnett build a fire for me. Cleaning up the bathtub was a terrible chore because the coal was so oily. I don't think I told anyone about that debacle, but as I look back on it, it was a worse fright than the "explosion."

In September or October of 1943 I got a job as an engine lathe operator in a small machine shop that produced aircraft parts for the war effort. Industrial Service Engineers was the ponderous name of this greasy little loft upstairs of a garage, with its old-fashioned, belt-driven heavy machines and its crew of maybe a dozen people, five or six of whom were grizzled old-timers, too old to be drafted (the young ones had gone to war). Still, the product was needed for the war effort, and the shortage of labor as the young men volunteered or were drafted compelled the employers to hire women. The older guys, mostly naturalized German immigrants in their fifties or sixties, were skilled and helpful to the new hires.

I was one of three girls who got jobs there. One of them, ignoring the safety rules that required women to keep their hair closely covered when on the shop floor and to shut off moving machinery whenever it was not actually in use, had a terrible accident with a whirling drill press not long after she was hired. Her loose hair got caught in the drill and she was partially scalped. Her screams could be heard echoing down the stairs as the boss rushed her out of the building and to the nearest hospital. She left a trail of blood which we quickly and silently cleaned up. They told us she got stitched up and would be OK, but she never came back to work.

The other was Florence Thompson, from Philadelphia, who became my friend. I never knew much about her, but in one of our lunchtime conversations she made a comment that clanged like a gong in my nineteen-year-old mind: "My mother once told me, you're born alone and you die alone," she said. It was a lugubrious notion, and she was sort of a cheerless person, but there she was, living all alone in Chicago with no family around, so it certainly seemed to apply to her. Though we ate our bag lunches together every day and enjoyed each other's company, we knew very little about one another.

One of the first lessons I had to learn was how to get to work on time. We punched in on the time clock, which mercilessly recorded the hour and minute of our arrival and departure. I had never learned the importance or necessity of punctuality, but George, the foreman, informed me firmly that I'd lose my job unless I could be on time like everyone else. So I learned.

Jan, my "big sister" from Scripps, showed up in the city after I was settled and working at the machine shop. She had landed a newspaper job at the *Chicago Sun-Times* and was involved in an affair with one of the editors. She said he was the Best Ever, and she wanted me to observe them in action—part of my education for when Harry came back? What did she think I was going to learn from *that*? My conviction was immovable: in our situation, irrespective of what Harry did in Australia or wherever he was out there, I was waiting for HIM.

62

The Maui's soldier-passengers disembarked in Brisbane, Australia, on August 16, 1943. They had a few weeks to prepare for their new life, during which they were allowed a last hurrah of shore leave. There are two stories from that Australian interlude, one of which became family lore. It was at a dance, where Aussie girls mingled with the GIs. Harry was not a naturally gifted or enthusiastic dancer, so I'm not sure whether the girl in question was dancing with him or one of his buddies, but after a few songs' worth of wild swinging, his dance partner announced, "I'm all knocked up. Go jazz my sister." Aussie slang was different from ours.

The other story, which Harry told me after the war, was that for the first (and probably last) time in his life, he visited a prostitute. I imagine a few beers relaxed his inhibitions and that the camaraderie of being one of the boys was a factor, as well as the no-tomorrow fever of wartime. And just curiosity: we had both been virgins when we got married. It didn't bother me. All he said about it was that it was "educational." I didn't ask what she had taught him. I figured it would be more fun to learn by doing.

The 583rd had orders for New Guinea, where it would set up its aircraft warning equipment and function as a sort of clearing house for the secret operations of the Battalion. After a period of making ready: getting troops and supplies organized, the 583rd reached Port Moresby, New Guinea, on September 19. There's no mention of how they were transported from Brisbane, but I suspect that, given the number of men, they traveled by ship. In Port Moresby, presumably, they drilled, got acclimated, and trained for jungle life. On November 25, they headed to what was presumably their first "destination" in the jungle, Oro Bay, arriving on November 27, 1943, their base until March 31, 1944, when they "relocated" to Nadzab. (From his letters I knew it only as "Station Secret" — Harry could never tell me where he was. If he mentioned anything that could be remotely identifiable, that part of his letter was blacked out by the gimlet-eyed censors. I pieced together his unit's itinerary for this account, from Army records that are now publicly available online.)

The campsite was some roughly cleared land on the shore of a body of water: a broad river , bay, or lake. The setup included a clearing with several rows of tents that would be "home" for the men; remote from the restrictions of rank in this jungle outpost, they had the luxury of organizing their own living arrangements, choosing tentmates based on affinity and friendship rather than on alphabetical order. Many of them had been together since Tacoma and McChord Field. (Among the names I have, from letters or from meeting them, are Schooner Friant; Doc Combs, battalion physician; Charlie Naftzinger; Major Sam Spann; Buck Croyle; Mike Mishkin.) The men of a construction unit put up a Battalion Headquarters, a structure of corrugated sheet metal, two or three steps above ground level to deter "varmints." The unit set up its aircraft warning equipment back in the bush, in an area near the camp.

Details of all that were military secrets, but I know about the corrugated metal HQ building because Harry described one electrical storm in which a ball of lightning entered through an open window. It made a hissing, sizzling sound and smelled of brimstone, and sizzled its way around all four interior walls before exiting, still sizzling. The men were terrified and transfixed, Harry recalled, not sure whether the lightning might cause an explosion or a fire, but apparently it simply visited the Battalion HQ and departed. Nothing like it ever happened again.

And so began the long, often monotonous work of being in the military backfield, so to speak. The bitter and costly battles for control of New Guinea and surrounding islands had been fought the year before, on land, sea, and air; the Americans, with their superior air power and food supply, had turned the tide in the battles of Midway and Guadalcanal in the summer of '42, and had driven back Japan's occupying forces. Harry's unit was the eyes and ears of the operation to hold that territory; their mission was to watch for and warn of enemy incursions.

Harry could not and did not describe what his duties were, but the pace of life in this small camp was only infrequently overwhelmingly busy and tense. Their area was so remote and the jungle so dense that there was minimal danger from enemy flyovers. "Station Secret" had a low level of military protocol and formality, it would appear: I never got news from Harry about regular drills. The best work time was early morning. By midday it was often steamy hot, so from then till after dark was time for light work, not requiring heavy thought or going from one place to another, and for leisure activities, including swimming, ball games, and reading. Then they might work again after the sun went down and it cooled off. Twice-a-week movies were shown in the open air of night, which not everyone appreciated because theirs was an early-to-bed routine: they had to be up by dawn.

The Army seemed aware of the risks of such remote deployments to soldiers' "morale." Psychiatric evacuations from New Guinea were "much higher" than from the European theater, and twice those even from Australia, according to a retrospective government report published in the 1960s, *Neuropsychiatry in World War II: Overseas Theaters*. Was it Atabrine—the antimalarial drug all the soldiers dreaded but had to take? Or was it the setting: isolated and still, humid and leafy, stalked by strange noises and insidious tropical diseases? "The elements of a civilized community which make for feelings of security and personal satisfaction are strikingly absent in New Guinea," the Army psychiatrists wrote. "In addition to these deprivations, the soldier in this area must often contend with heat, rain, mud, insects, poor food [lots of tinned Spam and peanut butter, Harry wrote; alcohol, even beer, was rare], and lack of recreational facilities. . . . Jungle warfare has certain disturbing aspects" (here the medics waxed almost poetic): "the confusing but ever-present jungle sounds, the whispering breezes through the trees, the crackling limbs, the whistling birds, the clatter caused by land crabs, and the numerous night sounds, which are often misinterpreted as indicating that . . . danger is present. The basic training of every soldier should include the recognition and proper evaluation of jungle sounds at night."

But they weren't in the middle of nowhere. The camp was set in among the villages of the area's original residents — natives who'd inhabited this land for who knows how long. The U.S. Army had just moved in on their territory; if there were diplomatic negotiations, very little about them became public. Probably other nations had done so before the U.S. as well — the Dutch, the Japanese. The natives were fascinated by these white men who played basketball and volleyball and swam, and who all had guns, but never seemed to shoot them. That could have seemed odd to people whose survival depended on being able to hunt and fish for their subsistence. They'd come and stand shyly at the edge of the camp and watch. The soldiers had a building in which they worked, writing things on paper and sending papers back and forth to other places. Occasionally one of them would board a small boat and visit another island or outpost with soldiers, but they didn't shoot or fight one another. They just handed papers back and forth.

As it turned out, the 583rd had among its soldiers some who had the ability to make nonverbal, cheery contact with these "hosts": a smile, a nod. And then there was Willie Steckman. I am not sure when he joined the 583rd, but by the time the men were living among or near Native villages, Willie was among them. I don't know what his rank was, but it didn't matter: a gregarious and approachable person, he took the lead in making friends with some of the natives. Willie had a knack for inspiring positive responses from even the shyest little children. He made gestures of friendship in the international language of friendly voice, smile; he shook hands, a gesture with which the natives were not familiar. He found extra garrison caps, or shirts, or almost any item of clothing stamped U.S. ARMY, inspiring others to root around in their luggage in search of little trinkets or souvenirs.

Pretty soon quite a few of the soldiers got on a cordial status with these shy, dignified, barefoot "landowners." There was a good feeling around the camp. Harry sent me an epic photo (now lost, alas!) of four bare-chested soldiers beaming proudly in front of their tent, resplendent in native grass skirts. I suspect that the natives must have helped out in some fashion—in a very unofficial way. They could run the occasional errand; they often brought bits of woven cloth. Once, Harry wrote me, two young soldiers built rickety little sailboats and took them out for a sail; caught in strong winds or currents, the boats fell apart. The two were a couple of miles from shore, by their account, but luckily both were strong swimmers. When they finally crawled ashore, one of them was too exhausted to walk. Kind natives nearby helped the castaways to their village and put them up for the night in the chief's tent (the soldiers were surprised that this group had tents) with his wives and the pigs. Next morning, they led the chastened argonauts past some enemy encampments and back to their own outfit.

The soldiers improvised all kinds of ways to fill their off-work hours, to stave off boredom and the quicksand of longing for home. They played baseball, basketball, possibly football; one or two tried fishing, but without much luck. Some of the men made toys and trinkets out of wood or scrap metal, whatever was at hand. Reading was, for some, an important pastime. Poetry had been a shared joy for us, and a thick anthology of poetry I'd given Harry accompanied him to the Pacific theater and back. We kept it, more as a keepsake, because its stay in the jungle tropics had warped and mildewed it beyond help. But we treasured it as a sort of talisman of that hard and lonely time.

The single most significant morale builder and antidote to loneliness was the mail: veritable lifeblood for these young men. I wrote to Harry pretty much daily, but he didn't get letters every day. Mail to New Guinea was irregular, often interrupted; the ships that carried it had to dodge enemy submarines, and at least one mail and supply ship was sunk, the Japanese way to threaten the troops' morale. There were times when there would be long lapses in mail delivery, and it was terrible for these soldiers. Then a whole bunch of mail would come all at once, the big event of the men's days. Mail *to* the U.S. was steadier. Over the almost twenty months we were apart, Harry and I wrote each other a letter a day. He saved the letters I wrote to him, and I saved the letters he wrote to me. We had two big barracks bags full of letters—almost a thousand between us. Of these, only a couple of hundred survive.

Writing this account, I realized that physical separation had played an influential role in the courtships and marriages of our family across the generations. Maybe the patriarch Abraham Gottlieb, and certainly his son and grandson, the two Harrys, conducted their courtship by mail. A coincidence? Rosie was likely promised to Abraham before he left Domažlice for Prague at about age ten; there is no mention of his shopping around for a suitable wife, and one infers that that was a done deal from way back, as was customary. They waited for each other until he left the employ of the Archduke, when the railroad was completed and running. He was twenty-eight and she was twenty-one when they married. If they got to know each other through letters, those have not survived. But we do have Harry Sr.'s several years of correspondence with Dot as he languished and convalesced out West. And finally, Harry's and my two-part epistolary chronicle: me at Scripps and Dogface Harry the draftee—the turning point, Tacoma—and finally our letters after we were married and endured that twenty-month separation.

Did I write to Harry about the most appalling drunken episode I ever suffered? I may have, to entertain him. In any event, I remember it indelibly. It occurred while I was working as an engine lathe operator at Industrial Service Engineers.

It was the Christmas party at the job that was almost my undoing. The boss took us all to a little Italian restaurant near the shop where we were to have dinner, having closed up a little early. I can't remember whether, once the machines were turned off, the boss brought out a couple of bottles of wine, or whether we did all the drinking at the restaurant. Somehow I think we must have had a head start on the alcohol. So there we were, twelve or fourteen of us, sitting at this long table in the restaurant. There was George, a big beefy guy who looked like Daddy Warbucks (of *Little Orphan Annie* comic strip fame); Al, a little old expert machinist who used to say, "Sit down on the floor and let your legs hang over," and then smile angelically as he waited for people to laugh. I always laughed. I liked Al, and he was generous when it came to helping his fellow workers. And Florence was there, too.

There must have been rather a lot more wine to drink before we ever got around to the food. Just before the dishes were set on the table, I rose to my feet (unsteadily, I am sure) and started to make an impassioned and eloquent speech about The Brotherhood of Man. I felt it all so deeply, so powerfully, I was sure that my words were beautiful and expressive. And then, the next thing you know, with no warning, no nausea, nothing, I threw up all over the table, all over me, all over the dish of Italian whatever-it-was that had just been placed in front of me.

There was a scuttling and a scurrying, and Florence (it must have been Florence) hustled me off to the ladies' room and cleaned me up. I really don't remember anything except for little snapshots: me, feeling less drunk but not quite sober, sitting silently at the table, emphatically not eating, while everyone else tucked into the delicious Italian dinners. Then stepping out into the black cold winter night — the cold air was a benediction as it cleared my head — and going in someone's car back to my apartment at 33 E. Division Street.

George walked me up the three flights of stairs to my door, and then he tried to come inside my apartment with me. That was when I snapped back to sobriety completely. He was big and strong, and there wasn't anyone else there, but I knew I didn't want or need him in my house, and I managed to shove and shoulder him out and slam the door. Never mind if he was going to fire me — for what? Insubordination for not allowing him to lay me? Off-hours drunkenness was not in itself cause for dismissal. Chronic tardiness for work was (I'd already gotten that kink in my on-the-job punctuality straightened out with a warning).

The next morning I suffered the excruciating shame and

embarrassment of the sobered-up drunk: I wondered how I could ever face my fellow workers again after having disgraced myself and made a spectacle of our entire group. I considered not going back to work for a few days (if ever!), but I really liked my job. It was modest both in significance and pay (I think I made somewhere around 35 to 60 cents per hour), but I was a participant in the War Effort. In 1943 these small aircraft parts probably went to the European theater.

So, with some trepidation, I went to work on Monday morning. No one sniggered; no one made snide remarks; George was aloof and businesslike; Al, that dear, gentle guy, was just as reassuring a presence as ever, and Florence? We just took up where we had left off, having our bag lunches together. Another Learning Experience!

63

The 583rd's next encampment was almost 200 miles north of Oro Bay, in Nadzab—captured from the Japanese in September 1943—where they arrived on March 31, 1944.

By that time, the men of the outfit were trying to keep normally imperturbable George Greider from going crazy with anxiety as they waited in the jungle for word of the birth of his and Cassie's baby, half a world away. The baby *was* somewhat late arriving, but the news was further delayed by the slow mail service from Ohio to New Guinea, and George—generally mild and unflappable—was beside himself awaiting word of the long-delayed debut of this infant, referred to as "the Ten-Month Baby." It wasn't till late May or early June that word of George Jr.'s birth on April 22, FINALLY finally reached his father. (Festive April 22 reunions in Fort Myers Beach have been staged with George Jr., now a graybeard, and his wife, Gayle Krantz, in commemoration of that event.)

Harry could, of course, tell me virtually nothing of what he or the unit were doing—other than that Willie Steckman had once again led the way in forging friendly relations with natives who lived nearby, and had nicknamed the two "principal" men Cornelius and Corbus. Beginning June 1, and for the rest of 1944, records show that 1st Lt. Harry N. Gottlieb held the position of "Commander of the Headquarters Detachment of the 583rd Signal Aircraft Warning Battalion." In practice, as a lieutenant, that meant that he was not issuing orders, but executing orders from above. Harry would have worn the title lightly—*commanding* was not his style—but it must have carried heavy responsibility, much of it logistical and bureaucratic, but also for the lives and well-being of his friends and all the men under his command. An example of the humane way he could use his authority (I learned later) was the time when he cut orders for Willie to deliver an important message to an island where Willie's brother just happened to be stationed. Harry might have been remembering the commanding officer who slipped him six day-passes in Tacoma, and the one who shooed him off the parade ground at Fort Monmouth to get married.

The battalion relocated again, to the recently retaken port town of Hollandia, along the far northwest coast of New Guinea, on July 25. But shortly before the unit was to depart Nadzab, the natives, who had become invaluable participants in camp life, invited their mentor and interpreter, Willie Steckman, to round up a few of his closest buddies to be honored with a feast in their home village. It was nearby — dugout canoeing distance from the camp — and they would paddle over and ferry their guests to the village. One of the advantages the 583d had was autonomy: knowing the natives, knowing that they would be safe and well-treated, they could accept such an invitation, which was prohibited as "fraternization" under Army regulations and protocol. If the brass had known what Willie was doing, he would have been court-martialed.

But they never knew, and the feast in the village was a memorable experience. Here is Harry's account, dated August 18, 1944.[3]

Willie Steckman and the Aboriginal Feast

Last Sunday I was telling you about our trip to a native village and I think the letter got us just about to the door of the hut where we were to have chow, the hut [in] which Cornelius and Corbus, their wives and their families, lived. When we sat down there was some not very savory looking rice, one whole fish (head, tail, and all), and some very weak looking tea on the table. The crockery was largely GI, and there wasn't enough of it to go around. The tablecloth was a bit dingy. Well, we thought, these characters are kind enough

---

[3]The earlier letter he refers to appears to have gone missing.

to put out this stuff, which to them probably represents a feast, so we might as well plow in, and we did.

We broke the fish with our fingers, and found that it was smoked and quite tasty. The rice wasn't too good, but suddenly some fried bananas appeared, which we mixed with the rice, and it went well. By that time we were hep to the fish, and I guess our hosts could see it, for suddenly all sorts of characters appeared in the hut, each bringing one or two fish. By that time we were in full stride, all smiles, tackling the meal with gusto. The natives beamed, because they knew we were pleased. More natives walked in, some bearing fresh fish, some a stalk of luscious looking bananas, some, of all things, bringing large fresh oranges. These were the first fresh oranges most of us had seen in New Guinea. They are not abundant here, also came some of the delicious paw-paw, and a few coconuts, by this time it was a gala affair. The natives peeled the oranges for us. I am a sucker for coconut milk, so a native opened up a coconut for me, and when the milk was gone he shredded it and let us get at the meat of it. For one solid hour we ate, babe. I had at least two whole fish, three big bananas, two oranges, many slices of fried bananas, a little rice, the milk and most of the meat from a coconut, and a good slice of paw-paw. That was a better meal than anything I had in Sydney.

Finally we staggered over to shore in another little canoe, looked at their very neatly built combination church and schoolhouse, and at the trough which brings them fresh water from way back in the hills. Then we sat around in the doorway of one of the huts that happened to be at dry land and had a little song. Willie had taught some of the natives Pistol Packin' Mama, so we tried that, and soon had a good portion of the male population joining in. One old codger ran up excitedly waving a pencil and paper. We thought he wanted the words to the song, so we started to write them down. NO, NO, that isn't what he wanted. The old bloke wanted us to write down the music! I was wondering how the guy ever learned his trebles and base [sic], and was very dubious about the whole thing. He seemed to sense my doubt, so he grabbed the pencil and wrote down Dutch, symbols for do ra me fa so, etc. From that I proceeded to try to write the music for him.

We were getting along very well when there came an interruption. Another native came up in a canoe and made Malayan noises at us. It seems that he is one of the guys who worked for Art Tatman, another member of our party. He had seen that Willie Steckman's boys had fed us royally. Now he wanted us to come and eat at his house! Being good natured blokes (and liking their food very much), we hesitated not at all, but climbed into the boat and went to his house. We must have looked a little green in the face, for the quantity wasn't quite so huge this time, but we couldn't even eat all of what they put before us. It was exactly an hour after we had finished our last meal with Cornelius and Corbus. This time I only made off with a few slices of fried banana, one fresh banana, a slice of coconut, and a slice of paw-paw. How are my bowels, you say? Fine, lass, they never were better. I can't understand it either.

Remember the beads and stuff you bought for me to give to natives before I left Tampa? Well, I took them along, and Corbus' and Cornelius' wives got the prettiest ones. They were quiet, serenely pretty girls who hovered a bit in the background. They were fully covered with clothing, at least as much as Dorothy Lamour wears, and they were easily the nicest native women I've seen in this year. To the men we gave tobacco, a few cigarettes, some safety pins (no, they went to the women too), and to the black mission boy we gave much paper and a few pencils to use in the school. We gave it out of gratitude after the meal, more as one would bring a box of candy to a nice hostess than anything else. Remember the big penguin and the four little penguins you sent me last Christmas? Well, most of them have perched on my desk with their little red scarves till this last move, when most of them somehow had their heads broken. But the big one survived except for a slight rupture about the feet, so I took him along. In the afternoon we ran across the little pocked boy who had worked so hard to paddle us to the village in the morning. I gave him the penguin and showed him how to patch up the little stand. Never have I seen so much pure joy over a gift. The kid leaped in the air, kicked his feet together, made noises like he thought a penguin made noises, said thank you in English, and dashed off shrieking.

Like all good dinner guests should, we were careful not to stay too long. Corbus and Cornelius got out a boat big enough to haul all five of us. Four of the guys sat up on an elevated sort of platform they'd built on the boat, sort of like the things they sit on in the movies when they ride on elephants. I sat on the narrow canoe, which is not quite as wide as my broad fanny, shirtless and with my bare feet dangling happily in the water. We had a few grenades along so we tossed them at fish hopefully (I didn't throw any, as I like my fishing with hook and line). All they got was small ones, minnowlike. Corbus had a forked spear he was going to try, but we never got close enough to anything worthwhile. Then we were back waiting for the LCM [Landing Craft Mechanized]. On the way back in the LCM Corbus came along just for the ride. The ride took quite awhile, for a big Liberty Ship was coming into the bay. The skipper of the ship had obviously never been in there before, so the little LCM had to show the way. It was a good day, babe, a heap good day.

It was an unforgettable experience for the lucky few who glimpsed—and were welcomed into—the world of a now-vanished way of life.

I worked at Industrial Service Engineers for almost a year, but after the summer of 1944, I had really had it. That loft, like most such workplaces in the early '40s, had no air conditioning, just exhaust fans. It was *hot* in the summer, with not only the heat from those nineteenth-century machines, but also being on the top floor of this rather rickety old loft building on West Lake Street. Furthermore, it looked as though Harry would be in the Pacific at least until after the war in Europe was concluded, which seemed a long way off. I decided it was my chance to go back to school. (Florence stayed on at the machine shop after I left.)

The University of Chicago Extension, under the U of C's innovative president Robert Maynard Hutchins, was offering a new, accelerated bachelor's degree alternative known as the Great Books continuing education program. Designed to offer people who might not have been able to go to college a quick, affordable, but intensive and high-class education, it had received a fair amount of publicity, and it appealed to me. I enrolled without any trouble. The course was in four parts: humanities (literature and philosophy), social sciences (history, sociology, politics, current events), physical and biological sciences. At the end of the year you took four-hour comprehensive exams ("comps") in each of the areas, and (if I remember rightly) you could earn a bachelor's degree in two years instead of four.

I had a wonderful time. The classes were small, with deep and wide-ranging discussions; the student body, all adults, was varied; the social studies "tutor," as they called all teachers regardless of academic rank, was especially brilliant and articulate. Three days a week I'd take the IC (Illinois Central) train from 33 East Division Street along the lakeshore to the South Side for classes, and I'd work on assignments in the library. I made some good buddies in that program, girls named Roseann "Rodie" Siegler and Charlotte "Schatzi" Getz. I became the third leg of that triumvirate. They both came from musical families: Rodie was going to teach me to play the piano, and Schatzi's family knew Lenny Bernstein. (Harry and I once later shared a packed, festive cab with Schatzi, Rodie, and the undeniably charismatic Lenny on the way up to Schatzi's family home on the North Shore.)

I even invited two young professors I liked to come over

to my apartment for dinner (one at a time). They knew I was married, but each one thought it was going to be one of those evenings when they'd get me into bed. They knew my husband was overseas and assumed I was looking for a little male company. I was, but not in bed! I was just lonesome, and I missed cooking dinner for a man. They got the message, and it was fun.

I went through the course, kept up with the work, wrote all the papers, and did very well—except in the physical sciences. I had no interest in that and wasn't good at it. I knew I'd never get through the comp exam for that one. As it happened, life crashed in, and I never took the exams. That was my last attempt at formal education until our youngest child, David, started school. Then—no quitter!—I tried to go back and finish what I'd started twenty years before, but the University of Chicago wouldn't let me in. They said, "Get yourself a bachelor's degree, and then come back." So I did, in the new Degree Completion Program at Mundelein College, a Catholic college, taught by nuns, that had opened its program to "all women over 26 years of age who seriously wish to continue their education." Diploma in hand, I went back to the University, where my wish proved serious enough to propel me through a master's degree and then a PhD.

64

It may have been within a few months of the Battalion's September 1943 arrival in New Guinea that Harry got his first taste of tropical illness.[4] His earliest mention of being "under the weather" is in a letter of January 1944; he didn't specify the symptoms. At first it was just a trip to the medic, but as the year wore on, letters began to mention midday siestas, a couple of hours during the heat of the day when he'd just lie around and read.

It was not unusual for men serving in the tropics to have fevers, gastrointestinal ailments, mysterious aches and pains, exotic insect bites, "jungle rot" — what happens to skin you can't keep dry — "New Guinea crud" or "the creeping cruds," catch-alls for tropical skin diseases. These conditions were ubiquitous, and very little was known at that time about what they were: malaria, dengue fever, jaundice (a symptom of several disorders, rather than a disease), dysentery, filariasis, schistosomiasis. I think Harry must have had an array of those bugs! They all did. He may have known about them, but this was not subject material for letters. He did not like to complain or to worry the home front.

He did write about "feeling bum" for several days, and on one occasion, after a stubborn headache and fever, he wrote me that he "went for a swim, took a cold shower, and drank three shots" of his precious stash of whiskey.

It's good that we didn't know what became clear only after the war: "Despite medical advances, for every two men lost to

---

[4]I went back to our letters of 1944 and '45 to trace the chronology of Harry's illness. They have been my only source of information; because he tended to be taciturn on the subject, I've had to do some creative extrapolation.

battle in the Southwest Pacific theater . . . five men were lost to disease." "Illness accounted for the overwhelming majority of Allied casualties during the Pacific War. Malaria was the main culprit, but dengue, scrub typhus, and other tropical diseases, together with FUO ('Fever of Undetermined Origin' . . .), took their toll as well."

It appears that Harry began being sick in earnest in the late fall of 1944. It was as though he'd fought off a lot of this stuff earlier, and it finally wore his resistance down. By this time the 583rd was preparing to leave the sylvan isolation of New Guinea for the island province of Leyte in the central Philippines, where the Armed Forces had just driven out the Japanese occupying force—in October—and were undertaking a massive building project in the mud of the rainy season, readying for a potential invasion of Japan.

Headquarters Detachment's work continued as they prepared for the move, but Harry had days when he was barely fit to work. "Maybe I was already getting sick—not in A-1 shape," he'd admit only later. In his effort to keep his parents and me informed of his general outlook on life, he felt, rightly, that he shouldn't conceal from us the bouts of illness, though he assiduously underplayed them, I now realize: no information on symptoms—probably fever; who knows what else? Most of his letters are filled with trivia about how much he enjoyed the midday siesta, reading books like Eric Knight's *Lassie Come-Home*, the classic about a collie dog.

The Battalion left Hollandia on November 8, 1944, and arrived in Leyte a week later. "From New Guinea to the Philippines is two quick jumps by air; one long, slow haul by sea," Harry wrote. The Philippines were very hot and muddy. They were encamped in Dulag, Leyte, till December 10, when they relocated about six miles north to San Roque.

By December 14, at the end of their first month in the Philippines, Harry was sick enough so that he had to go to the hospital. He was suffering recurring bouts of headache, fever, diarrhea, loss of appetite, and jaundice. Since all the men were required to take Atabrine, the antimalarial drug, everyone's skin had a sort of yellowish cast, but if a soldier developed jaundice, a symptom of a disordered liver, the difference was visible. Harry was evidently hospitalized for at least ten days, first on bed rest, and finally allowed up to regain strength. Then he was released—but he kept having to be briefly readmitted, more than once. (It probably didn't help that his concerned buddies were bringing him beer to nourish him—good for his morale, but not for his liver. The yellow would fade fairly rapidly when he didn't drink it.) George Greider, steady and knowledgeable, took over Harry's duties on a temporary basis whenever he had to stay in the hospital for more than a couple of days. John Solon was another important figure, about whom I know next to nothing. The letters mention that he had been Harry's assistant at Nadzab, and public records show that John J. Solon succeeded Harry as Commander of Headquarters Detachment at the end of December.

Their camp site was in an area where a new, larger airfield was under construction in preparation for invasion of Japan, and the hospital was in the same general area. Construction was pretty much a twenty-four-hour activity, resulting in conditions that were not restful for the many sick and wounded patients. Harry complained of the round-the-clock noise outside his window.

His was an endless case of stubborn recurrences. They'd treat him, prescribe strict bed rest, his test results would get better, they'd send him back to his outfit—and two weeks later he'd be back again with fever and all the symptoms, and they'd have to start him on the regimen again, and he'd get better . . . the same thing, on and on for quite some period. He kept relapsing at shorter and shorter intervals: out one day, back a couple of days later. Handwriting tells a lot: his went downhill from his characteristic plain, clear almost-printing to a soft, much less well-defined hand that bore no resemblance to his usual script.

Philippines, January 1, 1945: "Tried to write New Year's Eve letter but feel lousy."

January 2: "Feel a little better."

January 5: "In hospital; will feel better in 3 or 4 days."

January 11, a hopeful turn: "I'm not half as yellow as I was a week ago and my appetite will rapidly regain what weight I lost, as I am hungry almost all the time now."

January 16 he was strong enough to write more: "Your intuitive self has probably figured out that I'm not in A-1 shape yet, and it's a bit frustrating not to be, as I am essentially such a healthy guy. Well, this stuff lingers no matter what, so I am going to do more resting than working for awhile again. Gonna lie on my back and read and sleep and read and sleep and drink fruit juices until this yellow bug hauls ass out of here. Might be a good idea not to worry the folks . . . They're very likely to magnify it. . . . Until I'm back to 100% again I will continue to be sort of tired, ornery, and cantankerous . . . it doubtless creeps into my letters."

The "yellow bug" now had a diagnosis: acute infectious hepatitis. Harry Senior, frantic with worry (as Harry Jr. had feared), somehow got hold of a special experimental medication for the ailment and made elaborate arrangements to send it to his last living child, who was now in a hospital farther behind the lines, in the Netherlands East Indies (NEI). The Army was moving hospitals out of the anticipated war zone. I don't think the medicine ever got through.

On February 16, 1945, Harry wrote: "Medic est. be in hospital until 3/20."

NEI, it turned out, was his last stop. From there, they were shipping home sick ones who weren't going to be able to return to duty fairly soon. And Harry was clearly one of those. You can see that he was losing ground.

65

On February 23, 1945, Harry wrote: "Be of good cheer . . . on this anniversary day, darling. [We'd gotten married May 23.] Know that I am always very close to you, and becoming closer each day . . ." Was he giving me a hint? Did he know something? That never occurred to me at the time. A doctor had predicted that he'd be in the hospital until March 20!

In early March, Harry's father suffered a stroke and was taken by ambulance to Michael Reese Hospital. It turned out to be a mild stroke, and Harry Sr. wasn't desperately ill, but he was in frail health. I think he was kept at Michael Reese for as long as a week. There is a long explanatory letter from me to Harry, with an enclosure from his mother, explaining fully the events that led to his father's hospitalization. A letter or two written by Harry Jr. to me were on Red Cross letterhead. Had they made a request for emergency leave for Harry Jr.?

Whether or not the Red Cross was a player in this drama, he was evacuated from NEI to Salt Lake City. It may have been a hospital plane. He remembered a stopover at night in Hawaii, then on to San Francisco. Then there was some delay. Harry was low priority: there were Colonels going somewhere.

In any event, we received a telegram on March 5, 1945:

> Utah banning me, so will arrive Municipal Airport Chicago
> via United Airlines 10:55 tonight. Bring hot water bottle.
> Love, Harry

So Dot and I drove out to what is now Midway Airport, in a state of anticipation that beggars description. It was a rainy night, and we drove out 55th Street, or Douglas Blvd. (originally named Grand Blvd.), an imposing nineteenth-century parkway divided by its broad, tree-lined green median. That was a grand neighborhood once, and it still bears the dignity of its past splendor in its generous proportions and fine old trees.

We must have parked the car and gone into the terminal. I remember none of this. Did we talk, Dot and I? We were good, close, affectionate pals, the two of us — but we were in our own roiled worlds of emotion: anticipation and grief. The February 28 anniversary of Alan's death had just passed; had THAT had anything to do with Harry Sr.'s stroke? That, and his fears for Harry?

We must have sat in the waiting area near the gate. I have no memory of there being crowds of people: it was almost 11:00 p.m., after all — not the busiest time in the airport. In those days you could still smoke cigarettes anywhere and everywhere, and Dot and I both smoked — nervously. (So did Harry Jr., of course; all the soldiers got free cigarettes.) Did they announce the arrival of his flight from Salt Lake City? I have no recollection of any of that — nor of crowds, or noise. It was as if all of that had simply been erased from my sensory equipment. And then . . .

Here comes this young soldier in his khakis — holding his hat? Not wearing it. That shade of thick black sort-of-curly hair — Was he walking fast? Slowly? My eyes were fastened on him, seeing him move firmly but not fast. I was holding him and pulling him toward us with the power of my eyes. The airport was silent and empty — just Harry and me, nothing else. I don't remember whether he embraced Dot first, after all she'd been through these last few days. I don't know if she was crying or not. I was fastened on this man. Yes, he was pretty yellow. And then his arms embraced me.

We held on to each other, afraid we were going to fall over — but oh, how wonderful that so-long–absent embrace! He was thin through his overcoat; I could feel how thin he was. And then we kissed — and kissed — and couldn't believe it was true. And then we all three sat down in one of the rows of those airport chairs and held hands and looked at each other.

Dot asked him did he want something to eat — was he hungry? "No, let's go home," he said. He was so very skinny — AND yellow. We got Harry's luggage, a barracks bag, I think — I don't remember anything else. We got to the car — nothing seemed crowded. I'd erased all the other people but us three, I guess. And there was no trouble finding the car and getting out of the airport and back onto beautiful Douglas Blvd.

It was still raining lightly — the street lights were blurry from the rain. Harry and I are sitting together — very close together — in the back seat, and Dot is driving. And first Harry and I are holding hands — his so warm and meaty — the memory and the now jump together like attracting magnets — and the space between those months apart and now snaps shut, disappears, and all that's left is Now.

And then we look up — a lot of cars honking and headlights in our faces —

"Mom," Harry says, "I think you're going on the wrong side of this boulevard!"

Cars are veering and honking — their headlights smeary in the rainy night. "Oh my God!" Dot says. She begins inching over to the right, so that at the next cross-street opening she can get the car into its proper place in among the cars heading toward downtown and away from the airport.

And then we're in the dark of cars going along with us and no more honking and we are now kissing deliriously in the calm of "going with the flow" of cars in the obedient night. We hold hands and look at each other. Is this real? We talk to Dot to let her know we're still here and in the world — and something about Alan swirls around a little chill, perhaps? And then we're at our "home": 33 E. Division St. — the place with the cute little fireplace that Harry has never seen. But first we hug and kiss Dot: what a trouper! Can she make it home to 190 E. Chestnut OK? "Sure!" — a big smile.

And Harry faces the daunting challenge of climbing three flights of stairs. It took him quite a while: maybe thirty minutes altogether. I don't remember how we got his luggage upstairs. We stopped at landings; we stopped between landings, we sat on the stairs and held hands and looked at one another: unbelieving—and smiling because it's REAL!

I think I'd opened up the couch that turned into a double bed and had it all ready to get into. I helped Harry undress. He was so exhausted! Never mind brushing your teeth if you're too tired. A glass of water? Warm milk? "Water," he says. I help him hold the glass and just feast and feast, looking at him. My clothes piled on a chair, into the nightgown, into bed—I am lying beside him. Is it REAL? Yes! Skinny and weak, he still radiates a warmth that springs back to familiarity, that radiant warmth. Our arms and heads and legs and feet, bellies and breasts—every contact point thrills through us. And then, lights out; eyes fall shut. He is used up, my brave one.

And when we open our eyes tomorrow, our REAL LIFE will have begun.

Stern Family

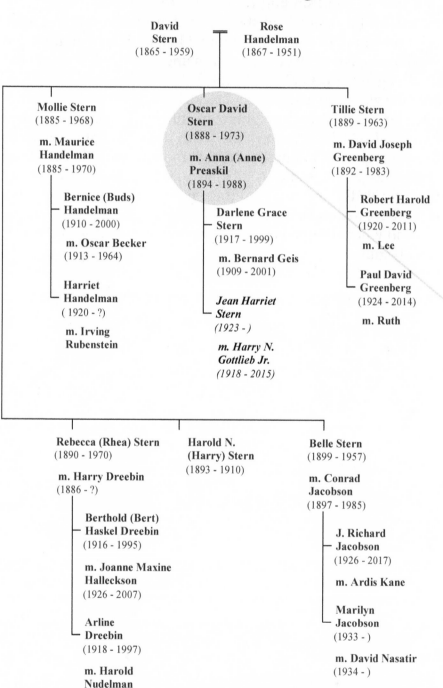

David
Stern
(1865 - 1959)

Rose
Handelman
(1867 - 1951)

Mollie Stern
(1885 - 1968)

m. Maurice
Handelman
(1885 - 1970)

  Bernice (Buds)
Handelman
(1910 - 2000)

  m. Oscar Becker
(1913 - 1964)

  Harriet
Handelman
(1920 - ?)

  m. Irving
Rubenstein

**Oscar David
Stern**
(1888 - 1973)

m. Anna (Anne)
Preaskil
(1894 - 1988)

  Darlene Grace
Stern
(1917 - 1999)

  m. Bernard Geis
(1909 - 2001)

  *Jean Harriet
Stern*
(1923 -)

  *m. Harry N.
Gottlieb Jr.*
(1918 - 2015)

Tillie Stern
(1889 - 1963)

m. David Joseph
Greenberg
(1892 - 1983)

  Robert Harold
Greenberg
(1920 - 2011)

  m. Lee

  Paul David
Greenberg
(1924 - 2014)

  m. Ruth

Rebecca (Rhea) Stern
(1890 - 1970)

m. Harry Dreebin
(1886 - ?)

  Berthold (Bert)
Haskel Dreebin
(1916 - 1995)

  m. Joanne Maxine
Halleckson
(1926 - 2007)

  Arline
Dreebin
(1918 - 1997)

  m. Harold
Nudelman
(1924 - 1980)

**Harold N.
(Harry) Stern**
(1893 - 1910)

Belle Stern
(1899 - 1957)

m. Conrad
Jacobson
(1897 - 1985)

  J. Richard
Jacobson
(1926 - 2017)

  m. Ardis Kane

  Marilyn
Jacobson
(1933 -)

  m. David Nasatir
(1934 -)

Preaskil Family

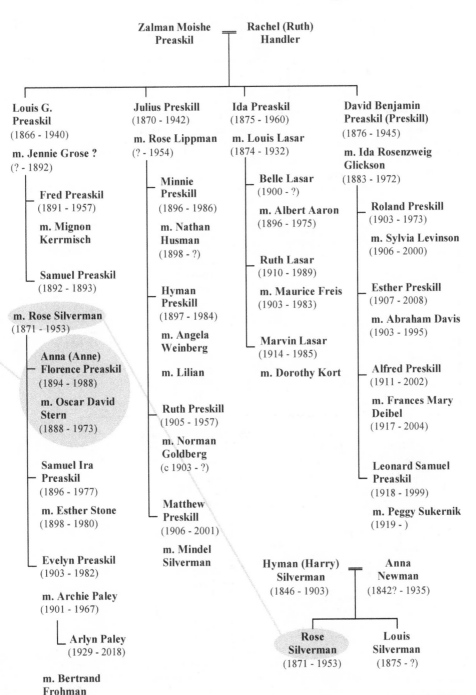

Zalman Moishe
Preaskil
—
Rachel (Ruth)
Handler

**Louis G.
Preaskil**
(1866 - 1940)

m. Jennie Grose ?
(? - 1892)

   Fred Preaskil
   (1891 - 1957)

   **m. Mignon
   Kerrmisch**

   Samuel Preaskil
   (1892 - 1893)

m. Rose Silverman
(1871 - 1953)

   **Anna (Anne)
   Florence Preaskil**
   (1894 - 1988)

   **m. Oscar David
   Stern**
   (1888 - 1973)

   **Samuel Ira
   Preaskil**
   (1896 - 1977)

   m. Esther Stone
   (1898 - 1980)

   Evelyn Preaskil
   (1903 - 1982)

   m. Archie Paley
   (1901 - 1967)

      Arlyn Paley
      (1929 - 2018)

   **m. Bertrand
   Frohman**

Julius Preskill
(1870 - 1942)

m. Rose Lippman
(? - 1954)

   **Minnie
   Preskill**
   (1896 - 1986)

   **m. Nathan
   Husman**
   (1898 - ?)

   **Hyman
   Preskill**
   (1897 - 1984)

   **m. Angela
   Weinberg**

   m. Lilian

   Ruth Preskill
   (1905 - 1957)

   **m. Norman
   Goldberg**
   (c 1903 - ?)

   **Matthew
   Preskill**
   (1906 - 2001)

   **m. Mindel
   Silverman**

Ida Preaskil
(1875 - 1960)

m. Louis Lasar
(1874 - 1932)

   Belle Lasar
   (1900 - ?)

   m. Albert Aaron
   (1896 - 1975)

   Ruth Lasar
   (1910 - 1989)

   m. Maurice Freis
   (1903 - 1983)

   Marvin Lasar
   (1914 - 1985)

   m. Dorothy Kort

**David Benjamin
Preaskil (Preskill)**
(1876 - 1945)

**m. Ida Rosenzweig
Glickson**
(1883 - 1972)

   Roland Preskill
   (1903 - 1973)

   m. Sylvia Levinson
   (1906 - 2000)

   Esther Preskill
   (1907 - 2008)

   m. Abraham Davis
   (1903 - 1995)

   Alfred Preskill
   (1911 - 2002)

   **m. Frances Mary
   Deibel**
   (1917 - 2004)

   **Leonard Samuel
   Preaskil**
   (1918 - 1999)

   m. Peggy Sukernik
   (1919 -)

**Hyman (Harry)
Silverman**
(1846 - 1903)
—
**Anna
Newman**
(1842? - 1935)

   **Rose
   Silverman**
   (1871 - 1953)

   **Louis
   Silverman**
   (1875 - ?)

Gottlieb Family

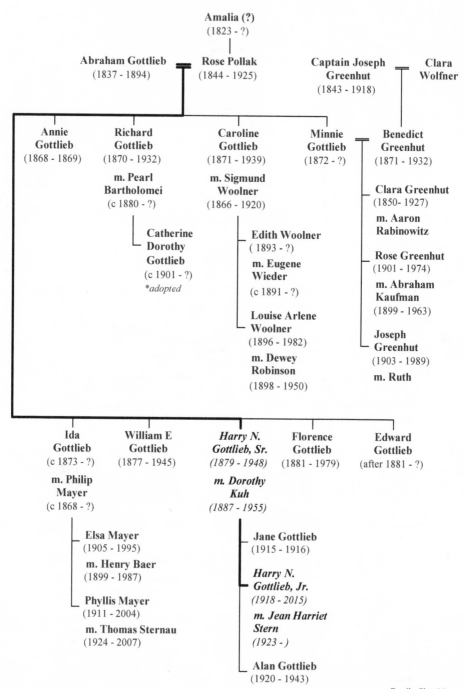

Amalia (?)
(1823 - ?)

Abraham Gottlieb
(1837 - 1894)

Rose Pollak
(1844 - 1925)

Captain Joseph
Greenhut
(1843 - 1918)

Clara
Wolfner

Annie
Gottlieb
(1868 - 1869)

Richard
Gottlieb
(1870 - 1932)

m. Pearl
Bartholomei
(c 1880 - ?)

Catherine
Dorothy
Gottlieb
(c 1901 - ?)
adopted

Caroline
Gottlieb
(1871 - 1939)

m. Sigmund
Woolner
(1866 - 1920)

Edith Woolner
(1893 - ?)

m. Eugene
Wieder
(c 1891 - ?)

Louise Arlene
Woolner
(1896 - 1982)

m. Dewey
Robinson
(1898 - 1950)

Minnie
Gottlieb
(1872 - ?)

Benedict
Greenhut
(1871 - 1932)

Clara Greenhut
(1850- 1927)

m. Aaron
Rabinowitz

Rose Greenhut
(1901 - 1974)

m. Abraham
Kaufman
(1899 - 1963)

Joseph
Greenhut
(1903 - 1989)

m. Ruth

Ida
Gottlieb
(c 1873 - ?)

m. Philip
Mayer
(c 1868 - ?)

Elsa Mayer
(1905 - 1995)

m. Henry Baer
(1899 - 1987)

Phyllis Mayer
(1911 - 2004)

m. Thomas Sternau
(1924 - 2007)

William E
Gottlieb
(1877 - 1945)

*Harry N.
Gottlieb, Sr.*
(1879 - 1948)

*m. Dorothy
Kuh*
(1887 - 1955)

Jane Gottlieb
(1915 - 1916)

*Harry N.
Gottlieb, Jr.*
(1918 - 2015)

*m. Jean Harriet
Stern*
(1923 -)

Alan Gottlieb
(1920 - 1943)

Florence
Gottlieb
(1881 - 1979)

Edward
Gottlieb
(after 1881 - ?)

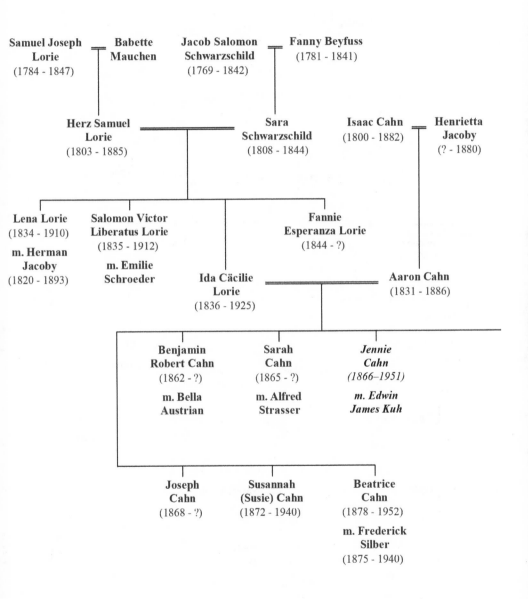

Kuh Family

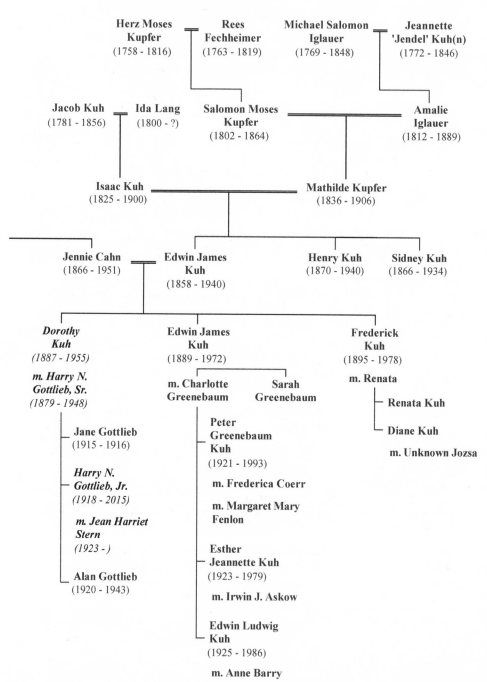

Herz Moses Kupfer (1758 - 1816) ═══ Rees Fechheimer (1763 - 1819)

Michael Salomon Iglauer (1769 - 1848) ═══ Jeannette 'Jendel' Kuh(n) (1772 - 1846)

Jacob Kuh (1781 - 1856) ═══ Ida Lang (1800 - ?)

Salomon Moses Kupfer (1802 - 1864) ═══ Amalie Iglauer (1812 - 1889)

Isaac Kuh (1825 - 1900) ═══ Mathilde Kupfer (1836 - 1906)

Jennie Cahn (1866 - 1951) ═══ Edwin James Kuh (1858 - 1940)

Henry Kuh (1870 - 1940)

Sidney Kuh (1866 - 1934)

Dorothy Kuh *(1887 - 1955)*

m. Harry N. Gottlieb, Sr. *(1879 - 1948)*

Edwin James Kuh (1889 - 1972)

m. Charlotte Greenebaum   Sarah Greenebaum

Frederick Kuh (1895 - 1978)

m. Renata

├ Renata Kuh

└ Diane Kuh

m. Unknown Jozsa

├ Jane Gottlieb (1915 - 1916)

├ **Harry N. Gottlieb, Jr.** *(1918 - 2015)*

  m. Jean Harriet Stern *(1923 -)*

└ Alan Gottlieb (1920 - 1943)

┌ Peter Greenebaum Kuh (1921 - 1993)

  m. Frederica Coerr

  m. Margaret Mary Fenlon

├ Esther Jeannette Kuh (1923 - 1979)

  m. Irwin J. Askow

└ Edwin Ludwig Kuh (1925 - 1986)

  m. Anne Barry

APPENDIX A

From the memoir of Ida Lorie Cahn (1837–1923)
Dated: Pasadena, California, February 11, 1913

It was on the 10th of March, 1844, that we three children, Lena, Victor and I, were told upon awakening that a baby sister had arrived and was named Fannie Esperanza Lorie. After this event, my mother was a great sufferer and I can only remember her reclining in a chair; on October 22, 1844, she was carried to her grave. They took us to her coffin, a simple wooden box, and we saw her face for the last time; never will I forget that impression. After that an elderly woman came to us—a sort of housekeeper, who also cared for the baby. Things went along this way for some years, when father found it necessary to take a more educated person into the house; and it was then that Fräulein Wolfers came from Hanover to us,—she was both housekeeper and educator for us.

At that time in Frankfurt there was a Jewish school, one of the best in Germany, having important Professors at its head; to this school my mother had also been sent. We three children went there. The school also had a department for Jewish children without means. . . .

My brother Victor made quite a record in various courses in school, especially in drawing. With the aid of his teacher, Herr Schlösser, the plan to become an artist ripened in him. . . . My father was antagonistic to this idea and insisted that his only son must enter his business, as he needed him. The business—carpets and linens—was going badly at the time. Just at this time came the Revolutionary period for Germany and Austria. Frankfurt am Main was then a Free City, as were Hamburg, Bremen, and Lübeck. In 1848 a Council of the German State convened in Frankfurt and representatives from Germany and Austria were sent on. The Parliament meetings were held in the "Paulskirche" quite near our home and my father rented some of his best rooms to the representatives. This parliament consisted of the Left Wing (called red republicans) the Center and the Right Wing, the latter consisting of "Yunkers" and economists, largely of the nobility. A certain Franz Raveaux, representative from Cologne, lived with us; he was a staunch Republican. I remember that there were many meetings in our house and later on we were told that the socalled "Revolution of Baden" was concocted in our rooms. It was on September 18th, 1848 — that the Revolt of the Citizens of Frankfurt occurred and huge barricades were erected in various streets, by the insurgents. Just before our house one was put up, and then came the trouble makers, bringing stones and oil to the first and second floor, fortifying the windows, while the Austrian Militia was stationed at the other end of our street, with drawn bayonets. At 2:00 o'clock a regular battle occurred; the shooting began and by 4:00 P.M. it had grown worse. The insurgents used guns while the militia returned their fire with "Kartätchen" — or grape-shot. The house we lived in was owned by an old aristocratic family. They lived on the first floor, we occupied the two others. These gentlemen (there were many brothers) became frightened, left their apartment to the insurgents and fled. My father, who felt entirely differently, sympathized with the citizens. As darkness came on, the Austrians moved nearer and stormed the barricade. The insurgents threw stones down and poured hot oil on the militia. But they saw that their cause was hopeless and fled to a court yard belonging to the house (below us there were laundries, etc.) Not long after, the barricades fell and the militia stormed our house because they knew that the insurgents were hiding there; thirteen were taken prisoner and one corpse was found on the first floor. As the Austrians were about to smash the door, my father descended in his dressing gown and called to them that he would open, if an officer would step forward. When the officer entered, my father told him that they could search everywhere, but must shield his family. Meanwhile we were all hidden in a small room on the fourth floor, a huge wardrobe moved in front of the door, as father feared the wrath of the soldiers. Often father related that they poked their bayonets into and under the beds. After quiet was restored the next day, the populace came to view the remains of the victim and our beautifully painted walls, riddled with bullets. The thirteen prisoners were sentenced to two or three years in prison and later went to America. . . .

Parliament was dissolved, peaceful times came and Frankfurt was incorporated in Prussia, which did not suit the citizens at all. I think it was in 1851 that my father returned from a short trip with Frl. Bertha and told us that from now on she would be a second mother to us; we should simply call her "Bertha." We children accepted it quietly enough, only brother Victor expressed opposition, but was soon set right by father. My paternal grandmother, however, was very angry and threatened to disinherit father, even starting a law-suit about it, a useless affair and very unpleasant for us children, as we had to appear as witnesses — but we had only good things, nothing evil, to say.

Years passed and Victor began his career at the Städel Institute, under the famous Prof. Steinle, a Catholic, who painted largely "holy" pictures, following the schools of Raphael and Murillo. There Victor worked hard for four years, copying the pictures in the Staedel Gallery in water colors and oils. But he realized that to become a real artist he would have to get out into the world — a difficult matter, on account of lack of money. . . . At that time my school days ended and I left with many marks of honor. I was presented with a large Album, in which my teacher wrote [a] poem (her own) . . .:

[*excerpt*]

. . . With yourself be ever truthful;
To yourself be just and say,-
If to God and self I'm faithful —
He will always point the way.

These words have accompanied me through life, and to this day I recall them, though that book with everything that I valued, was lost in the Chicago fire of 1871.

My father did not believe in having his daughters submerged in domesticity, so while Lena helped him [in the business], I was sent to learn dressmaking; the course took six months and was very expensive, but it gave me an excellent foundation, so that I could copy anything and make my own clothes and underwear for many years. When Victor was twenty years old, he went to Paris, where he had a hard time. He became a Cartoonist for a humorous paper; later he met people of the best Jewish circles in Paris, sons of wealthy bankers and business men of Frankfurt, who had been his school mates and who were only too pleased with his companionship. He studied with the famous Prof. Centurie and soon exhibited his own picture which he called: "Wine, Woman and Song." He sold it and better times began for him. I myself kept up a secret correspondence with him, owing to our father's objections to his studies; once he became very ill in Paris and wrote that only the wealthy could permit themselves the luxury of being ill in Paris; so I sent him heavy underwear and paid for it from my pocket money. His friends, who soon realized his talent, helped him in every way and secured orders for portraits for him, so that he saved enough money to make a trip to Italy in his twenty-fifth year—Italy, the promised land of the artist.

Meanwhile in 1856, my sister Lena married Herman Jacoby, an American Citizen, who had a leather factory in New York. When Lena left, I took her place in the business, and was there from morning till night. . . . The business was going badly— not enough capital, my father did not get along well with his employees—these were bad times for me. Sister Lena suffered from homesickness in New York, her marriage was unhappy and she begged me in every letter to come to her. One day I had trouble with father and I told him I was going to New York because Lena wanted me and that my grandmother was giving me the money for the trip. Sister Fannie had left school and could take my place in the business, and so on August 3rd, 1859, accompanied part way by father, I left for Paris, where Victor met me and took me to Havre. I landed in New York in nine days — it was the only boat that made the trip in that short time. I was so ill for five days that I saw no one, but on the sixth day I came on deck, was well and had pleasant days. . . . We entered the harbor of New York by night and the lights were marvelous — I never forgot that impression. — I found my sister much changed after three years of marriage and I realized there was no happiness. H. J. was a tyrant at home and I was unhappy, but I kept it to myself. . . . It was then that Aaron Cahn, a nephew of H. Jacoby, came to New York to do his buying and was often with us at supper. His quiet fine manner impressed me and a friendship resulted. In 1860 we became engaged; then in 1860–1861 the Civil War broke out and as no one knew when the call to colors might come . . . my brother-in-law did not permit us to marry until better days came. On August 25th, 1861, we were married at their house on 19th Street between 2nd and 3rd Ave. From that time began a happy time for me . . . Aaron's sisters and brothers were dear people and we had a happy home. Soon we had prospects of a family of our own and on August 26th, 1862, our son was born.

I received most interesting letters from Victor from Italy. He became the intimate friend of the family Oppenheim . . . especially Gustave, who lived in Alexandria, where Victor also spent much of his time. . . . Gustave's wife, nee Lagare (of Lagare Freres) was involved in an affair with the Viceroy of Egypt — she was very beautiful — who had her kidnapped from her box at the theater; Victor was the principal person to whom she owed her escape. In 1870 Victor was invited by the Count de Lesseps to attend the opening ceremonial of the Suez Canal — very few were thus honored. . . . As a friend of the Turks, he wanted to be in Constantinople. . . . [Settling there,] he . . . painted many portraits of the Ministers, which I hear are to be seen at the Museum there, having been purchased by the government. In 1876 the Turko-Russian war broke out and the Turks lost the Schipka Pass and fled to the fortress of Pleona, where they were besieged for four months until forced to capitulate. Victor joined the forces, as correspondent of the Frankfurt newspaper and became very intimate with the Defender of Pleona, Osman Pasha. He entrusted Victor with a dangerous mission, and disguised as a peasant, he had to make his way through the army, to bring the Sultan news of Osman Pasha and at the same time to ask of Queen Victoria of England, help for the starving soldiers. He was given 10,000 pounds sterling; the Sultan's gratitude was demonstrated by the gift of a cup set in diamonds, which he personally presented as a testimonial. Osman Pasha gave him a very fine write-up for his courage. The fortress of Pleona was taken as the army was dying of hunger and typhoid.

Victor became acquainted while at a concert at the Pyramid, with Emilie Schröder of Berlin . . . the divorced wife of a Prussian Baron and Lieutenant of the army; she was an important artist; her first husband did away with her fortune. Victor and she were married before the outbreak of the Russo-Turkish war and after Victor's return from the war, they moved . . . to Montreaux, where they led a quiet life. . . . There I met them frequently on my journeys to Germany. My last visit with my brother was in 1911, in Montreaux, in April; at that time he was a great sufferer— it was about one and one-half years after his wife's death. At that time I knew I would never see him again. He died on December 13th, 1912, tenderly cared for by his old servant and nurse, Jennie Rochat, who received a life pension from him. His life was a stirring one— most interest[ing] and honorable. . . .

Our life the first ten years of our marriage was very exciting; until 1868 I had a baby every two years.

APPENDIX B

From the diary and letters of Alan Gottlieb
(April 28, 1920–February 28, 1943)[5]

Sept. 1, 1942
Remembering 1939-41

Three years ago. It was a cool Vermont night with the snap of late summer in the air. I probably made the transition from my heavy outdoorish clothing to bed with near-lightning speed. My room was the refurnished, reconstructed one above the porch – my favorite. The bed is tremendous, simple in design, and yet beautiful because the wood was so well finished. . . . Somehow the worn whitish rug on the floor was deeper and softer than other Vermont rugs. I was well wrapped in my quilt for that would be necessary on Aug. 31, 1939.

It was barely morning – say 6 AM – and mother's familiarly hurrying footsteps came up the stairs into the room. She half-sat on the edge, half-kneeled by the side of the bed with choked tears, an unusual thing, in her voice. "It's happened," she said and instantly I was wide awake. For a fleeting second, a flashing instant, I thought of Dad – had he had a heart attack? I'd never thought of that possibility, but somehow that thought streaked

---

[5]This selection, focusing as it does on Alan's flight training and thoughts about the war, gives a skewed picture of his young man's mind and preoccupations. He also wrote about women, sex and love, parties, friends, visits with family, books, and shrewd analysis of people. Clearly a leader in training, he studied the personalities and tactics of leaders he admired or didn't, and thought about how to elicit the best from the various human types he now was just one of, but might one day lead. —AG

through my mind like a blazing arrow. Almost without pause mother continued – "They've done it again!"

Then I knew.... A queer, cold thrill shook me ... and my whole being felt sinisterly glad that fascism now was to be challenged. Poland had been invaded; so the world war's uneasy armistice was terminated. The fight was on and well it was for it could not have been avoided – at least not by the time 1939 was with us.

I did not have a sense of personal involvement in the struggle at that time. Indeed, I soon felt the war was being prosecuted as no war should be and that England and France should be left to muddle through to victory without too great expense on our part. But that too changed . . . There was little that had not changed in my mind by the time I returned from a lovely weekend [to a government internship in Washington] . . . and caught the "Fall of bombs on Pearl Harbor" announcement Dec. 7 in the early afternoon.

Jan. 29, 1942 – Thursday

"So be it" may sound like a foolish title for a diary, but in my mind it means much. Here I am embarking on what should be an entrance into the post-collegiate career of job, wife, and home hunting. But . . . law, public administration – any type of career – all must yield to the role of being a "soldier" . . .

There is no need to mope and regret my inability to get on with the task of amassing money, reputation, or whatever I choose to be my goal. On the contrary, were the war to cease suddenly as if it were a nightmare, I would find the ground even more unsure beneath my feet.

Feb. 7, 1942

Love is too tough for me to analyze, but I suppose definitely I'm not in it.

Feb. 13, 1942

Friday the 13th is supposed to be a day of horror and conservatism for the superstitious minded. . . . I headed to the Naval Air Station and became Alan Gottlieb seaman 2nd class . . . No longer am I the free self-controlled individual who with careless abandon indulged himself for 21 years 9 2/3 months. Now I am part of the great, massive collective group who with suppressed fury at their own lot, expressed fury at the Axis rise up toward a new concept of world freedom not fully grasped as yet by any human being. The process of enlistment took 2 1/2 hours and at the end there was simply a brief "Congratulations, Mr. Gottlieb." . . . Extremely tired. Small-pox vaccination better behave.

Feb. 15, 1942

Mother phoned from Chicago and said dad was in Tacoma and that the Harry-Jean romance was blossoming into a formal engagement announcement. I immediately whipped a wire out to the pair.

Jean is alarmingly young in age – a frosh in college. But she has a precocious sophistication, a delightful appearance and personality. I figure she'll be a good counterpart to Harry's mild social isolationism. He's not a retiring person, but like Pa the social grace of a wife like Jean will brighten his existence, pull him out of the anti-gregarious moods which do occasionally materialize. I wish I knew her better and don't anticipate any lessening of the bonds which link Harry and me together. Rather will Jean become a member of what I would call a select company. . . .

This battle is *not* yet a total war and it looks like greater danger is required to adapt our way of life to the needs of warfare. It isn't super-imposition as we are now doing – it is real change.

March 16, 1942

Mother and I went to see a picture at the Del Lago earlier Saturday – "Son of Fury" . . . With it was something called "International Squadron" which I wanted to take Ma from because of its morbid philosophy of an aviator's brief but heroic existence. She can't take that along with my flying with the desired lack of demonstrated emotion.

March 26, 1942

The days of leisure are thoroughly finished. . . . This AM at 8 I reported to the Naval Reserve Aviation Base and the subsequent chapters will be of ALE

IN

THE

NAVAL

AIR

CORPS.

Thursday, March 31

Our regimen has by now become a regular cadence and the newness gradually is giving way to an interested familiarity. We're up at 5:45, muster at 6:15, exercise until breakfast at seven (before which our bunks are made up), study from 7:30 to 10:30 (Aviation indoctrination, radio, theory of flight, Aircraft Identification), drill and recreation until noon, classes from 1–4:30 (Math., Physics, Principles of Navy Life), wiping down planes 4:30–5:00, supper, and radio class an hour in the evening.

The interest in flying makes the ground school hard to elevate to its desired level of importance. . . .

Got a swell letter from Jeanie, but does that loving lass know

Harry is occasionally grouchy, indrawn, and uncommunicative at times? A loveable guy, but he would be the first to climb off the pedestal.

April 22 – Wed.

We are nearing the end of ground school as abstracted from flying. Monday we cease to do both morning and afternoon spells at the books. We will fly about an hour-a-day in the morning or afternoon, study the other period. . . .

For what do people vote? Not issues certainly. . . . The inability of voters to respond with any ready pressure against obsolete ideas, men, and machines is an indictment of democratic processes. An indictment that is unanswered. If unsolved, it will weigh heavily against democracy in a post-war world which requires a continually dynamic progressivism to avoid revolutionary chaos.

Thursday – April 30th

Three hours of flight completed by today. I felt for the first time the carefree joy that comes with graceful movement through the air. Tension was markedly reduced although I grabbed the stick too tightly and jerkily. Turns and level flight were achieved without smoothness, but also without a desperate battle in which the plane acted as a determined enemy. Best of all was the perfect ease of stomach and absence of the little headaches I got previously. "S" turns, landings and take-offs were tackled with not unreasonable results; simulated forced landings were essayed with the most dire consequences looming up were not Evans to give her the gun. . . .

Clifton, Gregory, Thompson . . . They're a good crew without the heavy emphasis on the lewd and lascivious. Thompson has lulled himself into a violent cynicism which I suppose is actually a refuge from figuring out the curious problems he faced due to a hidden physical deformity (back.). Ordinarily such a guy, intelligent as he is, would find solace in ardent belief, some cause. In a way maybe his cynicism is a weak, unresolved cause. He actually brings himself to the point where he says the Naval Air Corps is only a "creditable suicide" for him.

Monday, May 11

War time is really here in a material form. We can see it in an outstretched palm, feel it in the unsweetened taste of coffee, and deduce its presence from thrifty thought in transportation procedure. Ration cards for sugar are already in use, gas rationing becomes severely enforced this week; and price ceilings on most retail goods have arrived. We must sacrifice to win and the actuality of that sacrifice stuns many of us even in the armed forces. It tends to end the disturbing feeling that this war is [a] nightmarish charade in which the unlucky few suffer, the multitude prosper. Maybe we really are all in it—may be even "total war" will not continue to be just the myth, ironic catch-all phrase I once thought it. Not much complaining; more disbelief than anything. . . .

Telephone and telegraph wires were reported flooded with Mother's Day messages. God knows our mothers deserve to hear our good cheery words because war can never be as casual nor comprehensible to the mother-at-home as to the son-at-the-front.

Tuesday – May 12

"Merde!" as Flip would so emphatically say. On my tender 9 hours of flight was heaped a solo check with Elldredge who turned a downward thumb. It was a bit premature for me to come up and I did not do badly, as Elldredge later confided to Longworth, but a quantity of little mistakes added to some fairly serious errors swung an adverse balance. The system operates on a two-check basis. The instructor followed by another instructor not acquainted with the student seek to ascertain the student's fitness for solo flight. Two downchecks are serious and may lead sooner or later to rapid departure. However, my work has not been bad enough to put me in jeopardy although naturally my determination and concentration are pretty fierce tonight. . . . Naturally I am a little tense and perturbed . . . but also pretty confident.

Monday – May 18

Made my second – and improved – solo flight today with the favorable assistance of a resurgent confidence and light winds. . . .

Going up alone began last Friday. Being sharply cognizant of my inexperience and my slowly developing coordination, I was nervous and tense comparable only to my first flight. . . . My landings and air work were poor last Friday, but pleasantly different today. I still lack the indescribable assurance of which pilots emerge – a confidence and cool maturity in meeting the ever changing circumstances of flight. However, today I revived the inner spark which keeps aglow the faith that I can be a damn good pilot – as I think I can be a damn-good-anything when I concentrate this hard. God knows there is nothing I'm holding back at this stage of endeavor.

Tuesday – May 19

My feeling in regard to soloing has fully passed from uneasy tenseness (except for the moment of rectifying mistakes just prior to landing) to a peaceful alertness as would exist in reading an exciting book. The pleasure of controlling a powerful machine, of adapting myself to something worthwhile in a physically minded world, of turning a mind useful in the social sciences to new fields — these make up the mental satisfaction that goes with the physical peace of rapid motion and lofty altitude.

Thursday – May 21

One of my reactions to a talk with Jeanie was of this being a figment of my ample imagination: Jeanie was too young; Harry was too uncommunicative; the whole situation precluded romance. That none of the above was true I knew, but the events assuring me of that moved as if they consisted of shadowy charades on a screen. However, it is all so good and wonderful that I must believe it and enjoy it for the blessings which it brings. Jeanie is wonderful and will be a good counterweight to bring out Bro's indrawn characteristics. And god know she draws something damn hard to beat. A gentle Puritan with more stuff inside than anybody I know except maybe his father.

Monday – May 25

Back "home" again. . . . In *Flight to Arras*, Saint-Exupéry describes how the passage of tense or momentous occasions are marked at the time only by a sequence of details without much significance. It will take time for the marriedness of Harry and Jean to lend completeness to the past weekend. However, the reunion, the jolly spirits, and the lovely lass joining our tribe were a source of continual pleasure. . . .

Had my first flight in an NSN today. An NSN is a Naval biplane trainer, 225 H.P. (Cub is 55), heavier, faster, and truer than a Cub. It's really an airplane. Evans gave me 1 hr. and one-half of everything one should know to run the thing. He remarked that I was progressing well although admittedly it took time for me to catch on to the change from cub to the new craft. The cockpits are open; one wears glasses; the instructor is in a separate cockpit forward, not in front of you in a single cockpit. In general, the affair is just more airplane. Longer time to take off; less extra landing space; more gadgets — wobble pump, mixture control, tab control.

In an NSN already the feeling comes over one that you can

rely less on *seeing* and must just *know* what to do and *feel* the rest. With a speed of 80 knots that feeling is little more than in embryo; in a fast ship one will feel a greater dependence, a greater subservience to the machine. . . .

Russia's survival is not certain; it alone may be said to be the key to the war. . . . Important also is a rumored Russian post-war plan guaranteed "to startle" her allies as well as the Nazis. Russia is our main hope and I will not find it easy to criticize their suggestions as to what to do with an enemy they shall have beaten.

Wed. – May 27

Alan described witnessing an experiment in rocket-aided takeoff, and the risk of what would happen if the rocket didn't fire again after launch:

The plane would be 20 to 40 feet up without flying speed and greedily awaiting a chance to plummet earthward. Oh for the life of a test pilot!

Tomorrow I solo in an NSN for the first time on the strength of 3 hrs. instruction of which today's hour and a half was half straight and level. I can do no worse, I trust, than Folz (forced landing – lost), Hazard (pulled fire ext. handle seeking to lock tail wheel), Gregory (off runway into swamp), and Leggett (bounce-bounce almost into tree stumps). Still all the above seems to indicate we are soloing before we are really ready in capacity and confidence to do so. Maybe it will require a *bad* accident to have them organize log books carefully and stretch our NSN dual instruction.

Friday – May 29

My first hour and a half NSN solo was sloppy, disquieting, and yet not so much worse than I anticipated. . . . On the last landing . . . in abysmal ignorance, I unlocked the tail wheel. The effect was to send the plane wildly to the right gradually turning into a ground loop. I had slowed up sufficiently not to be worried, but the lower wing tip struck the ground which alarmed me no end until inspection revealed no damage. Not good flying in a way that reflects both on my understanding of the ship and the amount of instruction given us before soloing. Then came the payoff, the clincher.

I was musing over my sins, sitting reflectively with the crash-truck driver. I thought that watching NSNs land might help me to get my bearings. For a time only Cubs waddling sluggishly around the pattern met my eye. Then an NSN sought to come in, was forced to circle again, finally found an opening in the pattern and dipped under good control over the trees. As it approached the runway I noticed the pilot was obliged to correct for a poor final turn which had taken him beyond the wind line.

But the correction was never made although it looked feasible, even easy to do. By supreme misfortune the pilot was hitting off the runway precisely in the only swampy section of Hybla Valley. A last effort to back into the air resulted in the simultaneous increase of speed and impact of plane against water. A fountain of water geysered 20 feet into the air and as it fell away, the plane could be seen to end a brief hesitation on its nose and to flop over on its back. The crash truck didn't start for maybe 20 seconds, but we scooted to the scene in less than a minute. Clifton (first solo) was the pilot and fortunately emerged without a scratch. Releasing his safety belt when upside down had plunged him headlong into the water and rendered him drenched as well as shamefaced.

Sunday, July 12

. . . By Sunday night Joan and I had driven a hot, tiring trek to Long Branch, N.J. where we supped and swam with

Harry and Jeanie. It was my first real opportunity to get to know Jeanie as a person, rather than as a bride or an objet d'art, and I was impressed by her intelligence, grace, and the way she and Harry could and do make a team. There was a stolen, carefree flavor about the visit which was invaluable. Somehow our moods all clicked — from the Beach at Long Branch to the peanut butter sandwiches gulped on the floor of Mrs. Reagan's and washed down with a plentitude of milk.

Aug. 14, 1942

. . . Oh, well, I'm young, 22, ardent about the war so why not fly a dive bomber?

Aug. 23, 1942

My assignment came through last week and proved to be USB or dive-bomber duty from a carrier. . . .

Dive-bombers usually don't live long and while I have many reasons for wanting to live my thoughts dwell quite frequently on my prospects honestly without fear. I have many ideas and plans for what I can do with a long life, but my mind is at peace with the knowledge I am using myself with all my physical and mental energy to bring about an improved world situation. If the cause is sufficiently just, the cost utilized in a purposeful manner, careful hands using the commodity of life constructively, then my chances whatever they may be are fitting and just.

Sept. 20, 1942

. . . Harry has his commission now – a vacation-honeymoon to boot. . . . With Bro assigned to duty in Tampa, I should be able to see him when I'm commissioned and en route to operational training.

October 1, 1942

Slowly I'm getting the feel of the SNI-4 and have passed from the A phase (familiarization) to the B – stunts. It is wearing on my stomach and quite nerve-wracking but I don't mind it too much. This has been my toughest mental conditioning so far since the thrashing around of this speedy ship is a bit on the uncomfortable [side] and causes me to worry at my lack of enthusiasm. Flying can be done well only when there is eager confidence. Dread of a hop and mild distaste do not promote success. However, I think I have gotten control of my outlook fully . . .

Nothing is written in the diary between October 26, 1942 and January 5, 1943. On January 5, Alan attributes this silence partly to "the Navy decree against keeping 'em. I begin again because there's no other way to keep track of this fast moving life and I think I have now a proper understanding of what the Navy does not want talked about." Even so, passages of the last pages have been snipped out as a condition of preserving the diary, itself a rare exception to the rule, as noted in a different handwriting at the end and signed by the Naval Censor, Lt. A. H. Wood. The sparse entries in the diary here are supplemented by Alan's last letters to his parents, brother, and friends.

January 4, 1943 *[to Harry Jr.]*

At this minute—8:08 pm—I am loafing only because my dive-bomber belched forth 2 gallons of oil on the first dive and the instructor waved me home for a bath.

January 5, 1943

To review world events of 40 days is impossible. The opening of the African front in November, the virtual annihilation of Rommel, the successful Russian offensives based on their triumph at Stalingrad, the assassination of Darlan following his "conversion" to the Allied cause, the total occupation of France by the Nazis are a part of the curious mosaic which now takes on a more pleasing hue for the Allies.

Personally I dragged my heels through the seemingly interminable weeks necessary to earn my wings and finally was commissioned Dec. 4th. Since then, Miami has been my bill of fare although there was a happy interlude with the folks in Pensacola . . . and a day or two with Harry and Jeanie in Tampa. . . .

My flying and my confidence in it went up a great deal. In gunnery – machine gun work and dive bombing – I started slowly but wound up above average. Navigation and scouting were much easier for me. Now down here I'm currently battling away at dive bombing and have counted about 6 hits in 24 tries in the last week. We fly a lively BT airplane and zoom in from 8,000 feet to the attack. . . . With a combination of dive bombing and night flying we have been hecticly active down here. That plus a curriculum too disciplined for newly blossomed ensigns tends to modify our full approval of this delightful environment.

Bill White showed up today after his Brewster (FSA) crack-up recuperating leave. He's none the worse for wear. . . . Several of my friends have not been so lucky in the last two months. Ray Barnett . . . got killed dive-bombing; [Fie?] Mercer, Winnetka lad and long time friend, was killed in a terrible P-boat crack-up; Syl Bouché, flying at Bronson while I was, disappeared last week while instructing there. Isolated cases of how training programs take their toll close to home no matter how capable the flyer or freakish the accident. . . .

As for now a night's sleep before going back to the heavy but enjoyable work of dive bombing those circles of 100 ft. radius outlined by white pegs.

January 8, 1943 *[to his parents]*
5 PM

After today's flying which has included an advanced formation flight check and will include night flying, we have only fairly short day flights the rest of our stay. I may have to work tomorrow as a safety pilot, which is actually more harrowing than sitting beside a mediocre auto[mo]bile driver, but in any case that will definitely end my night duty. Safety pilots are actually passengers who are alert for approaching planes and prepared to take control of the plane should the pilot be subject to "vertigo" – night flyer's occupational disease.

Although our hops are short and sweet from now on they are that way with a definite motive. We're practicing carrier landings on a field and such precision is required that they do not permit those learning them to fly more than an hour a day. We use a landing procedure which enables us to put the plane down on a dime. Not gently on a dime, but down even if the landing looks rough to the unknowing observer. It is in this stage that we start working with a signal officer who by waving flags quickly informs us of our least tendency to depart from the landing "groove." We must be a certain altitude, at a slow speed, with our plane's nose elevated just to the right degree. Then he gives us a motion to cut off our engine which must be instantaneously obeyed. The result is a fast settling of the plane so that it bounces quite a bit, but stops quickly.

Many people ask how on earth navy pilots land on the short deck of the carrier. What they do not know is that *never* is as much as half the deck space available and rarely even a third! That's why the landings have to be precise with a capital P.

January 18, 1943 *[to his parents]*

. . . The carrier landings are tough and I'm not getting them

520

fully under control as quickly as I should be doing. Consequently, in the little flying I do I have to bear down as hard as I can. Indeed I'm a little bit discouraged. . . .

Feb. 3, 1943

[censored]

. . . Zac Russom, who had gone with me to the President's Ball in Fort Pierce last weekend, had time only to radio "Emergency. Going down south of field!" when his engine cut out on him at 800 feet. No time to jump. No time to lower flaps. We searched for him for the remaining hours before dark and had given up for the evening with great reluctance. In the operations office, I wasn't there, Lt. Caldwell was outlining his suggested pattern of search for tomorrow's operations. The door opened while Caldwell talked, but he was engrossed, thinking, and did not look up. Lt. Simmons looked up and sat listening with a stupefied appearance. Finally he sputtered – "Russom's here — here's Russom!"

"Aren't you glad to see me?" Zac asked.

It turns out that he crashed the plane, was unhurt despite the fact that his plane was demolished and knocked down a lot of good sized trees. He walked and rode back the 10 miles to the field. His main fear, as far as I can make out, was that there might be alligators, snakes, or crocodiles in the tall, swampy weeds in the two miles intervening between himself and civilization. I guess now I won't have to get a new partner for fishing this weekend – Zac and I had counted on doing it together.

Feb. 3, 1943

The Brewster Buccaneer . . . has proved a wonderfully promising ship, but a woeful menace in its present form. . . . We make high speed dives up to and above 450 m.p.h. However, when we try it there are some disconcerting noises and almost inevitably a piece of wing, tail, or engine goes drifting back into space . . . enough pieces come off to be very nerve-wracking. Also the engines are temperamental and the emergency landings last week were too frequent for comfort.

As a result there is talk of returning the planes to the factory, transferring us elsewhere, keeping us here while SBD's (current fleet weapon) are transported, and, finally, getting some Brewster men down from New York to patch up and reinforce certain elements of the plane. The only thing we object to is patching up the plane because our confidence in the ships is one notch below zero and none want ever to see them again.

Feb. 3 *[to ?]*

Our main difficulty is that the fancy new airplanes are rather deficient in certain features and our superiors are quick to ground all planes for repairs and reinforcements when the need becomes apparent. In the long run these planes may prove wonderful, but our combination task of training in them while trying them out will be no short or easy task.

Feb. 3 *[to Lerner]*

It is fast, heavy, and powerful in guns and bombs, but unfortunately there are such a multitude of uncorrected "bugs" that we aren't too enthusiastic over it. It's called the Brewster Buccaneer — SB2A officially. . . .

It seems like a long road to have come in about a year, but whether we be transformed for better or for worse, flying is going to change a lot of us. I know well that the experience has done me a lot of good and I'm looking forward to the opportunity which I should get late this year of putting a year's endeavor to constructively destructive usage. . . .

Somehow flying helps to give one a bird's eye view of life in general.

Feb. 7, 1943 *[diary]*

Harry has been promoted to 1st Lieutenant. The little half of the duo bows low or better yet salutes humbly. A mighty rapid promotion. Maybe Jeanie is a military climber – bah! Somebody must have recognized that Harry has a real ability to command accompanying a rather lengthy list of virtues. It looks like I'd better snag a Yap cruiser or I'll not keep the pace. Yoicks!

Feb. 12, 1943 *[to Marty Stein]*

It seems that I've gotten out of Miami only to be planted in a more isolated, less attractive portion of the Florida quagmire. . . . Vero Beach . . .

We have some of the Navy's most powerful new dive bombers here and are performing a dual task of polishing our techniques and testing the durability of the planes. It is a good break to become familiar at this stage with as powerful a plane as will be used in the fleet for years to come, but at times nerve wracking when certain areas prove to be too feeble. We cavort about in these ships — known as Brewster Buccaneers in service jargon – at speeds up to and occasionally above 400 m.p.h. I find myself rather occupied with flying when diving at such speed, but we have some birds here who watch their speed indicator and have noted motion up to 500 m.p.h.

A lot of people wonder how it feels to make a dive-bombing run . . . The best simile I can think of is that of an elevator boy moving down rapidly, but yet seemingly not so rapidly as would make your stomach queasy. When you're in a dive, the pilot stands on the rudder pedals and thusly feels as if he were in a very normal posture. Seeing the ground come toward you and feeling the support of the safety belt are about the only things to dispel the illusion. There are no handy reference points like the walls of an elevator shaft so your feeling of motion is practically nil. When I think about it – and I don't often in a dive – there is only the top-heavy weight of your body (gravity pulls you toward the windshield), the whistle of the wind, the slight discomfort to your ears, and the two visual focuses of the whirling altimeter and the target growing in size in the bomb-sight. That isn't a good description, I suppose, because your mind and body are quite active and poised. So much of the feeling comes from within you and bears no relation to the physical elements involved. Then, too, pushing into the dive and pulling out are a multitude of discordant stresses which are in your mind the whole time of the dive.

I don't know why I should throw paragraphs like the above at you, but I enjoy trying to reconstruct the feeling and know you are a gal of tolerance and curiosity. . . .

You'd be surprised how early I get to sleep – 9:30 to 10 PM – and how late I sleep now – 7 AM. The old days are gone temporarily, but I hear they get up at 3 AM on a carrier. Yours for sleep while I can.

Love,
Alan

Feb. 18 *[to Howard Coare]*

The pleasure in breaking in something new far outweighs the anxiety over construction errors included in the planes. . . .

March 8, 1943
from U.S. Naval Air Force records

The pilot took off at about 0921, E.S.T., February 28, 1943, from the U.S. Naval Air Station, Vero Beach, Florida, on a dive bombing training flight. He returned to the field prior to completion of the flight after discovering failure of the hydraulic system of his plane. He remedied the trouble to the extent of lowering and locking his landing gear mechanically but complete failure of the hydraulic system prevented use of landing flaps or brakes. The pilot overshot the runway, landed, and attempted another take off. Failure of the engine to accelerate properly, however, did not allow the plane to become airborne, and it crashed through a fence, bounced over a railroad track and ended on its back in a canal with the cockpit submerged in about eight feet of water. The pilot was extricated about thirty-five minutes later and artificial respiration and later a resuscitator were used without effect. Death from drowning was pronounced at 1420. Identification was positive as no disfigurement occurred.

Commander H. L. Young to Alan's parents

Alan lost his life at the end of a routine training flight. He had had trouble getting his wheels down before landing, but managed – coolly following instructions – to get them locked down. However, the brakes of his plane were defective and he was unable to stop when he landed. Seeing that he might crash, he attempted to take off again, but, apparently, decided to do this too late to get off the ground. He struck a railroad embankment with such great force that he was knocked unconscious. The plane jumped over the embankment and ran into a drainage canal, turning upside down in the water. Because of the nature of the terrain, it was extremely difficult to extricate Alan from the plane and he remained under water for thirty-five minutes. The doctor worked on him for over two hours, the last hour using mechanical resuscitator. Alan did not suffer when he died, as he was undoubtedly unconscious when the plane entered the water.

In the short time that he was on duty at this station, he established himself as an outstanding young officer. His record here was excellent and he made many friends. I, and the other officers here, thought highly of him. We have lost a good friend and fellow officer and the nation has lost a well-trained and capable flyer of high character.

IN GRATEFUL ACKNOWLEDGMENT

Ezra Geis, to whom this book is dedicated

Julia W. Kramer

Annie Gottlieb

Sara Monroe

Martha Gottlieb

Janet Sailian

Alan Gottlieb

David Norman Gottlieb

Peter Geis

Stephen Yaakov Geis

Ed Geis

Hannah Geis

Mary Kuh Ambulos

Anne Kuh

Audrey Kuh Straight

Cathy Askow Thompson

Rowie Gray

Ruth Lazarus

Joan D. Levin

Marilyn Nasatir

John Preskill

Eileen Ielmini, University of Chicago Library Department of Special Collections

Kim Ostermyer, the Wyoming Room, Sheridan Public Library, Sheridan, Wyoming

Christine Hagenberger

Susan Owens

Karli Ledkins, Family ChartMasters

David Collins, WingSpan Press